BOSS RULE IN SOUTH TEXAS

Boss Rule
in South Texas
THE PROGRESSIVE ERA

by Evan Anders

 UNIVERSITY OF TEXAS PRESS, AUSTIN

For Betty, Robert, and Cecily

Publication of this book was assisted by grants from
  The University of Texas at Arlington and
  The Littlefield Fund for Southern History,
    The University of Texas at Austin.

LIBRARY OF CONGRESS CATALOGING IN PUBLICATION DATA
Anders, Evan, 1946–
  Boss rule in South Texas.
    Bibliography: p.
    Includes index.
    1. Texas—Politics and government—1865–1950.
  2. Progressivism (United States politics)
  3. Wells, James B., 1850–1923.   4. Parr, Archie,
  1860 or 61–1942.   I. Title.
  F391.A5   976.4'06   82-2701
  ISBN 0-292-70763-0 (pbk.)

Contents

Introduction

DURING THE DECADES following the Civil War, boss rule emerged as the pervasive pattern of politics for American cities. Characteristically, the political boss centralized government authority by filling city offices with men willing to follow his orders. Patronage became the lifeblood of the machine. The prospect of political jobs attracted a large following of campaign workers, while the assessment of contributions from the salaries of city officials and employees filled the party coffers. Business allies received lucrative contracts and franchises for public utilities and repaid the machine with kickbacks. Although contemporary reformers attacked the bosses for destroying the professional standards of the city bureaucracies and for looting the public treasuries, historians and social scientists have recently rehabilitated the reputations of these much maligned politicians. Without contesting the charges of corruption, modern analysts argue that the urban chieftains often provided desperately needed services for their diverse constituencies. At the same time, historians are reevaluating the claims of the progressive reformers that their sole motivation was a disinterested commitment to protect the public interest.

Social scientist Robert Merton has supplied the basic model for overhauling traditional interpretations of boss rule. In addition to indulging in graft, the urban machines also performed a variety of constructive functions: social welfare benefits for the downtrodden, particularly immigrants; a channel of upward mobility for ambitious members of these suppressed groups; special privileges for businesses, such as franchises and the elimination of red tape. Recent historians have argued that boss politics was the inevitable product of the rapid, chaotic process of urbanization during the late nineteenth century. Suffering from the crippling diffusion of power among city officials and from the interference of rural-dominated state legislatures, municipal governments could not meet the needs of the mushrooming urban populations. To overcome this paralysis the bosses used their influence with the party leaders at the state level and imposed their own tightly controlled machines on the fragmented city administrations. Irrespective of the formal lines of authority, city officials submitted to the boss' dictation because they depended on his campaign organization for reelection. As one further service, the machines defended immigrant life-styles against nativist attack. The result of all these activities was support for boss rule from both influential businessmen and massive voting blocs of immigrants.[1]

This form of government came under sharp attack during the Progressive Era. Reformers denounced the bosses as corruptionists and tyrants, who squandered public funds and subverted the democratic process by monopolizing power and manipulating the ignorant immigrant voters. Despite the progressive promises to bring the government closer to the people, Samuel Hays argues that reform campaigns in many cities transferred power to newly formed business and professional elites, whose influence had remained limited under the boss system. Instead of legitimizing all the necessary functions of the machines, the municipal insurgents promoted structural changes in government, which restricted the political participation of the lower classes, reduced government expense and waste, and advanced their own economic interests. The moralistic appeals of the progressive crusaders for clean, democratic government masked fundamental social and economic conflicts.[2]

Although Hays, Merton, and other students of machine government have limited their studies to urban politics, their findings provide an analytical framework for examining boss rule in a quite different setting—the South Texas counties of Cameron, Hidalgo, Starr, and Duval during the late 1890s and the early twentieth century. The problems of governing in these rural, small-town communities were much less complicated, but there emerged a system of Democratic machines that broadly conformed to the Merton model.

The network of county organizations provided basic social and economic services to an economic elite of ranchers and merchants and to a lower-class mass of Mexican American laborers, farmers, and ranch hands. Political success rested upon control of the Hispanic votes and access to patronage. Even though the bosses had faced recurrent Republican opposition and Democratic factional divisions since the end of the Civil War, the challenge to machine domination in South Texas assumed new force during the Progressive Era. The insurgents' own efforts to manage Mexican American voting blocs and their reliance on the federal customs house as an organizational base reflected the continuity of twentieth-century agitation with past opposition. Yet two developments transformed the political landscape. The challengers eventually embraced the popular reformist rhetoric of the period, and, more fundamentally, they rode the tide of an economic revolution in South Texas. With the completion of a railroad network through the region and the advent of large-scale irrigation, the citrus and truck farming boom swept the Lower Rio Grande Valley and attracted thousands of new settlers. In accordance with the Hays analysis, the reform movement represented an upwardly mobile economic class, and its main aim was to restrict the political participation of the lower-class voters, who had sustained the established order. As a result of these forces, political conflict in South Texas came to a head during the first two decades of the twentieth century.

To be complete, the study of South Texas politics must explore not only the mechanics of the county rings and the nature of their local opposition but also the careers of the Democratic bosses who organized the machines, the influence of these men on state and national politics, the special relationship between the bosses and the Texas Rangers, the role of Mexican Americans in shaping regional politics, and the prevalence of violence and racial tension along the border. Four figures stand out in the political drama that unfolded in this volatile frontier setting: James Wells, who consolidated boss rule in Cameron County and emerged as a leading spokesman for the conservative wing of the state Democratic party; Archer (Archie) Parr, whose ruthless tactics and misuse of public funds in Duval County established him as one of the most notorious corruptionists in the history of the state; Manuel Guerra, a Mexican American rancher and merchant whose authoritarian domination of Starr County was indistinguishable from the practices of his Anglo counterparts in the other border counties; and John Nance Garner, who served the interests of these bosses during the formative years of his congressional career. To understand these politicians and the partisan battles that they waged during the Progressive Era, one must first review the social and economic history of South Texas and the operation of boss rule before 1900.

The four counties of Cameron, Hidalgo, Starr, and Duval fall within the Trans-Nueces region, which is bordered by the Nueces River on the north and the Rio Grande on the south. The first three counties lie along the Rio Grande and form the Lower Rio Grande Valley, occupying the southeastern corner of Texas. The Valley takes shape as the flood plain of the Rio Grande expands into a broad delta plain, which follows the twisted course of the river for 250 miles to the Gulf. (Two hundred and fifty miles is the navigational distance of the river from the point at which the Lower Rio Grande Valley forms in the west to the mouth of the river, and this figure includes the measurement of all the twists and turns in the river. All other river measurements in the book are navigational distances.) Until the county reorganizations of 1911 and 1913, Duval County bordered the western-most Valley county of Starr on the north. Irrigation converted most of the Lower Rio Grande Valley into a fruit and truck farming bonanza, but before 1900 grasslands and stretches of chaparral covered the whole Trans-Nueces region. Modest rainfall limited earlier agricultural development, and cattle and sheep ranching dominated the South Texas plains.

During the periods of Spanish and Mexican rule, the Trans-Nueces region remained sparsely settled, but by 1836 the two governments had divided most of the territory into land grants. The allotments varied in size from the *porciones* of a few thousand acres, which were distributed among the settlers in the early towns along the Rio Grande, to later grants of hundreds of thousands of acres. After the War for Texas Independence, both Mexico and the new republic claimed the land between the Nueces and the Rio Grande, and control of the area remained in dispute until the United States annexed Texas and defeated Mexico in the war of 1846–1848. Although the United States agreed to respect the existing land grants, Mexican ranchers in the northern half of the Trans-Nueces plains abandoned their holdings. Beset by both Indian raids and Anglo and Mexican marauders, they sold out cheaply to future Anglo ranch barons like Richard King and Mifflin Kenedy. Squatters also invaded South Texas and established homesteads without any legal claim to the property.

Despite these pressures, many landowners in the Lower Rio Grande Valley refused to yield. With their lands near the border, they felt more secure and usually demanded high prices—if they were willing to sell at all. The complexity of clearing land titles in the border region served as another deterrent against a complete Anglo take-over. Mexican pioneers had occupied the Lower Rio Grande Valley long before the distribution of the northern grants, and, with each generation, these families had subdivided the ownership of their lands. Although a family might hold the original grant together as a single ranching enterprise, the purchase of the tract, or any part of it, would require the concurrence of numerous collective owners. The proliferation of the smaller *porciones* and even some communally owned municipal properties in the vicinity of Mexican border

South Texas in 1910

South Texas in 1921

towns further complicated the accumulation of vast stretches of land by Anglo businessmen. For all these reasons, only a handful of Anglos bought ranches in the Valley during the 1850s. After the Civil War, Anglo landholding steadily expanded, but much of the area remained under Mexican American ownership.

Regardless of whether they sold their land or stayed, the Hispanic proprietors of the largest land grant estates left a legacy of feudalistic rule, which had important implications for the future politics of South Texas. A pattern of *patrón-peón* relations existed between the landowner and most of his laborers. As *patrón*, the rancher exercised almost complete social and economic control over his *peones*. The submissive workers could not quit their jobs or own property, and they needed their master's permission to marry, to leave the ranch, or to summon a doctor or some other outsider. The *patrón* also served as the local judge, who settled disputes among his *peones*, maintained order and discipline, and even assessed punishments. The workers' financial indebtedness partly accounted for their subordination. Paid minimal wages, forced to buy food and other supplies at the ranch-operated store, and charged for medical treatment and other services, the *peones* invariably fell into debt, and the debts were passed on from one generation to the next. But just as important as this economic bond was the arrangement of mutual obligations that held the *patrón* and his *peones* together. Responsibility as well as power defined the rancher's social role. He provided the laborers with living quarters and other necessities, protected them from Indian and bandit raids, offered fatherly advice, and sponsored fiestas, weddings, and funerals. So long as the *patrón* fulfilled these obligations, the *peones* loyally served him. Some of the cowboys, or *vaqueros*, were sons of small landholders, and they managed to maintain their independence. The bulk of the work force, however, submitted to the *patrón*'s complete domination. Even with the elimination of the legal sanction for peonage after the collapse of Mexican rule, the tradition of paternalistic responsibility and willing subservience continued.

Anglos first arrived in the Lower Rio Grande Valley in the late 1820s with the establishment of the town of Matamoros near the mouth of the Rio Grande on the southern bank of the river. Along with other foreign merchants from France, Spain, and England, the American businessmen participated in the trade between New Orleans and northern Mexico. After the Texas Revolution, the Americans withdrew from Matamoros because of Mexican hostility, increased tariffs and taxation, the threat of Texan privateering against shipping from Mexican ports, and the outbreak of Indian raids along the Rio Grande.

Not until the U.S. military occupation of the Trans-Nueces region during the war with Mexico did the American presence become permanently established. The stationing of troops at Corpus Christi transformed that modest trading post at the mouth of the Nueces River into a boom town. During the decade following the war, Anglos purchased fourteen of the fifteen land grants in Nueces County to consolidate their domination over the northern half of the Trans-Nueces plains. The question of power and influence remained more complicated in the Lower Rio Grande Valley.

With the invasion of northern Mexico, American merchants returned to Matamoros, and, at the end of the war, Charles Stillman and his business associates organized the town of Brownsville directly across the Rio Grande from Matamoros and adjacent to an army post, Fort Brown. Despite early fluctuations between boom and bust, Brownsville replaced Matamoros as the dominant trading center for northeastern Mexico. The American annexation of the harbor of Brazos de Santiago at the mouth of the Rio Grande contributed to the growth of Brownsville, but the resourcefulness of local businessmen also played an important role. The merchants recognized the advantage of shipping goods to Brownsville and then smuggling them across the Rio Grande to avoid paying the high Mexican tariffs. The Anglo monopoly of steamboat traffic further strengthened Brownsville's position. To facilitate the movement of soldiers and supplies during the Mexican War, the U.S. Army had introduced steam navigation to the Rio Grande, and by 1852 the merged steamboat interests of Charles Stillman, Mifflin Kenedy, and Richard King monopolized river transportation. Although turmoil and political instability on both sides of the border disrupted trade after 1850, commerce remained the bulwark of the Lower Rio Grande economy through the first three decades of American rule. Not until the construction of railroad lines from Corpus Christi and San Antonio to Laredo in the early 1880s did Brownsville and the other Valley communities lose their grip on the lucrative trade with northern Mexico.

The impact of the commercial activity in the Valley reached beyond the border towns of the Rio Grande. With the sizable profits from smuggling, legitimate trade, and steamboat shipping, many of the Anglo entrepreneurs invested heavily in land. Mifflin Kenedy, Richard King, and others assembled vast ranching empires during the 1850s. These men eventually revolutionized the economics of

South Texas ranching with the introduction of fencing, cattle drives to Kansas, large-scale sheep raising, and the scientific breeding of livestock. At the same time, however, they patterned their social conduct after the conservative model of the Mexican *patrones*. Because of the difficulties of purchasing large tracts of land in the Lower Rio Grande Valley, some Anglo businessmen married into wealthy Hispanic families and adopted the life-style of this established elite. In the cosmopolitan community of Brownsville, racial barriers within the upper class broke down as Mexicans, Spaniards, Englishmen, Frenchmen, and Americans intermingled. Even in the northern reaches of the Trans-Nueces, where most land was available for outright sale and racial tensions were more pronounced, ranchers usually learned the Spanish language and assumed the role of *patrón* in their relations with Mexican ranch hands and laborers. The pattern of rigorous social control and paternalistic responsibility characterized Anglo as well as Hispanic ranching operations throughout South Texas.

Despite the survival of Hispanic landownership near the Rio Grande and the cultural adjustment of Anglo ranchers, racial strife still haunted the South Texas plains. Many Hispanics resented the separation of this territory from their homeland, and they greeted the establishment of Anglo authority with deep suspicion. The racism of some newcomers, double standards in the courts, and the abuses of the Texas Rangers reinforced their uneasiness. When a foreign *patrón* failed to fulfill his paternalistic obligations of care and protection, *peón* submissiveness sometimes gave way to malingering and other acts of quiet defiance, which reinforced the Anglo-held stereotype of the indolent, lazy Mexican. Anglo relations with upper-class Hispanics also showed signs of strain. Families who had lost their land accused the Anglo purchasers of intimidation, violence, and fraud. Although the courts held out the promise of redress for these grievances, all too often this alien legal system not only invalidated the land claims of the Hispanic proprietors but also overwhelmed them with ruinous lawyers' fees.

Even in the Valley, where Anglo acquisitions remained limited before the Civil War, Hispanic discontent had an explosive potential. After the withdrawal of U.S. troops from Fort Brown and the other South Texas outposts in early 1859, Juan Cortina, a notorious cattle rustler and an heir to sizable landholdings, attacked Brownsville and occupied the town for several days. Although his original aim was to kill the city marshal and a former Anglo partner in cattle stealing, Cortina soon proclaimed himself the champion of the oppressed Hispanic population. He cited the theft of land and the physical abuse of lower-class Hispanics as the justification for his raids against ranches and border towns. Before a Texas Ranger offensive forced Cortina to retire across the Rio Grande, his band grew to several hundred men, and he gained considerable popular support.

The Cortina War exposed the powerful currents of racial antagonism in South Texas society, but the episode was also clouded with ambiguities. After Cortina withdrew from Brownsville, Mexican troops from Matamoros occupied the American town to prevent the bandit's return, and a wealthy landowner named Francisco Yturria organized a company of Mexican American militiamen to join with the Anglo minority in battling the marauders. Hispanic landowners along with the Anglos evacuated their ranches during the upheaval and later pressed damage claims. Even Cortina displayed some ambivalence on the question of racial conflict. Instead of promoting the reunification of the Trans-Nueces region with Mexico, he expressed faith in the commitment of governor-elect Sam Houston to ensure legal protection for the Hispanic residents of Texas. Nor was Cortina completely isolated from the local Anglo community. Before his campaign of terror, he had cooperated with Democratic politicians to mobilize the Mexican American vote, and a decade later some of his old allies lobbied for a state pardon for the former desperado.

Following the American Civil War and the collapse of French intervention in Mexico, racial strife again flared in the Trans-Nueces territory. The absence of political stability and effective military control in northern Mexico led to another outbreak of lawlessness along the border. Discharged soldiers from the Mexican armies and veteran rustlers crossed the Rio Grande and terrorized ranchers throughout South Texas. Some Mexican Americans served as informants for the bandits and even participated in the raids, but most shared the alarm of the Anglo settlers at the mounting violence. The bands of desperados showed little disposition to differentiate along racial lines in choosing their victims. Unfortunately, companies of Anglo militiamen perceived the upheaval as a racial conflict and turned their rage against countless innocent Mexican American victims. This tragic pattern of bandit attacks and indiscriminate retaliation continued through the mid-1870s. The appointment of Juan Cortina as the military commander for the state of Tamaulipas in 1870 aroused American suspicions that the neighboring Mexican authorities were even encouraging the disorder. With General Porfirio Díaz's consolidation of power in Mexico and the removal of Cortina, the two countries at last stamped out the border raids. Still the racial hostility and bloodshed of the 1860s and 1870s left a bitter legacy for South Texas.

The mixed pattern of discord and accommodation, which characterized the Anglo intrusion into the Trans-Nueces, created both formidable opportunities and obstacles for stable political organization. The overwhelming majority of the population consisted of lower-class Mexican Americans, who had no experience in democratic politics, but the survival of *patrón-peón* relationships on Anglo- and Hispanic-owned ranches provided the means for ensuring their participation in elections and for controlling their votes. Yet what politician could feel entirely secure with a constituency whose normal submissive behavior concealed racial resentments that might erupt at any time? The first priority of any viable political organization would have to be the reinforcement of the bonds that held the races together and the amelioration of the tensions that threatened open conflict.

BOSS RULE IN SOUTH TEXAS

1. The Wells Machine

AMERICAN POLITICAL AFFAIRS in South Texas began with the end of the Mexican War and the establishment of the counties of Cameron and Starr in 1848 and Hidalgo in 1852. During the pre–Civil War years, concern over the legal standing of land claims dominated politics. Hispanic and Anglo landowners alike agonized over the validity of their titles because of competing claims, the complications of collective family ownership, the unfulfilled terms of some grants, the imprecisions of others, and the destruction of records in Mexican archives with the recurrent outbreaks of armed conflict. In addition, some Anglos had secured their lands under dubious circumstances. Aggressive land speculators, squatters, and even the Texas state government appeared threatening. The state designated thousands of acres as part of the public domain on the grounds that the heirs of original grantees had abandoned their properties or had committed other violations of the grant provisions. Communal lands, which the residents of Mexican towns like Matamoros had held jointly, also came under state control. When the legislature established a special commission in 1850 to evaluate the legality of land titles south of the Nueces River, the ranchers' uneasiness gave way to panic. Perceiving a plot to take away their land, they organized protest rallies and even petitioned the U.S. government to detach the region from Texas and to form the Rio Grande Territory. Both Anglos and Hispanics joined the separatist movement, and the furor subsided only when the judges demonstrated their commitment to guaranteeing genuine claims.

Although the legislature validated all the titles that the commission had approved, land disputes remained a perplexing problem. Some property holders had failed to press their claims before the tribunal, and, incredibly, the commissioners lost all their field notes when the steamboat *Anson* sank in the Rio Grande. Under pressure from South Texas politicians, the legislature laid down ground rules in 1860, 1870, and 1871 for judging still unconfirmed titles. These laws instructed the district courts to relax requirements for field notes and precise surveys in land grant cases and to respect "the laws, usages, and customs of the government from which the claim is derived and the principles of equity applicable thereto."[1]

Not surprisingly, the leading expert on Texas, Spanish, and Mexican land laws emerged as the most influential politician of the border region. With a background in diplomacy and New York law and politics, Stephen Powers arrived in the Lower Rio Grande Valley in 1847 as a lieutenant in General Zachary Taylor's army. A year later Powers settled in Brownsville and opened his law practice. Over the next three decades, he held the positions of postmaster, customs collector, mayor of Brownsville, Cameron County judge, district judge under the Confederacy, state representative, and state senator. His political success rested on his mastery of land litigation and his commitment to defend the interests of both Mexican and American ranchers. Despite his own acquisitions of thousands of acres and his service as a purchasing agent for Richard King, Powers never advocated complete Anglo domination of South Texas. As a lawyer, he represented the landed Hispanic families along with the Anglo settlers; as a politician, he supported candidates of both races. His principal political strategy was to call on his rancher allies to mobilize the vote of their *peones* and *vaqueros*. Even Juan Cortina regularly delivered forty to fifty votes for the Powers tickets during the 1850s.

Prior to the Civil War, almost all the South Texas politicians were Democrats, despite factional splits over the separatist movement of 1850 and over a prolonged court fight to determine the ownership of the Brownsville town site. After the war, Democrats still quarreled, but the emergence of a Republican threat generated efforts to bolster Democratic unity and organization. Although the Democrats still carried Cameron County and its thinly populated neighbor, Hidalgo, the Republicans of Starr County prevailed during the early 1870s and won a respectable share of the local offices during the 1880s. At the close of Reconstruction, the GOP totals in Cameron County stood at nearly 40 percent—only to collapse for the remainder of the 1870s. Yet even Cameron County Democrats had to take the Republican challenge seriously. In two consecutive congressional elections following Powers' death in 1882, the GOP claimed sizable percentages of the county vote, and, in the first of these contests, the Republican candidate, Thomas Peck Ochiltree, swept the district. Except for the congressional race of 1882, Duval County stood firmly in the Democratic column from the date of its formal organization in 1876 through the 1880s. After 1890, however, the lo-cal Republican party expanded its base of support and gained a slight edge over the Democrats. Not until 1906 did the Duval Democrats reestablish their domination.

During the 1870s and the early 1880s, Republican presidents filled the federal offices in South Texas with partisans who played active roles in local politics. The local customs house and the post offices provided an organizational base for recruiting party workers. Paradoxically, the very character of the manipulated Mexican Amer-ican vote also offered opportunities for Republican gains. Whenever a Democratic leader defected because of the temptation of a federal appointment or because of his defeat in some factional squabble, he might carry scores of controlled votes into the Republican camp. Recognizing the threat of disunity to Democratic dominance, Ste-phen Powers and his close associate James G. Browne tried to stabi-lize the system of loose Democratic alliances with the establish-ment of a formal organization, the Blue Club of Cameron County. Under this arrangement, the party leaders hammered out compro-mise tickets, and the rank-and-file membership of several hundred voters unanimously supported the candidates. The Republicans countered with the formation of the Red Club, and comparable com-peting groups developed elsewhere in South Texas. This identifica-tion with colors was designed to facilitate party recognition on the part of the illiterate Hispanic voters.

Despite the organizational advances under Stephen Powers, boss rule did not reach fruition until the ascendancy of James B. Wells, Jr., Powers' protégé in law and politics. Wells was born in 1850 on St. Joseph's Island along the Texas Gulf Coast just north of Aransas Pass. Both of his parents came from New England seafaring families, and his father, James B. Wells, Sr., participated in the Texas Revolu-tion as a privateer. Following the war, the veteran sea captain headed the naval yard of the Texas Republic at Galveston, and then settled on St. Joseph's Island to raise cattle and to operate a merchant schooner. Reared in an isolated environment both on the island and at a later home on the mainland, James B. Wells, Jr., received most of his basic education from his mother. After managing the family ranch for a few years, he studied under a Galveston attorney in 1873 and then attended the University of Virginia Law School. Wells launched his law practice at Rockport but shortly moved to Corpus Christi, where he also engaged in land speculation. The young law-yer's performance in an important land suit impressed Powers, and adversity drew the two men together in 1878. Powers' junior partner was killed in a duel, and Wells had to sell all of his landholdings to cover his father's economic reverses. Desperate for a fresh start, Wells readily accepted Powers' offer to form a partnership.

With his dramatic debut of twenty victories in twenty-one land suits before a single term of the Cameron County District Court, James B. Wells won Powers' confidence and assumed political responsibilities. In 1880 Wells married Powers' niece, Pauline Kleiber. A series of marriages bound the Powers, the Brownes, and several other prominent Democratic families together, and Wells now joined the inner circle. The young lawyer even converted to his bride's religion, Catholicism. By the time of Powers' death in 1882, Wells had emerged as his chief lieutenant and heir apparent. Enjoying the support of the leading ranchers of the region, Wells consolidated his control over the Cameron County Blue Club and eventually extended his influence over the Democratic organizations of Hidalgo, Starr, and Duval counties. In each of these counties, Wells oversaw the rise of bosses who ran their own local machines but who acknowledged Wells' leadership on regional, state, and national questions. Although the Brownsville attorney won the election to public office only once, he stood as the central figure in South Texas politics as early as the mid-1880s, and he continued to exercise power as the Cameron County Democratic chairman until 1920. His associates like Archie Parr of Duval County and Manuel Guerra of Starr County established even more durable machines. The longevity of boss rule in the Trans-Nueces owed much to the artful maneuvering of Wells and the other leaders, but the real basis for its success was the satisfaction of constituent needs. The Wells machine, which served as the model for the other Valley organizations, provided basic services for the powerful ranchers, the Brownsville merchants, and the Mexican American majority and received their support in return.

Within this coalition, the ranch owners played the most important role. By 1890, ninety ranchers maintained tracts of over 1,000 acres and controlled 97 percent of the land in Cameron County. The Kings and the Kenedys held over 300,000 acres each, and James G. Browne controlled 114,000 acres. Nineteen other ranches contained over 10,000 acres each. The population of Cameron County stood at 14,000, and half of the residents lived in the countryside—outside the county seat of Brownsville and the two smaller towns of Santa Maria and Point Isabel. The overwhelming majority of the rural population consisted of Mexican Americans, who worked as ranch hands, farm laborers, sharecroppers, and small ranchers and farmers. Because of the survival of the *patrón-peón* relationships, the large landowners were able to deliver the votes of their lower-class Mexican American employees and neighbors. Toward the end of his political career, James Wells offered the following explanation for the pattern of bloc voting that characterized South Texas politics:

> I suppose they [the King ranchers] control 500 votes, and they [the Mexican American people] go to their major domos, and they go to Mr. Caesar Kleberg, and to Robert Kleberg, and to Captain King—while he was living—and ask him whom they should vote for. The truth is, and very few people who don't live in that county know it, that it is the property owners and the intelligent people who . . . really vote Mexicans. . . . The King people always protected their servants and helped them when they were sick and never let them go hungry, and they always feel grateful, and they naturally don't need any buying, or selling or any coercion—they went to those that helped them when they needed help. . . . The Mexican naturally inherited from his ancestors from Spanish rule, the idea of looking to the head of the ranch—the place where he lived and got his living—for guidance and direction.[2]

Wells also turned to his rancher allies for financial contributions when assessments from candidates, appointed officials, and other politicians failed to cover all the campaign costs.

To maintain the consistent support of most of the influential landowners in the county, James B. Wells performed legal services, promoted favorable state legislation, used his influence to hold down property taxes, promoted railroad development, and lobbied for the deployment of Texas Rangers and U.S. troops to maintain order along the border. The defense of land titles remained the paramount concern. With the close of Reconstruction, the Trans-Nueces confronted another crisis on this issue. Under pressure from land speculators, the Texas constitutional convention of 1875 passed a measure that threatened to curtail the validation of still unperfected land grant titles. By the terms of the constitutional provision, landholders could not submit as evidence in legal suits any documentation that had not already been recorded at the county seat or in the state General Land Office. To the relief of many South Texas stock raisers, Powers and Wells won a series of cases, in which the courts ruled that the Texas Constitution did not nullify land titles that had been recorded with the Mexican government but not with Texas or county authorities. In a final effort to eliminate the uncertainties plaguing landownership, Wells oversaw the passage of a land act in

1901 that allowed the ranchers themselves to bring suit to determine the validity of their unconfirmed Spanish and Mexican land grant titles. Permissible evidence in these proceedings would include papers from the Mexican archives as well as county and state records. The original version of the bill, which Governor Joseph Sayers vetoed, contained provisions that would have provided a legal defense for even the most suspect claims. (For a full discussion of the 1901 land legislation, see Chap. 6.) In his campaign to uphold land grant claims in South Texas, Wells represented both Anglo and Mexican American clients.

Low property taxes also attracted rancher support for the Wells county machine. The legislature set uniform rates for state ad valorem taxes and allowed the county governments to determine local taxes within a specified range. During the 1890s, the state property tax averaged 30¢ on each $100 valuation, while the additional Cameron County taxes ranged from 50¢ to 60¢ per $100 valuation. Although the combined tax rate for Cameron County property owners stood at the relatively high level of 91⅔¢ in 1900, the county officials provided substantial savings for their rancher constituents through the valuation of property for tax purposes. During the 1890s and into the first decade of the twentieth century, the Cameron County commissioners' court defined six classes of taxable land—each with a single rate of valuation. The county-rendered values ranged from $25 an acre for improved land near the Brownsville city limits to 50¢ per acre for unimproved land on the coastal islands within the county. Most of the pasturage fell within the second-cheapest category—valued at $1.00, even though the sale price of private pastureland before 1900 varied from $1.50 to $3.00 an acre, and county and state school land sold for $2.00 to $3.00 an acre. With 342,617 acres and 304,779 acres, respectively, the King and Kenedy families were the largest landholders in the county. Despite fencing and other improvements, the county government set the value of all their land at $1.00 per acre. These ranchers benefited as well from low assessments of the value of their livestock.

Favoritism also shaped the taxing policies of Cameron County. Wells' critics charged that the local officials penalized Republicans and independent Democrats with tax valuations that exceeded those for the loyal supporters of the machine. In addition, the county administration seldom demanded prompt tax payments from regular Democrats. The delinquent taxes of some ranchers accumulated for several years before the sheriff applied any pressure. Wells himself regularly fell behind on his taxes.

Satisfied with the low level of taxation, the Democratic ranchers of Cameron County even tolerated a modest level of graft. Although Wells and his associates generally exercised more restraint than the bosses in neighboring counties, one major scandal surfaced in Cameron County before 1900. In 1882, the commissioners' court authorized a bond issue to pay for the construction of the county courthouse and jail. By the time of the refunding of the debt in 1899, the county had collected $98,000 in taxes to cover the bonds. Despite the fact that the expenditures for that purpose had totaled only $60,000, all the money in the special sinking fund had disappeared. County officials never did account for the missing money. With the heavy influx of Anglo voters after 1905, the Democratic organization tried to improve its image and abstained from the outright theft of large sums of public revenue.

Security along the border was just as important to the Valley ranchers as low taxation. Although cattle raids from Mexico declined dramatically after Porfirio Díaz assumed power in the mid-1870s, the stockmen still harbored fears of the revival of rampant lawlessness. To provide at least a measure of protection, Wells used his influence with state officials and congressmen to maintain the presence of both Texas Rangers and U.S. Army troops in the Trans-Nueces. The Cameron County boss developed close ties with the conservative Democratic administrations that dominated Texas politics from 1895 through 1906, and many of the Rangers serving in South Texas received their appointments on the basis of Wells' recommendations. As a result, the Ranger force readily responded to Wells' appeals for intervention to quell disorders and to crack down on cattle rustling. Wells demonstrated his loyalty to the agency when a 1900 attorney general ruling denied the legal authority of Ranger privates and noncommissioned officers to make arrests. With the Rangers facing complete paralysis, Wells mobilized South Texas legislators to fight for the corrective legislation that salvaged the force.

Despite Wells' confidence in the Rangers as a safeguard against disorder, these lawmen hardly administered evenhanded justice. Both Democratic and Republican politicians applied pressures to shield party loyalists from arrest and prosecution. In addition, the Rangers were notorious for their abuses against the Mexican American population. During the cattle raiding era of the 1870s, Captain L. H. McNelly expressed concern for the innocent Hispanic victims of Anglo vigilante action, but his own tactics included hanging suspected rustlers without a trial. Gun battles between Rangers and respected Mexican American citizens in Webb County in 1885 and Cameron County in 1902 heightened racial tensions. With the resumption of large-scale bandit raids from Mexico in 1915, the state lawmen and local vigilante groups launched a reign of terror against the Hispanic residents of South Texas. At least two hundred Mexican Americans, and possibly many more, were killed. Yet Wells and his allies failed to protest the Ranger mistreatment of the Mexican American population until 1918, when Governor William Hobby used the officers to discourage Hispanic voting. In fact, throughout his political career, the Cameron County boss provided free legal services for Rangers facing criminal charges.

The failure of the Valley politicians to curb Ranger misconduct revealed the depth of Anglo insecurity in the midst of the Mexican American majority. The Anglo residents had adapted to the Mexican social system and culture and had welcomed Hispanic political participation, but the memories of the racial violence of the first three decades of American rule lingered. The Cameron County Democrats still placed a premium on the presence of an Anglo police force that had demonstrated its effectiveness in battling Mexican raiders and intimidating the general population.

The U.S. Army served as another frontier defense. Federal troops had intervened against the Mexican raiders in the 1870s, and, in 1886, they rebuilt and occupied Fort Brown on the outskirts of Brownsville. When the War Department contemplated closing the post in 1901, Wells persuaded Governor Joseph Sayers, U.S. Senator Charles Culberson, local Congressman Rudolph Kleberg, and several other members of the Texas congressional delegation to campaign for the retention of troops at Brownsville. Even the Texas Legislature passed a resolution protesting the planned evacuation. The War Department submitted, and Fort Brown remained.

Between the close of the cattle raids of the post–Civil War period and the turn of the century, the abortive Garza Revolution posed the most serious threat to stability along the border. Catarino Garza was an exile from Mexico who established a South Texas newspaper and sharply criticized both legal injustices against Mexican Americans in the Valley and the repression of the Díaz regime in Mexico. A crisis developed when Garza organized an armed band on American soil in 1891 and staged raids against Mexican garrisons in the neighboring state of Tamaulipas. Although Garza's force showed no inclination to attack Texas ranches or settlements, the Americans became apprehensive. They feared that Garza's appeals might attract widespread Mexican American participation in the campaign, provoke raids from Mexico, and usher in a new era of lawlessness. To counter this threat, James Wells canvassed the Valley counties to make personal appeals to his rural Mexican American constituents to avoid involvement with Garza. He also persuaded Governor James Hogg to dispatch a special force of Rangers when the regular army failed to crush the small but elusive band of raiders. After the capture of most of his men, Garza apparently fled the Valley.

The ranchers of South Texas did not limit their attention to the essentially defensive policies of maintaining public order, holding down taxes, and preserving their land titles. They also embraced visions of rapid economic development. The construction of a railroad line from Corpus Christi into the Lower Rio Grande Valley would serve as the catalyst for the transformation of the region. Mifflin Kenedy's son John, Robert Kleberg, who managed the King Ranch after the death of his father-in-law, Richard King, and other powerful landholders planned to organize towns along the railroad system and to subdivide stretches of pasturage into small farm sites. With the introduction of large-scale irrigation to convert the arid plains into productive farmland and with the availability of the railroad for transporting the produce, new settlers would flock to the Trans-Nueces, and property values would soar.

Brownsville merchants and bankers also rallied behind the cause of railroad development as a means to revive commerce in the Lower Rio Grande Valley. The first railroads to the border region by-passed the Valley and dealt a devastating blow to the local economy. With the completion of railway lines from Corpus Christi, San Antonio, and Monterrey, Mexico, to Laredo in 1882 and 1883, Brownsville's domination of trade with northeastern Mexico collapsed. In 1875, the value of exports and imports passing through the Customs District of Brazos de Santiago, which included Brownsville and the other border towns of the Valley, totaled $3,743,016; by 1885, the sum stood at $1,404,102; by 1892, $764,693. Those businessmen who remained in Brownsville viewed the proposed extension of rail service to their community as the only hope for full recovery.

As the agitation of ranchers and merchants grew, James B. Wells assumed an active role in promoting railroad construction. In 1889, Wells threw his support behind Colonel E. H. Ropes, who proposed a grandiose scheme to build a rail network from Corpus Christi, across the border at Brownsville, and onward through Mexico, Guatemala, El Salvador, Nicaragua, Costa Rica, and Panama. The Cameron County boss invested his own money, solicited funds from others, and conducted negotiations to gain control of a Mexican railway concession. In the face of mounting evidence of mismanagement and deception, however, Wells abandoned Ropes and helped to persuade the Boston capitalists backing the project to organize a new company, the Pan American Railway Company. Even with the acquisition of the Mexican concession and a charter from the Texas government, the Pan American Railway Company collapsed because of crippling litigation, instability within the firm, and the loss of investor confidence.

The record of repeated failures and frustrations did not come to an end until Uriah Lott and Benjamin F. Yoakum organized the St. Louis, Brownsville, and Mexico Railway in 1903. One year later, the company completed the railroad from Corpus Christi to Brownsville, as work continued on a branch through Hidalgo County and on the northward extension of the main line to Houston. Serving as a member of the board of directors and as the general counsel for the St. Louis, Brownsville, and Mexico Railway, Wells handled the acquisition of land titles and the formulation of needed changes in the company charter. With his participation in this enterprise, Wells advanced the interests of his constituents and pursued personal profit, but he also contributed to a social-economic revolution that would eventually reshape the political environment that he had mastered.

James B. Wells' responsiveness to the needs of Brownsville businessmen went beyond his support of railroad projects. During the two decades of economic decline after 1880, the Democratic machine maintained low rates of municipal taxation. Except for 1889, city revenue did not exceed $15,000 in any year during the 1880s, and the sum of ad valorem taxes and special occupation and market taxes for businessmen averaged only $9,000 annually. To hold the line on taxation, the city government sacrificed public services. The single largest expenditure each year was approximately $4,000 for the maintenance of a police force of ten men. By the turn of the century, Brownsville still lacked a water works, an electric power plant, and a telephone system. With the construction of the railroad and the subsequent business recovery in Brownsville, however, Wells would emerge as one of the leading promoters of modern public utilities to meet the needs of the growing and prospering community.

The lower-class Mexican Americans constituted the third component of the Democratic constituency of Cameron County, and Wells' power ultimately rested on the votes of these people. In Brownsville as well as in the countryside, they formed a solid majority of the population. Apart from the influential Mexican American families, who operated stores and other businesses, most of the Hispanic residents of Brownsville worked as common laborers, although a minority held jobs as craftsmen, street vendors, and even clerks. Wells relied on the ranchers and businessmen to mobilize their workers and tenants for elections, but his ties with the Mexican American majority were not just secondhand. The Cameron County boss touched the lives of his constituents with the same kind of paternalistic activity that characterized the operations of the big-city machines. Facing criticism in 1919 for his manipulation of South Texas elections, Wells defended his relationship with the Mexican American voters: "So far as I being a boss, if I exercise any influence among those people because in the 41 years I have lived among them I have tried to so conduct myself as to show them that I was their friend and they could trust me, I take no advantage of them or their ignorance. I buried many a one of them with my money and married many a one of them. It wasn't two or three days before the election, but through the years around, and they have always been true to me."[3] Several years earlier, a close associate described Wells as the "Father Confessor" for "a people . . . whose notes he has endorsed and paid, whose babies he has played with, whose tangles he has untangled, and whose troubles he has made his own for more than thirty years."[4] When the severe drought of the early 1890s threatened hundreds of poor Mexican Americans with destitution and starvation, Wells contributed generously from his own pocket and supported a county drive to raise relief funds. With this display of leadership, he won the gratitude and loyalty of the Hispanic community. Like the *patrón-peón* bond, political leadership and support entailed more than the simple exercise of power. Political relations also depended on an understanding of mutual obligation.

The South Texas boss offered further assistance when Mexican American laborers faced problems with the law. Wells defended *peones* for minimal fees or no charge at all, sometimes arranged their release from jail without the formality of a trial, and even used his influence with Texas governors to secure pardons for men convicted of serious crimes. Mexican American constables, elected with machine backing, frequently dispensed an informal brand of justice, which circumvented the courts altogether. Although these officials assessed and pocketed fines on their own, the offenders escaped more serious legal punishments and accepted the arrangement. Wells and his organization stood as a buffer between the populace and an alien legal system, which they neither understood nor fully trusted. This willingness to tamper with the law would take on more sinister overtones when the defendants were important political figures and the charges were as serious as murder.

The Mexican American constituents were receptive to Wells' gestures of friendship and support. Lacking any tradition of participation in electoral politics, they did not view themselves as inde-

pendent voters or as an aggrieved interest group with the potential
power to organize and force their demands on public officials. Instead, the heritage of peonage conditioned the Hispanic workers and
farmers to define their political role in terms of personal obligation.
They voted for a particular candidate, not because of his qualifications or campaign promises, but because they felt indebted to the
candidate or to Wells or to their employers, who supported the machine ticket. The reciprocity of the old feudal system survived. In
exchange for jobs, help in time of need, or just small favors, the Mexican American workers submitted to the authority of the boss and
his allies. Certainly, the voters were vulnerable to economic and
physical coercion. Even so, the cultivation of loyalty and trust was
as important as the application of force. The past outbreaks of racial
strife revealed the dangers of taking Mexican American subservience
for granted, and the more perceptive politicians and ranchers understood the need to satisfy the popular expectations of paternalistic
support and protection. Even as followers, the Hispanic majority
strongly influenced the pattern of political conduct.

Despite Wells' informal system of welfare and legal assistance,
boss rule did not produce any general upturn in the living standards
of the Mexican American workers and farmers. Burdened with debts
and receiving as little as $5.00 to $15.00 wages per month during the
1870s, the ranch hands and farm laborers of South Texas struggled
just to subsist. By the early 1890s, the average farm wage in Cameron County stood at only $8.15 per month, and, in 1901, Wells re-
ported to a prospective land purchaser that "an abundant supply of
good labor . . . could be obtained at 50¢, or less, per man, per day."[5]
Although the ranchers often provided their employees with housing
and other support, the lower-class Mexican American families still
endured severe poverty. Wells and his associates generally limited
their aid to covering special expenses, such as weddings and funerals, and to meeting individual or general emergencies. These paternalistic practices might prevent an individual from succumbing to
complete destitution, but the prospects for advancement remained
bleak.

Outside Brownsville, even the public school system failed to
offer any promise of improvement for the children of the poverty-
ridden families. A competent teaching staff and a special program to
teach Mexican American children English over a three-year period
reflected the commitment of the Brownsville school board to a sound
educational program, but political patronage destroyed the effectiveness of the county schools. Wells' opponents repeatedly charged that
graft on the part of the county school superintendent and the ap-

pointment of semiliterate political cronies to teaching positions reduced education in the rural areas to a farce.

Although Hispanic politicians held positions of influence, the
Wells organization afforded only marginal opportunities for upward
mobility for the mainstream of the population. The machine sometimes recruited common laborers, small-time farmers and ranchers,
or members of their families for the low-ranking jobs in the county
and city governments and the party hierarchy, but they seldom rose
to higher posts. In comparison with the depressed level of agricultural
wages in South Texas, income from some of the full-time patronage
jobs was substantial. For example, in the early 1890s, Brownsville
patrolmen, all of whom were Mexican Americans, received $25 per
month, and county teachers received $45 per month. On the other
hand, campaign workers, election officials, and other temporary employees collected only a few dollars. The chief reward for these appointees was heightened prestige as a result of their identification
with the local power structure. With fewer than one hundred full-
time local patronage positions available to Mexican Americans, only
a small percentage of the population experienced even these modest
advances.

All the Hispanics who exercised political power came from
well-to-do families with established business and ranching interests.
They served in such important posts as county commissioner, county
treasurer, county attorney, justice of the peace, and city councilman.
Despite their influence, these politicians did not represent an independent force committed to the advancement of the Mexican American population as a whole. As the heirs of a long-standing aristocracy, they failed to identify with their *peones* and employees.
Instead, the Mexican American elite faced the reality of Anglo power
and decided that their interests lay with the Anglo landowners and
businessmen. Although many Mexican families had retained their
land, the economic balance had clearly shifted to the Anglo side by
the 1870s. With their enormous profits from the Civil War cotton
trade along the border, the Anglo entrepreneurs had expanded their
landholdings and commercial interest in Cameron County. In the
political arena as well, the local Anglo practitioners enjoyed important advantages: greater familiarity with the rules and tactics of electoral competition and monopolization of the contacts with higher
governmental authority at the state and national levels. Facing these
odds, the Mexican American *patrones*, businessmen, and politicos
became preoccupied with winning respectability and acceptance
from the Anglo power holders.

Rather than offering an open society with abundant opportunity for improved living standards and upward mobility, the Wells machine won Mexican American support by embracing the survivors of the Mexican elite and sustaining a social system to which most of the population was accustomed. That system was certainly exploitative with the relegation of most Mexican Americans to low-paying manual labor. Still the continuation of a familiar culture, the low level of overt racial discrimination, and the availability of paternalistic aid offered some compensations. Without proposing alternative benefits, later reformers would attack even these concessions to the hard-pressed populace.

To mobilize their Hispanic support fully, the Cameron County Democrats took advantage of lax election laws and engaged in practices of questionable legality. By the terms of the Treaty of Guadalupe Hidalgo that settled the war with Mexico, all Mexican citizens who chose to remain in the territories brought under American rule automatically became U.S. citizens unless they reaffirmed their allegiance to Mexico within one year. During the decades following the war, thousands of additional Mexicans migrated into South Texas, and many were able to participate in elections without ever attaining U.S. citizenship. Under the provisions of the 1876 Texas Constitution, a male alien could vote if he simply declared his intention to become a naturalized citizen "at any time before an election" and established his residence in the state for one year and the county for six months. The number of Mexicans submitting declarations of intent to the Cameron County administration skyrocketed during election years. Wells' opponents accused him not only of voting local residents who never intended to become citizens but also of recruiting aliens who lived south of the Rio Grande.

Another source of controversy was the practice of "corralling voters" on election day. On the afternoon before the election, both the Wells Blue Club and the opposition Reds rounded up their respective voters and plied them with barbecue and liquor through the night. The next morning the party organizers led their followers to the polls en masse. Before the election reform laws of the early twentieth century, the election officials prepared separate red and blue ballots, and the usually illiterate Hispanic voter simply indicated his color preference. To complete the process, campaign workers sometimes distributed cash bribes after the party loyalists had cast their votes.

Because of its reliance on these improper tactics to maximize the Hispanic vote, the Wells machine vigorously opposed all efforts to enact election reforms. The first serious challenges came in 1895 when the state legislature established regulations for party primaries, which included criminal sanctions against buying votes and bribing election officials. The legislature and the electorate also passed a constitutional amendment that required aliens to declare their intentions to become citizens at least six months before voting in an election. This added time requirement had little effect on the participation of Mexican nationals in the border elections. During the same legislative session, Wells' allies managed to block passage of the Australian ballot and limitations on assistance to illiterate voters. Despite the statewide furor over election abuses along the Rio Grande, none of the reform initiatives of the 1890s curtailed the manipulation of Hispanic voters, and the demand to clean up South Texas elections became a rallying cry for progressive insurgents during the first two decades of the twentieth century.

Catering to the demands and needs of the ranchers, Brownsville businessmen, and Hispanic voters was the fundamental requirement for sustaining the power of the Democratic machine, but James B. Wells' political success depended on more than sensitivity to constituent interests. He also had to be able to handle his fellow politicians. Despite their deference to Wells as the boss of Cameron County, he never exercised absolute authority over his party. With the division of most of the electorate into controlled blocs of voters, individual politicians could develop independent power bases by consolidating the support of a few ranchers or businessmen. Although policy differences within the Democratic Blue Club were rare, personal rivalries for the limited number of local political offices repeatedly threatened party unity. To counter these divisive tendencies and to maintain his own position of leadership, Wells practiced the politics of compromise and consensus. Rather than dictating the party ticket, the boss consulted factional leaders and the powerful ranchers loyal to the Blue Club. Because of the scope of his personal support and his control over state and sometimes federal patronage, Wells exerted more influence than the other politicos, but the emphasis was on accommodation. Until 1906, the Cameron County Democrats conducted nominating conventions instead of direct primaries, and weeks of intense negotiation sometimes preceded the formal ratification of the ticket at the convention. Even after the introduction of primary elections, Wells tried to minimize open competition for the nominations by arranging political trade-offs and persuading some candidates to withdraw. Wells' skill as an arbiter not only enhanced Democratic unity but also made him the party's indispensable man.

These efforts at accommodation did not always succeed, however. In 1892, Cameron County Sheriff Santiago A. Brito broke with

Wells in a dispute over the gubernatorial race between James Hogg and George Clark. Eight years later, factional feuding prevented another sheriff, Emilio Forto, from reclaiming the nomination, and he defected to the Red Club. When disgruntled Democrats rejected compromise and rebelled, Wells' conciliatory posture turned to bitter opposition. As he explained to his friend Colonel E. M. House on one occasion, "I have done all in my power to conciliate and I shall now devote doing all I can to crush, and I am too old a frontiersman to even think of wounding a snake—kill it or leave it alone."[7] In fact, Sheriff Brito was murdered by unidentified assailants after he challenged Wells' leadership. Despite charges by some of Brito's allies and a Laredo newspaper, no evidence ever materialized to implicate Wells or any of his associates. Nevertheless, the assassination of the Cameron County sheriff was one of the earliest in a series of murders with political overtones that blackened South Texas politics during the 1890s and the first two decades of the twentieth century.

Another source of Wells' political strength, besides his adeptness at compromise and his careful cultivation of constituent support, was his influence over patronage. By the 1890s, the county and city governments had created over one hundred appointive jobs, most of which went to either teachers or law enforcement officers. Projects, such as road improvements and the construction of public buildings, provided additional temporary work for scores of laborers. Like the determination of local slates of candidates, the distribution of patronage entailed concessions to contending factions, but Wells as the party unifier exercised the dominant influence. From the ranks of the political appointees came a cadre of loyal supporters and campaign workers—men who submitted completely to Wells' authority because their livelihoods depended on his benefaction. Still, the South Texas boss recognized that this power also posed problems. Throughout his career, job seekers hounded Wells, and some of his most determined opponents were frustrated spoilsmen. Wells' exasperation surfaced when he confided to a friend that every appointment produced eleven enemies and one ingrate.

Because of his close association with the "king maker" of Texas politics, Colonel Edward M. House, James Wells enjoyed a near monopoly over the distribution of state patronage among Valley residents. From 1894 through 1902, House engineered the election of three conservative governors and rewarded his political allies like Wells with patronage favors. Not only did Wells decide the appointments of the limited number of state officials serving in the Valley counties, but he also exercised an indirect veto over the applications of South Texas citizens for any state government positions. Only a

Wells endorsement assured serious consideration for an office seeker from Cameron, Hidalgo, or Starr counties. Further patronage benefits accrued to the Rio Grande Democrat with his election as state Democratic chairman in 1900 and 1902. From this influential post, he assessed campaign contributions from officeholders throughout the state government to finance South Texas as well as statewide races.

The single most important patronage prize in the Lower Rio Grande Valley was the federal customs service for the district of Brazos de Santiago. The customs collector at Brownsville selected and supervised a force of almost thirty men, who patrolled a 250-mile stretch of border from the coast to the town of Roma in Starr County. The president of the United States appointed the collector on the advice of the secretary of the treasury, whose department oversaw the Customs Service. During the two Democratic administrations of the Gilded Age, President Grover Cleveland and his advisers relied on the recommendations of Congressman William H. Crain for patronage choices for South Texas, but the determination of Valley appointments ultimately rested with James B. Wells. The Cameron County boss spearheaded Crain's first campaign for the House of Representatives in 1884 against strong opposition, and the freshman congressman repaid Wells with complete control over local federal patronage.

In 1885, Wells arranged the selection of J. J. Cocke as the Brownsville collector, and Cocke proceeded to appoint subordinates loyal to Wells and his allies in Hidalgo and Starr counties. When the Democrats regained the presidency in 1893, another machine applicant, John A. Michel, assumed the position. Wells' control of federal patronage proved to be a short-term phenomenon, however. For twenty-two of the thirty-eight years that Wells reigned as the boss of Cameron County, Republicans occupied the White House and filled the local federal offices with partisans hostile to the Democratic machine. Republican activists like Rentfro B. Creager used the customs house as a political base for recruiting supporters and organizing election campaigns. Even with the election of Woodrow Wilson and the restoration of national Democratic power in 1913, Wells failed to reassert his dominance over the federal bureaucracy in the Lower Rio Grande Valley. Instead, independent Democrats secured the postal and customs appointments and upheld the tradition of federal opposition to the Wells organization.

Despite the recurrent challenges of the so-called customs house parties, James B. Wells remained the dominant force in Cameron County politics through World War I. With the dramatic rise of truck and fruit farming and the arrival of new settlers toward the end of the first decade of the twentieth century, the opposition developed considerable strength and scored several election breakthroughs, but Wells retained the chairmanship of the Cameron County Democratic party until 1920. From this base of power in his home county, the Brownsville political leader extended his influence over the two other Rio Grande Valley counties, Hidalgo and Starr, as well as Duval County. Alternating competition and cooperation marked his relations with the Democratic machines to the north and west of the Valley, the Nueces County Democrats at Corpus Christi and the Webb County Democrats at Laredo. For some district and state races, Wells intervened in the campaigns of counties as distant as Zavala, Dimmit, La Salle, Frio, Atascosa, McMullen, and San Patricio.

The preeminence of James B. Wells among Valley Democrats was hardly surprising. The social conditions of Cameron, Hidalgo, and Starr counties were nearly identical. Mexican Americans formed overwhelming majorities in all three counties, and powerful ranchers controlled vast tracts of land. Mexican cultural patterns prevailed throughout the region. In fact, Anglo penetration of Starr County was so limited that the bulk of the land remained in Hispanic hands at the turn of the century. Within this common social setting, Cameron County assumed a position of leadership. Of the three counties, Cameron had the largest population, and Brownsville stood as the center of commercial activity for the whole Lower Rio Grande Valley. Political relationships both reflected and reinforced the dominance of the county. Cameron County Democrats established the first formal political organization along the border, and, with the death of Stephen Powers, Wells took command of the machine that served as a model for other county parties. The law practices of Powers and Wells enhanced their political standings, as both men defended clients throughout South Texas and won the direct support of ranchers and merchants beyond the boundaries of Cameron County.

Throughout his career, James B. Wells intervened in the political affairs of Hidalgo and Starr counties. During the 1880s and 1890s, factional dissension and armed confrontations wracked the Democratic party of Hidalgo County. To preserve his influence in the midst of this turmoil, the Brownsville boss constantly shifted tactics. At different times, he promoted reconciliation, backed one side against the other, and finally supported the moves of Sheriff John Closner to destroy the power of the combative factional chiefs and to provide alternative leadership. Similarly, Wells shepherded the early career of Manuel Guerra in Starr County and helped to arrange an alliance between Guerra and Sheriff W. W. Shely. These two men exercised joint control for more than a decade until Shely's retirement in 1906, and then Guerra emerged as the sole master of Starr County politics. Closner, Shely, and Guerra all benefited from Wells' willingness to delegate patronage authority. Wells allowed these associates to name the state appointees stationed in their counties and even customs officials when Cleveland held the presidency. In return for this support, the three politicians faithfully followed Wells' lead in state and district races.

A close political relationship also developed between the Brownsville attorney and Archie Parr of Duval County, northwest of the Lower Rio Grande Valley. Wells consulted with Parr on patronage choices as early as the 1890s, but the Duval rancher did not establish his dominance over county politics until 1908. The Duval Republican organization won a respectable share of the local offices and regularly delivered the county for GOP congressional candidates from 1892 through 1904. Despite his late emergence as a county boss, Parr eventually forged the most powerful and lasting machine in the Trans-Nueces. Paternalistic oversight of his Hispanic constituency, voter manipulation, rampant corruption, and political violence all contributed to Parr's ascent. Even as Parr's influence surpassed that of James B. Wells, during the waning years of his career, the two men remained staunch allies.

For four decades, Wells stood at the center of South Texas politics. At the height of his career, he managed the Cameron County Democratic party, influenced the political evolution of three other counties, cooperated closely with the U.S. congressmen from his district, and distributed state and sometimes federal patronage for the Lower Rio Grande Valley. Wells' main concern was always the consolidation of his power at the local and regional levels, but he also showed interest in two other political endeavors. Beyond arranging patronage appointments and battling election reforms, the South Texas boss sought to influence the general policies of the state and national governments. In addition, he used political leverage to create business opportunities for himself and his friends.

On most of the state and national issues of the 1890s and the early twentieth century, James B. Wells held conservative views. He embraced the standard Bourbon Democratic doctrines of limited government, reduced tariffs, and the restoration of the gold standard. With his background of railroad promotion and frequent participation in other corporate enterprises, Wells viewed government regulation of the economy as a deterrent to business expansion and a possible threat to his own self-interest. In 1892, the South Texas boss conducted a vigorous preconvention campaign against Governor

James Hogg, whose foremost achievement had been the establishment of the Texas Railroad Commission. Wells later opposed the successful gubernatorial bid of another leading progressive Democrat, Thomas Campbell. During the twelve-year interim separating these reform-minded administrations, Wells participated in the loose coalition of probusiness conservatives who dominated Texas politics and resisted the challenges of both Hogg Democrats and Populists. The Brownsville lawyer's opposition to prohibition also reflected his aversion to government regulation, and his Catholic constituency shared his disapproval of this drive to impose pietistic Protestant standards of personal morality through government sanctions.

At the national level, Wells remained loyal to Representative William Crain, who consistently supported the conservative policies of President Grover Cleveland during the depression of the 1890s. Even in the face of the dramatic public reaction against the Bourbon administration and the growing strength of the free silver movement within the Democratic party, Crain cast one of only four Texas congressional votes in favor of Cleveland's proposal to repeal the Sherman Silver Purchase Act. When Crain died in 1896, Wells threw his support behind Rudolph Kleberg, whose advocacy of silver coinage at election time masked his real commitment to the gold standard.

Despite his consistent preference for conservative doctrines and policies, political principle did not dictate Wells' actions. He regularly sacrificed ideological commitments for the sake of expediency. Always sensitive to constituent pressures, Wells and his congressional protégés compromised their support for low tariffs with demands for protection for wool, hides, and other locally produced commodities. Nor did his belief in the Jeffersonian ideal of limited government deter the Brownsville politico from agitating for federal harbor projects along the South Texas coast or for federal and state aid for irrigation development.

Adaptability characterized Wells' relations with state Democratic leaders as well. Although he objected to Hogg's regulatory policies, the Valley boss refused to abandon the regular Democratic party after the governor's renomination and to endorse the independent candidacy of conservative George Clark in the general election. Similarly, Wells reached an accommodation with Governor Thomas Campbell and supported him for reelection in 1908. In each of these cases of reconciliation, party loyalty, the desire to retain influence within the state Democratic organization, and concern for patronage prevailed over ideological qualms.

Allegiance to the Democratic party was the only principle that

Wells refused to violate. When the free silver forces gained control of the state party in 1896, James B. Wells, a staunch gold Democrat, rejected appeals to bolt and offered the following affirmation of his faith in party loyalty: "I am just as much of a 'sound money' man as ever or more so if possible, but I have no patience with the 'holier than thou' crowd calling themselves 'Democrats' who are giving direct aid and comfort to the enemy by deserting and betraying our party. I shall give my heartiest support and my best efforts to our party and its nominees. Should we suffer defeat, I prefer a 1000 times to go down with our flags flying with it than to survive with our enemies."[8] Despite his claim that he would be willing to suffer defeat for the sake of Democratic fidelity, Wells did not insist on party loyalty because of some emotional or doctrinaire commitment to the Democratic party. Instead, practical political considerations underlay his steadfast allegiance. Wells wanted to salvage his influence within the state organization and to avoid weakening the party. His experience in South Texas politics shaped his assessment of political priorities at the state and national levels. Policy disagreements rarely materialized among Valley Democrats before 1900, but factional disputes over the distribution of patronage and elective offices posed a recurrent threat to the local dominance of the party. As a result, Wells came to value party unity over ideological purity. For the veteran campaigner, party organization and cohesion were the foundations of power, and the exercise of power, not policy commitments, was the essence of politics.

Politics alone did not monopolize Wells' attention. Besides the practice of law and railroad promotion, he engaged in ranching, land speculation, irrigation development, and numerous investment ventures ranging from oil exploration to life insurance. Inevitably, Wells' political and business interests overlapped. While his success in land title cases helped Wells to consolidate the political support of powerful ranching interests, his influence as a politician attracted legal clients. The Brownsville boss regularly represented ranches, railroads, and other businesses before the county boards of equalization, which reviewed complaints about property valuations for tax purposes. Political allies doubled as business associates. Wells loaned money to Manuel Guerra, received loans from Archie Parr, persuaded Colonel House to invest in Brownsville utilities, and joined John Closner in promoting irrigation, land speculation, and town development schemes. Throughout his career, Wells maintained close political and economic ties with the King family. After the death of Stephen Powers, Wells assumed the role of lawyer and purchasing agent for this mammoth ranching enterprise. He also received personal loans and campaign contributions from the Kings and the Klebergs and consulted with them on countless political matters.

The Valley politico's personal interests usually coincided with those of his constituents. As a rancher, Wells benefited from the low tax policies of the county governments. As an investor in irrigation projects, he profited from his own lobbying campaign to promote state legislation that would settle competing water-rights claims and facilitate the organization of irrigation districts. With the revival of the Brownsville economy after the turn of the century, local businessmen pressed for the construction of modern utilities, and this legitimate public need afforded Wells his most promising business opportunity. The Brownsville city council initially awarded engineer John W. Maxcy with the franchise to establish a waterworks, an electric light plant, and a telephone system, and Wells invested heavily in the enterprise. When Maxcy failed to meet the deadline for starting construction because of a shortage of capital, the city council refused to grant an extension and transferred the franchise to Wells, who received two extensions over the next year and a half. Although the Cameron County boss failed to fulfill the terms of the franchise, he helped to organize the two companies that subsequently secured new franchises and provided Brownsville with the needed utilities.

Despite this interplay of political influence and business activity, James B. Wells did not amass a personal fortune from politics. The veteran campaigner was a compulsive speculator, whose business career was riddled with repeated failures. Constantly borrowing, investing, and even loaning money, he faced mounting indebtedness from the mid-1880s on and nearly succumbed to bankruptcy on three separate occasions. In 1884, one of his law partners warned Wells to stop "throwing money away right and left," and a later associate conceded that Wells displayed no financial aptitude in his own business affairs, despite his sound advice to clients.[9] The economic rewards of political power could not offset this record of ineptitude. Politicking entailed its own expenses, as Wells spent money for campaign financing and paternalistic care for his impoverished constituents. Apparently, the limited amount of embezzlement from the Cameron County treasury did not even cover the costs of these undertakings, let alone make Wells and his cronies rich men. The Cameron County Democrats never engaged in the kind of continuous, large-scale thievery that characterized the political operations under John Closner, Manuel Guerra, and Archie Parr.

Making money was certainly a secondary motive behind Wells' ceaseless political campaigning and maneuvering. Political power itself and the attention that it brought were what mattered to the Brownsville lawyer. In economic terms, not only the Kings, Klebergs, and Kenedys but numerous other South Texas entrepreneurs overshadowed James B. Wells. Even as a highly esteemed lawyer, he served as the agent of more successful men. Only as a political leader did Wells stand on an equal footing with the powerful figures of the Trans-Nueces region. Two of his allies in state politics, Colonel House and Frank Andrews, marveled at the enthusiasm that the Valley boss mustered for his campaign efforts, and his political correspondence was filled with extravagant pledges of support. Wells did not merely campaign for a candidate; he performed "a labor of love."[10] This enthusiasm did not stem from any commitment to policies or doctrines, since Wells compromised his ideological beliefs throughout his career. Nor did personal loyalties fully account for his excitement. He remained close to some allies over the years, but many were lost in the shuffle of shifting alignments. This seasoned professional thrived on the mechanics of the political process. Political power had made him an important man, and he relished the demonstration of that power in campaigns and factional battles.

2. The Customs House Gang

HEATED CONTROVERSY SWIRLED around the issue of patronage during the Gilded Age. Reformers denounced the appointment of political cronies to government jobs as corruption. Men secured public positions, not because of their competence or expertise, but because of their party affiliation, their willingness to submit to the control of their political sponsors, and their agreement to kickback part of their salaries as campaign contributions. At the national level, the struggle to eliminate patronage abuses culminated with the passage of the Pendleton Act, or the Civil Service Act, in 1883. The legislation authorized the Civil Service Commission to administer merit tests for appointments and promotions to 10 percent of the federal offices and empowered the president to expand the range of coverage at his discretion. The law also strengthened the ban against collecting assessments from federal employees. Mugwumps and their fellow crusaders hoped that the reform would lay the groundwork for an efficient, professional bureaucracy, immune to political manipulation.

The professional politicians viewed patronage from a different perspective. Ideally, the practice of awarding political appointments embodied the democratic concept of making all government officials accountable to the electorate. When the elected representatives of one political party met defeat, strict adherence to the rules of patronage ensured the removal of the appointed personnel as well. The spoils system stood as a barrier against the creation of an entrenched government aristocracy. In more practical terms, patronage provided a mechanism for political organization. Through the skillful management of patronage, politicians could reward their loyal followers, discipline rebels who challenged party leadership, and appease competing factions.

For the Republicans of South Texas during the late nineteenth and early twentieth centuries, federal patronage constituted their main political resource. Only when Republicans held the presidency and controlled the distribution of federal jobs was the local GOP able to challenge Democratic dominance in the Lower Rio Grande Valley. Republican officeholders participated in local, state, and national campaigns, and the party leaders sometimes induced defections from the faction-plagued Democratic organizations with offers of national appointments. Even with the influx of new settlers after 1905 and the rise of a sizable constituency hostile to boss rule, Republicans and, later, independent Democrats continued to rely on federal patronage to create their organizational base.

The nationally appointed officials who served in South Texas included postmasters, internal revenue commissioners, and various law enforcement officials, but the customs collector for the district of Brazos de Santiago overshadowed all others in the exercise of political influence. Charged with the responsibility of collecting duties on imported goods and preventing smuggling, the collector appointed and managed a force of almost thirty men. With his headquarters at Brownsville, he selected deputy collectors to operate customs stations at the towns of Point Isabel and Santa Maria in Cameron County, Edinburg in Hidalgo County, and Rio Grande City and Roma in Starr County. Even at the customs house in Brownsville, the collector provided only general oversight, while his special deputy collector handled the administrative details. To combat smuggling, especially the herding of livestock from Mexico, twenty mounted inspectors patrolled the 250 miles of borderland from the mouth of the Rio Grande to the western boundary of Starr County.

The Pendleton Act required the Treasury Department to organize competitive examinations for subordinate customs employees only in districts with fifty or more jobs. Even with the partial extension of this system to the district of Brazos de Santiago in December 1894, civil service reform had limited impact on the practice of making partisan appointments. Of all the employees under the control of the Brownsville collector, only certain deputy collectors, two female inspectors, and the male inspectors exempt from mounted patrol duty had to take exams to qualify for appointments. Instead of raising the level of competence among customs officials, the introduction of merit tests had the paradoxical effect of forcing the collector to select some men barely able to handle their duties. Seventy-five to 90 percent of the passengers on the ferries crossing the Rio Grande were Mexicans who could not speak or understand English, but the civil service exams contained no questions for measuring proficiency in foreign languages. As a result, the collector frequently had to choose ferry inspectors from "eligible lists" that included no

Spanish-speaking applicants. The impracticality of this arrangement became so obvious that the Treasury Department allowed the Brownsville collector to abolish the classified positions for male inspectors in 1905, to hire additional mounted inspectors exempt from testing, and to rotate the ferry duty assignments among the mounted inspectors.

The collector exercised some discretionary authority even over those few posts covered by the system of competitive testing. The results of the examinations did not dictate appointments but only designated the eligible candidates, among whom the collector could make his choices. Throughout the Gilded Age and the subsequent Progressive Era, political calculations took precedence over civil service guidelines in the appointment of almost all customs officials.

Nor did civil service reform curb the intervention of customs appointees in local political campaigns. The prohibition against political assessments applied to all federal employees, not just the classified personnel subject to competitive examinations. Still the law contained a glaring loophole. While the Pendleton Act forbade federal officials from forcing subordinates to make political donations, employees were free to make voluntary contributions to solicitors outside the government. The customs house officials in the Valley regularly donated money to local Republican organizations. These men claimed that they acted voluntarily, but their dependence on the collector for their jobs clouded the distinction between voluntary and coerced behavior.

The civil service restrictions against active campaigning were also ambiguous. The Pendleton Act outlawed the pressuring of federal employees into political action, but only implied that the appointees should avoid voluntary partisan agitation. Although the Civil Service Commission eventually formulated guidelines banning involvement in political campaigns, the rules lacked legal sanction and applied only to the competitive classified service. In practice, the national administrations imposed a double standard on the Brownsville collectors. The Treasury Department removed the appointees of previous opposition administrations for interference in local politics but usually tolerated such activity on behalf of the party in power, as long as the campaigning did not interfere with the performance of official customs duties.

In the absence of rigorous enforcement of the restrictions on political agitation, the Republican customs collectors at Brownsville spearheaded the assaults against Democratic rule in South Texas. The GOP insurgency followed an erratic course. After scoring impressive gains during the transitional period between the death of

Stephen Powers and the consolidation of Wells' power, the local Republican party experienced a nearly fatal collapse with the election of Grover Cleveland in 1884 and its loss of control over federal patronage and only partially recovered during the next Republican term under Benjamin Harrison. The Republican challenge finally revived with the election of 1896 and reached its peak during the administrations of William McKinley and Theodore Roosevelt. In 1900, the party fell just a few votes short of a popular majority in Cameron County. Six years later, a full-scale offensive in Starr County produced not only a close election but also an armed confrontation, two political assassinations, and federal indictments against the Starr County Democratic boss and the sheriff for conspiracy to commit murder. By 1910, demographic changes had laid the groundwork for further gains against machine domination in both Cameron and Hidalgo counties, but the local Republican party ceased to exist as a distinct organization. After the election of 1908, the Republicans discarded their party label and fused with maverick Democrats to form the Independent party.

Although the GOP mounted its most serious challenges around the turn of the century, the earlier Republican customs collectors set the precedents for political activism. From 1884 through 1896, James O. Luby and Robert B. Rentfro dominated Republican politics in South Texas, and both men served as Brownsville collectors. When Luby applied for the post toward the end of the administration of Chester Arthur, Rentfro promoted Luby's candidacy with a forthright admission of their partisan ambitions: "We need only a skillful hand to make this entire border Republican beyond doubt. Luby . . . is endowed with remarkable political sagacity, and has always succeeded in overthrowing the 'Bourbon' element in every community in which he has hitherto resided."[1] At the time of Luby's appointment, Rentfro practiced law in partnership with James B. Wells, but their joint enterprise came to an abrupt end in 1884 when Rentfro announced his plans to run as a Republican against Wells' candidate for Congress, William H. Crain. Converting the customs house into a combative political machine, Luby managed Rentfro's campaign and supported local Republican candidates throughout the Valley. Incensed Democrats accused the collector of offering patronage jobs to sway voters, promoting dissension within their party, and conducting a libelous newspaper campaign against Democratic candidates. Although these efforts fell short of victory, Rentfro collected a record number of Republican votes in Cameron County and even carried Starr County. After Luby's removal during the Cleveland administration, he returned to his home county of Duval, engineered an insurgency within the local Democratic party, and won election as county judge. He subsequently revived the Duval Republican organization, which scored several impressive victories over the Democrats from 1892 through 1904.

Despite his defeat in the congressional race, R. B. Rentfro retained his influence among Cameron County Republicans, and received the collectorship when Benjamin Harrison reclaimed the presidency for the GOP in 1889. Rentfro's mobilization of the customs force produced some modest gains in Starr County but failed to broaden the Republican base of support in Cameron County. This stagnation resulted not only from Wells' success in fashioning an efficient Democratic machine but also from dissension within the Republican minority. When several local party members accused the collector of secretly collaborating with Wells, Rentfro lashed out at his critics. He condemned individual Republicans for smuggling, postal fraud, participation in the Garza Revolution, drunkenness, and gambling. The combination of these charges and countercharges created the image of a party filled with ne'er-do-wells, political opportunists, and common criminals. The prestige of the Rentfro administration sank even lower in 1890 as the result of his association with a Hidalgo County judge who tried to stay in office after an election defeat through the use of armed force and whose wife killed the victor in the election.

Rentfro's removal as customs collector did not alter the basic pattern of Republican politics along the border. Factional splits and wild fluctuations in vote totals continued to plague the GOP, but, with the Republican sweep at the national level in 1896, the local party members started a resurgence that culminated in two dramatic campaigns, the Cameron County election of 1900 and the Starr County election of 1906. In the wake of the factional dispute over Rentfro's stewardship, Valley Republicans embraced a new candidate for the Brownsville collectorship, C. H. Maris. Maris' aggressive campaigning and recruitment of Democratic defectors led the Republicans to their strongest showing in Cameron County since Reconstruction and produced modest gains in Hidalgo and Starr counties. Like his predecessors, however, C. H. Maris eventually fell victim to sharp Democratic counterattacks and internal Republican feuding.

During the 1880s, C. H. Maris moved from Ohio to Victoria County, Texas, where he held the position of county attorney, and then settled at Brownsville in 1891. Maris joined E. H. Goodrich's law firm and real estate dealership as a junior partner. Although Goodrich had bolted the Republican party and had won election as the superintendent of county schools on the Democratic ticket, Maris assumed an active role in local Republican politics. In 1892, he served as acting U.S. district attorney for the closing term of the federal court in Brownsville, and, two years later, he ran as a Republican candidate for the Texas Court of Civil Appeals. By 1897, Maris was ready to take charge of the Cameron County GOP.

As a result of Grover Cleveland's economic and political bungling during the depression of the 1890s, Republican success in the presidential election of 1896 seemed assured. The prospect of again sharing in federal patronage attracted wayward Valley Republicans back to the party fold, and GOP strength in Cameron County returned to the thousand-vote level. With his vigorous campaigning for the Republican ticket, C. H. Maris won the respect of his fellow party members. The chairman of the Republican executive committee for the South Texas congressional district even singled out Maris as the man most responsible for doubling the Republican vote along the border.

Having demonstrated his skill as a political organizer, the Brownsville lawyer lobbied for the customs appointment, and local, Texas, and out-of-state GOP leaders rallied behind his candidacy. Maris received endorsements from over 110 groups and individuals, including the chairmen of the Cameron and Hidalgo County Republican executive committees, five members of the state committee, and seven U.S. senators and representatives. Only the Starr County Republican organization remained loyal to Rentfro and opposed Maris' appointment. Maris' defenders emphasized his adeptness at campaigning over any claims that he might have had to administrative competence. According to the Hidalgo County Republican chairman, the selection of this relative newcomer to the political battleground of the Valley could result in an incredible increase of two to three thousand votes for the GOP, while Rentfro's appointment threatened to "sound the death knell for the Republican Party on the frontier."[2] Other endorsements cited Maris' ability to restore unity to the local party organizations. In light of these openly partisan appeals to boost his candidacy, C. H. Maris interpreted his appointment as a mandate to revitalize and lead the Republican forces of South Texas.

When Maris assumed the post of Brownsville customs collector in June 1897, one of the leading merchants of Brownsville, Henry Field, held the chairmanship of the Cameron County Republican party. As a longstanding critic of Rentfro's leadership, Field had promoted Maris' appointment, but competition for control of the county organization later destroyed their alliance. Other GOP organizers also posed problems for the new collector. Although GOP rhetoric condemned the Democratic politicos as grafters and criminals, the Republicans' own claims to respectability lay open to question. Besides influential businessmen like Field, the party ranks included a number of unsavory characters who regarded their political affiliation as a license to commit illegal acts. The most notorious of these men was W. B. Linton, R. B. Rentfro's brother-in-law and a former customs official. According to the report of a special Treasury agent, Linton devoted most of his time to gambling and "skinning suckers and drunkards."[3] For Linton and his barroom associates, employment in the customs service represented an opportunity to engage in smuggling. When Maris refused to appoint the former inspector, Linton made arrangements with the deputy collector, Alfred Thornham, to discourage the investigation of smuggling operations and to release confiscated goods. The Texas Rangers arrested other Republican loyalists for cattle rustling, but these suspects frequently escaped punishment because of the intervention of their political allies, who provided legal counsel, paid bail, and even cast partisan votes on juries.

The Republicans were not alone in their tolerance of disreputable party members and the obstruction of justice. As the controllers of local government, the Democratic machines also rigged trials and practiced selective law enforcement. The cooperation of county officials with the Texas Rangers to thwart cattle stealing occasionally lapsed when the culprits turned out to be Blue Club members, rather than raiders from Mexico, Republicans, or unaffiliated Anglo rustlers. Because political campaigning along the border sometimes led to violent confrontations, both parties recruited men who could provide armed support, irrespective of their backgrounds. In this frontier community where even many respectable businessmen and ranch owners had made their starts through smuggling, rustling, or dubious land deals, a permissive attitude toward the law prevailed, but Republicans and Democrats alike had to be careful to defend the interests of their constituents. Failure to protect the property of Democratic ranchers could prove disastrous for James B. Wells and his organization.

Within two years of his appointment, C. H. Maris had filled all but a handful of customs jobs with GOP loyalists, including the president of the Red Club of Cameron County, Robert A. Lieck, and a former Republican newspaper editor, Jasper A. Maltby, who had waged a vigorous campaign against Wells' system of boss rule in the mid-1890s. An important exception to this pattern of selecting Republicans was Maris' retention of Alfred Thornham, the deputy

collector for Brownsville under the previous Democratic administration. Both Thornham's administrative competence and his willingness to forsake his Democratic commitments and to campaign
for the Republican party impressed Maris. In fact, he allowed his
deputy considerable latitude in running the Brownsville office. Although Thornham's later exposure as an embezzler and a collabora-
tor with smugglers would embarrass and outrage the collector, the
ex-Democrat's dishonesty had the paradoxical effect of initially en-
hancing Republican unity. Maris rejected the applications of W. B.
Linton and his cohorts, but their opposition to the new customs collector subsided when Thornham agreed to protect the Brownsville
smuggling activities. The complications arising from the deputy's
dismissal in 1904 would split the local Republican organization and
provoke demands for Maris' removal.

Despite the disintegration of the Republican voting bloc in Starr
County because of feuding between the Maris and Rentfro camps,
the GOP gained almost four hundred additional votes in Cameron
and Hidalgo counties in the election of 1898. The most dramatic
surge for Maris and his allies, however, came with the Cameron
County contest of 1900. The combination of Wells' absence and
Democratic factional division brought the Republican party to the
verge of victory in this bastion of Democratic power.

James B. Wells' participation in Cameron County politics slack-
ened around the turn of the century. With the forced resignation of
the state district judge for the Valley counties in 1897, the Democratic boss accepted the gubernatorial appointment to serve the remainder of the judicial term. Preoccupied with his new responsibilities, Wells only belatedly reentered the political fray in 1898 and
devoted most of his attention to the congressional and gubernatorial
races. One year later personal tragedy struck when Wells' oldest son
was killed in a shooting accident. Wells succumbed to intense depression and withdrew from both politics and his law practice for
several months. Even when the boss' interest in politics revived, the
focus was again on state, rather than local, matters. At the state
Democratic convention in August 1900, Colonel House and his conservative allies arranged Wells' selection as chairman of the state
Democratic executive committee. From August through the November election, Wells resided in San Antonio, where he managed the
party headquarters.

In the absence of James B. Wells' steadying influence over the
Democratic organization of Cameron County, factional tension
came to a head in 1900. The party wrangling centered on Emilio
Forto, a native of Spain who had won election as Cameron County

judge in 1882 and sheriff in 1892. After holding these two prized county offices for eighteen years, Emilio Forto stood as one of the most influential men in the Democratic machine, but in 1900 he confronted challenges from two directions. A number of Hispanic ranchers attacked Forto for openly condoning Texas Ranger harassment of the Mexican American population. As an alternative to the veteran Spanish politico, these insurgents promoted the candidacy of Celedonio Garza for sheriff. This unusual display of independence among the Mexican spokesmen hardly represented a break with the Wells organization, since Garza was a party regular who had previously served as county treasurer for fourteen years. The prosperous Hispanic merchant also enjoyed the secret support of James A. Browne, the son of the cofounder of the Cameron County Blue Club and a politician eager to expand his power at Forto's expense. As the contest for the party nomination heated up, both candidates claimed to have the backing of James B. Wells. At the same time that Forto came under attack for his insensitivity to Ranger abuses, a Ranger captain confided to several Brownsville businessmen that the agency suspected the sheriff of collaboration with the "criminal class" in the Valley.[4] A later Treasury Department report identified Emilio Forto as "the recognized friend, aide, and abettor of smugglers."[5] In the past, the association of Democratic politicians with either the Rangers or suspected criminals had posed manageable risks, but now Forto fell victim to simultaneous backlashes.

Facing both a Republican resurgence and the split between powerful factions in his own party, the long-time Democratic county judge Thomas Carson took the unprecedented action of negotiating with the Red Club to choose a compromise slate of candidates for several county offices. The rank and file of the Blue Club, however, protested the selection of Forto as the fusion nominee for sheriff. Although half of the countywide candidates, including Robert B. Rentfro, Jr., the son of the former collector, ran unopposed, a bitterly contested campaign for sheriff ensued. Trying to exploit the deepening tensions among the Democrats, Collector Maris and his deputy Thornham encouraged both Forto and Garza to defect to the Republican side. With his standing inside the Democratic party uncertain, Forto accepted the offer. Even after the incumbent sheriff's nomination at the GOP convention, dissension plagued the Democrats, and only belatedly did a party caucus choose Garza as its candidate. Despite desperate appeals to Wells to intervene to settle the feuding, he remained at the state headquarters in San Antonio and held to a position of awkward neutrality. Wells recognized the scope of the reaction against Forto's performance as sheriff, but he also feared that the Spaniard still held the balance of power in county politics. For this reason Wells failed to repudiate his former ally in 1900, and the Democratic party approached the elections without its customary advantages of unity and strong leadership.

Emilio Forto's candidacy also produced a rift within the Red Club when County Chairman Henry Field refused to endorse the incumbent sheriff because of his alleged criminal connections. Most of the local Republicans, however, followed the campaign leadership of C. H. Maris, and the addition of Forto's followers raised the GOP vote to a rough parity with the Democrats. Ironically, Sheriff Forto, whose defection accounted for the sudden GOP upsurge, trailed the other Republican candidates in the returns, since Field persuaded some of his allies to support Garza. While the ex-Democrat lost by two hundred votes, most of the GOP state nominees fell only ten votes short of a majority, and the Republican candidate for lieutenant governor actually carried Cameron County by a single vote. The Republican congressional nominee trailed by seventy votes in the county returns, and the electors for President William McKinley lost by just two votes. In addition, the partial fusion agreement on the local ticket enabled R. B. Rentfro, Jr., to win the post of county attorney and another Republican to claim a seat on the county commissioners' court. In Hidalgo and Starr counties, the Democrats retained power by safe margins, but the combined Republican balloting for the two counties reached the record level of thirteen hundred votes.

In the aftermath of this setback for the Cameron County Democratic organization, James B. Wells reasserted his leadership and launched a campaign to force Maris' removal from office. Wells and two of his political cronies, District Judge Stanley Welch and District Attorney John Kleiber, charged that Maris was guilty of collusion with cattle thieves and demanded a Treasury Department investigation. The accusation was a political contrivance. To support their claims, the Democratic leaders cited a Cameron County grand jury report that called for an expansion of the local Ranger force to cope with the mounting problem of cattle rustling. The report did not mention the Brownsville collector or the Republican party. Beneath the rhetoric that Maris' conduct was "socialistic in its encouragement and protection of violators of the law," the Democrats could offer only one specific charge: Maris had served as defense counsel for men accused of rustling.[6] For a judge, a prosecutor, and an experienced attorney to condemn a fellow lawyer for defending his clients was simply ludicrous.

In response to a Treasury Department inquiry, a Texas Ranger

acknowledged that Republican jurors often sabotaged criminal prosecutions by casting partisan votes, but he failed to implicate C. H.
Maris in the practice. Although the peace officer cited the collector
for "helping out" Red Club members in trouble with the law, he did
not indicate that this assistance went beyond providing a legal defense in court. The law officer further undercut the credibility of the
Democratic case with his claim that Blue Club loyalists were just as
guilty of politicizing the judicial process: "If you get a few Reds on
the jury, you can't convict a Red, and if you get a few Blues on the
jury, you can't convict a Blue."[7]

The effort to oust Maris from his position not only ended in
failure but also revealed Democratic abuses far more serious than
the charges leveled against the Brownsville collector. In presenting
his defense, Maris argued that the Democratic professions of concern for the legal process were hypocritical. He cited two cases in
which local officials obstructed justice to protect their political allies. In 1900, several Republican spokesmen, including the successful GOP candidate for the county commissioners' court, J. E. Keller,
accused the Democratic school superintendent, E. H. Goodrich, of
embezzling public school funds, and they collected affidavits to document the wrongdoing. Despite the prospect of a grand jury investigation into the superintendent's conduct, District Judge Stanley
Welch appointed Goodrich as one of the jury commissioners who
would select the grand jury members for the upcoming court session
in September 1901. Not surprisingly, Goodrich packed the grand jury
with his sympathizers. Instead of taking action against the superintendent, the jury indicted all the witnesses, who had testified
against him, for "false swearing," and Judge Welch suspended Commissioner Keller from his duties just before the county commissioners' court initiated its review of the finances of the county school
system.[8]

During the same session of the district court, Lawrence H.
Bates, the Brownsville city marshal and one of Wells' closest confi-
dants, faced murder charges for shooting a black man, who had not
died immediately but had survived for several days. The case against
Bates collapsed when District Attorney John Kleiber, Wells' brother-
in-law, failed to introduce evidence that the victim had died from
the wounds inflicted by Bates, and Judge Welch ordered a verdict of
"not guilty" even before the defense had a chance to present its case.
Both the Democrats and the Republicans shared responsibility for
the distortion of justice along the Rio Grande, but with its control
over local government the Wells machine had greater opportunity to

indulge in legal manipulation, and the machine exploited that opportunity fully.

In the face of this campaign to discredit the collector, the local Republican organization stood united in his defense, and both Henry Field and R. B. Rentfro denied the Democratic claims that Maris was responsible for the obstruction of effective law enforcement in the Valley. In January 1902, President Theodore Roosevelt ordered the dismissal of the charges and informed Maris of his nomination for reappointment with the admonition that "there must be no improper political activity that would cause scandal."[9]

The presidential warning did not deter Maris from continuing his aggressive campaigning, and in April 1902 the Brownsville collector tried to convert the killing of a Hispanic rancher into a political issue. While investigating the rustling of cattle from the King Ranch land in Cameron County, Ranger A. Y. Baker sighted a Mexican cowboy branding a calf. According to the lawman's account, he shot the suspect in the head only after the man had opened fire and had killed the Ranger's horse. The identification of the victim as Ramon de la Cerda, a small rancher who owned property adjoining the King Ranch, and the revelation that the body had been mutilated revived Hispanic resentment against Ranger abuses. Although the Cameron County sheriff went through the motions of arresting Baker and his two partners for murder, the King family and several other influential Democratic ranchers immediately paid the $10,000 bond, and the Rangers remained on duty. In a telegram to the Texas adjutant general, who commanded the Ranger force, James B. Wells reaffirmed the support of the local Democratic party for the "faithful and successful services of Baker and his men."[10]

With the Wells machine openly aligned with the Texas Rangers, Maris and Forto made a play for the support of the Hispanic ranchers by condemning Baker and his fellow officers as murderers. Forto's past record of tolerating Ranger abuses cast doubt on the sincerity of the appeal, however, and the political rhetoric appeared as an incitement to the pattern of mounting violence that followed. On September 9, 1902, a band of gunmen ambushed Baker, another Ranger, and an employee of the King Ranch. Although Baker escaped with a slight wound, his partner was killed, and a subsequent Ranger investigation led to the arrest of six men, including Ramon de la Cerda's brother, Alfredo. After Ranger reinforcements thwarted a move to lynch the suspects, Alfredo de la Cerda went free on bond. A few days later he was killed by A. Y. Baker in yet another gunfight. The following year, in two separate trials, the Ranger faced murder charges for the Cerda killings, but won acquittals on grounds of self-defense. Wells served as his defense attorney.

The involvement of the Red Club in the controversy over the Ranger abuses and the series of shootings failed to enhance the party's popularity. The Mexican American distrust of Forto remained intact, while the Republican attacks against the Texas Rangers alienated many of the Anglo ranchers previously aligned with the Spanish politician. Following the election of 1900, James B. Wells had abandoned his neutral stand toward Emilio Forto and had moved to revive the unity of the Cameron County Democratic party. With many of Forto's past followers back in the Democratic fold, the Wells organization reestablished its traditional dominance in the campaign of 1902. When the returns revealed that the Republican totals for Cameron County had fallen to the one-thousand-vote level and that most of the GOP candidates had lost by over six hundred votes, C. H. Maris charged that the Blue Club had committed election fraud. As insurance against a Republican victory in the event of another close race like the 1900 contest, the election officials had refused to allow Red Club members to observe the vote count, but the reunification of the local Democratic party and the depletion of Forto's support probably accounted for most of the dramatic decline in Republican voting strength.

The contest of 1902 represented Maris' last serious challenge to Democratic boss rule in Cameron County. Internal Republican conflicts immobilized the party for the 1904 election and nearly forced Maris' removal from office. County Chairman Henry Field had long resented the collector's dominant role in GOP campaigning, and other local leaders shared the chairman's dissatisfaction with Maris' failure to consult with them on customs appointments. The confrontation within the Republican party came to a head with the firing of Special Deputy Collector Alfred Thornham on charges of embezzlement and shielding smugglers from prosecution. Although the Treasury Department investigation exonerated Maris of any involvement in the corruption, the Brownsville collector suffered politically from the scandal because of the reaction against his choice for Thornham's successor.

Following the death of R. B. Rentfro in December 1901, C. H. Maris, Henry Field, and Emilio Forto stood as the leaders of the contending GOP forces. The seven-member Republican Executive Committee for Cameron County reflected the balance of power in the aftermath of the disappointing campaign of 1902. Although neither man sat on the committee, Maris controlled two votes, and Forto three. Chairman Field enjoyed the support of Committeeman

W. B. Linton, who had opportunistically cast about for an ally after the death of his brother-in-law, R. B. Rentfro. Despite their past differences, Field and Forto formed an alliance to limit Maris' influence in early 1904, even before the removal of Thornham as special deputy collector. At the March county convention to choose delegates to participate in the presidential nominating process at the state level, their two factions blocked the selection of Maris as a delegate. With the firing of Thornham in May, Emilio Forto set the price for reconciliation: Maris had to appoint either Forto or one of his allies to the vacated post. When Maris rejected the ultimatum and promoted the customs house cashier, Ira Killough, to serve as his deputy, the split in the party became irreparable. Not only did the collector reject the demands of his rivals for a voice in the management of the customs service, but Maris and Killough immediately launched a crackdown on smuggling, which further antagonized Forto, Linton, and other Republican participants in the illegal border trade.

With the battle lines firmly drawn, Maris made his own move to take control of the Republican county organization. When Chairman Henry Field departed for the hot springs at Topo Chico, Mexico, to improve his health, the Brownsville collector's two allies on the executive committee, Jasper A. Maltby and Tomas Cortez, wrote the Republican state chairman, Cecil A. Lyon, and charged Field with dereliction of his party responsibilities. Because the county chairman's absence threatened to prevent the party from meeting the deadline for filing legal notice of its nominating convention, the two committeemen proposed the removal of Field and the appointment of a replacement. After conferring with Collector Maris in Houston, Lyon suspended the county chairman and directed Maltby to serve as acting chairman. The Field and Forto factions refused to abide by this action on the grounds that Maris had deceived State Chairman Lyon. According to Field, he had appointed W. B. Linton to act as chairman during his absence with full authority to arrange the county convention, and had even returned to Brownsville the day before his suspension to file the required notice with the county judge. Maltby, however, refused to relinquish his authority, and the two sides proceeded to organize rival county conventions. Neither faction nominated local candidates, but both chose delegates to attend the state convention. Although the convention at Fort Worth recognized the Field group as the "regular organization," the state leadership granted equal voting rights to the competing delegations to avoid a floor fight.

With the question of the legitimacy of the two county organizations still unresolved, W. B. Linton and three other Republicans pressed charges against Maris and demanded his ouster from the collectorship. The accusations against the Brownsville collector included usurping the authority of the regular Republican organization, lying to the Republican state chairman, trying to bribe local Republicans with offers of customs appointments, forcing his employees to make political contributions, and allowing his men to leave their customs posts unattended while they participated in his county convention. Treasury Department investigator J. C. Cummings cleared Maris on all counts, except the charge of maneuvering to establish his dominance over the local Republican party. The agent conceded that even this action was at least partially defensive since the rival GOP leaders were conspiring to destroy the collector's influence. Cummings questioned whether Field had actually appointed Linton as acting chairman, and he speculated that the chairman and his allies were willing to sabotage the 1904 campaign in order to undercut Maris' reputation as an effective political organizer and thus to discredit him in the eyes of state and national Republican leaders. Rather than attacking the Brownsville collector, agent Cummings leveled his severest criticism against Forto, Linton, and several other plaintiffs, whom he characterized as disgruntled office seekers, gamblers, smugglers, and "barroom loafers."[11] The investigator concluded his report by citing Maris' recent efforts to curtail smuggling and recommending the collector's retention for the final year and a half of his term.

The election returns of 1904 reflected the disarray within the Republican party. With the failure of the opposing Cameron County organizations to field local candidates or even to campaign, the state and national nominees received less than one hundred votes. Even in Starr and Hidalgo counties, where the customs house factions faced no serious challenges to their campaign leadership, the GOP vote plummeted to less than one third of the 1900 totals. Maris' fight to hold his position and to salvage his influence in Cameron County had paralyzed his political operation throughout the Lower Rio Grande Valley.

Although Maris retained the collectorship until the expiration of his term in 1906, he never recovered from the bitter Republican infighting of 1904. The rival factional chiefs refused to accept the Brownsville collector's leadership or even to cooperate with him in organizing campaigns. Maris was a skillful politician, who had maximized Republican voting strength during his first six years in office, but his political career ultimately collapsed before the same forces that had frustrated his predecessors: entrenched Democratic power and Republican dissension.

Until the arrival of thousands of new settlers toward the end of the first decade of the twentieth century, the population of the Rio Grande counties remained static. Through a combination of traditional social controls, sensitivity to constituent needs, and strong-arm tactics, the Democratic machines maintained tight control over the bulk of the electorate. Declining to challenge the existing social system, the Republican insurgents had to play by the rules of their Democratic opponents. Instead of promises of alternative public policies, the Republicans relied on patronage and political organizations. Like their counterparts in local and state government, the customs officials "corralled" the Mexican American employees of sympathetic ranchers at election time, organized unaffiliated voters, and provided armed support when political violence flared. Although the customs service constituted the single largest source of patronage in the Valley, the Republicans could not compete with the Democrats in the distribution of political appointments. The Democratic-controlled local governments of Cameron, Hidalgo, and Starr counties employed at least 250 people, while the Brownsville collector oversaw a force of 30 men. The postal service provided a few more federal jobs. In the face of this organizational imbalance, the only hope for GOP success rested with Democratic defections. However, even the conversion of Emilio Forto, perhaps the second most powerful politician in the Wells machine, failed to transform the balance of power. Once Sheriff Forto met defeat in the election of 1900 and lost his influence over local government policies and patronage, the ranks of his supporters thinned rapidly.

The heavy reliance of the local Republicans on the customs service for patronage rewards placed the collector in an untenable position. He constantly had to make difficult choices among competing political needs: appeasing rival Republican leaders, tempting disgruntled Democrats, and building a cohesive machine with the appointment of men personally loyal to him. Failure to strike a proper balance could spell disaster. Maris fashioned an efficient campaign organization at the expense of the other uses of patronage and provoked a rebellion within his own party that eventually destroyed his effectiveness as a politician.

Despite the collapse of Republican campaigning in Cameron County at the end of Maris' term, opposition to Democratic machine rule was far from dead. The influx of new residents with the rise of large-scale fruit and vegetable farming in the Valley would revitalize the insurgent movement. Even before irrigation and the consequent demographic changes transformed the political landscape of the Lower Rio Grande Valley, a wealthy South Texas rancher, Edward (Ed) C. Lasater, launched his own development project in the northern section of Starr County, which lies outside the Valley. For the first decade of the twentieth century, Lasater and his growing constituency of settlers at Falfurrias waged a dramatic struggle against the Democratic boss of Starr County.

3. Assault against the Guerra Machine of Starr County

THE ANGLO PENETRATION of Starr County began during the war with Mexico, but by the beginning of the twentieth century, Mexican Americans still comprised over 90 percent of the population. The extension of the steamboat service along the Rio Grande in the late 1840s sparked the rise of two trading centers, Rio Grande City and Roma. With the formal organization of Starr County in 1848, Rio Grande City became the county seat. The first Anglo settlers engaged in both legitimate trade and smuggling, and some of the newcomers married into the wealthy Mexican families who owned most of the ranchland of the county. A few purchased property outright.

Despite their limited numbers, the Anglo merchants, ranchers, and lawyers controlled local politics until the 1890s. Personal rivalries and shifting alliances among these men produced an erratic political pattern. The Democrats carried the county for most of the 1870s, but neither party was able to establish its dominance from 1880 through 1884. After 1884, the Democrats exploited their control over the county commissioners' court to manipulate the election process and to ensure Democratic victories in 1886 and 1888. Since both parties relied on the mobilization of illiterate Hispanic laborers, the Democrats and Republicans adopted the Cameron County practice of using color labels, but the colors were reversed. In Starr County, red represented the Democratic party, and blue the GOP.

Although members of the Mexican American gentry occupied government posts and participated in the Democratic and Republican organizations, racial antagonism developed over the Anglos' near monopoly of countywide offices. The tension reached a peak in the late 1880s with the agitation of newspaper editor Catarino Garza, who condemned the abuses against Mexican Americans in the Valley and eventually organized the ill-fated Garza Revolution against the Díaz regime in Mexico. In the face of this pressure, the Republican party selected a Mexican American to run for sheriff in 1888. During the campaign, a former U.S. marshal wounded Garza in a gunfight on the streets of Rio Grande City, and mob violence erupted. The leaders of the Red Club even received reports that a militant Hispanic faction was planning to launch armed attacks to disrupt the election in two Democratic precincts. Although the insurrection never took place, the Republicans apparently won a narrow popular majority. The Democratic county commissioners, however, threw out enough votes to allow the Red Club candidates to claim most of the countywide offices. The commissioners also overturned the election of the GOP nominee for sheriff on the grounds that he could not speak English.

For the duration of the Garza Revolution, which culminated with Garza's raids into Mexico in 1891 and then collapsed the following year, the Republican party continued to make strong showings in Starr County elections. At the same time, however, Mexican Americans assumed a much more influential role in the Democratic party, and Manuel Guerra emerged as one of the commanding figures in the Red Club. Midway through the opening decade of the twentieth century, Guerra would win recognition as the Democratic boss of Starr County.

The presence of the Guerra family in the Lower Rio Grande Valley dates from 1767 when Don José Alejandro Guerra received two Spanish land grants that extended into Texas. Manuel Guerra was born in 1856 at Mier, Mexico, across the river from Roma. At the age of fourteen, he moved to Corpus Christi to study the English language and to gain business experience working for an American merchant. Seven years later he settled in Roma, where he opened his own store and eventually took control of the Guerra ranchlands in Starr County.

By the mid-1880s, Manuel Guerra had established his political base at Roma and had gained the support of James B. Wells, who allowed the Mexican entrepreneur to influence the selection of state and federal appointees for Starr County. Yet Guerra remained a secondary figure in county politics until the 1890s. His breakthrough came in 1894 when Wells intervened to end the factional and racial infighting that had contributed to the Democratic setbacks of 1888, 1890, and 1892. By the terms of the truce, Guerra and Sheriff W. W. Shely, the boss of the Red Club of Rio Grande City, agreed to share patronage and party nominations. In the election of 1894, the Democrats reasserted their domination over Starr County politics, and Manuel Guerra won a seat on the county commissioners' court, a position that he held until his death in 1915. The election of John R. Monroe as county judge in 1900 completed a ruling triumvirate. Five years later, failing health forced Shely from office, and Guerra moved to consolidate his leadership over the county Democratic organization. This power play revived dissension within the party and provoked the strongest Republican challenge of the Progressive Era—a challenge that ended in political violence and the indictment of Manuel Guerra for conspiracy to commit murder.

The reunification of the Democratic party, its concessions to the Hispanic gentry, and the appointment of a Democratic customs collector in 1893 after the election of Grover Cleveland to the presidency reduced the Republican party of Starr County to a manageable minority. The Blue Club experienced a revival at the end of the decade, however, as a result of the return of the customs service to Republican control and the emergence of a new forceful GOP leader, Edward C. Lasater of Falfurrias. Lasater's efforts to promote the economic development of the northern section of the county attracted new settlers resistant to Democratic boss rule and provided a financial base for Republican campaigning. Rather than competing with the Brownsville collector for political leadership, as his counterparts in Cameron County did, Lasater cooperated with C. H. Maris and his successor, John W. Vann, to maximize Republican strength.

Ed C. Lasater was the son of a small-time rancher, whose career was marked by repeated economic setbacks and mounting indebtedness. When his father was murdered in 1883, Lasater sacrificed his ambitions to study law, assumed responsibility for the family debts, and struggled to support his invalid mother and his sister. Despite his modest success as a cattle buyer, the drought and panic of 1893 left him propertyless and again heavily indebted. Paradoxically, the hard times of the 1890s also afforded Lasater an incredible economic opportunity. Unfamiliar with the technology for drilling deep wells, the ranchers of Starr County suffered the loss of thousands of cattle, and many faced financial ruin. With borrowed capital, Lasater purchased huge tracts of land in the northeastern corner of the county from fifteen Hispanic families at giveaway prices and organized a ranch of 380,000 acres. Over the next few years, he stocked his ranch with twenty thousand head of cattle, began experimenting to improve the breed of his livestock, and established a network of artesian wells to sustain his ranching operation even during periods of drought. Ironically, these moves to modernize the agricultural economy of Starr County took place outside the richer lands of the Lower Rio Grande valley, which comprised the southeastern part of the county.

By 1900, Ed C. Lasater ranked as one of the most successful ranchers in the nation, and his ambitions for fostering the economic development of northern Starr County soared. Two years before the completion of the St. Louis, Brownsville, and Mexico Railway to the border, he persuaded the managers of the San Antonio and Aransas Pass Railroad to extend their line to his ranch holdings. At the location of the railroad station, Lasater established the townsite of Falfurrias. The South Texas promoter envisioned the conversion of the surrounding pastureland into a community of dairy, truck, and citrus farms. To lure settlers to the region, he subdivided sixty thousand acres of his property into small farm sites, made the land available for sale, and announced plans for extensive irrigation and the establishment of a dairy plant at Falfurrias. During the next two decades, his scheme prospered: more than six hundred families eventually purchased his farm lots; the population of Falfurrias rose to 2,500 by 1920; and the state legislature organized a new county with Falfurrias as its county seat in 1911. For the first few years of the twentieth century, however, the population growth of the area remained limited, and Lasater had to contend with a county government hostile to his interests. The new settlers came from other parts of Texas, the Southeast, and the Midwest, and their aversion to boss rule and to what they perceived as Mexican domination heightened tensions.

Resentful over discriminatory tax policies and his lack of influence at the county seat of Rio Grande City, almost ninety miles from Falfurrias, Ed Lasater threw his financial support behind the local Republican insurgency. With his initiation into Starr County politics in 1900, he received a valuable lesson in Democratic tactics. The Democrats had to overcome the handicaps of a critical shortage of campaign funds and the defection of a veteran party organizer. Shortly before the election, Sheriff W. W. Shely arrested his Republican opponent for conspiracy to commit murder. Although the district judge later dismissed the charge as groundless, the resolution of the case came after the election. For additional insurance, Manuel Guerra and his allies recruited aliens from Mexico to vote and stationed armed guards at the polling places to intimidate GOP voters. The Democratic party carried the election by almost four hundred ballots, despite the active campaigning of the customs officials and Lasater's generous contributions. By 1904, Republican election strength had fallen to less than half the 1900 totals, as the factional feuding in Cameron County neutralized the customs house as a political force. Undeterred by these defeats, the Blue Club stood ready to exploit the factional strife that overtook the Democrats in 1906.

The three-man Democratic rule of Manuel Guerra, W. W. Shely, and J. R. Monroe ended abruptly in 1905 when Sheriff Shely withdrew from politics because of a debilitating nervous disorder. Although Shely retained the position of sheriff until July 1906, he left the county half a year earlier to undergo medical treatment. The competition to succeed the longtime Democratic leader split the party. With the support of County Judge Monroe, Manuel Guerra maneuvered to tighten his control over county affairs by promoting the nominations of his cousin Deodoro Guerra for sheriff and his son H. P. Guerra for tax collector. Manuel Guerra's brother Jacobo already held the post of county treasurer. The prospect of the Guerra family occupying four major county offices aroused protests from other Democrats, especially the incumbent tax collector and deputy sheriff, Gregorio Duffy, who planned to run for sheriff. When Duffy formed a common front with the county tax assessor and a former county commissioner to oppose the Guerra take-over, Manuel Guerra expelled the dissidents from the Democratic county ring.

Recognizing the difficulty of challenging the Guerra family in the Democratic primaries, the three insurgents made overtures to the Republican party. The GOP organizers responded by presenting to District Judge Stanley Welch a petition, which demanded the suspension of the incapacitated Shely and the promotion of Deputy Duffy to sheriff. To counter this move, County Judge John Monroe secured a letter of resignation from Shely and called a special session of the commissioners' court to appoint Deodoro Guerra as his successor. The intrigues continued when Duffy's allies circulated reports that Wells and Guerra had fallen out and that the Cameron County boss planned to support Gregorio Duffy. With Wells' public endorsement of Manuel Guerra's leadership, Duffy and his associates gave up all hope of prevailing within the Democratic party and formally defected to the Republican camp. All four Guerras swept the Democratic primaries, and the GOP convention nominated Duffy to run for sheriff.

In the ensuing campaign the Republicans posed as reformers with their attacks against Manuel Guerra's boss rule, the alleged incompetence of Mexican American officeholders who could barely speak English, and the use of the public schools as a patronage boondoggle, but county finance emerged as the central issue. Through his own newspaper, the *Falfurrias Facts*, Ed C. Lasater charged that the Democratic administrations discriminated in the assessment of property taxes. While some landowners faced "double assessments," others escaped taxation altogether because of the absence of their properties from the tax rolls.[1] The taxpayers shouldered the additional burden of covering the interest on the enormous public indebtedness that had accumulated through repeated bond sales. In defense of Starr County government against these charges of mismanagement, the Democratic chairman, Francis W. Seabury, who had served as Speaker of the Texas House in the previous legislative session, wrote two detailed articles for the *Brownsville Daily Herald*. Seabury cited the low rates of per capita taxation, the modest salaries of county officials, and the efficient use of tax money in building one of the best road systems in the state. Although he conceded past tax irregularities, the Democratic county chairman blamed these abuses on the incumbent tax collector and the assessor who had just switched to the Republican party. Seabury also argued that the Republican county officials of the late 1880s and the early 1890s were responsible for most of the county debt. Despite the forcefulness with which Seabury advanced these arguments, three years later a state investigator confirmed Republican charges of pervasive corruption in Starr County.

This extended debate over public policy posed a striking contrast to past election campaigns and reflected the interest of both parties in the independent voters, who were migrating to Starr County from the Midwest and other sections of the country. By 1906, almost three hundred residents of the Falfurrias area had registered to vote. Although the margin of victory for the Democratic party had not fallen below four hundred ballots in any election since 1892, Guerra and his allies were not willing to concede the entire bloc of newcomers to the Republican camp. Still both sides relied mainly on strong organizations to mobilize the vote of the Mexican American laborers. With the appointment of a new Brownsville collector, John Vann, the customs force was again available for active Republican campaigning.

Republicans and Democrats alike believed that the election of 1906 would have repercussions beyond Starr County. The GOP organizers aimed their attacks not only against the Guerra family but also against James B. Wells. They vowed to rid the county of "outside dictation."[2] The combination of winning the support of the incoming settlers and repudiating the leadership of one of Wells' closest allies could revitalize the Republican party throughout South Texas. Recognizing the seriousness of the threat, Manuel Guerra's brother Jacobo called on Democrats to "knock the Republican move in the head now and kill it so dead that it will not rise to trouble us again."[3]

With the stakes so high, the two parties were willing to resort to almost any tactics. In 1902, the Texas electorate had ratified a constitutional amendment that made the payment of the poll tax a prerequisite for voting. In violation of the spirit if not the letter of this amendment and the election laws that followed in 1903 and 1905, the Republican and Democratic leaders of Starr County paid the poll taxes for hundreds of lower class Mexican Americans. Moreover, both sides recruited Mexican nationals to vote and made preparations for "corralling" their supporters the night before the election. The ultimate recourse, however, would be the use of armed force.

Texas law prohibited persons, except for lawmen and authorized election officials, from carrying guns within one-half mile of polling stations. The Red and Blue clubs proceeded to circumvent the ban, and a pattern of paramilitary escalation developed. In response to reports that armed gangs from Mexico were converging on Starr County, District Judge Stanley Welch deputized twenty-four special officers for the ostensible purpose of maintaining order on election day, but the appointments reflected his partisan bias. All twenty-four deputies were active members of the Red Club. To counter this buildup of Democratic strength, a Rio Grande City county commissioner, who had joined the rebellion against Manuel Guerra's leadership, selected thirty Republicans to serve as guards at the courthouse, where the local balloting was to take place. The day before the election, Welch again intervened and authorized the presiding election judge at Rio Grande City to name another twenty officers. The combination of these special appointees and a sheriff's force of nine deputies provided the Democrats with a legally sanctioned army of over fifty men, while the Republican ranks, which included the seven customs officials for the county, totaled almost forty. The two political clubs also hired additional undeputized gunmen. Although the Red forces held a numerical advantage for the whole county, the Republicans concentrated their armed recruits in Rio Grande City, the scene of the election-day showdown.

Many Republicans believed that Judge Stanley Welch posed the most serious threat to their campaign. He was responsible for the dramatic increase in the number of Democratic deputies, and rumors circulated that he intended to block the voting of all the Republicans who had not paid their own poll taxes. With political acrimony intensifying and GOP resentment focused on the district judge, violence struck. The night before the election, Stanley Welch was shot to death as he slept in his bed. District Attorney John Kleiber, the only other occupant of the house in which Welch had been staying for the duration of the court term, did not discover the body until eight o'clock the next morning. Earlier that same night, a gang of thugs had pistol-whipped a local Republican leader and had "left him for dead" outside his house, but the murder of Judge Welch overshadowed all other news.[4]

The reports of the killing stunned Democratic leaders, left their organization in Rio Grande City in temporary disarray, and provided the Republicans with an opportunity to take the initiative. As news of the tragedy spread, fifty armed men, apparently under the command of Duffy, took control of the courthouse and demanded that the voting begin. Fearing the outbreak of a full-scale battle, other Blue Club spokesmen had second thoughts about this power play and negotiated with Democratic Chairman Francis W. Seabury an arrangement for conducting a peaceful election. No gunmen could approach or occupy the courthouse, and two officers, representing both parties, would supervise the balloting on the second floor of the building. In the midst of drunken rioting, Republican gangs repeatedly violated the agreement by regrouping in front of the courthouse and even seizing the ground floor. Within Rio Grande City, the Blue Club gunmen outnumbered their Democratic counterparts, and the cutting of the telegraph lines to Roma early in the morning prevented the prompt dispatch of Red Club reinforcements. Although the Democratic leaders in both Rio Grande City and Brownsville wired desperate appeals to Governor S. W. T. Lanham and Adjutant General John Hulen to order the intervention of the Texas Rangers, these law enforcement officers arrived only after the election had ended.

The Republican show of force and the outbreaks of rioting deterred over 120 Democrats from voting in Rio Grande City, and the outcome of the election hinged on the votes in outlying communities, like Roma and Falfurrias. Ranger Captain William B. McDonald and his four subordinates not only tried to restore order in Rio Grande City but also assumed responsibility for the delivery of the ballots to the county seat for the official canvass of the returns. Two days after their arrival, violence erupted again. At night along the road connecting Rio Grande City and Roma, the force of Rangers encountered a wagon occupied by several armed Hispanics. Without warning, the gunmen opened fire. When McDonald and his men took cover and identified themselves, the attackers cursed the Rangers and continued shooting. In the battle that followed, the law enforcement officers killed four of the Hispanics, and a sheriff's posse later captured two other suspects. Some Red Club leaders initially suspected a GOP plot aimed at killing the Rangers, blocking the collection of votes from Democratic precincts, and consolidating Republican armed rule, but the authorities concluded that the assault had resulted from a drunken spree. The gunmen were intoxicated when they left Rio Grande City earlier that evening, and they failed to take advantage of the thick brush along the road to stage an ambush. Although the assailants were Republican partisans, no evidence indicated a prearranged scheme to intercept and murder the Rangers for political purposes.

In the wake of this gunfight, Governor Lanham took decisive action. He doubled the number of Rangers at Rio Grande City and dispatched a cavalry force of forty Texas national guardsmen under the personal supervision of Adjutant General John Hulen. Afterward an armed standoff between three Rangers and seven Hispanics developed on the edge of town, but no further violence occurred. Within a few days of the arrival of the state troops, the gangs of gunmen retreated from Rio Grande City and the neighboring ranches and crossed into Mexico. The process of disarmament also included the confiscations of the caches of weapons at the Republican headquarters and the local saloons. Even with the restoration of order, the lawmen remained apprehensive. One week after the election, ten Texas Rangers occupied the courthouse to forestall any possible disruption of the official tabulation of the votes.

In the presence of Adjutant General Hulen, U.S. District Attorney Marc McLemore, and State District Attorney Kleiber, representing both political parties and three levels of government, the Starr County commissioners' court canvassed the returns. Despite a Republican majority at the county seat, the Democrats narrowly carried the election. Deodoro Guerra defeated Gregorio Duffy in the sheriff's race by sixty-three votes. The Republican successes were limited to the election of a Falfurrias constable and three precinct-level officials for Rio Grande City including County Commissioner T. W. Kennedy. The Democratic party profited from a landslide vote at Roma and an unexpected victory at Falfurrias. Apparently, news of the murder of Judge Welch had produced a backlash among the newcomers to the northern section of the county. On the day of the election, the residents of Falfurrias organized a mass meeting to pay tribute to Welch and to demand the apprehension of his assassin. This local Democratic breakthrough proved to be short-lived, however, since the voters of Falfurrias reemerged as the mainstay of the GOP insurgency in subsequent elections.

In the immediate aftermath of the 1906 campaign, the murder of Judge Stanley Welch remained unsolved. Regional Democratic politicians and newspapers blamed the Starr County Republican party. The day after the election, James B. Wells asserted that the district judge "was assassinated because he did his duty in trying to enforce the law, and that this was the legitimate result of Republican-

Customs House politics on the Lower Rio Grande."[5] According to the *Brownsville Daily Herald*, "'reform,' revolver in hand and murder in heart, has swooped down upon us with all the fervor and malignity of utter, howling anarchy."[6] Despite the proliferation of politically inspired attacks, the identification and arrest of a murder suspect proved to be a slow process.

Even with the posting of rewards and the cooperation of the authorities in the Mexican border towns, the Texas and local law enforcement officers failed to charge anyone with the killing of Judge Stanley Welch for eight months. From the outset, contradictions and twists marked the investigation. Dr. A. M. Headley, one of the two physicians who examined Welch's body, concluded that the murderer must have fired his gun directly over the victim. The doctor, a Republican, even accused the district attorney, John Kleiber, who shared the house with Welch, of committing the crime. Ignoring both Headley's medical findings and his charge, the sheriff and the Rangers proceeded on the assumption that the assailant had fired the fatal shot from a nearby window. This contention rested solely on the discovery of a dent in the window shutter and on speculation about the path of the bullet, which Headley rejected. No powder burns appeared on the shutter. The coroner's jury summoned neither of the examining doctors, and the only testimony at the inquest came from Kleiber. For the first half of 1907, the leads in the case were limited to the identification of several gunmen who had crossed the border immediately after the murder and to interviews with people who suspected their relatives or neighbors of involvement in the crime. Finally, in July, Starr County Deputy Sheriff E. P. Guerra arranged for the Mexico City police to arrest Alberto Cabrera, a Republican organizer who had worked as a bartender for Duffy's half-brother. Another suspect, who had traveled to Mexico with Cabrera, eluded the Mexican officers and a bounty hunter that the Valley Democrats hired.

After a change of venue from Starr County, the trial of Alberto Cabrera took place in Cuero, Texas, in June 1908 and attracted statewide attention. Texas Lieutenant Governor A. B. Davidson served as one of the prosecuting attorneys, while a leading Brownsville Republican, Rentfro B. Creager, headed the defense team. Both Ed C. Lasater and Customs Collector John Vann attended the proceedings and provided Cabrera with moral support. The state's case rested heavily on the testimony of Mrs. Jesusa Peña, who claimed to have witnessed the crime and who identified the defendant as the murderer. Mrs. Peña had withheld this information from the authorities for several months. To undercut the credibility of the star witness, three men, including two relatives of the Peñas, testified for the defense that Mrs. Peña had confided to them that she and her husband had been asleep at the time of the killing. Other individuals provided Cabrera with an alibi, but all the defense witnesses acknowledged their Republican loyalties. The prosecution also suggested that Gregorio Duffy had conspired with Cabrera, but the state attorneys failed to offer any convincing evidence.

The trial reached a climax when Ed Lasater interrupted Lieutenant Governor Davidson's closing argument. As the two men engaged in a heated argument and verged on an exchange of blows, Collector Vann and his customs agents reached for their pistols. Although the Rangers and the local lawmen were able to prevent the outbreak of violence, many spectators fled from the building in panic. In the midst of this tension-filled atmosphere, the jury found Cabrera guilty and sentenced him to life imprisonment. Despite continuing accusations of a GOP conspiracy behind Welch's murder, no one else was ever charged or tried for the crime. The Republicans argued that Cabrera was the victim of political persecution, and they made the unsubstantiated charge that the Democrats were responsible for the killing. In 1912, Cabrera escaped from prison and fled to Mexico, where he joined Venustiano Carranza's Constitutionalist army and eventually advanced to the rank of lieutenant.

Legal action growing out of the Starr County political confrontation of 1906 did not end with the Cabrera trial. In January 1907, with local investigators still baffled over the Welch murder, another key participant in the 1906 campaign was killed, and the resultant litigation continued until February 1910. This second series of investigations and trials revealed both the influence of the Democratic bosses over the local grand juries and state courts and the tenacity of Republican federal officials in challenging the power of the South Texas machines.

After his narrow loss in the race for sheriff, Gregorio Duffy consolidated his influence within the Republican organization and secured an appointment to serve as the customs inspector at Roma. Because of his participation in the armed occupation of the courthouse on election day and his suspected involvement in the murder of Judge Welch, Starr County Democrats regarded Duffy as their most dangerous foe. From this new position, he posed a threat not only to Manuel Guerra's hegemony over Roma politics but also to the smuggling operations from which Guerra and other merchants profited.

On the night of January 26, 1907, Sheriff Deodoro Guerra and two of his deputies, Juan and Gabriel Morales, followed Gregorio

Duffy as he made the rounds of the Rio Grande City bars. With two Rangers and a number of Democratic and Republican politicos present, the sheriff engaged the customs inspector in a conversation at the saloon operated by Duffy's half-brother. When the Republican organizer left to relieve himself behind the building, Guerra accompanied him. The two deputies were waiting outside, and a few minutes later shooting erupted. Hit in the shoulder, spine, and abdomen, Duffy fell to the ground mortally wounded. The Rangers inside the saloon thought that they had come under attack, and they began firing through the backdoor. In the midst of this confusion, the Morales brothers fled to the county jail.

Deodoro Guerra and Gregorio Duffy with his dying declaration offered conflicting versions of the violent outburst. According to the sheriff, a drunken brawl developed between Duffy and Juan Morales, and the customs agent provoked the gunplay by striking Morales on the side of the head with his pistol. As Guerra struggled to break up the fight, the two combatants stepped back and began firing. Morales shot Duffy several times in self-defense and escaped serious injury only because the Mexican coins in his pocket deflected a bullet that struck his side. Although Deodoro Guerra drew his gun, he did not fire. As he lay dying, Duffy contradicted this account. He contended that Juan and Gabriel Morales shot him without warning or any provocation on his part. An eyewitness, who worked for Duffy's half-brother, supported this testimony with his claim that Duffy was still buttoning his pants when the firing started. Another observer recalled that the sheriff rushed through the front door of the saloon after the gunfire had ended and "asked what all of the shooting was about."[7]

The physical evidence also undercut the credibility of Guerra's story, but ambiguities remained. Duffy's wounds indicated that gunshots had struck him from three different directions. The next morning the Rangers located the dead man's pistol and determined that it had not been fired recently. Since the lawmen had searched for the weapon earlier without success, the sheriff's defenders argued that someone had removed Duffy's gun and had replaced it with an unfired pistol of the same caliber, .45. As proof that the customs inspector had used his gun, the Democrats cited Juan Morales' slight wound, the discovery of a .45 caliber shell in the yard, and the identification of two bullet holes in the wall behind the spot where Juan Morales had apparently stood. All other identifiable bullets were .38 caliber, matching Sheriff Guerra's and Gabriel Morales' pistols. Juan Morales, the only man whom both Guerra and Duffy accused of firing shots, had a .44 caliber gun. Further investigation uncovered the weapon that Gabriel Morales had dropped as he scaled a wall behind the saloon to flee the scene of the killing. The .38 caliber pistol had several empty chambers and fresh powder marks. Again Guerra and his sympathizers protested that their enemies had tampered with the evidence.

Assistant U.S. District Attorney Noah Allen, an aggressive GOP partisan, conducted his own investigation of the incident and drew the following conclusions: Sheriff Guerra and the Morales brothers had all shot Duffy in an act of premeditated murder; Manuel Guerra had participated in a conspiracy with these three men to arrange the assassination. For several days prior to the fatal encounter, the two deputies had made repeated inquiries about Duffy's whereabouts and had tried to track the inspector as he scouted along the border. While drunk, Juan Morales had even bragged of his plans to kill Duffy. Allen argued that on the night of the shooting Sheriff Guerra and his deputies had followed Duffy with the intention of cornering him alone and committing murder. The linking of Manuel Guerra to the crime rested on the ambiguous testimony of Candelario Hinojosa, who claimed that the Starr County boss had approached him with a proposition "to put Duffy out of the way."[8] Later, Duffy's widow alerted the assistant U.S. attorney to the possible existence of more damaging evidence. According to Mrs. Duffy, a policeman from Monterrey, Mexico, Julio Cantu, had informed her husband, about a month before his death, that Manuel Guerra had written Cantu a letter offering to pay him to kill Duffy. The federal authorities failed to secure Cantu's testimony.

The Starr County grand jury for the state district court consisted of Guerra loyalists, and they were reluctant to indict anyone for the killing of Gregorio Duffy. Only under pressure from Noah Allen, who threatened to seek federal indictments, did the grand jury take action. It charged Juan and Gabriel Morales with murder but still refused to implicate either Deodoro or Manuel Guerra. The conduct of the district judge and the district attorney also disturbed the Republican prosecutor. With the consent of District Attorney John Kleiber, Judge W. B. Hopkins, Welch's successor and a staunch Wells ally, authorized the release of the Morales brothers on $2,500 bond. When Noah Allen asked permission to participate in the prosecution of the case, the judge abruptly ordered a change of venue to Laredo, without even receiving a motion from the defense. Kleiber then dismissed the federal agent's request on the grounds that the district attorney for Webb County was now in charge of the case.

The judge at Laredo promptly granted a six-month continuance, and Allen received reports that District Attorney John A. Valls had no intention of conducting a vigorous prosecution.

Because of the evasive actions on the part of the state officials, Noah Allen and his superior, U.S. District Attorney Lock McDaniel of Houston, appealed to the Justice Department for authorization to press for federal indictments against both the Moraleses and the Guerras. Allen and McDaniel argued that conspiring to murder Duffy to prevent him from discharging his duties as a United States customs inspector constituted a violation of federal law. They also portrayed Duffy as a determined champion of clean government pitted against the forces of corruption. In the face of these claims, the Justice Department agreed to federal intervention, and later even President Roosevelt expressed an interest in the prosecution of "that outfit of assassins down there who killed Duffy."[9]

In May 1907, U.S. Attorney McDaniel persuaded the federal grand jury at Brownsville to return murder and conspiracy indictments against Manuel and Deodoro Guerra, Juan and Gabriel Morales, and a fifth man, Desiderio Perez. At the time of the killing, Perez served as a Texas Ranger at Rio Grande City, and he subsequently joined Sheriff Guerra's staff as chief deputy. He allegedly participated in the planning of Duffy's murder. Of all the defendants, only Juan Morales, who was already serving a forty-day sentence for smuggling, remained in jail. Within a half-hour of their arrests, the Guerras and Perez were free on bond. Gabriel Morales avoided arrest and fled to Mexico, where he took refuge on the ranch of William Hanson, a former U.S. marshal and close associate of James B. Wells.

With Gabriel Morales under arrest but still awaiting extradition from Mexico in January 1908, the court officials at Laredo decided to proceed with the state trial of his brother Juan. District Attorney John Valls belonged to the Republican machine that dominated Webb County politics for the first decade of the twentieth century, but he occasionally cooperated with Wells and other Democrats on legal and political matters. After some initial equivocation, Valls agreed to allow Noah Allen to assist in the presentation of the state's case. Unfortunately, according to Allen, Valls "lost his nerve, and when it came to the closing argument, he was frightened out of his wits and hardly touched on the case."[10] Despite Valls' "lack of backbone" and the agitation of local Democratic leaders, the jury voted eleven to one for conviction on the first ballot and remained deadlocked at that count for almost a week until the end of the court term when the judge had to declare a mistrial. Lock McDaniel blamed the outcome on the infiltration of a "fixed" juror.[11]

The Justice Department officials and U.S. Attorney McDaniel had originally agreed to schedule the conspiracy trial after the resolution of the state case against the Morales brothers, but repeated postponements in the state courts forced the hand of the federal authorities. Further delay could only weaken their case as witnesses moved away, or died, or faced harassment from state and local law enforcement officers. Ever since the indictment of the Guerras, the Rangers had engaged in a campaign of intimidating the Hispanic witnesses. McDaniel attributed the interference of the South Texas Rangers to their dependence on James B. Wells for their appointments. To salvage the prosecution of the Starr County boss and his cohorts, the U.S. attorney proposed the prompt setting of a trial date, a change of venue from Brownsville, and the hiring of John Vann, who had recently lost his job as customs collector, to provide protection for the prospective witnesses and to ensure their compliance with the court subpoenas.

More than two years after the death of Gregorio Duffy, the federal trial opened in Victoria, Texas, with James B. Wells and Francis W. Seabury representing the defendants, and Lock McDaniel and Noah Allen handling the prosecution. To counter the government charges of conspiracy to commit murder, the defense argued that the shooting stemmed from a spontaneous fight between Duffy and Juan Morales and that Morales shot the victim in self-defense. According to the Guerras, the surveillance of the customs inspector and any conferences among the defendants were related to the investigation of the murder of Judge Stanley Welch. The jury accepted this version of the killing and voted for acquittal. When Juan and Gabriel Morales finally went to trial in state court in May 1910, the judge dismissed the case on grounds of double jeopardy. After two grand jury investigations, extradition hearings, three trials, and repeated continuances and changes of venue, the state and federal authorities failed to win any convictions for the killing of Customs Inspector Duffy.

Because of the ambiguity of the evidence and the partisanship that permeated the courts of South Texas, definitive judgments on the guilt or innocence of individual suspects in the Welch and Duffy murder cases are impossible. Certainly the evidence against the Guerra brothers was strong, if not conclusive. Yet, even if the Republican and Democratic leaders did not give explicit orders to commit murder, these men were still guilty of creating a political atmosphere that encouraged acts of violence. Both sides systematically flouted the voting laws and made preparations to carry the election through the use of force. The line between hiring gunmen to intimidate the opposition and sanctioning shootings or murders was thin indeed.

Although the leading figures of both parties escaped either indictment or conviction for the violence of the 1906 campaign and its aftermath, the resultant legal battles took a political toll. Sharp fluctuations in Starr County politics closely paralleled the progress of the ongoing litigation. By the late summer of 1908, the legal tide appeared to be running against the Republican party: the state murder trial of Juan Morales had ended with a hung jury; Blue Club loyalist Alberto Cabrera had received a life sentence for the murder of Judge Welch; and more than a year after the indictments of the Guerras, the federal judge had not even scheduled their conspiracy trial. With little immediate prospect of breaking the Democratic machine through court action, Ed Lasater decided to negotiate an accommodation with Manuel Guerra for the upcoming election. A pronounced shift in the balance of power at Rio Grande City also influenced the calculations of the GOP leader. Following the shooting of Duffy, at least fifty Republicans had moved away from the county seat because of their fear of further bloodshed. All hope for continued Blue Club success in that town vanished. The inflated Republican majority at Rio Grande City in the 1906 contest had stemmed from the intimidation of Democratic voters. The Red Club would be prepared for any future armed confrontation there. Now Falfurrias stood as the only bastion of Republican strength. Despite its steady growth, that community could not prevail over the rest of the county.

Still facing the threat of eventual federal prosecution, Manuel Guerra was eager to avoid a repetition of the volatile campaigning of 1906. Another outbreak of violence and the accompanying revival of adverse publicity about political conditions in Starr County could only complicate his legal problems. The opportunity to forego heavy campaign spending also encouraged the Democratic boss to arrange a truce, which would leave him in control of local politics. By the terms of the understanding between Ed Lasater and Manuel Guerra, the Republicans abstained from running a countywide ticket, while the Democrats withdrew their opposition to Lasater's choices for precinct officials for Falfurrias. The compromise provided the Blue Club with a single representative on the governing body for the county, the county commissioners' court. J. A. Brooks, a former Ranger captain and the Democratic candidate for the Texas House of Representatives, participated in the negotiations and agreed to support Lasater's scheme to organize a new county centered at Falfurrias. The proposed county would include not only the northern section of Starr County but also smaller parts of Hidalgo, Duval, and Nueces counties. As early as 1907, the Republican rancher had lobbied before the state legislature, but he had met defeat at the hands of South Texas Democrats. Starr County officials realized that the loss of Falfurrias with its valuable farmland and dairy ranches would radically cut county revenues and force tax increases for the remaining property owners. In making his commitment to the formation of Falfurrias County, Brooks acted on his own initiative and misrepresented the intentions of his fellow Democrats.

Just two weeks before the November election, several Falfurrias Democrats threatened to sabotage the agreement by challenging Lasater's handpicked candidates at the precinct level, but James B. Wells intervened to block the move. Fortunately for Ed C. Lasater, the armistice held through the election. Although the Republicans received only one seat on the county commissioners' court, they retained their insider's view of the often closed operations of the Starr County government. In defiance of state law, the commissioners' court had failed to publish any comprehensive reports on county finances for several years. The new GOP county commissioner, B. T. Henry, like his predecessor, T. W. Kennedy, was able to penetrate the veil of secrecy and observe Democratic fiscal management firsthand. With the collapse of the political truce in 1909, this opening would prove to be a valuable resource.

Three developments revived the conflict between the Red and Blue clubs of Starr County and precipitated a new Republican assault. When Representative Brooks introduced the bill for the creation of the new county of Falfurrias during the 1909 legislative session, the other South Texas legislators mobilized opposition to the measure and blocked its passage. In the view of Ed Lasater, the Democrats had reneged on one of the main provisions of the 1908 agreement. Political tensions also mounted because of the callous response of the Starr County government to the outbreak of a smallpox epidemic at Falfurrias. Before the arrival of the county health officer, Dr. C. Solis, local physicians had organized a "pest camp" for the quarantine of the patients. Solis took charge of the operation for a brief time, and his administration turned the quarantine into a shambles. He even fired the guards at the detention hospital. When local residents protested to the state health officer, Solis retaliated by selling the hospital, which was county property. Finally, with the scheduling of the federal conspiracy trial for Manuel Guerra and his codefendants, Lasater became convinced of the vulnerability of his opponents, and he decided to take the political offensive again.

Armed with information gathered by the Republican member of

the county commissioners' court, Ed Lasater and his allies inundated Governor Thomas Campbell with complaints about political abuses in Starr County and made preparations to file suit in the state district court to force the ouster of Manuel Guerra, Sheriff Deodoro Guerra, and County Judge John R. Monroe. The plaintiffs' petitions characterized Commissioner Guerra as a "political boss" and offered the following description of his control over local government: "The defendant is a man of dominating character, inordinate ambition, and soulless purpose. He is surrounded by a weak, ignorant, incompetent, and yielding set of men, who constitute the remaining members of the Commissioners' Court. . . . The defendant, by virtue of his political dictatorship, controls the elections of the county and places in office those, and only those, agreeable to his purposes, and by virtue of his official position as County Commissioner, the defendant disburses the funds of the county to the end that the political machine may profit thereby, and that he may personally profit thereby."[12] Most of the specific charges concerned the manipulation of public finances. Without any legal sanction, the county commissioners' court created an all-purpose "County Salary and Expense Fund" and transferred appropriations from duly constituted accounts to this contrived fund. Manuel Guerra and his associates regularly drew money from the fund, far exceeding their official county salaries, to cover political and personal expenses. As another ploy to loot the county treasury, Guerra arranged the appointment of one of his tenants to the post of superintendent of public roads. For a three-month period ending in February 1909, the county boss collected over $2,800 from the "Road and Bridge Fund." Other officials submitted inflated bills for expenses that they had incurred in the performances of their duties. Besides the embezzlement of county funds, the petitioners also cited the hiring of unqualified teachers for political purposes, the appointment of Mexican aliens, the assessment of public employees for campaign contributions, the establishment of a special police force to intimidate voters on election day, the expansion of the sheriff's force beyond the legal limit, and the illegal appointment of elected county officials as deputies.

In response to the mounting protests from Falfurrias citizens, Governor Campbell dispatched a personal representative, Monta Moore, to investigate Starr County politics. After conferring with the new Brownsville customs collector, Rentfro B. Creager, and other Valley insurgents, Moore vouched for the validity of the charges in the ouster petitions and condemned the "cabal" for manipulating the local courts "to grant immunity to their supporters for any outrage they may perpetrate and to indict and punish . . . those who give trouble though guiltless of crime."[13] The current grand jury included two members of the Guerra family, two sons-in-law of County Judge Monroe, and the judge's son, who served as foreman. According to the governor's agent, even District Judge W. B. Hopkins, a loyal Democrat who resided in Corpus Christi, feared for his personal safety during the court session at Rio Grande City because of the impending legal action against the Starr County government, and he demanded the presence of the Texas Rangers.

Not surprisingly, Hopkins refused to institute ouster proceedings. Less than a week later, the jury at Victoria found Manuel Guerra, his cousin Deodoro, and the other defendants innocent of the federal charges of conspiring to murder Gregorio Duffy. With the collapse of these court challenges to the power of Manuel Guerra, Governor Campbell gave in to pressures from South Texas Democratic leaders and abandoned his own investigation of Starr County.

Having weathered all the Republican assaults from 1906 through 1909, Manuel Guerra appeared completely secure in his domination of local politics, but his response to developments outside the county produced another crisis in 1910. This renewal of political turmoil finally convinced Guerra of the advisability of allowing Ed Lasater and his Falfurrias supporters to form a separate county. The enormous influx of settlers into Cameron County after the introduction of large-scale irrigation strengthened the opposition to the Wells machine and produced a dramatic breakthrough in 1910, as the Independent party, consisting of Republicans and maverick Democrats, triumphed in the Brownsville city election. Throughout the turbulent first decade of the twentieth century, Manuel Guerra had turned to Wells for assistance in combating the Republican insurgency. With Guerra's mentor and protector now on the defensive because of major demographic changes, the Starr County boss panicked. His instinct for political survival prevailed over his sense of gratitude to Wells. To the shock of longtime allies like County Judge J. R. Monroe, Manuel Guerra opened negotiations with Lasater and Wells' nemesis in Cameron County, Collector Rentfro B. Creager, to form a fusion ticket for the Starr County election of 1910. Although the bargaining eventually collapsed because the two sides failed to agree on the distribution of public offices, Guerra's maneuver produced a political upheaval.

For County Judge Monroe and his friends, the negotiations with Lasater and Creager represented both a betrayal of Wells and a threat to the survival of the Democratic organization of Starr County. Monroe expressed his anguish over the machinations of the Guerra family when he delivered the following warning to James B. Wells:

"Manuel Guerra, your best friend, has gone into this combination, knowing beyond question that you are opposed to it. . . . It means he has gone into a combination to ruin politically one of the truest and best friends he ever had, a man who has stood by him like a brother."[14] In an effort to salvage their party, the Monroe faction challenged the leadership of the Guerra family and organized their own straight Democratic ticket for the July primary. After the abandonment of the fusionist scheme, Manuel Guerra announced a competing slate of candidates. The ensuing confrontation nearly shattered the supremacy of the Democratic party in Starr County.

Desperate to stave off defeat within his own party, Manuel Guerra portrayed the campaign as a struggle for racial domination between Anglos and Hispanics and appealed to the solid Mexican American majority to embrace his cause. Jacobo Guerra even warned that "Starr County won't be a good place for Americans after the November election."[15] This demagogic rhetoric hardly reflected the political realities of Starr County. The Monroe forces had nominated Mexican Americans to more than half the major county offices. Besides, the Guerras, not their rivals, had tried to make a deal with the Anglo-dominated insurgent movement at Falfurrias. J. R. Monroe and his backers responded to this attack with charges that the Guerras were traitors to the Democratic party. Despite the bitterness of these exchanges, both camps suffered lapses of confidence shortly before the July election and urged James B. Wells to choose a compromise ticket. When the Brownsville politico failed to act, the two sides met head-on in the Democratic primary.

Although the Monroe faction carried Rio Grande City by a sizable majority, the Guerras won the election with almost unanimous votes of support at Roma and several smaller communities. Amid charges of election fraud and voter intimidation, many of Monroe's followers openly expressed their hatred of Manuel Guerra and even threatened to bolt to Lasater's new Independent party. Fearful of a massive defection, the Guerra family again appealed to Wells to act as a party unifier. On Wells' advice, the Starr County boss agreed to scrap the slate of primary winners and to settle for a compromise ticket, which included J. R. Monroe as the nominee for county judge. This reconciliation assured the triumph of the Democratic party in November, but serious strains remained.

As long as lingering antagonisms endangered party unity, Ed Lasater and his Falfurrias constituents posed a real threat to take control of the county. For the sake of his own political security, Manuel Guerra withdrew his opposition to the campaign to organize a new county. In 1911, the Texas Legislature established Brooks

County with its seat of government at Falfurrias. Lasater continued to challenge Democratic dominance in South Texas, but, in the years that followed, his main target would be Archie Parr of Duval County. The separation of the Falfurrias region restored the homogeneous character of Starr County with its overwhelming Hispanic majority and its economy geared almost exclusively to ranching and commerce. The agricultural development along the Rio Grande that transformed the southern parts of Cameron and Hidalgo counties did not reach Starr County during the Progressive Era. Within the traditional social-economic environment of the westernmost Valley county, Manuel Guerra reasserted his supreme authority. He even managed to force J. R. Monroe from office in 1914. When the Starr County boss died in 1915, his sons inherited his political power, and the Guerra family continued to rule until the post–World War II era.

The Republican insurgency of Starr County that Ed Lasater spearheaded represented a prelude to the broader-based political uprisings that would threaten the Democratic machines of Cameron and Hidalgo counties during the second decade of the twentieth century. Like the later Independent parties, the Lasater Republicans drew strength from incoming Anglo settlers and posed as reformers. The GOP activists were reformers in the narrowest sense, however. Their commitment to change focused on eliminating corruption and mismanagement in local government, and all too often their demands reflected racial and cultural biases. Even before the uncovering of evidence of pervasive corruption within the Starr County administration, the Blue Club agitated for the removal of Hispanic officeholders who had failed to master the English language, even though these men were representative of the Mexican American electorate and sensitive to their constituents' needs. Nor did the Republicans' adoption of Democratic campaign tactics enhance their reformist image. They regularly paid the poll taxes for Mexican American laborers, "corralled" their voters on election eve, and plied them with liquor and barbecue until the polls opened the following morning. For the climactic contest of 1906, the Blue Club leaders even resorted to armed force to carry the election at Rio Grande City. Only later, after years of frustration in competing with the Democratic machines for the Mexican American vote, would the Republicans and independent Democrats of South Texas embrace the cause of "purifying" elections. In practical terms, this brand of reform meant the disfranchisement of the mass of the Hispanic voters.

Both sides in the Starr County political wars were able to engage in illegal and even violent actions because of the absence of a nonpartisan judicial system. Despite the tenacity of the federal prosecutors in the Duffy murder case and the later collection of evidence of widespread corruption in Starr County government, Manuel Guerra and his henchmen escaped conviction for their offenses. The influence of the Democratic bosses over the judges, district attorneys, grand juries, and petit juries precluded any evenhanded administration of justice. Even for the Republicans, the legal risks were minimal. Although Cabrera received a life sentence for the murder of Judge Welch, none of the GOP organizers faced prosecution for their armed take-over of the county courthouse during the 1906 election. Rather than relying on cumbersome litigation that might drag on for months or even years, the Red Club was more likely to recruit its own armed force and to resort to election fraud to counter a Republican threat.

The battle for power in the Lower Rio Grande Valley hinged not only on local legal and political conditions but also on politicking at the state and national levels. The Republicans and the maverick Democrats relied heavily on federal patronage, while Wells' close ties with Texas congressmen and senators served as a counterweight to the hostility of the national administrations. No comparable balance of strength existed in state government. Although several South Texas Republicans ran for state office, none could compare with James B. Wells in the exercise of influence over Texas politics. After all, the Democratic party reigned supreme, and Wells was a force to be reckoned with inside that party.

4. Wells and State Politics:
The House Years

THE LEGACY OF RECONSTRUCTION, the level of economic development, ethnic conflicts, the upheavals of the 1890s, and the political leadership of Colonel Edward House, Joseph Bailey, and James Hogg shaped the political environment in which James Wells maneuvered to exercise statewide influence. With the collapse of Reconstruction in the mid-1870s, the Democratic party consolidated its dominance over Texas politics. The Bourbon leadership of the party embraced the principles of white supremacy, states rights, and limited government. With no viable Republican opposition at the state level, the racist sentiment of the Democratic electorate prevailed. Social custom, extralegal violence and repression, local governmental action, and, later, state legislation shaped a segregated order in which blacks experienced the abridgment of legal and political rights and the loss of opportunities for social and economic advancement. Fear of federal intervention to block the restoration of a racial caste system reinforced the traditional Democratic aversion to a strong national government. The alleged abuses of Republican rule during Reconstruction served as a rationale for limiting the role of the state government as well. The constitution of 1876 imposed sharp restrictions on the powers of state officials, especially the governor, and the Democratic-controlled legislatures after 1872 dramatically reduced government expenditures, even for such vital public services as education. Although the lobbying of the Grange delegates forced the inclusion of antimonopoly provisions in the constitution, the state government abstained from any rigorous regulation of corporations for almost a decade and a half. Despite periodic uprisings, such as the campaigning of the Greenback party in 1878 and 1880, the conservative Democrats faced no serious opposition until the 1890s.

During this period of unchallenged Democratic control, the state experienced spectacular growth as its population increased 40 percent between 1880 and 1890, but its social make-up reflected few changes. By the closing decade of the nineteenth century, Texas remained overwhelmingly rural, and cattle and cotton production dominated the economy. The majority of the population consisted of Anglo, evangelical Protestant farmers, who were either native-born Texans or recent arrivals from other southern states. The concentration of blacks in East Texas, the German settlements of Central Texas, and the Hispanic population of South Texas posed the most striking exceptions to this general pattern. Despite the retention of their distinctive culture and their record of political independence, the Germans won the acceptance and even the respect of the rest of the citizenry of the state. Only the struggle over prohibition and the later anti-German hysteria of World War I generated tensions. The blacks and Mexican Americans, on the other hand, faced deep-rooted hostility. The Hispanics of the Trans-Nueces escaped the racist stigma of biological inferiority that plagued the blacks, but the Anglo majority of Texas still regarded the Hispanic population as an alien force that threatened the basic decency of society. Distrust of Catholicism, the popular stereotype of the indolent, subservient Mexican *peón*, the corruption of the Hispanic vote, the periodic outbreaks of banditry along the border, and the Mexican American opposition to prohibition all sustained the widespread Anglo prejudices.

These unassimilated ethnic and racial groups represented no threat to the dominance of the Democratic party. By 1890, blacks formed only 25 percent of the total population. Even before the establishment of the state poll tax in 1902, which reduced the black electorate to a range of 10 to 25 percent of the black adult male population, local white repression had limited the voting strength of blacks. The independent-minded Germans, who split their votes between the Republican and Democratic parties, comprised a much smaller fraction of the population, and the sizable Hispanic community of South Texas rallied behind the Democratic banner. Between 1876 and 1890, the Democratic vote increased steadily from 150,000 to 260,000, while the combined opposition of the Republicans and various third-party movements surpassed 100,000 votes in only two elections. As long as Bourbon Democracy maintained the support of the overwhelming majority of the white, evangelical Protestant farmers of Texas, its success was assured.

This political consensus collapsed in the late 1880s with the onslaught of a nationwide agricultural depression, which demolished cotton, corn, wheat, and beef prices. Hard-pressed farmers throughout the eastern, northern, and central regions of the state flocked to the Populist party. This new party condemned banks, railroads, and other business interests as exploiters of the farm population and promoted free silver, the state ownership of railroads, and federal loans to relieve agricultural distress. The Populists of Texas were among the most militant in the country, and they waged three vigorous campaigns against the Democratic party from 1892 through the climactic election of 1896. To forestall massive defections to the insurgent movement, the Democratic governor, James Hogg, embarked on a program of moderate reform. While refusing to endorse government farm loans, Hogg oversaw the creation of the Texas Railroad Commission, endorsed free silver, and indulged in anticorporation rhetoric. Despite the Bourbon resistance to Hogg's reelection in 1892, many conservative Democrats made their own pragmatic adjustments to cope with the agrarian upheaval. Hogg's more conservative successor, Charles Culberson, reversed his position on the currency issue to become a leading advocate of free silver. Even die-hard gold Democrats like James B. Wells acquiesced to the passage of a free-silver plank at the 1896 state convention and supported the candidacy of William Jennings Bryan for the presidency. To halt the Populist surge, Democrats also resorted to election fraud, voter intimidation, and race-baiting. Despite a strong showing in the state races of 1896, the Populist party of Texas collapsed as a potent political force before the turn of the century. Democratic tactics, internal dissension, the disintegration of the national party organization, and the improvement of economic conditions sealed the fate of the third-party movement.

The subsidence of farmer unrest undercut not only Populism but also the reform-minded Hogg wing of the Democratic party. By 1901, conservative Democrats had regained complete control of state politics. Despite occasional reform gestures, the promotion of business growth and the attraction of outside capital investment took precedence over corporate regulation in a state where the annual gross income from agriculture was twice as great as the value of industrial output. The relaxation of restrictions on the issuance of railroad stock, the tolerance of an escalating pattern of railroad consolidation, the slack enforcement of antitrust legislation, and opposition to increased corporate taxation typified the direction of state government during the late 1890s. Many of the leading political figures invested heavily in the developing industries of Texas, and some even served as corporate officials. Not even former Governor Hogg could resist the temper of the times, as he represented

Southern Pacific in an antitrust suit, organized the Hogg-Swayne Oil Syndicate, and solicited financial support for his company from Pittsburgh oil magnate Andrew Mellon.

Instead of machinelike regimentation, factional competition and makeshift alliances characterized the organization of the conservative wing of the Texas Democratic party. Within this fluid system, two men, with contrasting political styles, exercised the most influence. Colonel Edward M. House managed the successful gubernatorial campaigns of Charles Culberson and Joseph Sayers from 1894 through 1900 and the election of Culberson to the U.S. Senate in 1899. A masterful political technician, House perfected the strategy of arranging early primary and county convention victories for his candidates to generate a bandwagon effect, which frequently drove the competition from the field. For each campaign, he fashioned a loose coalition of regional and county leaders to handle the grass roots organization. Because of his role as confidant to a succession of conservative governors, the Colonel was able to reward his campaign allies with patronage concessions, assured access to the chief executives, and appointments to key party positions. Despite his considerable influence, House neither dominated Texas politics nor personally controlled any bloc of voters. His power rested on his reciprocal understandings with party organizers across the state.

In contrast to Colonel House's penchant for behind-the-scenes manipulation, the other commanding figure in state politics, Joseph Weldon Bailey, excelled at public oratory and aroused the emotions of Texas voters as no other campaigner of his era could. With a secure base of support in the rapidly growing region of North Texas, Bailey served in the U.S. House of Representatives for ten years and even secured the post of Democratic minority leader. The congressman's sweep of the county conventions and preferential primaries of 1900 assured his election to the Senate, but that same year his political reputation suffered serious damage with the exposure of his involvement with the Waters-Pierce Oil Company. In March 1900, a court order forced the corporation to forfeit its charter to operate in Texas because its ties with the Standard Oil Company violated the state antitrust laws. At the request of the company president, Henry Clay Pierce, Bailey participated in the reorganization of the firm and then assured Governor Sayers and Attorney General Thomas Smith that the company had withdrawn from the Standard Oil trust. When the Texas secretary of state renewed the charter for the corporation, a storm of protest erupted. Although the uproar failed to block Bailey's promotion to the U.S. Senate, additional revelations revived the controversy six years later, and charges of impropriety hounded the North Texas politico for the remainder of his career.

Both Edward House and Joseph Bailey combined generally conservative outlooks with occasional displays of ideological flexibility, but again their political styles clashed. Preoccupied with the mechanics of organizing campaigns, the Colonel preferred compromise and consensus over controversy and avoided public commitments on volatile issues. He rarely participated in the shaping of legislation and confined his policy-making role to the unpublicized drafting of planks for state Democratic platforms. Bailey, on the other hand, thrived on political combat. He broke with the Cleveland administration over the issue of free silver, condemned American imperialistic expansion, opposed prohibition and women's suffrage, and defended the entanglements of politicians with corporate interests. Throughout his career, though, Bailey reserved his most extravagant oratory for the conservative Democratic concepts of states rights, limited government, and white supremacy. Even his infrequent forays to promote reforms like national railroad regulation entailed theatrical performances on the floor of Congress. As the controversy over Bailey's connections with the Waters-Pierce Oil Company and other corporate powers intensified, the senator himself became an emotionally charged issue. Bailey's disruptive influence on Texas politics made House uneasy, and the two men never fully trusted each other. Their cooperation in waging statewide campaigns represented a marriage of convenience and masked underlying tensions within the dominant conservative Democratic coalition.

Despite his indulgence in speculative oil ventures, James Hogg remained the leading advocate of reform within the Democratic party. At the state nominating convention of 1900, he even persuaded the delegates to override the Bailey-dominated platform committee and to endorse legislative submission of three constitutional amendments aimed at curtailing corporate influence over Texas politics. Rather than reversing the conservative tide that had swept the state, Hogg's dramatic performance constituted a rearguard action for his rapidly retreating forces. In 1898, Joseph Sayers had overwhelmed the Hogg candidate in the competition for the gubernatorial nomination, and, two years later, Congressman Bailey forced U.S. Senator Horace Chilton, another ally of the former governor, to withdraw from his race for reelection. Only East Texas with its tradition of political protest and its widespread poverty remained a stronghold of support for agrarian Democratic reformers. As his political power receded, James Hogg maintained surprisingly cordial relations with Colonel House, who had served as one of his campaign organizers in 1892. At the same time, Hogg's criticism of Bailey's role in the Waters-Pierce affair generated a bitter personal feud. Even though conservative Democrats held all the major state offices after January 1901, the personal relations among House, Bailey, and Hogg had an unsettling effect on Texas politics. Clashes of temperament, style, and ambition did not always coincide with differences over policy.

Both Joseph Weldon Bailey and Edward House relied on James B. Wells to mobilize South Texas support for their campaigns. The election totals of the Lower Rio Grande Valley counties represented only a tiny percentage of the statewide Democratic vote, but several elements enhanced the influence of the Brownsville politico. The machine domination of the Mexican American electorate facilitated the implementation of House's strategy of conducting early primaries and conventions in counties where his candidates were assured of success. When Culberson and Sayers ran for the gubernatorial nomination for the first time in 1894 and 1898, respectively, Wells delivered timely convention victories in Cameron, Hidalgo, and Starr counties to the House-sponsored candidates and monitored campaign activity as far north as Victoria. At the Democratic state conventions of the 1890s, the fifteen to twenty Valley delegates voted as a unit under Wells' direction.

As the Populist threat to Democratic supremacy mounted, even the general election along the border took on importance. Because of the nativist reputation of the Populist party and the rigid control of the mass of the Hispanic voters by both Democratic machines and a few Republican county organizations, the agrarian insurgency failed to make any headway in South Texas. In 1894, the Democrats carried the state by only 55,000 votes, and the Democratic landslide in the sparsely populated region south of the Nueces River supplied almost 15 percent of the margin of victory. The Valley counties alone provided Charles Culberson with a majority of 4,845 votes to one vote over his Populist opponent, while the Republican nominee collected 1,070 votes. Two years later the combination of GOP strength in Duval and Webb counties and the fusion of the Populist and Republican tickets for the state races reduced the scope of the Democratic victory in South Texas, but Wells and his allies still routed the opposition in Cameron, Hidalgo, and Starr counties, 4,646 to 1,457.

James B. Wells' record of unfailing party loyalty also bolstered his standing among state Democratic leaders. During the 1892 struggle for the Democratic gubernatorial nomination, Wells favored the conservative railroad lawyer George Clark, who charged that Governor Hogg's regulatory reforms would wreck the Texas economy. At the tumultuous state convention, however, the Valley chieftain refused to bolt the party with the other Clark delegates, and he threw his support behind Hogg in the general election. Nor did the triumph of the free-silver forces at the 1896 conventions undermine Wells' commitment to the regular Democratic organization. In fact, he accepted the party platform, won admittance to the state Democratic executive committee, and condemned his fellow gold Democrats who called a separate protest convention. As defections from both the right and the left sapped the strength of the Democratic party during the 1890s, Wells' steadfastness impressed even his ideological adversaries. When the veteran campaigner announced his candidacy for the Democratic state chairmanship in 1900, James Hogg overlooked their policy differences and acquiesced to Wells' election "because I know you to be a Democrat of unquestioned loyalty to the party."[1]

His power base in South Texas and his reputation as a die-hard Democrat made James B. Wells a formidable force in state politics, but his rapid rise through the party hierarchy after 1894 depended ultimately on his close association with Edward House. The two politicians respected each other as campaign managers, shared generally conservative beliefs, and valued political success over ideological purity. In evaluating prospective candidates and assessing political conditions, House consulted more freely with his chief troubleshooter Joe Lee Jameson, Houston corporate lawyer Frank Andrews, and Congressman Albert Burleson than with Wells. Nevertheless, the Rio Grande boss still belonged to that inner circle of House associates, known as "our crowd," whose adherence to the Colonel's leadership was unquestioned. In exchange for Wells' dependable support of gubernatorial and other state candidates, House sponsored the promotion of his South Texas organizer to key party positions. In 1898, House arranged the election of the Brownsville lawyer as temporary chairman at the state convention, and two years later the Colonel invited Wells to run for the chairmanship of the Texas Democratic party. Despite the outbreak of acrimonious debate over Hogg's proposed constitutional amendments and Bailey's ties with the Waters-Pierce Oil Company, Wells secured the post by acclamation at the conclusion of the convention.

Political controversy did not deter James B. Wells from embracing the cause of the other leading Texas conservative, Joseph Weldon Bailey. When the North Texas congressman decided to run for the U.S. Senate, Wells joined the ranks of early Bailey supporters and remained loyal in the face of attacks against the candidate for his role in the relicensing of the Waters-Pierce Oil Company. At the nominating convention of 1900, the South Texas boss served on the platform committee, which refused to condemn the decision to allow the oil company to resume its operations in Texas.

At the price of antagonizing the East Texas reformers who had abstained from challenging his impending election to the state chairmanship, Wells also sided with the Bailey forces in their assault against the proposed Hogg constitutional amendments, which called for the outlawing of corporate campaign contributions and free railroad passes for public officials. Prior to the 1900 Democratic gathering at Waco, Colonel House had assured the former governor that he would accept the inclusion of the measures in the state platform. Because of House's refusal to take part in the battle over the amendments, Hogg prevailed on this single issue. Despite the continued domination of the conservative factions of the Democratic party, Wells' close identification with Bailey at the 1900 convention adversely affected the South Texan's future political plans.

The final challenge to Bailey's candidacy came at the opening of the regular session of the Texas Legislature in January 1901, and again Wells provided valuable support. Although the congressman's only serious opponent, incumbent Horace Chilton, had already withdrawn from the race, pressure mounted for the legislature to investigate the rechartering of the Waters-Pierce Oil Company before electing a U.S. senator. In response to urgent appeals from Bailey partisans, Wells traveled to Austin to lobby personally for the North Texan's cause. Two of Wells' closest legislative allies, Francis W. Seabury of Starr County and John Nance Garner of Uvalde County, played key roles in limiting the scope of the inquiry. As chairman of the pro-Bailey caucus, Garner submitted amendments to water down the accusations of impropriety in the resolution calling for a review of the case, and Seabury served on the investigating committee. After imposing a two-day deadline for summoning witnesses and after hearing testimony from only four witnesses, including Bailey and Attorney General Smith, the House committee authorized Seabury and two other members to draft a report. Not only did these legislators find the senatorial candidate innocent of the charges of using undue influence and covering up continued corporate links between Waters-Pierce and Standard Oil, but they also lashed out against Bailey's accusers for their "cruel, vindictive, and unfounded attack."[2] The full House deleted this indictment of the congressman's critics but upheld the committee's exoneration of Bailey's conduct. Just two weeks after the start of the session, the Texas Senate and House elected Joseph Bailey to the U.S. Senate with only six dissenting votes.

Until 1900, James B. Wells had never aspired for election to public office. Even after his appointment to a district judgeship in 1897, he refused to run for the position in 1898, although he was assured of victory. With the resurgence of conservative Democratic control of state politics and with his elevation to the rank of state party chairman, Wells' ambitions soared. He wanted to become the governor of Texas. Having cultivated close ties with both Colonel House and Joseph Bailey, Wells believed that his prospects for succeeding Governor Sayers in 1902 were excellent. However, a combination of regional rivalries, cultural tensions, conflicting personal ambitions, and expedient political calculations destroyed Wells' dream. Even though the Rio Grande boss withdrew from the race almost a year before the nominating convention, his abortive campaign was important because it revealed the tensions that plagued the conservative wing of the Democratic party.

As early as the state convention of 1900, at which Governor Sayers won renomination without opposition, House and his colleagues began to evaluate possible gubernatorial candidates for 1902. The Colonel believed that James Wells deserved serious consideration, but Congressman Albert Burleson dismissed the South Texan's prospects as remote because of the interaction of sectional and ideological conflicts. Burleson focused his attention on the growing power of North Texas politicians. By the turn of the century, the twin cities of Dallas and Fort Worth and the rich farmland of North and North Central Texas claimed almost a third of the state population, and the distribution of state offices reflected the dramatic development of the region. Both U.S. senators and seven of the sixteen popularly elected state officials came from a tier of counties, three to four counties wide, stretching northward from Waco to the Red River. Only three of the officeholders resided in counties farther south than Waco, and only one as far south as San Antonio. Even conservatives from other sections objected to this allocation of elective offices, not because of policy differences, but because of the limitations on their opportunities for political advancement. As a Central Texas representative with ties throughout South and Southwest Texas, Burleson shared this resentment and offered a solution for the upcoming gubernatorial race: "If the governorship is permitted to go to North Texas in 1902, it will be two decades before our section of the state will regain control of state governmental affairs. But if we can effect an alliance with the Democrats of East Texas, the Democrats south of a line drawn through McLennan County [Waco] can name who will be governor at the expiration of Sayer's second term."[3] By unifying the House forces with the remnants of the Hogg movement against the North Texas conservatives, the proposed coalition would cut across ideological lines, but Burleson still intended for the conservatives to retain control of state politics: ". . . I have made it plain to everyone of them that East Texas at this time is under the ban of disapproval and that no East Texas man could hope to succeed in securing a nomination for state office, but that if an understanding could be effected and we could succeed in putting into the office of governor a South or Southwest Texas man, that four years from now a few slices of pie might be handed to the East Texas crowd, and strange to say, in every instance they have readily assented to the suggestion made."[4]

James B. Wells' activism at the 1900 Democratic state convention destroyed any possibility of his leading the conservative-reformist coalition that Burleson envisioned. The Valley boss' close association with Joseph Bailey and his opposition to the Hogg amendments completely alienated the East Texas delegates. Nor could Wells turn to his conservative allies in North Texas for support. Congressman Burleson argued that these men planned to name their own candidate for the governorship and to complete their sweep of the major state offices. Confronted with the power of North Texas, political organizers either had to forge alliances with the leaders of that region or to unite the rest of the state in opposition to North Texas dominance. Neither alternative appeared viable for the prospective candidacy of James Wells, who was caught in the crossfire of regional rivalry and debate over public policy.

Colonel House realized that the concentration of electoral strength in North Texas would shape the campaign strategies of 1902, but he rejected Burleson's suggestion of forming an alliance with the Hogg reformers. House's main concern was not the consolidation of North Texas control over state government but instead the fragmentation of the conservative vote, which might allow the East Texans to make a strong showing on their own. As Burleson's analysis forecast, a united conservative front necessitated the choice of a North Texas candidate, but House hoped to find one whom he could control. Initially he favored the nomination of Texas Supreme Court Justice Thomas Jefferson Brown, and, after his withdrawal from the race, House turned to Congressman S. W. T. Lanham. At the same time, the Colonel flagrantly misled James Wells.

While giving Wells tentative assurances of support in the summer of 1901, Edward House recruited Andrews, Burleson, and Joe Lee Jameson to discourage the South Texan from running. Although

House's early assessment of the Wells candidacy was less pessimistic than Burleson's judgment, the "Texas king-maker" anticipated a grueling struggle, which he was unwilling to undertake. Having suffered from recurrent poor health, the Colonel wanted to reduce his involvement in state politics and to devote more time to his business interests. However, nothing short of an all-out effort by House and his organization could salvage the campaign of his Valley ally.

Besides the difficulties of winning over political leaders in both North and East Texas, House worried about two other drawbacks to Wells' candidacy. James Wells was a Roman Catholic in a state where Protestants formed the overwhelming majority of the population. The evangelical Southern Baptists and Methodists, who set the religious tone for the state, were notorious for their nativist, anti-Catholic prejudices, and Wells' identification with the Hispanic population of South Texas threatened to intensify the cultural backlash. When House first raised the issue, he expressed regret over the influence of religious bigotry on Texas politics. Later, as his desperation to dump the South Texan grew, the colonel directed his criticism toward Wells and his family: "I am told that they are Catholics of so rabid a type that Mrs. Wells will not enter a Protestant church even to attend a funeral or a wedding. Two of his sisters are nuns and they are about as extreme as people ever get to be. If you do not think this is going to hurt him . . . you are greatly mistaken."[5]

One other problem disturbed House. Despite Wells' mastery of South Texas politics, the Colonel questioned his understanding of the requirements of running a statewide campaign: "It is almost impossible to control Wells in as much that you cannot reach him and when you do you cannot make him write letters or see people. At this stage of the game Governor Sayers had written several thousand letters to his friends throughout Texas. I doubt whether Wells has written as many as a dozen. He does not seem to have the remotest idea how to organize a campaign or direct it."[6]

By September 1901, the Texas power broker concluded that Wells' cause was hopeless and that any further association with the campaign would reduce "our crowd" to "political bankrupts." Even as he maneuvered to force Wells' withdrawal and to embrace the Lanham candidacy, House still professed respect for the Rio Grande boss: "I would not give Wells's little finger for the whole of Lanham's body, and outside of yourself [Andrews] I would rather see him governor than any other man in Texas . . . but after going over the situation fully I do not believe that he can win."[7] Political realism prevailed over personal friendship.

Although Wells never publicly announced his candidacy and assumed a noncommital posture even in private, he spent the spring and summer of 1901 surveying political sentiment around the state and soliciting support. His preparations for the formal campaign were not as thorough as House had expected, but Wells was hardly inactive in his pursuit of the governorship. In fact, the initial correspondence from political contacts outside South Texas was encouraging. The men assured Wells that he could surmount the "petty jealousies" among the different sections of the state, force other conservative Democrats like Judge Brown from the race, and eventually win the backing of Senators Bailey and Culberson.[8]

Unaware of Colonel House's duplicity, Wells first realized that his campaign faced serious obstacles when he received reports that Joseph Bailey had thrown his support to Thomas Jefferson Brown. On Wells' behalf, Jeff McLemore, the secretary of the state Democratic executive committee, conducted a thorough review of political conditions across the state. In early July, McLemore confirmed that both Bailey and Culberson were promoting Brown's candidacy. He also relayed Governor Sayers' belief that self-serving calculations motivated the two senators. They were afraid that "a younger man" like Wells, with more ambition and vigor than the aging Brown, "might aspire to one or the other's seat in years to come." Incensed by what he regarded as a betrayal of his friend, the Democratic secretary heaped scorn and ridicule on the claim of Brown's North Texas promoters that they were "saving" the state from "Hoggism."[9] In McLemore's view, political greed rather than ideological commitment accounted for the North Texans' vigorous support of Judge Brown: ". . . while the fact that they already have both Senators, two Supreme Judges, and other state officers ought to induce them to be generous toward some other portion of the state, yet the effect is just the opposite and having most of the big offices they seem to think it is their divine right to grab and have them all."[10] Although McLemore assured Wells of House's continuing support, "as far as I can learn," Wells' confidence crumbled, and he bitterly complained to the Colonel about the tactics of the Brown camp.[11] Wells added that he would not "break [his] back" to reunite the party behind Brown.[12]

Not even the withdrawal of Brown and a private vow of support from Culberson could revive Wells' hopes. As soon as Judge Brown stepped aside, the North Texas politicos united behind S. W. T. Lanham. On instructions from House, members of "our crowd" labored to convince Wells that his chances for success were slim, especially since the Colonel would be unable to devote his full attention to the contest. Finally, in September, the South Texan informed House of his decision to terminate his campaign, and, one month later, Wells reluctantly pledged his support to Lanham. The choice of Congressman Lanham as the consensus candidate of the conservative wing of Texas Democracy reflected political cynicism. Besides his residence in North Texas, he had no qualifications for the governorship. All the major party leaders regarded him as an inept politician, but he fit into their political calculations. Joseph Bailey and Charles Culberson endorsed his candidacy because he posed no future threat to their Senate careers, and Edward House perceived an opportunity for "our crowd" to continue to manipulate the executive branch of Texas government. The most contemptuous appraisal of Lanham came from Burleson, as he described his fellow congressman's response to a complimentary letter from House: ". . . he was as pleased at the receipt of it as a child with a new toy. He repeatedly said to me how gratifying it was to him that a man of your wide experience and thorough knowledge of the political situation should have given such a ·sweeping approval of his speech, without suggesting a single change."[13] Despite his obvious defects as a political leader, S. W. T. Lanham faced no serious opposition. When several northern counties, known to favor the front-runner, scheduled early primaries, Lanham's remaining competitor, a reformer named Thomas Campbell, also withdrew.

With the resolution of the governor's race even before the start of the county conventions and primaries of 1902, James Wells returned to the front lines of the Texas political battles. As compensation for his failure to win the gubernatorial nomination, Edward House decided to promote the reelection of the Rio Grande boss to the chairmanship of the state Democratic executive committee. This proposed break from the tradition of one-term service at the head of the party machinery provoked strong opposition. The protests focused on Wells' refusal to use his power as state chairman to institute uniform primaries.

The House strategy of generating political momentum for his candidates with early primary victories in safe counties had proven to be an effective campaign weapon but had also aroused considerable resentment. Hogg reformers and independent politicians argued that this practice minimized the role of public debate in deciding elections and placed a premium on organization. Only those candidates with close ties to the county rings across the state could influence the scheduling of primaries to advance their causes. When Thomas Campbell withdrew from the gubernatorial race in January 1902, he pointed out that, as a newcomer to statewide campaigning, he needed time to gain public exposure and to explain his positions on the important issues facing the Texas voters. He had no realistic hope of preparing for the February primaries in several populous northern counties where Lanham enjoyed the support of the local Democratic organizations.

Even some conservative Democrats, who shared the views of the House-sponsored candidates, developed their own reservations about the manipulation of the nominating process. The scheduling of winter and early spring county primaries to benefit a single state-wide candidate, or at the most a handful of candidates, placed not only their opponents but also aspirants for other offices at a disadvantage. Harried candidates at the state and district levels had to contend with different primary dates for different counties and date changes from year to year. These complications made advance planning difficult, and the extension of the primary season over several months increased campaign expenses. Texas congressmen were particularly hard pressed. Serving in Washington, over a thousand miles from their home districts, they were often caught off guard by the rescheduling of primary contests and had to make hasty choices between fulfilling their legislative responsibilities and rushing back to Texas to campaign.

As the attacks against the existing primary system escalated, even Colonel House expressed his willingness to accept reform. He continued to arrange early primaries as long as the party regulations permitted such action, but he declined to organize any opposition to proposed rule changes. As a result, the delegates at the 1900 state convention passed a resolution that directed the executive committee to order the holding of primary elections and conventions for the selection of state officers "upon the same date throughout the state."[14] The committee also received instructions to disallow the official counting of returns from counties that failed to comply with the uniform scheduling. Apparently on his own initiative, Wells resisted the implementation of the convention mandate. His delay in calling a meeting of the state Democratic executive committee to consider the question stirred criticism not only from reformers but also from the Texas congressional delegation. In correspondence to Colonel House, Albert Burleson claimed that "every Congressman I have heard mention the matter has deplored the procrastination of Wells, for the reason that they are anxious to have a primary upon a uniform date." Wells was so obstinate in his refusal to take any action that Burleson wondered whether he was deliberately creating political mischief as revenge for "what occurred last summer."[15]

By the time that Wells finally yielded to the mounting pressure and assembled the state Democratic executive committee, four heavily populated North Texas counties had either conducted or scheduled their 1902 primaries. At the February 27 committee meeting, Wells led the fight against the imposition of a mandatory uniform primary date and suggested that his committee "recommend" rather than "order" the holding of county primaries on a specified date. He argued that the enforcement of the sanctions that the 1900 state convention had prescribed for noncompliance would result in the disfranchisement of part of the Democratic electorate. According to Wells, only the state convention had the authority to evaluate the validity of primary returns and to rule on the eligibility of county delegates who would cast convention votes in accordance with those returns. The past convention had simply erred in delegating these powers to the executive committee. One of Wells' allies at the session, John Nance Garner, took an even more extreme stand, as he asserted that "each county was sovereign within itself,"[16] and that not even the state convention could enforce rules for the scheduling of primaries. To the proponents of uniform primaries, this claim of local sovereignty appeared ludicrous. Moreover, they argued that, since the state executive committee was the creature of the convention, the committee was obligated to carry out whatever instructions it received. After more than an hour of heated debate, Wells mustered a fourteen-to-thirteen majority against setting a mandatory date, and the executive committee "recommended" that the counties across the state conduct their primaries on June 14.

In the immediate aftermath of this vote, James Wells began to maneuver to secure reelection to the state chairmanship. He pressured a majority of the executive committee into giving him a vote of confidence for his present leadership and endorsing his bid for a second term. When Colonel House decided to appease the Valley boss by backing his candidacy, Albert Burleson protested and reported that Senator Bailey also frowned upon any commitment to the South Texan because "it is impossible for us to elect Wells."[17] Despite these objections, House recruited his most reliable organizer, Joe Lee Jameson, to mobilize statewide support for the Brownsville politico. Jameson was a political realist like his mentor, and, at the outset of the campaign, he warned Wells not "to make a fight at [the state convention] against the uniform primaries for 1904."[18]

The Hogg forces and several influential conservatives like Senator Culberson threw their support behind the candidacy of Joseph Cockrell of Dallas, who had battled for uniform primaries as a member of the state executive committee. Congressman Lanham remained publicly neutral because of his misgivings about Wells' loyalty. Even after Campbell had withdrawn from the gubernatorial race, Lanham complained to Burleson that "he suspected that Wells was anxious to see a 'tie up' in the convention, in hopes that he [Wells] would be selected as the most available man to unloosen the complication."[19] Although Wells continued to favor optional rather than compulsory uniform primaries, he appeared to have a clear-cut edge over his opponent by the opening of the July state convention. Bailey, all of House's associates, including Burleson, and even Lanham's campaign manager were aligned with the South Texan. Still, the sentiment for election reform was so overwhelming that Wells felt compelled to make the incredible claim that "nothing that I have said or done in the discharge of my duties can be fairly constructed to place me in antagonism to [uniform primaries]."[20] When the veteran campaigner carried the convention by a vote of 619 to 388, Jameson commented that the victory was "so complete" that "Lanham knows now who is running things in Texas."[21]

The convention delegates also reaffirmed their commitment to uniform primaries. The party platform set the second Saturday in July as the date for state primaries, denied participation in the organization of the next convention to those counties that failed to comply, and explicitly instructed the state executive committee to "enforce this provision."[22] Action by the state legislature, however, relieved Wells of any responsibility to take the initiative on this matter. The Terrell Election Law of 1903 provided legal sanctions for the enforcement of the uniform primary date. The meeting of the Democratic executive committee on April 22, 1904, to order the holding of nominating elections and conventions for state and district officials on July 9 was a mere formality.

James B. Wells' second term as state chairman passed uneventfully, and at its conclusion he voluntarily stepped down. Although he still harbored ambitions to run for the governorship, Wells' influence over state politics declined after 1904. While remaining a leading organizer and spokesman for South Texas Democrats, he did not secure another major party position at the state level until 1916, when he served as the platform chairman for the Democratic convention. The cultural and regional tensions that frustrated his gubernatorial aspirations in 1901 continued to plague Wells, but after 1904 he faced an even more formidable obstacle: the collapse of conservative Democratic domination and the rise of a viable progressive movement in Texas. Along with his fellow conservatives, James Wells engaged in a rearguard action for the remainder of the decade. Even with the revival of conservative fortunes in 1910, he stayed on the defensive in statewide political competition.

5. Wells and State Politics: The Progressive Challenge

S. W. T. LANHAM WON reelection in 1904 without serious opposition, but within two years progressive Democrats gained sufficient strength to wrest the governorship from conservative control. Although the Old Guard of the party reclaimed the office in 1910, progressivism remained a formidable force in state politics through the second decade of the twentieth century. Like reformist campaigners across the nation, the Texas progressives agitated for government regulation of corporations, fairer distribution of the tax burden, the elimination of political corruption, and improved public services. The need for business controls was not as pressing in Texas as in the more industrialized states, however. Tax inequities, conflicts between giant interstate and smaller local companies, mistreatment of industrial workers, and corporate corruption of public officials all existed but on a modest scale because of the economic underdevelopment of the state. The efforts of the conservative Democratic leaders to attract outside capital investment and to promote industrial growth with probusiness policies had met with only limited success. Even with the rise of the oil industry after the discovery of the Spindletop field in 1901, cotton production, cattle ranching, and other agricultural pursuits still dominated the Texas economy for the duration of the Progressive Era. The supremacy of oil over the political and economic affairs of the state lay in the future. Nor did the railroads, the traditional targets of Texas reformers, pose any dire threat to the public welfare. Despite the acceleration of railroad consolidation after 1896 and the maintenance of rates above the national average, the companies provided satisfactory service for farmers, ranchers, and other shippers. To a large extent, the commission established during the Hogg administration had tamed the railroad menace, as it held down intrastate rates, combated rate discrimination, and policed the issuance of stock.

In the absence of an all-powerful corporate villain, Texas progressives proceeded to enact needed but modest economic reforms and to personalize the issue of corporate abuse as they launched repeated crusades to destroy the political influence of one man, Joseph Weldon Bailey. From the progressive perspective, Bailey stood as the symbol of the corrupting influence of big business on politics. In addition, the reformers turned their attention to issues like prohibition and election reform, which reflected the social and cultural concerns of the electorate. The drive to outlaw alcoholic beverages drew its strength from the rural, Anglo, Protestant majority, who were determined to impose their pietistic values on the city dwellers and the ethnic minorities of the state. Most progressives embraced this cause because of their belief that the liquor and beer industries constituted dangerous special interests that not only undermined personal morality but also corrupted the political system through bribery, campaign contributions, and intensive lobbying. Likewise, the promotion of stronger state regulation of primaries and general elections combined a passion for honest government with cultural biases. Many of the proposed reforms were aimed at curtailing the political participation of blacks and Mexican Americans. Even the campaign for women's suffrage stemmed, at least in part, from the desire to strengthen the electoral majority of the white evangelical Protestants and to broaden the base of support for prohibition.

Several factors accounted for the dramatic turnabout in Texas politics after 1904. The gathering momentum of progressive agitation at the national level and the rise of reform-minded interest groups among farmers, industrial workers, businessmen, women, and preachers at the state level had an impact, but just as critical was the weakness within the conservative camp of the Texas Democratic party. During Lanham's first term as governor, Edward House's influence over state government declined. Surprisingly, Lanham rebelled against the domination of "our crowd," and the Colonel spent most of his time in New York City and at his retreat in Magnolia, Massachusetts. After playing a minor role in Alton Parker's drive for the Democratic presidential nomination, House withdrew almost completely from participation in Texas politics. Preoccupied with various business ventures, he remained politically inactive until the presidential campaign of Woodrow Wilson in 1912. House's departure created a crisis of leadership for the Democratic Old Guard.

Without the Colonel's steadying influence and artful maneuvering, Texas conservatives failed to agree on any consensus candidate to succeed Governor Lanham, and factional strife intensified. No other politician could fill House's role. Joseph Bailey lacked Colonel House's organizational skills, and the senator's controversial career encouraged dissension rather than unity. With the revival of the Waters-Pierce scandal in 1906, Bailey devoted all of his attention to his own political survival. Senator Charles Culberson suffered from debilitating health problems, and Governor Lanham never displayed any leadership capability. Nor did any of the members of "our gang" move to take House's place as the "king-maker" of state politics. James B. Wells remained a provincial South Texas figure unable to control the ambitious politicians of the populous northern counties. When the progressive forces captured the governorship with the election of Thomas Campbell in 1906, three North Texas candidates divided the conservative vote.

Even before that fateful gubernatorial contest, the state legislature of 1905 advanced the progressive cause with the enactment of several important reforms. Ironically, one of Wells' Valley allies, Francis W. Seabury, held the all-important position of Speaker of the House of Representatives and contributed to the legislative breakthrough. A native of Virginia and a graduate of the University of Virginia, Seabury migrated to South Texas in the early 1890s. After serving as the city attorney of Brownsville, he moved to Rio Grande City. From 1895 through 1906, Seabury represented Cameron, Hidalgo, and Starr counties in the Texas House, and for two terms he chaired the Rules Committee. At the conclusion of the 1903 legislative session, the Rio Grande lawmaker launched a campaign to win the speakership. He toured the state and solicited support from both incumbents and prospective new members of the House. Finally displaying a willingness to concede an influential government post to their allies along the border, the Bailey loyalists of North Texas promoted Seabury's candidacy. By the opening of the legislative session in January 1905, the South Texan's support was so overwhelming that no one contested his election.

Despite his conservative views and his long-standing record of cooperation with James Wells, especially in opposing election reforms, Francis Seabury did not act as Wells' pawn during his service as Speaker of the House. In campaigning for the office, Seabury had cultivated political contacts throughout the state, and he tried to appease all segments of the Democratic party. Although conservatives received a majority of the committee chairmanships, Seabury's appointments provided progressive Democrats with strong representation on four important committees, which handled bills relating to taxation, the conduct of elections, business regulation, and the supervision of railroads and telephone and telegraph companies. Reformers chaired three of the four committees. The leading beneficiary of Seabury's concessions to the progressive camp was Dallas representative Thomas B. Love, who secured the chairmanship of the committee on private corporations and served on the taxation and election committees. Even Wells endorsed Love's appointments. When Thomas Campbell later won the governorship, the South Texas boss turned to Love as his liaison with the reform wing of the Democratic party.

Seabury's determination to streamline the operation of the legislature also facilitated the outburst of progressive activism. At the end of his second term as chairman of the Rules Committee, the veteran lawmaker sharply criticized the inefficient management of legislation in the House of Representatives. Limited to biennial sessions of roughly four months' duration and occasional special sessions, the legislators faced a tight schedule for conducting their business. Yet the House members usually proceeded at a leisurely pace for the first half of the biennial gathering, meeting in full session only two to three hours each morning. The inevitable result was a flood of haphazardly considered legislation at the close of the term. The failure of committees to prepare explanatory reports on bills, the overlapping jurisdiction of different committees, the lack of communication with the Senate, and the free movement of visitors and lobbyists through the House chamber all added to the confusion and indirection. As Speaker, Seabury instituted a number of procedural reforms to alleviate these problems: replacing the short morning sessions with four-to-six-hour afternoon sessions; reorganizing the standing committees and clarifying their legislative responsibilities; requiring the committees to provide printed assessments of the bills that they planned to return to the floor for the consideration of the full House; and restricting nonmembers' access to the floor. With the holding of committee hearings both in the morning and at night, the House of Representatives functioned from 9:00 A.M. to midnight at least five days a week and sometimes on Saturdays as well. According to the *Dallas Morning News*, the lower chamber assumed the appearance of a "three-ring circus."[1] The aggressive reformers took advantage of the expanded legislative schedule to study a broad range of issues and to propose an impressive array of progressive measures.

At the outset of the 1905 regular session, few observers anticipated the rush to pass reform legislation. According to the *Dallas Morning News*, "there is no evidence of any great uprising of the people, no thundered popular demand for radical changes in the methods and the laws of the state."[2] On the opening day of the session, the *News* noted the "judicial and conservative disposition of the Legislature," but just eleven days later, the paper drastically revised its evaluation and reported the emergence of strong anticorporate sentiment in the House.[3] Even the business lobbyists failed to prepare for the revival of reform agitation. During the second week of the session, the Dallas newspaper observed that "the 'lobby' is less numerous [than in former legislatures] and without apparent definite organization."[4]

This outburst of progressive activism did not divert Seabury from his commitment to maximize the capacity of the House to pass legislation. When his fellow lawmakers pressed for an early adjournment to the regular session, the Speaker blocked the move. In a speech before the House, he cited the long list of bills still under consideration and ridiculed the claim that the members should not have to serve beyond the first sixty days of the term when their salaries fell from five dollars to two dollars per day. With the exception of election reform, Seabury declined to take a stand on any of the substantive issues facing the legislature, and his colleagues praised his evenhanded conduct. The South Texan appeared to be almost totally absorbed in the mechanics of the legislative process.

During the regular session of 1905 and the special session that followed immediately, the House and the Senate passed a number of reforms. Confronted with a deficit in government spending from the preceding biennium, the lawmakers focused their attention on expanding the tax base of the state. Four measures shifted a larger share of the burden to corporations with the imposition of taxes on the intangible assets of corporations, on their profits and stocks, and on the gross receipts of railroads and insurance companies. Despite Seabury's behind-the-scenes resistance, the legislature also enacted a major revision of the election laws. There were limits to the progressive offensive, however. Proposed reforms that met defeat included a pure food and drug bill, prohibitive liquor license fees, the supervision of private banks, and the municipal regulation of water, gas, light, and telephone rates. The drive to eliminate the spending deficit also resulted in sizable cuts in appropriations for public institutions, such as the epileptic colony, the home for destitute Confederate veterans, and various asylums. In fact, even James Wells expressed satisfaction with the performance of the legislature after the trimming of the appropriation bill during the called session.

The 1905 term of the Texas Legislature represented only a preliminary skirmish. The progressive challenge to conservative Democratic rule came to a head with the gubernatorial race of 1906. Again James Wells contemplated running for the governorship. As early as the fall of 1904, he publicly announced his intention to become a candidate, but he received little encouragement beyond pledges of support from other South Texas political leaders and the general counsel of the fastest growing oil corporation in the state, the Texas Company. The Valley boss' only chance for victory was to monopolize the conservative vote in a contest against several reform candidates. In the view of one Wells strategist, a single conservative contender could control at least a third of the delegates to the state convention and possibly win on the second ballot if the progressive forces remained divided. The scenario proved to be illusionary, however. From the outset, the Brownsville politico faced competition from former Attorney General C. K. Bell for the allegiance of Old Guard Democrats, and even two of the so-called progressive candidates attracted conservative support. After considerable indecision, Wells declined to launch a formal campaign and endorsed Bell for governor.

Despite his respectable record of enforcing antitrust laws when he served as attorney general from 1901 through 1904, C. K. Bell emerged as the most conservative spokesman in the field of four gubernatorial candidates. With the spread of reformist agitation across the state, all the contestants at least paid lip service to the cause of controlling corporate power, but Bell tempered his progressive pronouncements with praise for the Lanham administration and with denials of widespread corruption in Texas politics. Furthermore, he opposed statewide prohibition and enjoyed the support of most of Colonel House's close associates, including Frank Andrews, Albert Burleson, and Wells. The progressive credentials of two other candidates were also open to question. During his erratic career, Oscar Colquitt had supported Hogg in the early 1890s, had agitated against tax reform at the end of the decade, and had pressed for lower transportation rates and a ban on free passes after his election to the Railroad Commission in 1902. For the present campaign, he combined advocacy of modest economic reforms with strong opposition to prohibition. The third contender, Criminal Appeals Judge M. M. Brooks, favored prohibition, but he was conservative enough on other issues to secure the endorsements of Joseph Bailey and Charles Culberson.

In the eyes of many voters, Thomas Campbell stood out as the only bona fide progressive candidate for the governorship. Despite his service as a railroad lawyer in the 1890s and his past cooperation with Colonel House's organization, he had consistently championed reformist causes since the turn of the century. Campbell established his reputation as a maverick Democrat at the conclusion of his abortive gubernatorial campaign of 1902 when he condemned the influence of giant corporations and political machines over state government. In the years that followed, he prepared for the 1906 race by carefully cultivating the support of former Populists, his fellow East Texas Democrats, and the new progressive organizations. Only Campbell's effort to straddle the prohibition issue tarnished his progressive image.

The reactions of Wells and his allies to Campbell's forceful progressive rhetoric were mixed. As early as 1901, one Wells loyalist had characterized Campbell as a politician "with a knife up his sleeve for railroads . . . and . . . corporations of any magnitude."[5] During the 1906 campaign, another alarmed correspondent forecast the downfall of conservative Democracy before the forces of class prejudice and political demagoguery. While conceding that the Democratic party faced a choice between conservatism and radicalism, James Wells abstained from strident ideological pronouncements and concentrated on the mechanics of the campaign. The Brownsville boss planned to deliver solid primary victories for C. K. Bell in the Lower Rio Grande Valley, but his strategy did not entail the waging of a holy war against the front-runner. Still a pragmatic calculator, Wells had no intention of foreclosing the possibility of some future accommodation with the faction that might take control of the state Democratic party. Having weathered the Hogg and free-silver triumphs of the 1890s, he did not yet equate defeat in a statewide election with impending political doom. Only later, when his regional as well as his state influence had waned, did Wells indulge in hysterical harangues against the opposition.

In the July Democratic primary, Thomas Campbell captured a plurality of the popular vote. Campbell's success stemmed in large part from the growing support for progressive reform and from the fragmentation of the still sizable conservative vote in the state, but regional factors also influenced the result. All the opposing candidates lived in North Texas and split the returns of this populous region, while Campbell swept most of the counties of East Texas and received enough support elsewhere to muster a 20,000-vote lead over his closest rival, Oscar Colquitt. Although C. K. Bell finished last in a closely packed field, he overwhelmed his opponents in the three Valley counties, collecting all but 70 of the 1,746 ballots cast. The legislative sessions of 1901, 1903, and 1905 had produced landmark election reforms, which included the poll tax, detailed regulations for eliminating voting fraud, and mandatory uniform primary elections. These laws, however, failed to change the basic pattern of South Texas politics. Wells and his allies paid the poll taxes for their

Mexican American constituents and controlled the primaries as handily as they had managed the county nominating conventions in the past.

Thomas Campbell claimed the Democratic nomination on the second ballot at the August state convention. Apparently signaling his abandonment of the fading candidacy of Judge Brooks, Joseph Bailey forecast the outcome of the hard-fought contest when he brought the convention delegates to their feet with the rallying cry "the Campbells are coming."[6] Even in the face of Bailey's opportunistic switch to the Campbell camp, the Bell forces tried to form a united front with the backers of Brooks and Colquitt against the East Texas progressive, but the strategy failed. During the primary campaign, bitter personal exchanges had flared among the three candidates as they competed for the support of essentially the same conservative North Texas constituency, and the antagonism persisted through the convention. When Colquitt faced the prospect of elimination on the second ballot, he endorsed Campbell for governor and ensured the front-runner's victory.

James Wells attended the convention with delegate credentials from all three Lower Rio Grande Valley counties. As a diehard Bell backer, he exercised little influence, however. Although Wells served on the platform committee, the list of party commitments hardly reflected his conservative concerns. The document contained an impressive number of reform proposals, including "the just rendition of all property for taxation at its full value," additional increases in corporate taxation, and bans on lobbying, corporate campaign contributions, nepotism, and the operation of insolvent companies in the state. The only significant concession to Old Guard Democrats like Wells was a condemnation of the renewed criticisms of Senator Bailey's role in the Waters-Pierce Oil Company affair as "malicious and unjust."[7]

After Campbell's election to the governorship over weak Republican opposition, James Wells faced isolation from the center of state power for the first time since the Hogg administration. The south Texas boss had to admit to office seekers that he exercised no influence over Campbell's patronage choices. Instead of appealing directly to the chief executive on behalf of the applicants, Wells urged these men to present his letters of endorsement to "several of my strongly influential and esteemed friends in Dallas, such as . . . Hon. Thomas Love, who will be the next Speaker of our Legislature."[8] Despite his fall from favor, Wells avoided direct confrontations with the governor and remained open to any suggestion of accommodation. Rather than lobbying against the full range of

Campbell's progressive proposals, the Rio Grande politico focused his attention on legislation of local importance and allowed the Valley legislators a free rein on most other issues. The voting records of the two House members representing Cameron, Hidalgo, and Starr counties did not reflect uncompromising opposition to reform. The veteran lawmaker José T. Canales voted for a corporate disclosure bill, a corporate franchise tax, stringent regulation of the insurance industry, mine safety standards, the outlawing of nepotism in state government, and the establishment of the Department of Agriculture, while he opposed the full rendition tax bill, the inheritance tax, and the ban on free railroad passes. C. F. Elkins, who succeeded F. W. Seabury, showed consistency only with his high rate of absenteeism for roll call votes.

When Campbell ran for renomination in 1908, Wells and several other influential conservatives, such as Frank Andrews and former Governor Sayers, embraced his candidacy. As a political realist, Wells recognized the futility of renewed opposition to the East Texas progressive. Since the end of Reconstruction, every governor had won reelection to a second term, and the caliber of Campbell's only Democratic opponent, a sixty-nine–year–old blacksmith who had never campaigned for public office before, ensured the continuation of the tradition. The refusal of Governor Campbell to promote prohibition or to participate in the attacks against Joseph Bailey also attracted conservatives to his cause. Not even the rise of a self-styled progressive challenge to the Democratic machine in Cameron County deterred Wells from reaching an accommodation with the reformist governor. Although the Rio Grande boss failed to regain his lost influence over state government, Thomas Campbell eventually repaid Wells for his vigorous support in the primaries and the general election of 1908. A year later pressure mounted for state intervention to curb the political abuses in Starr County. Even when his own investigator condemned Manuel Guerra's county administration as corrupt and tyrannical, the governor refused to take any action beyond periodically dispatching Texas Rangers to quell outbreaks of violence. Following the example of his conservative predecessors, Governor Campbell tolerated the peculiar brand of South Texas politics that combined graft, voter manipulation, and armed confrontation.

Despite his opportunistic embrace of the Campbell administration, James Wells remained a leading proponent of conservative causes. On three basic issues, he fiercely resisted the progressive tide. The Valley boss never compromised his commitment to Senator Bailey, and he consistently opposed election reforms and prohibition. Proposals to strengthen the state regulation of elections posed a direct threat to Wells' political power, while considerations of personal loyalty and cultural resentment reinforced Wells' conservative stand on the other two questions.

With the exception of women's suffrage, the major election reforms of the Progressive Era became law before the administration of Thomas Campbell. In 1901, the Texas Legislature passed a state constitutional amendment that made the payment of the poll tax a prerequisite for voting, and a year later the electorate ratified the measure. The legislatures of 1903 and 1905 broadened the scope of political reform with the enactment of the Terrell Election Laws, which established comprehensive regulations for conducting both primaries and general elections. The dual purpose of all these measures was to combat corruption and to discourage certain types of voters from participating in the political process.

The battle over the poll tax took place before the progressive-conservative confrontation in Texas politics crystallized, and the controversy cut across ideological lines. Conservatives and reformers stood on both sides of the issue. Some Old Guard Democrats perceived an opportunity to reduce the voting strength of the impoverished farmers, who had rallied behind the banner of Populism in the 1890s. With the demise of the third party, these conservative leaders feared that the disaffected agrarians might return to the Democratic fold in large enough numbers to alter the balance of power within the party. East Texas Democrats viewed the poll tax as a means of reinforcing their local efforts to disfranchise the black population, which formed majorities in several counties of the region. For reformist proponents of the measure, the overriding concern was political corruption. In a series of editorials, the *Dallas Morning News* argued that the "idlers and floaters" who regularly sold their votes to the highest bidders threatened the integrity of Texas elections.[9] The *San Antonio Daily Express* made a similar appeal for the poll tax but defined the problem of political corruption in more specific terms when it asserted that "one effect of this amendment to the Constitution will undoubtedly be . . . to prevent the importation of voters across the border."[10]

Labor unions, Populist spokesmen, black Republicans, and representatives of the beer and liquor interests campaigned against the poll tax. The strongest opposition, however, came from South Texas conservatives. Although the poll tax hardly threatened to break the control of the Democratic machines over the Hispanic electorate, the enforcement of the amendment would make the delivery of that vote much more expensive. Except for John Nance Garner, James

Wells' allies in the Texas Legislature stood solidly against the measure. When the House tally fell three votes short of the necessary two-thirds majority, Garner joined two other representatives in switching his vote from "nay" to "yea." The legislator's home-county constituents overwhelmingly favored the poll tax, and Garner was apparently willing to cooperate with Wells on this issue only as long as his vote did not make the difference between passage or defeat. On the day that the Senate agreed to House revisions of the constitutional amendment and assured its legislative enactment, Representative Francis Seabury introduced a bill to reduce the poll tax from $1.50 to 75¢, but the proposal died in committee. In the general election of 1902, the poll tax amendment swept the state by a vote of 200,650 to 107,748 and carried 194 of the 221 counties. The only concentrated resistance appeared in South Texas. In Wells' home county, the amendment lost by the staggering margin of 1,831 to 270.

The statewide popularity of the poll tax amendment and the continuing pressure for uniform primaries, which Wells had resisted in his capacity as Democratic state chairman, sparked another legislative drive for election reform in 1903. The chairman of the House Committee on Privileges and Elections, Alexander Terrell, spearheaded the campaign. As a veteran crusader for reform causes, Terrell exhibited both a commitment to eliminate corruption and a racist distrust of black and Mexican American participation in politics. At the outset of the session, Terrell introduced a bill that called for mandatory uniform primaries and comprehensive regulations for the payment of the poll tax and for the management of primaries, conventions, and general elections. His committee then submitted a substitute measure, which retained the main features of his original proposal.

Although Francis Seabury led the floor fight against the Terrell bill, the South Texas legislators failed to maintain a united front. The Brownsville representative, William Russell, served on the subcommittee that framed the substitute proposal, and he sided with Terrell on every roll call vote. In the face of strong public support for election reform, conservative opponents recognized the impossibility of defeating the legislation outright and concentrated instead on forcing the adoption of amendments that would weaken the proposed regulations. One key fight centered on an amendment to allow citizens to pay the poll taxes for other voters and to collect the receipts. Terrell denounced the measure on the grounds that it would result in the manipulation of the black and Mexican American vote. To resolve the dispute, progressive representative Thomas Love offered a compromise amendment that would require voters to pay their poll taxes in person only if they lived in cities with populations over 10,000. In smaller communities, anyone with written authorization from the prospective voter could pay his poll tax, but the tax collector would mail the receipt directly to the voter. With Terrell's reluctant endorsement, the House passed the compromise. Since all the Valley towns had less than 10,000 residents, the Love amendment facilitated the efforts of Wells and his allies to finance the poll tax payments of their Hispanic constituents. Another provision prohibited a candidate or any of his active supporters from paying the poll taxes of other voters. After the enactment of the bill, the Democratic bosses simply ignored this restriction.

The House and the Senate adopted over 150 amendments. Although progressives as well as conservatives pressed for revisions, the overall effect of the rewriting of the bill was to provide openings for election manipulation. Instead of requiring primary elections, the final version of the law afforded party officials at the county level the option of organizing primaries or conventions to choose nominees for the general election. Other concessions to the opponents of meaningful reform included the exclusion of independent candidates from the November ballot, the elimination of the requirement that a representative from each party serve as a local election judge, and the scrapping of the provision providing for poll watchers and supervisors. Despite the enactment of carefully defined procedures for conducting conventions and elections, the loopholes in the Terrell law allowed the South Texas machines to continue to control the political process with minimum interference from the competing parties. Oversight by Republican and Independent Democratic election officials was essential to the effective enforcement of the new regulations.

Dissatisfied with the 1903 law, Alexander Terrell introduced a new proposal at the next regular session of the legislature. The revival of the campaign for election reform produced a bitter clash between Terrell and Francis Seabury, who now held the post of House Speaker. The veteran reformer accused his South Texas adversary of maneuvering behind-the-scenes "to amend the general election bill out of shape."[11] In a dramatic performance, Terrell took the floor of the House and displayed a list of twenty-five proposed revisions in the Speaker's handwriting. The submission of all these amendments, Terrell argued, would delay a final House vote until the end of the session and kill any chance for enactment. When two of Seabury's allies called for the substitution of the present election law for the pending bill, Terrell renewed his attack:

This move emanates from the Rio Grande, where Mexicans are induced on election day to swim across the Rio Grande and are voted before their hair is dry.

There has been a conspiracy from the time this session began to defeat this bill by some means or other.[12]

Although Francis Seabury resisted far-reaching election reform, his actions were not as sinister as Terrell portrayed them. Rather than using his powers as Speaker to ensure the defeat of the legislation, the Starr County representative made two important concessions to the proponents of reform. He appointed Terrell to the chairmanship of the Committee on Privileges, Suffrage, and Elections, and he fought for an extension of the regular session to allow the House more time to deal with the Terrell bill and other important bills.

Even with the postponement of the adjournment date, the Senate failed to complete its consideration of the Terrell bill before the session ended. Governor Lanham salvaged the legislation by submitting the issue of election reform to the special session that convened the next day. Because of prolonged wrangling over the proposal for a blanket primary, the fate of the bill remained uncertain until the final meeting of the extra session when the House voted to accept the conference committee report. The Terrell Act of 1905 corrected some of the defects of the earlier law by authorizing the listing of independent candidates on the general election ballots, requiring poll watchers and election judges from different parties, and replacing the option to hold county conventions with a mandatory uniform primary. At the local level, the primaries alone would determine the party nominees. District and state conventions would still be held, but the delegate voting was supposed to reflect the popular vote in the primaries. Despite these improvements, Seabury and his conservative allies managed to retain the loophole that allowed persons with written authorizations to pay for other voters' poll taxes.

With the passage of the Terrell Act in 1905, progressive concern over election corruption subsided. During the Campbell administration, the legislature enacted a measure that based party nominations at all levels solely on the popular vote in the primaries, but voter qualifications and the administration of elections remained unchanged. Not until the uproar over the defeat of a prohibition constitutional amendment in 1911 did Texas reformers again agitate for new regulations to curtail voter manipulation.

Although the Valley machines continued to deliver the Hispanic vote through a combination of coercion, bribery, and paternalistic care, the election reforms did have some impact on border politics. The poll tax increased the cost of preparing for elections to such an extent that Wells periodically had to appeal for outside assistance in financing his campaigns. Poll tax expenses may have contributed to the decline in the Democratic vote of Cameron County in 1904 and 1906, but, once the threat to Wells' control became serious, the Democratic turnouts rose dramatically. In addition, the presence of poll watchers and election judges from the opposition parties discouraged the falsification of returns and other forms of outright fraud, at least in general elections. The safeguards for primaries remained minimal. Ironically, the election regulations also posed problems for Wells' rivals. Citing infractions of the Terrell Law, Democratic officials instituted a legal suit against the Independent victory in the 1912 Brownsville city election and forced the removal of Independent party candidates from the November ballot that same year. The resourceful Wells not only survived the challenge of election reform but also learned to use the regulations to his own advantage.

James Wells' defense of Joseph Bailey was just as determined as his resistance to the enactment of election reforms. Bailey had weathered the initial public debate over his participation in the rechartering of the Waters-Pierce Oil Company, but the uncovering of new information threatened to undercut his campaign for reelection in 1906. After the North Texan's triumph in a nonbinding preferential primary, Attorney General R. V. Davidson filed suit against the Waters-Pierce Company to force its ouster from the state for violations of the Texas antitrust laws and to collect millions of dollars in penalties. Despite assurances from Joseph Bailey in 1900 that Standard Oil had relinquished its control over the Waters-Pierce Company, later antitrust litigation in Missouri revealed that the corporate ties remained intact. Even more damaging to the senator was Davidson's release of evidence that Henry Clay Pierce, the president of the oil company, had loaned Bailey $3,300 at the time of his intervention on behalf of the firm. This revelation reinforced the image of Bailey that the famous muckraker David Graham Phillips had presented in an earlier exposé for *Cosmopolitan* magazine. Phillips portrayed the Texas senator as a servant of big business, who had helped to arrange huge financial transactions for Standard Oil, Pierce, the lumber magnate John Kirby, and a syndicate of St. Louis investors. Between 1902 and 1906, Kirby alone had paid Bailey almost $150,000 for legal services. In the view of most progressives, the veteran legislator was guilty of unethical conduct and possibly even criminal acts. Although no one had challenged Bailey in the summer primary, pressure mounted for a delay of his formal election to the U.S. Senate until the state legislature had had an opportunity to conduct a full-scale investigation of the Waters-Pierce affair.

The renewal of attacks against Joseph Bailey produced a split among the members of "our crowd." While Colonel House remained aloof, one of his closest associates, Austin lawyer Thomas Watt Gregory, assisted Attorney General Davidson in preparing the legal case against the Waters-Pierce Oil Company. Albert Burleson expressed reservations about Bailey's record in his correspondence to constituents, but he declined to make any public criticism until 1908. Frank Andrews and James Wells, on the other hand, rallied to the defense of the beleaguered politician. Bailey's refusal to support Wells' gubernatorial bids had strained relations between the two men, but the senator had made a concerted effort to revive the loyalty of his Rio Grande ally. After some initial resistance, Bailey vigorously campaigned for Wells' reelection as Democratic state chairman in 1902. Two years later, the North Texan made a further concession with the promotion of Francis Seabury's candidacy for the House speakership. Just as importantly, Wells still admired Bailey as the most aggressive and articulate spokesman for Democratic conservatism in the state. In the face of mounting progressive agitation, James Wells assured Senator Bailey that "my whole heart's deepest friendship and pride are with you in repelling the base slanders that have been heaped upon you by your enemies."[13]

Before the opening of the 1907 legislative session, Wells informed Frank Andrews and other Bailey organizers that the two Valley representatives, the Nueces County representative, and the state senator for South Texas would all stand firmly behind Bailey's reelection. Only the Republican legislator from the Laredo district posed a problem. Unexpected dissension developed among Trans-Nueces Democrats, however. When a strong anti-Bailey movement emerged in Nueces County, Representative Russell Savage joined the opposition, and even State Senator John Willacy, a longtime Wells ally, showed signs of uneasiness.

After the introduction of a bill containing forty-two charges of impropriety against Senator Bailey, both houses voted to organize a joint investigation. Brownsville representative José T. Canales expressed the concern of the Bailey camp in the following letter to Wells: ". . . some of our friends are getting a little shaky and undecided. . . . They want to put the election off until after the Investigating Committee reports and that might take a month; there are a lot of weak knees who are carried away by such foxy practices."[14] Nevertheless, two days after the start of the committee hearings, the legislature proceeded to conduct the election of a U.S. senator on the date set by law. Delivering one of the seconding speeches for Bailey's nomination, Canales openly admitted that he would vote for the senator even if all the accusations against him were true. Despite the progressive inclinations of a majority of the thirtieth legislature, Bailey received 108 of the 147 votes cast. The senator's victory in the Democratic primary, his continuing popularity, his influence over the state party machinery, and the absence of a serious alternative candidate all influenced the legislators. In addition, the newly elected governor, Thomas Campbell, who had received timely support from Bailey at the state convention, refused to participate in the campaign to force the North Texan's removal from the U.S. Senate.

At the conclusion of a thorough, forty-day investigation, the Texas Senate voted for complete exoneration for Bailey without even allowing its own committee members to prepare a report. The House acted more judiciously, but the result was the same. By a vote of 70 to 41, the representatives approved the majority committee report that found Bailey "not guilty" on all counts. More persuasively, the minority of the committee members cleared the U.S. senator of "any act of corruption" but characterized his conduct as "inconsistent with sound public policy and indiscreet" and cited his "failure . . . to take the people of Texas fully into his confidence."[15] Rather than taking advantage of his vindication to promote unity within the ideologically divided Democratic party, Joseph Bailey delivered a bitter victory speech, in which he cast his critics as "infidels" and pledged "to bury them face down [in their graves] so that the harder they scratch to get out, the deeper they will go to their eternal resting place."[16]

With the battle lines tightly drawn, Bailey sought a vote of confidence from the Texas electorate. In 1908, the senator headed a slate of four candidates running for the delegate-at-large positions to the Democratic national convention. A coalition of progressives and prohibitionists chose an alternative ticket to challenge the North Texas demagogue in the May primary, and the contest quickly degenerated into an exchange of vicious personal attacks. The choice of a Democratic nominee for the presidency was irrelevant to the power struggle since both sides proclaimed their support of William Jennings Bryan.

James Wells impressed upon his supporters the importance of "doing everything possible to have our 'Bailey Primary' a great success."[17] The only stronghold of anti-Bailey sentiment in the Valley was Falfurrias. While urging C. M. Laughlin, the leader of the regular Democratic organization at Falfurrias, to conduct a fair election,

Francis Seabury reminded him that his special primary did not come under the regulations of the Terrell Act. Seabury also instructed Laughlin to discard the ballots of any voters who scratched out the pledge to support all Democratic nominees in the general election. The Falfurrias Democrat resorted to a much more effective expedient to limit the size of the anti-Bailey vote in Starr County, however. He simply refused to hold the precinct primary.

Bailey carried the state by a comfortable margin and swept the Lower Rio Grande Valley. The victory in Starr County was particularly impressive, 473 to 2. The Bailey forces also dominated the May state convention, which selected the remainder of the Texas delegation to the national convention. Although he won election as a delegate, James Wells failed to attend the gathering at Denver because of pending legal matters and a shortage of funds.

Despite his impressive triumph, Bailey's political fortunes declined after 1908. He never did escape the taint of the Waters-Pierce scandal, and he became increasingly disenchanted with the direction of both the state and the national Democratic parties. In September 1911, the veteran politician decided not to seek reelection, and the subsequent success of Texas progressives in promoting the presidential candidacy of Woodrow Wilson prompted Bailey to resign even before the end of his term. After delivering a farewell address to the Senate on January 2, 1913, he retired to a lucrative Washington law practice. James Wells always remained loyal to this champion of conservative causes. On those occasions when Bailey reentered the Texas political wars, Wells rallied to his side. During the second decade of the twentieth century, inconsistency characterized Wells' commitments to state leaders. At different times the Rio Grande boss backed and opposed most of the major figures in Texas politics—Oscar Colquitt, Thomas Campbell, James Ferguson, and William Hobby. Only Senators Bailey and Charles Culberson enjoyed Wells' unfailing support. The South Texan's loyalty to Culberson stemmed from the senator's readiness to lobby for Wells on patronage questions and other practical political matters. Bailey, however, was more than a reliable friend in Washington. He symbolized the traditional commitment of the Democratic party to the Jeffersonian ideals of limited government and states rights—concepts that Wells believed in despite his long record of expedient compromises and shifts.

The drive to establish statewide prohibition confirmed for many conservatives their worst fears about the ultimate outcome of the expansion of governmental authority. In the view of Wells and his allies, the public acceptance of progressive economic controls revived the threat of state regulation of the social mores of individual citizens. To counter the prohibitionist denunciations of the corrupting influence of the liquor and beer industries, the wet spokesmen raised the rallying cry of personal liberty. Even conservatives, such as Francis Seabury, who were concerned about the adverse effects of alcoholic consumption on society, objected to statewide prohibition because of their preference for local control. They believed that local option elections offered the only equitable solution. Since the defeat of the state prohibition amendment in 1887, local option campaigns had triumphed throughout North Texas, except for Dallas and Fort Worth, and had made inroads in East and Central Texas. South and Southwest Texas had stubbornly resisted the tide, however. For the state to dictate a particular moral code to unwilling communities, Seabury argued, was a blatant violation of the principle of popular rule.

Cultural factors also sustained the opposition of South Texas politicians to prohibition. As a ritualistic religion, Catholicism stressed adherence to institutional formalities and historic doctrines rather than demonstrations of pure behavior. The church did not demand abstinence from drinking liquor and beer, and the Hispanic population resented the efforts of the evangelical Protestants, who spearheaded the temperance crusade, to impose an alien standard of morality. Despite their complaints about election irregularities, the advocates of prohibition along the border conceded that the virtual unanimity of the Hispanic voters on the liquor issue stemmed as much from genuine conviction as from machine manipulation. The local dry leaders directed their appeals almost exclusively to the Anglo settlers who poured into the region after the introduction of large-scale irrigation. The escalation of ethnocultural tensions in the state as a result of the struggle over prohibition again placed the Valley bosses on the defensive. With the defeat of a second constitutional amendment in 1911, Texas progressives resumed their campaign to limit the political participation of Mexican Americans.

After the passage of an impressive number of economic reforms during Campbell's first term, the progressive movement focused its attention on prohibition. Despite their gains through local option elections, the dry forces realized that the large cities and the communities with Hispanic, black, and German majorities remained invulnerable to local assaults. Only state action could fulfill the dream of driving the beer and liquor industries from Texas. The imposition of statewide prohibition entailed a complicated three-stage process that worked to the advantage of the defenders of the status quo: pas-

sage of a nonbinding referendum in the Democratic primary; legislative enactment of a constitutional amendment; and submission of
the amendment to the electorate for ratification. By 1908, both sides
had organized fully, as the Anti-Saloon League and the evangelical
Protestant churches confronted the Texas Brewers' Association and
the Retail Liquor Dealers Association. The prohibitionists carried
the primary contest of 1908 by a narrow margin, but both houses of
the state legislature fell a few votes short of the two-thirds majorities necessary for the passage of a constitutional amendment. This
defeat set the stage for the climactic battles of 1910 and 1911, which
decided not only the fate of another constitutional amendment but
also the selection of the next governor of Texas.

Prohibition was the overriding issue in the gubernatorial race of
1910. After Thomas Campbell's decision to step aside at the end of
his second term, four serious candidates competed for the Democratic nomination. Longtime progressive activist Cone Johnson and
moderate dry William Poindexter, who received the formal backing
of Joseph Bailey, split the prohibitionist vote. Former Attorney General R. V. Davidson opposed the outlawing of beer and liquor but
managed to capture some reform-minded support because of his vigorous prosecution of the Waters-Pierce case. With the prohibitionist
and progressive forces hopelessly divided, Railroad Commissioner
Oscar Colquitt consolidated his position as the representative of the
wet, conservative element in the state. Despite his reformist posturing when he ran for the governorship in 1906, Colquitt now
launched a sharp attack against Campbell's progressive activism and
called for "rest from restrictive and harsh legislation."[18] On the all-
important liquor question, the candidate promised more-effective
enforcement of local option laws, but he vowed to oppose any move
to institute statewide prohibition. Not even Bailey's public endorsement of his close friend Poindexter undercut the Colquitt campaign,
since the U.S. senator privately encouraged his militant antiprohibitionist allies to back the railroad commissioner.

James Wells threw his support behind Oscar Colquitt, but the
Rio Grande politico failed to take charge of the campaign at the regional level as he had done for conservative candidates in the past.
Wells was simply too preoccupied with local crises. The Independent party had carried the Brownsville city election earlier that
spring and now posed a threat to Wells' control of county politics. In
addition, the infighting between J. R. Monroe and Manuel Guerra
provided an opening for the Falfurrias insurgents in Starr County.
Even Wells' longtime associate Francis Seabury, who had moved
from Rio Grande City to Brownsville in 1908, contributed to the po-

100 THE PROGRESSIVE CHALLENGE

litical disorder by promoting the candidacy of William Poindexter for governor while remaining loyal to Wells in the local struggle against the Independents. In the absence of the Brownsville boss' regional leadership, Duval County Democrat Archie Parr assumed the role of chief organizer for the Colquitt campaign for the whole Trans-Nueces. Wells' contribution to the gubernatorial effort was clearly secondary, as he limited his politicking to Cameron and Starr counties and relied on Parr as his contact with Colquitt's state headquarters.

The split in the prohibitionist ranks between Cone Johnson and William Poindexter proved to be decisive. Although the proposition on the primary ballot to submit a prohibition amendment to the voters passed by a margin of almost 30,000 votes, Colquitt won the gubernatorial nomination with 40 percent of the vote and a plurality over his rivals. The combined votes for the two dry candidates surpassed Colquitt's total by 9,000 ballots. Not surprisingly, the Trans-Nueces stood as a bastion for pro-Colquitt, antiprohibitionist sentiment. The railroad commissioner swept past the rest of the field with a majority of 3,000 votes in the seven southernmost counties of the state, and the submission proposal met defeat by a similar margin, 3,610 to 989. In preparing for a tough general election fight against the Independent party, Wells rolled up lopsided majorities in the Cameron County primary: 1,084 for Colquitt to 141 for the opposition; 1,108 to 99 against prohibition. Parr's performance in Duval County was even more impressive: a clean sweep of 773 to 0 for both Colquitt and the wet cause.

With the demonstration of popular support for submission in the 1910 Democratic primary, opposition in the Texas Legislature collapsed, and both houses passed a constitutional amendment by votes comfortably above the necessary two-thirds majorities. Even two South Texas legislators broke ranks and voted for the ban against the manufacture and sale of alcoholic beverages. The antiprohibitionists were not willing to concede popular ratification of the amendment in the special election set for July 22, 1911, and a bitter struggle ensued. The dry forces relied heavily on the activism of the Baptist and Methodist churches, while the liquor and beer interests financed the campaigning of wet politicians and even subsidized poll tax payments for thousands of black and Hispanic voters.

Because of overwork on business and legal matters and the strain of the local election contests of 1910, James Wells suffered a serious physical breakdown in November 1910, but he recovered in time to direct the 1911 antiprohibitionist campaign in Cameron County.

With financial support from outside liquor interests, Wells launched a drive to broaden the poll tax base among his Mexican American constituents. The county tax collector issued 3,509 poll tax receipts, almost 600 more than the total for the hotly contested 1910 election. In violation of the Terrell Act, the Wells operatives, who paid the poll taxes of the Hispanic voters, retained the receipts until election day. The stationing of dry observers around the polls and the prohibitionist threats to press for the prosecution of election law violators forced the Democratic machine to institute a complicated procedure of distributing the poll tax receipts that reduced the size of the Hispanic vote. According to prohibitionist witnesses, wagonloads of Mexican Americans arrived at a Brownsville store owned by the president of the Blue Club. After checking the names off a polling list, the Democratic organizers dispatched the voters in small groups along a route of side streets to a second store, where they received their receipts. Although the system of dry surveillance failed to prevent the illegal distribution of poll tax receipts, the oversight slowed the pace of Hispanic voting and probably discouraged more blatant forms of election fraud, such as the dispersal of unclaimed receipts to available but unregistered recruits. Less than half the citizens listed on the poll tax rolls of Cameron County voted.

With a statewide turnout of over 468,000, the dry forces lost the election by a margin of only 6,297 ballots. The less populous southern half of the state voted almost two to one against the constitutional amendment. Despite a drop in voter participation in all three Valley counties, Wells and his allies still delivered an impressive majority for the wet cause, 2,459 to 554. For the eight counties forming the southeastern corner of Texas, the antiprohibitionist lead totaled 4,055 votes, almost two-thirds of the statewide margin of victory.

Incensed over the outcome of the constitutional referendum, dry partisans charged that illegal poll tax payments and other election irregularities had produced their defeat, and they identified blacks and Hispanics as the main culprits. Thomas Ball, the state chairman of the 1911 temperance campaign, vented the prejudices of his fellow prohibitionists with his indictment of "the poor, ignorant negroes, deluded by designing white men, inspired by the liquor interests, and the Mexican vote, which Texas in 1836 declared unfit to govern this country."[19] The leader of the dry caucus in the House of Representatives questioned the legality of Mexican political participation all along the border from Brownsville to El Paso: "I was informed at the beginning of this year that thousands of Mexicans were being brought across the border for the purpose of getting poll tax receipts to vote in this election. . . . If such a report is true, an honest investigation will certainly disclose thousands of illegal Mexican votes cast against the amendment and more than enough to change the result from anti to pro."[20] The fact that eleven wet counties in the state recorded more total votes than poll tax receipts reinforced the suspicions of the antiliquor men. Exempt voters over the age of sixty could not account for all the discrepancies.

Many progressives concluded that the only way to overcome the political influence of the beer and liquor interests was to strengthen the Texas election laws. Just nine days after the defeat of the constitutional amendment, the legislature convened in special session, and both houses established committees to investigate the alleged irregularities in the submission election. At the conclusion of month-long hearings, the prohibitionist legislators, who dominated the proceedings, sharply criticized the campaign tactics of the wet forces and proposed stringent election reforms: detailed regulations for the issuance of poll tax receipts, including the requirement that each voter pay for his own poll tax; rules to facilitate the challenging of suspect voters; restrictions on providing assistance to illiterate voters; and limitations on corporate campaign contributions. The practical effect of most of these proposals would be to curtail the voting of impoverished, illiterate blacks and Mexican Americans.

The progressives managed to channel their anger and frustration over the result of the 1911 referendum into political action with their promotion of the Boehmer election bill. In February 1912, state Representative Joseph O. Boehmer of Eagle Pass organized a convention at Del Rio to advance the cause of voting reform. The delegates established a permanent body, the Ballot Purification League, and appealed to the Texas Legislature to pass two measures: a constitutional amendment requiring aliens to become fully naturalized citizens before they could vote; and a ban on any assistance to a voter in preparing his ballot, unless he was physically disabled. In defense of this second proposal, the reformers contended that their real target was the "purchasable" voter rather than the illiterate citizen per se. When their critics pointed out that thousands of honest illiterate whites would also be disfranchised, along with the Hispanics, blacks, and corruptionists, the proponents of election reforms dismissed such claims as "little less than insults to the state of Texas."[21]

At the start of the 1913 legislative session, Representative Boehmer introduced a bill to ban assistance to voters, and he freely admitted that his intent was "to disqualify the Mexicans of the Western and Lower Rio Grande Counties."[22] After the passage of the measure in the House by a solid majority, John Willacy, a Wells ally, led the opposition in the Senate. He submitted an amendment to allow two judges to assist voters in the presence of all the other judges, clerks, and supervisors, but his colleagues tabled the proposal and all other weakening revisions, except for a delay in the implementation of the bill until January 1915. Even this concession failed to win the approval of the conference committee, and the bill passed the legislature intact. Only the action of Governor Colquitt blunted the reformist offensive. Following the close of the session, Colquitt vetoed the measure on the grounds that it would purge thousands of honest citizens from the political process. As a leading opponent of prohibition, he recognized the necessity of maintaining the voting strength of the Hispanic population of South Texas.

Despite the election of a prohibitionist senator to replace Joseph Bailey in January 1913, the temperance movement lost momentum. The resistance of Governor Colquitt and his successor, James Ferguson, and the continuation of strong wet sentiment throughout the southern half of the state stymied moves to impose statewide prohibition for the next six years. The antiliquor movement finally achieved success at the end of the decade but only after two dramatic developments upset the balance of political power in the state: the impeachment of Ferguson and the unleashing of anti-German prejudices with American entry into World War I. Wells and Parr again came under attack when their uncompromising opposition to both prohibition and women's suffrage revived progressive demands for an end to the manipulation of the Mexican American electorate.

A shifting strategy of accommodation and opposition characterized the response of the South Texas conservatives to the first decade of progressive agitation. As Speaker of the House, Francis Seabury contributed to the early legislative successes of the reform movement by streamlining the procedure in the lower chamber. After the election of Thomas Campbell to the governorship, James Wells forsook uncompromising resistance to the full range of progressive reforms and allowed the Valley legislators to take independent stands on many issues. The border Democrats even embraced the candidacy of Campbell when he ran for reelection. Despite these concessions, the reformers still regarded the Rio Grande bosses as symbols of conservative obstruction and corruption because of their support of Joseph Bailey, their opposition to prohibition, and their flagrant indulgence in election abuses. Ethnocultural biases reenforced the hostility of the progressive activists. Most came from the ranks of the Anglo, Protestant majority and looked with contempt upon the social standing, life-styles, religion, and moral values of the Hispanic population upon whom Wells and his associates built their power.

James Wells withstood the repeated campaigns to curtail the voting of Mexican Americans, but his power at the state level declined appreciably during the Progressive Era. With the election of Campbell, he lost his influence over state patronage for South Texas. Not even the elevation of Colquitt to the governorship restored the absolute control that Wells had enjoyed during the reign of Colonel Edward House. Colquitt seriously considered Wells' recommendations for government appointments, but the chief executive did not automatically approve them. Despite his regular attendance at state Democratic conventions, the Brownsville boss also failed to maintain his influence within the party organization. The strength of his progressive opponents and the absence of a powerful promoter like Colonel House prevented Wells from competing for the important state party posts that he had once held. Even at the regional level, the power of Archie Parr came to rival that of Wells, as the Duval County Democrat cultivated close relations with Governors Colquitt and Ferguson and intervened in the politics of several Trans-Nueces counties.

The revival of local insurgencies paralleled the challenges of the statewide progressive movement to boss rule in South Texas. The partial enforcement of election laws and the influx of new settlers threatened to upset the balance of power in Cameron and Hidalgo counties, while the customs house continued to provide an organizational base for the Republicans and independent-minded Democrats. To combat the latter problem, James Wells relied increasingly on the congressman from the southernmost district of Texas, John Nance Garner.

6. The Election of John Nance Garner to Congress

WITH THE POLITICAL UPHEAVALS of the 1890s, the incumbent South Texas congressmen, who enjoyed the backing of James B. Wells, faced serious challenges. After supporting President Cleveland's demand for the repeal of the Sherman Silver Purchase Act, William Crain barely escaped defeat in the election of 1894. When Crain died two years later, Wells promoted the candidacy of Rudolph Kleberg, the brother of the manager of the King Ranch, Robert Kleberg. In the midst of deteriorating economic conditions, free-silver sentiment became so pervasive in the northern and western counties of the district that Kleberg reversed his position on the currency issue between the special April election to fill Crain's unexpired term and the regular November election of 1896. Having run as a gold Democrat in the spring, the new congressman championed the cause of free silver after William Jennings Bryan's triumph at the national Democratic convention. As the chief architect of Kleberg's nomination and election, Wells sanctioned this conversion, but the move was too transparent to be wholly successful. Despite his election victory, Kleberg managed to alienate substantial numbers of gold and silver Democrats, and he claimed only a plurality of the vote against Populist and Republican competition. The South Texan widened his margins of victory in 1898 and 1900, but he remained a vulnerable candidate, who faced strong opposition even with the subsidence of the depression of the 1890s and the collapse of the Populist party.

As the Republican forces of the Lower Rio Grande Valley gained strength under the leadership of Collector C. H. Maris, James Wells became increasingly dissatisfied with Kleberg's candidacy. The Brownsville boss wanted a congressman who would bolster the sagging fortunes of the Democratic party in South Texas. In addition, one of Kleberg's legislative initiatives alarmed Wells. The congressman proposed the construction of a series of dams across the Rio

Grande for irrigation purposes. Wells feared that any dams to the northwest of the Lower Rio Grande Valley would limit the amount of water available for the future development of his region. When an ambitious state legislator named John Nance Garner took advantage of congressional redistricting in 1901 to launch his campaign for Congress, Wells embraced Garner as his candidate. The two men remained close political allies for the next twenty years.

In 1889 when he was twenty-one years old, John Garner moved from his hometown of Clarksville, Texas, to Uvalde, a frontier community southwest of San Antonio and fifty miles from the Rio Grande. Although nearly two hundred miles separated Uvalde County from the Lower Rio Grande Valley, both areas fell within the same congressional district. Despite his youth, Garner was already a practicing attorney, and he quickly branched out into land speculation, banking, and other business ventures. After serving as a county judge for two terms, the Uvalde Democrat won election to the state legislature. In his new position, Garner advanced the traditional Democratic concepts of states rights and white supremacy and rallied to the defense of Joseph Bailey, but he was not an uncompromising Bourbon. He voted for antitrust reforms in 1899, proposed the regulation of the insurance industry, and sponsored an ambitious tax reform package in 1900. Both Garner's skill as a parliamentarian and his posture as a moderate earned him the respect of his colleagues in the Texas Legislature.

Through all his legislative maneuvers and his ideological compromises, John Garner remained committed to one central objective: election to the U.S. Congress. With the increase in the population of the state and the addition of three congressional seats for Texas, the lawmakers faced the responsibility of organizing new districts. Political careers hinged on the forms that the new districts would take and on the influence that prospective candidates exercised over the legislators.

Garner also had to appeal to the diverse Democratic factions of South Texas, but one individual assumed overriding importance in Garner's calculations, James B. Wells. The Brownsville boss had stage-managed the elections of William Crain and Rudolph Kleberg from 1884 through 1898. Not even the upsurge in Republican strength in the Lower Rio Grande Valley after 1896 and the distraction of his responsibilities as state Democratic chairman undercut his dominance over South Texas congressional politics. To secure the Democratic nomination and to win the general election of 1902,

Garner needed the backing of James Wells. Although Wells was more conservative than the Uvalde legislator, Garner's flirtations with reform causes did not disturb the veteran politician. As always, political success meant more to Wells than ideological purity. Republican aggressiveness along the border and the threat of the passage of the poll tax and other election reforms heightened Wells' determination to recruit an effective campaigner to replace Rudolph Kleberg. Garner's solid election victories in 1898 and 1900 and his growing influence in the Texas Legislature impressed Wells. Just as important, Garner had repeatedly demonstrated his willingness to cooperate with Wells on matters that the Rio Grande chief regarded as crucial to his interests.

Collaboration between James Wells and John Garner began with the congressional campaign of 1896. After initially supporting one of Rudolph Kleberg's rivals for the nomination, Garner joined the Kleberg camp, and Wells rewarded the Uvalde politician by arranging his election to the Democratic chairmanship of the congressional district. Two years later, Garner reclaimed the post with Wells' backing. The developing political partnership came to fruition during Garner's second term in the legislature. Both men played key roles in promoting Joseph Bailey's election to the U.S. Senate at the start of the regular session. Wells then focused his attention on three issues that affected not only the power of his political machine but also the preservation of the social and economic order of the Lower Rio Grande Valley: poll tax reform, the bill to reorganize the Rangers and to restore the authority of privates and noncommissioned officers to make arrests, and the measure to facilitate the confirmation of unperfected land titles stemming from Spanish and Mexican grants. Except for the final vote on the poll tax, John Garner cooperated with Wells on all of these matters. On the question of property titles, Garner took charge of the legislative campaign to safeguard the claims of South Texas ranchers and speculators.

A crisis over landownership developed in 1899 when the legislature authorized the appointment of two agents to investigate charges of illegal occupancy of public land. At the completion of the survey, the land commissioner reported to Governor Sayers that holders of forty-three tracts of land totaling over 1.1 million acres in five South Texas counties had never secured patents from the General Land Office. After the legislature voted to reaffirm the authority of the attorney general to file suit against these occupants to recover the land for the state, James Wells drafted a bill to bolster the legal defenses of his constituents, and John N. Garner introduced the legislation.

This special-interest measure related only to land located between the Rio Grande and the Nueces River and to claims emanating from Mexican and Spanish grants.

The most controversial provision of the bill liberalized the rules of evidence. A series of Texas Supreme Court decisions had assured the admissibility of evidence from the Mexican archives, but the titles of many ranchers in the Trans-Nueces remained insecure. Some claimants had resorted to illegal methods to secure their holdings, while others faced the threat of eviction because recurrent armed conflicts in Mexico had resulted in the widespread destruction of public records. To compensate for the absence of original documentation on Spanish and Mexican grants, Wells proposed that any records submitted to county officials and certified by the county clerks at least five years before the passage of the bill should stand as evidence of ownership. The origins and the authenticity of these documents would have no legal bearing on the cases.

Other features of the measure also favored the landholders. Previous state legislation dealing with Mexican and Spanish grants had applied only to those grants extended before the establishment of Texas independence in 1836. By the terms of the Garner bill, the state would have to recognize the validity of grants that the Mexican government had issued as late as February 8, 1848, the date of the signing of the Treaty of Guadalupe Hidalgo. Furthermore, the legislation would allow the claimants themselves to bring suit against the state to force the verification of their titles. The trials would take place in the ranchers' home counties, where the juries were likely to be sympathetic to the landowners' point of view. In the past, Austin had served as the site of land-case proceedings involving the state. The only concession to the state was to require the ranchers to pay for the court costs of those suits that they initiated, irrespective of the outcome of the cases.

During the legislative battle over the Garner land bill, Assistant Attorney General Reese exercised effective control over the Attorney General's Office as a result of a debilitating and eventually fatal illness that struck his superior, Thomas Smith. Although Wells consulted Reese and Land Commissioner Charles Rogan in preparing the legislation and received their approval, both men reversed their stands and raised objections to the revision of the rules of evidence and the location of the trials in the home counties of the claimants. To counter the argument that the bill placed the state at an unfair disadvantage, Garner and the Valley legislators cited the difficulties of securing documentation from the Mexican archives. They also warned that the revival of uncertainty over landownership could generate economic chaos throughout the Trans-Nueces and discourage the outside investment essential for economic development of the region. With Garner and State Senator D. McNeal Turner of Corpus Christi marshalling support, the legislation passed both houses by comfortable margins, but Governor Sayers vetoed the measure when Reese, Rogan, and the new attorney general, C. K. Bell, all recommended its rejection. Last-minute appeals from Garner and Wells failed to sway the usually dependable chief executive.

Still the practical politician, James Wells overcame his bitterness toward Bell and Sayers and invited the attorney general to participate in the formulation of a revised bill. C. K. Bell acknowledged the need to clarify the procedure for confirming titles, but he insisted on protecting the interests of the state. The two politicians agreed on a compromise, which formalized the admissibility of evidence from Mexican archives, recognized the legitimacy of documents inserted in the county records at least thirty years earlier, and rejected Mexican grants issued after 1836. The proposed bill also allowed landholders to institute their own suits but only in the district court at Austin. At the urging of Garner and Wells, Governor Sayers submitted the question of verifying land claims to the next special session of the legislature on August 20, 1901. Representatives Francis Seabury of Rio Grande City and J. O. Nicholson of Laredo introduced the new bill, which passed over nominal opposition. Although Wells and his constituents won some concessions from the state with the enactment of the measure, the chief beneficiary of the legislative confrontation was John N. Garner, whose performance as floor manager for the original bill was so impressive that he clinched Wells' support for his plans to run for Congress.

The Texas legislators tackled the issue of congressional redistricting during the same special session in which they passed the second land bill. More than a month before the opening of the August–September term, Garner informed Wells that he intended to use the reapportionment process as a springboard for his congressional campaign. Although Wells was willing to cooperate with Garner, the Brownsville boss had to take into account a wider range of concerns than his ally's congressional aspirations. Like Garner, Wells wanted to gerrymander the district to ensure conservative Democratic control, but his overriding objective was to prevent the inclusion of the Trans-Nueces in the San Antonio congressional district. With a population of over fifty thousand, San Antonio would dominate any district that encompassed the sparsely settled counties of South Texas. Fusion with the city would mean the loss of substantial political influence for Wells and his associates along the border. They could no longer dictate the Democratic choice for Congress or oversee federal patronage during Democratic administrations. Yet more than personal ambition and power was at stake. A clear-cut conflict of interest existed between San Antonio and the Rio Grande counties. Appreciative of the contributions of military spending to the local economy, San Antonio politicians and businessmen were agitating for the abandonment of the army posts in Cameron, Starr, Webb, and Kinney counties and for the concentration of all the South Texas troops at the city's own Fort Sam Houston, already the largest military establishment in the nation. The residents of the border region needed an independent voice in Congress to fight for the preservation of the U.S. Army installations that they regarded as essential to their security.

As a member of the House Committee on Congressional Districts, John N. Garner occupied a strategic position for advancing his own ambitions and the broader interests of his South Texas allies. Because of his friendship with the committee chairman, Garner also served on the subcommittee that drafted the initial version of the reappointment bill. Not surprisingly, the House measure conformed exactly to Garner's and Wells' specifications. The legislation created a district that included Uvalde and the Trans-Nueces but excluded San Antonio and the county with the largest electorate in the existing South Texas district, Guadalupe. The presence of an independent-minded German population and a sizable bloc of black Republicans made the politics of that county particularly volatile. In the past four elections, the Populists had carried the county once, and the Republicans had triumphed three times. Besides, Guadalupe was the home of a popular state senator, Joseph Dibrell, who had already indicated his intention to run for Congress. Another conspicuous omission from the proposed district was Dewitt County, the residence of Congressman Rudolph Kleberg.

In sharp contrast to the House bill, the Senate reapportionment scheme posed serious threats to Garner and Wells. The state senators attached the Trans-Nueces to a newly formed San Antonio district and relegated Uvalde to a district that stretched along the upper reaches of the Rio Grande to El Paso. The mechanics of the conference committee, however, worked to the advantage of the Uvalde politico and his allies. After two hours of unproductive debate, the committee decided to allow Garner, the state senator from San Antonio, and the two other South Texas committeemen to settle their differences among themselves. Garner organized a majority of three to override the San Antonio spokesman and to reconstitute the district generally along the lines of the House plan with one notable revision, the inclusion of Guadalupe County. Despite vigorous protests from the San Antonio legislators, Garner's version of the district realignment survived the votes of the conference committee, the House, and the Senate.

With Wells' full support, John Garner announced his candidacy for Congress in February 1902. Because of the exclusion of Rudolph Kleberg's home county from the new district, Garner faced only one serious competitor for the Democratic nomination, state Senator Joseph Dibrell of Guadalupe County. Having survived the turbulent politics of Guadalupe County in the face of strong Republican and Populist challenges, Dibrell entered the congressional race with the reputation of being a formidable campaigner. On national issues, the two candidates posed as moderates and shared many common views. Scrupulously avoiding the currency question, both men condemned the annexation of the Philippines, endorsed the construction of a canal through Central America, attacked business trusts, and supported tariff protection for raw materials. Despite their indulgence in rhetoric against the growing power of the national government, the Democratic rivals subordinated their conservative values to the special needs of the district and promoted federal financing of harbor projects and irrigation. Only in the field of taxation did the candidates express sharp differences. Garner proposed the replacement of the protective tariff with a graduated income tax, while Dibrell argued that "direct taxation by itself . . . would create a revolution inside six months in this country."[1]

John Garner and Joseph Dibrell participated in two widely publicized debates, which focused on national issues, but disagreements over public policy did not determine the outcome of the primary contest. Instead, the decisive factor was James Wells' intervention on Garner's behalf. The Brownsville boss used every resource at his disposal to advance Garner's cause. At the outset of the campaign, the candidate from Uvalde acknowledged his dependence on Wells: "I am always by you as I want my boy to always be by me, 'tell me everything and I can then better know how to advise him.' You must treat me as you would your own boy."[2] Garner also understood his obligation to repay Wells: "I can only say, the time will never come and the circumstances never exist, when it will not be my heart's greatest desire to serve you or yours, and I do sincerely and truly hope that you will command me."[3]

Although the Dibrell forces argued that Wells should remain

neutral because of his position as state Democratic chairman, the veteran politician openly endorsed Garner. Wells' action on the issue of uniform primaries aroused even more controversy. The Democratic chairman marshalled a one-vote majority on the state executive committee to block the imposition of a compulsory uniform primary date for 1902 and then proceeded to organize an early primary strategy for Garner. Lacking influence over the county organizations outside Guadalupe, Dibrell was unable to stall the Garner bandwagon by arranging timely primary dates for the counties in which he enjoyed solid support. Before the recommended primary date of June 14, party officials in nine of the twenty-two district counties conducted conventions, and Garner carried eight of the contests. The single victory for Dibrell occurred in Guadalupe County. Democrats in another Dibrell stronghold, Live Oak County, were eager to hold an early primary, but Wells stymied their efforts when he refused to appoint a replacement for the vacated post of county chairman. James Wells provided additional support for his protégé with his oversight of the conventions in the Lower Rio Grande Valley and Laredo. He also helped to preserve the unity of the Garner organization by mediating a dispute between Duval and San Patricio County leaders over the selection of a Democratic nominee for the state legislature.

Although early press reports had forecast a close race, John Garner built an overwhelming lead by mid-May, and the increasingly desperate Dibrell partisans responded with sharp attacks against the architect of their impending defeat, James B. Wells. In his speeches, Dibrell characterized Wells as a ruthless boss, whose domination of the congressional district was driving Democrats in Guadalupe and other counties into the Republican camp. Several South Texas newspapers participated in the campaign to discredit the Rio Grande chieftain. The *Eagle Pass Guide* offered the following assessment of Wells' leadership:

> When the Democrats of Texas made J. B. Wells chairman of the state executive committee, they did not expect him to run the Democratic party, regardless of everything and everybody. They did not expect him to use his position to intimidate citizens, to bulldoze subordinate organizations. His naming the congressman is . . . detrimental to the party and the state. When he said "with my corral I hold the balance of power and can dictate to the people of this district," he stepped beyond the bounds of democratic principles and good government. . . . His policy is not that of right and justice but that of force.[4]

The effort to convert the primary contest into a mandate against boss politics failed. On the recommended primary date, John Garner claimed six more victories, and Dibrell withdrew from the race. Although Garner formally received the nomination by a unanimous vote at the district convention, bitterness among Dibrell's supporters lingered. The Guadalupe delegation refused to attend the convention, and some disgruntled Democrats predicted a GOP landslide in that county.

To challenge John N. Garner for the congressional seat of the fifteenth district, the Republicans nominated Corpus Christi lawyer John C. Scott. Despite his consistent opposition to James Wells over the past twenty years, Scott had switched party affiliations twice. As the editor of the *Brownsville Daily Cosmopolitan*, he supported R. B. Rentfro in his 1884 congressional campaign against W. H. Crain and created a sensation with his scathing condemnations of the manipulation of the Hispanic vote. A decade later, he served as the platform chairman for the Nueces County Democratic convention, which endorsed the policies of the Cleveland administration. Subsequently professing disillusionment with the president's financial mismanagement during the depression of the 1890s, Scott returned to the Republican fold and ran for district attorney in 1898. Although he lost the election to Wells' brother-in-law, John Kleiber, the GOP candidate carried Corpus Christi and Nueces County, normally a Democratic bastion, by a three-to-one majority. With James O. Luby, the Republican boss of Duval County, acting as his campaign manager, Scott won the 1902 congressional nomination by acclamation at the district convention.

The Corpus Christi lawyer's erratic political career and his opposition to black participation in the Republican party disturbed a few GOP spokesmen, but no serious opposition materialized. Although blacks formed only a small percentage of the total population of the district, Scott's lily-white views still posed a problem because of the concentration of nine hundred black voters in the pivotal county of Guadalupe. The district organizers simply assumed that these traditional GOP supporters would remain loyal to the party, irrespective of Scott's rhetoric. With its white supremacy views, the Democratic party hardly offered a viable alternative for disenchanted blacks. In addition, campaign funds would be available to offset black apathy. Scott's reputation as an opponent of Hispanic voting was an even more glaring liability, which his backers also chose to ignore.

Although their party had lost every congressional election in South Texas since the triumph of Thomas Ochiltree in 1882, the

Republican organizers approached the 1902 contest with renewed hopefulness and determination. The GOP had established a solid base of support in five district counties, which had voted Republican in at least the past three elections. This group included the two counties with the largest populations, Guadalupe and Webb. The margins of victory in Guadalupe County had been narrow, but the discontent of Dibrell partisans raised the prospect of massive defections from the Democratic ranks. The Republicans also anticipated sizable gains in Nueces County, where Scott had demonstrated his popularity in the district attorney race of 1898. Even James Wells' home county of Cameron, the third-most populous in the district, appeared vulnerable. Since 1894, the Republican vote totals had risen from five hundred to fifteen hundred, and as few as fifteen votes separated the winners and losers in several races for county offices in the last election. With customs houses located at Corpus Christi, Brownsville, Laredo, and Eagle Pass and with post offices scattered throughout the region, John Scott and his allies had access to a patronage force of over 150 federal appointees, from which they could recruit campaign workers and assess contributions.

At the outset of the campaign, the South Texas Republicans also benefited from outside assistance. Although the GOP enjoyed a comfortable majority of forty-six seats in the U.S. House of Representatives, the Republican National Committee feared a possible Democratic resurgence and decided to make funds available to any Southern district in which the party's candidate was competitive. At a Galveston strategy conference, the state leaders agreed to funnel financial aid into three races, including the Scott-Garner contest. Even the White House provided an indirect boost for the congressional campaign. When factional infighting over patronage and the racial composition of the party threatened to paralyze the state Republican organization, President Roosevelt personally intervened to force a truce. The press reported that during a meeting with his political manager for the state, Cecil Lyon, the president expressed his "utter disgust" with the bickering "for the right to dictate a few petty post office appointments" and urged the Texas Republicans to concentrate on the congressional races.[5] Under pressure from Roosevelt, Lyon and two other factional leaders, ex-Congressman Robert B. Hawley and railroad magnate Edward Green, reached an accommodation at the state convention. Their commitments to waging a unified fall campaign were short-lived, however. The late October revival of intraparty feuds at the state level would have a devastating effect on Scott's drive for Congress.

Even with the assets of party harmony, abundant funding, and sound organization at the start of the campaign, John Scott faced an uphill struggle in this traditionally Democratic region of Texas. Two years earlier, James Wells' preoccupation with his duties as state chairman had prevented him from concentrating on local and regional politics. Now he was fully committed to maximizing the Democratic vote throughout the fifteenth district because of his enthusiasm for Garner's candidacy, his opposition to the popular ratification of the poll tax amendment, and his determination to reverse the Republican gains in the Lower Rio Grande Valley. Exercising his influence as Texas Democratic chairman, Wells pressured state officials and employees into contributing over $3,000 to the Garner campaign chest. The Brownsville boss also recruited speakers of statewide prominence, including Senator Joseph Bailey, who toured the district the week before the election.

James Wells did not overlook the need to pacify the dissident elements in the Democratic party. Despite the opposition of the Guadalupe delegation to Wells' reelection as state chairman, the Valley chieftain arranged Joseph Dibrell's appointment to the platform committee at the state convention. A month later the senator announced his intention to campaign for Garner. At the district convention, Wells agreed to the reelection of an original Dibrell supporter to the post of congressional chairman. With its indictment of business abuses and trusts, the Democratic platform for the congressional race reflected the moderate progressive views of Garner and Dibrell, rather than Wells' staunch conservatism. In another effort to attract reform-minded voters, ex-Governor James Hogg promoted Garner's candidacy in an appearance at Seguin, Texas, in Guadalupe County. By late October, the editor of the *Seguin Enterprise* reported that the campaigning of Dibrell and Hogg had turned the tide in Guadalupe County. Instead of a Republican sweep of the county, the newspaper now forecast a narrow victory for Garner.

During the campaign, Garner and Scott participated in two public debates, in which they focused their attention on the national issues of trust regulation and the tariff. Each candidate claimed to be a dedicated antitrust fighter and challenged the other's reform credentials. On the tariff question, the two politicians staked out more distinct positions. Scott defended the traditional Republican commitment to the protective tariff, while Garner denounced the tariff as the mother of the trust and a source of inflation. Even here, however, their differences became blurred when Garner asserted his commitment to the protection of raw materials so long as the inflated duties for industrial commodities remained intact. The contestants also debated whether a Republican or a Democratic congressman would be more effective at securing federal aid for irrigation and harbor improvements for the district.

Issues that were unrelated to Congress and national policy also surfaced. One controversy threatened to shake the loyalty of the Hispanic population to the Democratic party, but the Republicans failed to take advantage of this opening because of Scott's well-known prejudices. During the spring primaries, the Democratic organization of Frio County, adjacent to Uvalde County, had barred the participation of Mexican American voters. Although Garner had carried the county convention with the support of the local party leadership, he denied any responsibility for the exclusionist policy. Fearful of an adverse reaction among the Hispanic electorate, the Garner camp strongly condemned the action of the Frio County Democrats and incorporated a resolution into the platform of the congressional nominating convention that praised Mexican Americans for their "faithful support" of the Democratic party.[6] During the first debate with Scott, Garner took the offensive on this issue. After repeating his criticism of discrimination against Mexican American voters, he read an excerpt from the 1894 Nueces County Democratic platform, which John Scott had authored as chairman of the platform committee. The plank called for Mexican disfranchisement on the grounds that these people "are strangers to our institutions, laws, and customs . . . and are hostile to the prosperity and welfare of our government."[7] The Republican candidate failed to respond to Garner's remarks and never made a concerted effort to force a wedge between the Democratic party and its Hispanic constituency. In fact, at the outset of the campaign, Scott denounced the rival party for "kissing and hugging the Negroes and Mexicans and pulling them into their primaries."[8]

Although John Garner welcomed Mexican American involvement in the political process, he was just as racist as Scott in his attitudes toward blacks. At the second debate, the Uvalde legislator indulged in traditional Democratic race baiting as he attacked the GOP for selecting party officials that "were as black as the ace of spades."[9] Later the Garner camp described Scott's stand against black participation in the Republican party as a campaign ploy aimed at attracting German voters in Guadalupe County. According to the Democrats, Scott anticipated the solid support of the small black constituency in the fifteenth congressional district. Thus, the campaign offered the spectacle of a lily-white Republican and a white supremacy Democrat accusing each other of practicing racial tolerance.

As their hopes for an upset faded, the Scott forces turned in desperation to the issue of land litigation. In early August 1902, the new attorney general, C. K. Bell, filed eleven law suits against 130 land-holders in Cameron, Starr, Zapata, Duval, and Nueces counties in order to determine the validity of claims to over half a million acres. Eager to capitalize on the crisis, the Republican party charged that the attorney general's authority to take this action stemmed from the Garner land proposal. Without making any distinction between Garner's vetoed bill and the Seabury-Nicholson law, which passed during the special session of 1901, John Scott argued that the Democratic legislation sacrificed the interests of the Trans-Nueces ranchers for the purpose of assuring lucrative legal fees for land lawyers, like James B. Wells. A Republican newspaper in San Antonio even accused Wells and Garner of participating in a plot to defraud landowners of their property and to make it available to the railroads. Scott and his allies completely misrepresented the intention and substance of the original Garner bill and the subsequent law. Democratic spokesmen pointed out that the attorney general already had the power to sue for the recovery of land for the state and that the aim of Garner's measure was to protect South Texans from impending litigation. In fact, Governor Sayers vetoed the first bill because it provided too many concessions to the titleholders. The eventual law constituted a compromise between Wells and Bell, but it still bolstered the defenses of the ranchers. The Democratic rebuttal to Scott's accusations was essentially accurate, except for one distortion. Overreacting to sensationalistic claims of a Wells-directed conspiracy, Garner's apologists denied that the Rio Grande boss had played any role in the drafting of the 1901 law.

The Republican exploitation of the land controversy had little impact on the outcome of the election. Of far greater importance was the eruption of organizational and financial problems that extinguished the last hopes of the Scott supporters for political success. At the outset of the campaign, GOP strategists launched a drive to collect thousands of dollars in assessments from the federal appointees of South Texas. The collectors at three of the customs houses contributed $500 apiece and imposed a minimum donation of $50 for each of their employees. Difficulties arose, however, when President Roosevelt instructed the Civil Service Commission to combat political activity on the part of federal personnel holding classified jobs. Despite the lax enforcement of the new guidelines, the customs collector at Eagle Pass, R. W. Dowe, took the presidential admonition seriously because of the firing of his predecessor for alleged violations of the civil service rules. Collector Dowe refused to pay any money to the Scott campaign and encouraged his subordinates to follow his example. With the support of the Eagle Pass postmaster, Dowe held firm. Facing threats of political retaliation for their defiant stands, the two officials even counterattacked by openly gathering evidence against the federal appointees who participated in the congressional campaign. Once eager contributors in other parts of the district developed second thoughts, the level of funding fell far below the original expectations of the GOP organizers. The losses from Eagle Pass alone amounted to $3,000.

The renewal of infighting among state Republican chieftains also created havoc for the Scott campaign. While blacks remained a force within the Texas GOP, three white Republicans, Cecil Lyon, Robert Hawley, and Edward Green, emerged as the dominant figures in the party after 1900. At the state convention of 1902, these factional leaders arranged a temporary agreement on the distribution of power and patronage. With Green presiding over the convention, Lyon claimed the chairmanship of the executive committee, and Hawley retained his seat on the National Republican Committee. The truce collapsed in late October when Lyon maneuvered to take control of the Republican organization for the fifteenth congressional district. Both dissatisfaction with the management of the Scott campaign and a desire to improve his standing in the party motivated the state chairman. By salvaging the only possible Republican victory in Texas, he hoped to solidify his relationship with Roosevelt and to attract enough rank-and-file support to overpower his two rivals. Although Green consented to Lyon's action, Hawley rebelled. As a resident of Galveston, the national committeeman regarded South Texas as his sphere of influence, and he deeply resented the intervention of the North Texan Lyon. Local leaders also objected to the power play, but not because of any loyalty to Hawley. Instead, they simply wanted to preserve their autonomy against outside interference.

Although tension between the state chairman and the South Texas organizers reduced the effectiveness of Republican politicking, the fatal blow came from Robert Hawley. In his determination to thwart Lyon's scheme, Hawley sabotaged the whole Scott campaign by blocking the payment of $3,000, which the National Republican Committee had tentatively promised the Corpus Christi candidate. The combination of the withdrawal of this pledge of support and the loss of the contributions from the federal appointees at Eagle Pass spelled political doom for John Scott. As support for Garner mounted throughout the district, the GOP nominee's only chance for an upset was to claim overwhelming majorities in Guadalupe and Nueces counties. To achieve this goal, he needed thousands of dollars to mobilize the black vote of Guadalupe and to stage campaign blitzes in both counties. Because of the actions of Hawley and Collector Dowe, the money was not available.

In the last few days of the campaign, the Republican strategists acknowledged the hopelessness of their cause by making plans to contest Garner's impending victory if it fell short of a landslide. Leveling charges of "intimidation and fraud," the Scott forces hoped to persuade the Republican majority in the U.S. House of Representatives to disallow the Democratic votes of Cameron, Hidalgo, Starr, and Webb counties.[10] The public exposure of the assessment of federal officeholders along the border, however, discredited the Republican portrayal of John Scott as the honest alternative to corrupt Democratic bosses, and the legal challenge to Garner's election never materialized. In fact, the Garner forces unleashed their own self-righteous rhetoric, as they accused the Republicans of trying to buy the election. The hypocrisy of this exchange of charges reached its peak when the Democrats condemned the GOP for practicing "ward politics."[11]

John Garner won the congressional election with almost 60 percent of the vote, and he carried eighteen of the twenty-two counties in the district, including Scott's home county of Nueces. The Republican nominee prevailed in Guadalupe County but only by a margin of 174 votes. James Wells confirmed his dominance in the Lower Rio Grande Valley, as his Cameron County machine crushed the local GOP opposition by a vote of 1,644 to 1,084. Although Collector C. H. Maris protested that the Blue Club had resorted to fraud, he failed to contest the election in court. For the district as a whole, "fraud and intimidation" did not account for the scope of Garner's victory. Wells' organizational skills, the dissension among the Republican leaders, and Garner's ability to hold his own in the debates with Scott all contributed to the success of the Democratic campaign, but the key factor was simply the revival of unity within the long-standing Democratic majority. With the removal of Rudolph Kleberg from the political scene, the old animosities stemming from the currency battles of the 1890s disappeared. Despite a bitter primary contest, Wells and Garner were able to pacify disgruntled Dibrell supporters and the remnants of the agrarian reform movement with moderate progressive rhetoric and key party appointments. Once the Democratic party reunited, Scott's defeat was certain.

Following the election, James Wells observed that the result of the Garner-Scott contest "takes this district forever out of the doubtful column."[12] John Garner's seat was indeed secure. After 1902, Garner faced serious opposition only once in the Democratic primaries, and his vote totals for the general elections never fell below 60 percent. After 1910, his token opponents frequently received fewer than twenty votes. Despite his reliance on Wells for his initial election to Congress, Garner was not an ineffectual politician like his predecessors, William H. Crain and Rudolph Kleberg. While these men remained permanently dependent on Wells for their reelections, the new congressman eventually developed his own power bases in South Texas and Washington and emerged as an independent political force. By the end of the first decade of the twentieth century, the Brownsville boss was appealing to Garner for assistance at election time. Still Garner was deeply indebted to Wells for managing the 1902 campaign, and the Uvalde politico devoted much of his attention during his first four terms in Congress to repaying that debt. At the outset of his congressional career, John Garner was clearly Wells' man in Washington.

7. Trouble with Washington

WHEN JOHN GARNER ARRIVED in Washington, D.C., in 1903, the Republican party stood as the majority party of the nation. Theodore Roosevelt occupied the presidency, and solid Republican majorities dominated both houses of Congress. The Democratic party had still not recovered from the public backlash against Grover Cleveland's mismanagement of the economy during the depression of the 1890s. To make matters worse, the Democrats in Congress lacked effective leadership and regularly feuded among themselves over both major issues and pork-barrel legislation. The fortunes of the beleaguered minority party began to improve after 1908, however. As open warfare developed between the progressive and conservative wings of the GOP, two new congressional leaders, Champ Clark and Oscar Underwood, restored unity and discipline to the ranks of House Democrats. Minority leader Clark's skill at mediating Democratic differences and Underwood's shrewd parliamentary maneuvering served as perfect complements. In addition, the Democratic representatives agreed to make caucus decisions with two-thirds support binding on the whole delegation. When the GOP split produced a Democratic sweep of the House races of 1910, Clark, Underwood, and their followers were ready to exercise power responsibly.

John Garner profited enormously from the organizational patterns that reshaped the Democratic delegation in the U.S. House of Representatives. His political experience in South Texas, where success depended on cooperation with boss-run machines, had conditioned him to value sound organization over commitments to particular policies and causes. During his first few years in Congress, the Uvalde lawyer followed the commands of the party leadership on most issues, concentrated on learning the techniques of lawmaking, and formed friendships with influential figures like Champ Clark. His performance as a reliable team player paid off in 1909 when Champ Clark appointed Garner to serve as a party whip. Two years later, when the Democrats gained control of the House, the new majority leader, Oscar Underwood, retained Garner as a whip and also appointed him to the three-man Committee on Organization, which supervised the distribution of over three hundred jobs related to the operation of the lower chamber. This control over House patronage increased Garner's influence among his fellow congressmen, who were eager to secure appointments for their friends and constituents, but the Texas representative remained a legislative mechanic. He still played only a minor role in defining party positions on national issues. Garner's opportunity to serve as an important policymaker did not come until his appointment to the House Ways and Means Committee in 1913. In the years that followed, he contributed to the formulation of tariff and tax policies and emerged as a leading defender of Woodrow Wilson's plans for financing World War I.

While John Garner was familiarizing himself with the operation of Congress and winning the confidence of the Democratic leadership, he never lost sight of his obligation to advance the special interests of his South Texas constituents. The bulk of the measures that Garner sponsored, either as individual bills or as provisions of broader legislation, related to local concerns. Despite his agitation for economy in government, the Uvalde congressman became a dedicated practitioner of pork-barrel politics. Garner's famous comment, "Every time one of those Yankees gets a ham, I am going to do my best to get a hog," reflected the premium that he placed on arranging legislative favors for his district.[1] Although the total number of pensions, relief bills, and federal buildings that he proposed during his first ten years in Washington was hardly staggering, the U.S. representative promoted three projects that would eventually cost millions of dollars and speed the development of the whole region south of San Antonio: the construction of a coastal canal from Galveston to the Rio Grande and deep-water ports at Brownsville and Aransas Pass, just north of Corpus Christi. As a result of Garner's persistent lobbying, the federal government erected a new system of jetties at Aransas Pass and extended the coastal canal from Galveston to Corpus Christi by 1913. Unfavorable reports from the Army Corps of Engineers, however, thwarted Garner's efforts to arrange the creation of a deep-water port at Brazos de Santiago and the dredging of Laguna Madre, the hundred-mile channel that connects Corpus Christi and the mouth of the Rio Grande. The fulfillment of John Garner's grand design came only gradually over the next thirty-five years.

Despite his initial failure to win congressional approval of the channel and harbor improvements for Brownsville, Garner never faltered in his commitment to defend the interests of James B. Wells. His services for the Cameron County boss included sponsoring legislation for the construction of an international railroad bridge at Brownsville, lobbying for the retention of troops at Fort Brown, securing a federal soil survey for South Texas, arranging the location of a federal experimental farm just outside Brownsville, promoting the construction of post offices in the new towns of the Valley, introducing pension bills for Wells' associates, and proposing the establishment of a weather station at Brownsville. Garner also lobbied against a proposed treaty between Mexico and the United States that would have imposed limits on the amount of water from the Rio Grande that American farmers could use for irrigation. In the end, the outbreak of revolution in Mexico, rather than Garner's agitation, killed the treaty. Two other concerns, however, overshadowed all of these pork-barrel offerings: the 1906 Brownsville raid, in which a group of black soldiers allegedly launched an attack against the town, and federal patronage.

The Brownsville raid of 1906 aroused not only local passions but also nationwide political controversy. On July 25, 1906, three companies of black soldiers arrived in Brownsville to replace the white battalion that had previously occupied Fort Brown. The response of the community to the presence of black infantrymen was ambivalent. Between 1865 and 1891, black troops had regularly served at Fort Brown without provoking any serious incidents. In fact, two of the leading citizens of Brownsville, the merchant and Republican organizer Henry Field and the banker William Kelly, had commanded black units of the Union Army stationed along the Rio Grande at the end of the Civil War. Even the Democratic mayor of Brownsville, Dr. Frederick Combe, had served with black troops as an army surgeon during the Spanish-American War. According to Kelly, the town merchants welcomed black soldiers because they generally made more purchases than their white counterparts. He also claimed that the lower-class Hispanics, who formed the majority of the population, accepted blacks as social equals.

Although Brownsville hardly conformed to the image of the conventional southern community, where the overriding social concern was to keep the black man in his place, serious problems did exist. After the announcement of plans to assign the black troops to Fort Brown, Senators Culberson and Bailey and Representative Garner relayed constituent protests to the War Department. William Kelly attributed these complaints to a minority of the residents, "the people from the southern cotton states that have come in there recently," but other evidence indicated that racist sentiment was widespread among the Anglo population.² The black soldiers, their white predecessors, and their white officers all reported racial slurs and threats on the part of the townspeople. Two of the Anglo-owned saloons excluded blacks, and the other one offered a separate bar for them at the rear. Having escaped the strict enforcement of the color line during their four-year tour of duty at Fort Niobrara, Nebraska, the soldiers resented the segregationist policies of Brownsville. A form of southern social etiquette, which required public displays of black deference to whites, also extended to the border town. Ten days after the arrival of the three companies of the Twenty-fifth Infantry, one of the customs inspectors struck a private with his pistol for allegedly jostling a group of white women on the sidewalk. Even the Hispanic policemen of Brownsville abused the troopers. Because the soldiers usually had enough cash to cover fines while Mexican American laborers did not, the patrolmen sought out blacks who had been drinking, clubbed them, and hauled them to jail on charges of public drunkenness. The victims had to pay not only the regular fines but also additional assessments that the policemen divided among themselves. Despite the frequency of this kind of harassment, no major racial incidents occurred until August 12, when a white woman charged that an unidentified black soldier had assaulted her. The following day, Mayor Combe warned the commanding officer at Fort Brown, Major Charles Penrose, that "if you allow these men to go into town tonight, I will not be responsible for their lives."³

With the emotions of the citizenry already running high, shooting erupted just outside Fort Brown a few minutes before midnight on August 13. A force of fifteen to twenty raiders charged through an alley located between two of the main streets of Brownsville and fired indiscriminately into the nearby buildings, including a house where five children were sleeping. After wounding a police lieutenant and killing his horse, the marauders split into two groups. While some of the men crossed over to Washington Street, the others resumed their advance through the alley and directed a fatal volley into the Ruby Saloon. The shots killed the bartender and grazed one patron. Within ten minutes, the raid had ended, and the attackers had escaped.

From the outset, the townspeople assumed that black infantrymen had perpetrated the outrage. This sentiment cut across party lines. Republicans, such as Rentfro B. Creager, joined in the condemnation of the soldiers. Around 1:15 in the morning, Mayor Combe encountered an army unit that Major Penrose had dispatched to investigate the shooting spree. Combe returned with the troopers to their post to inform the major of the charge against his men. Having misinterpreted the gunplay as an attack against the fort, rather than the town, Penrose was skeptical about the allegation but agreed to call the roll of the soldiers and to order an inspection of their rifles and ammunition. Although the white officers failed to uncover any incriminating evidence, the major accepted the judgment of the Brownsville citizenry when Combe later presented a collection of shells and rifle clips that his colleagues had found along the path of the assault. The items had come from special Springfield rifles, which the army alone used. Yet, not a single soldier confessed any involvement in the raid or admitted any knowledge of who was responsible.

The residents of Brownsville were determined to apprehend the guilty parties among the 170 troopers stationed at Fort Brown and to ensure the safety of their community against a future uprising. When the two goals came into conflict, the townspeople opted for security over retribution. At a mass meeting held the day after the raid, Mayor Combe appointed a committee of prominent citizens, under the chairmanship of William Kelly, to investigate the affray and to appeal for outside assistance. In both of these pursuits, the committee experienced frustration. Of the twenty-two witnesses that Kelly and his associates interviewed, only five contended that they had actually seen black soldiers staging the raid, and none could identify any individual suspects. Despite his willingness to cooperate, Major Penrose failed to secure any additional information from his men. The whole case against the soldiers rested on the testimony of witnesses, who claimed to be able to recognize the skin color and uniforms of men at distances of twenty-five feet or more in almost total darkness, and on the recovery of the Springfield shells. Later army ballistic examinations revealed that the cartridges had probably been discharged during target practice at Fort Niobrara, Nebraska. Their appearance on the streets of Brownsville indicated that someone had stolen the spent cartridges from the storeroom at Fort Brown and had planted them at the scenes of the shooting in order to frame the infantrymen. Even at the time of their discovery, the shells appeared to be suspect evidence. Although both the soldiers and the civilians estimated that the raiders had fired over 250 shots, investigators retrieved only forty Springfield cartridges. An army officer found eighteen of the shells bunched together in a circular area of approximately eighty square inches. Ejection from a Springfield rifle would have dispersed the shells over an area of eighty square feet. Moreover, none of these shells matched the bullets lodged in the three nearest buildings. Still the citizens' committee and the townspeople persisted in their certainty that black soldiers had carried out the terrorist attack.

The main cause of civilian alarm was not the inconclusiveness of the committee investigation but instead the failure of the state and federal governments to take prompt action to prevent any possible recurrence of the raid. The citizens demanded both the intervention of white troops and the removal of the three companies of black soldiers. At the time of the shooting, James Wells was attending the state Democratic convention at Dallas. The next morning, three committee members telegraphed Wells, asking him to recruit the two Texas senators and Congressman Garner to lobby for the withdrawal of the black troops. The committee also urged Adjutant General John Hulen to dispatch the Texas militia and to conduct his own investigation of the Brownsville affair. On August 15, several local officials made direct appeals to President Roosevelt and Governor Lanham. In their telegram to Roosevelt, the community representatives revealed their sense of desperation: "We find that threats have been made by [the soldiers] that they will repeat this outrage. We do not believe their officers can restrain them, there being but five commissioned officers. Our condition, Mr. President, is this: Our women and children are terrorized and our men are practically under constant alarm and watchfulness. No community can stand this strain for more than a few days. We look to you for relief; we ask you to have the troops at once removed from Fort Brown and replaced by white soldiers."[4] Although Wells assured his constituents that "Senators Bailey and Culberson have wired the Secretary of War and [are] doing everything in their power to aid us," no reinforcements arrived, and the Twenty-fifth Infantry Battalion remained at Fort Brown.[5]

During the week following the raid, the War Department did nothing more than solicit reports from Major Penrose and dispatch Major Augusto P. Blocksom to investigate the matter more fully. Despite pressure from Bailey, Culberson, and Garner, the military was unwilling to transfer the black troops until the completion of a thorough inquiry and the identification of the culprits. Both the state and federal officials accepted Penrose's assurances that no further trouble was likely. After the state Democratic convention, illness incapacitated Governor Lanham at his hometown of Weatherford, and he failed to respond to the pleas for assistance for several days. Even when Lanham returned to Austin, his usual indecisiveness and Hulen's reluctance to challenge federal authority precluded any dramatic state action.

When James Wells returned to Brownsville on August 18, he found that indignation over the apparent indifference of the Lanham and Roosevelt administrations had swept the community. Since the night of the raid, the town had come to resemble an armed camp. Local merchants had sold hundreds of rifles and pistols. Perhaps as many as four hundred men now owned Winchesters, and a force of forty special deputies patrolled the streets at night. The families with houses near the fort had withdrawn to other parts of town or to Matamoros. The residents lived in fear that "the accidental discharge of a firearm, any overt act of an excited citizen," could provoke a bloodbath.[6] After renewed appeals to the president and the governor failed to produce any results, Wells warned the adjutant general that the citizens of Brownsville were preparing to mount a direct appeal to the people of Texas, which would embarrass the state administration.

Finally, the combination of the protests from the Texas senators and new recommendations from Majors Penrose and Blocksom forced a change of government policy. Both army officers acknowledged the continuing state of tension in Brownsville and endorsed the pleas of the local citizenry to remove the black troops as quickly as possible. On August 20, 1906, after consulting with President Roosevelt, the acting secretary of war, Major General F. C. Ainsworth, ordered a single company of white soldiers to replace the black battalion at Fort Brown. The black soldiers received instructions to report to Fort Reno, Oklahoma, where they would undergo further interrogation. Although these orders offered the relief that the townspeople sought, ill feeling toward the military and the Roosevelt administration did not subside. Penrose's published account of the Brownsville raid implied that the civilian population had provoked the attack with their discriminatory practices. In addition, several newspapers reported that the War Department intended to use the incident as an excuse for abandoning Fort Brown. Not even the danger of renewed violence disappeared. Before the three black companies withdrew, Captain William McDonald of the Texas Rangers arrived at the border town and precipitated a new crisis.

An inveterate grandstander and race baiter, William McDonald intended to take charge of the investigation of the raid and to bully the black soldiers into confessing their crimes. Accompanying McDonald on the last leg of his journey from Austin to Brownsville, District Judge Stanley Welch of Corpus Christi assured the Ranger that he had the power to arrest even members of the U.S. Army. Amid denunciations of the governor and the adjutant general for their failure to send the state militia, the citizens' committee welcomed McDonald and invited him, Welch, and District Attorney John Kleiber to join their ranks. After reviewing the evidence that the committee had collected, the Ranger captain proceeded to Fort Brown. Major Penrose allowed McDonald to interview several soldiers. Although none of these men revealed any new information about the affray, the Texas Ranger persuaded Judge Welch to issue arrest warrants for twelve troopers and one ex-soldier, who had operated a black saloon. The evidence against each suspect was either highly circumstantial or nonexistent. McDonald leveled charges against three men because of their absence from the fort on the night of the assault, one because of the discovery of his hat near one of the scenes of the shooting, two because of their involvement in altercations with local citizens, and the rest because of their service as sentinels and noncommissioned officers in charge of the quarters and guns. Operating on the assumption that black soldiers had committed the outrage, the Ranger captain concluded that these guards and noncommissioned officers must be aware of who had left the fort to participate in the raid. While refusing to surrender the accused men to the civilian authorities, Major Penrose ordered their confinement in the post guardhouse.

Despite McDonald's flagrant abuse of his authority to make arrests, no one raised any objections to the Ranger's conduct until he threatened to block the transfer of the battalion of black infantrymen. The company of white replacements had reached Fort Brown on the day of the Ranger captain's arrival, but the townspeople still harbored fears that another shooting spree might erupt. In their view, only the withdrawal of the black troops would ensure their safety. McDonald, on the other hand, was determined to prevent the removal of his twelve suspects from Brownsville. When he learned that Majors Penrose and Blocksom planned to move the prisoners with the rest of their men, the Texas Ranger ordered the local railroad officials to detain the special troop train. After McDonald refused to yield in the face of Penrose's protests, the local politicians arranged a meeting with the Ranger and Judge Welch. Even John Garner, who had traveled to Brownsville to attend the congressional district convention, was present. Under pressure from James Wells and others, Welch demanded that the captain allow the troops to leave without any further interference. Mayor Combe later recalled Wells' admonition to McDonald: "McDonald, I am a friend of yours, but you are only a Ranger captain, and if you keep along the way you are doing, you are going to precipitate us into trouble. You are zealous, you are a good officer, and you think you are doing right, but if you attempt to interfere with those soldiers down there, this matter will break out anew, and we will lose a great many lives. You must remember our wives and children."[7] William Kelly, Combe, and Welch all echoed these sentiments, but the Ranger vowed "to hold that bunch of niggers with those warrants until I hear from Governor Lanham."[8]

That evening Judge Stanley Welch and Cameron County Sheriff Celedonio Garza organized a posse to confront McDonald and to compel him to surrender the warrants against the twelve soldiers. Facing the threat of arrest himself, McDonald complied with Welch's demand. A timely telegram from Governor Lanham helped to defuse the crisis by providing the Ranger captain with a face-saving avenue of retreat. Although Lanham agreed with McDonald that the prisoners should remain in Brownsville, the chief executive instructed the Texas Ranger to "consult with the district judge and the sheriff and to act under and through them."[9] A force of fifty to sixty special deputies escorted the black soldiers to the train, and Mayor Combe announced that the police would arrest or shoot anyone who interfered with the departure of the troops. The withdrawal of the black battalion went smoothly, but bitter relations between Captain McDonald and the South Texas politicos persisted. McDonald publicly condemned the actions of the local officials and even suggested to Governor Lanham that the state legislature should impeach Judge Welch. After the murder of Welch in November 1906, James Wells appealed to the governor to dispatch the Rangers to Rio Grande City but cautioned him not to send McDonald.

The weakness of the Ranger captain's case against the thirteen accused men became all too apparent in September when the Brownsville grand jury conducted a three-week investigation of the raid. Shortly before the proceedings began, the announcement of War Department orders to abandon Fort Brown rekindled the townspeople's indignation, and Judge Welch's charge to the jury was hardly a model of judicial impartiality. He condemned the soldiers for their "fiendish malice and hate, showing hearts blacker than their skins," and for "the brutish hope on their part of killing women and children."[10] Despite this emotional appeal and the shared assumption that black soldiers had staged the attack, the grand jurors failed to hand down any indictments. Neither the citizens' committee, nor Captain McDonald, nor the witnesses appearing before the grand jury could provide enough evidence to support the prosecution of a single black trooper.

The failure of the local authorities and the U.S. Army to apprehend any of the participants in the Brownsville raid did not deter

President Roosevelt from imposing penalties. After the soldiers resisted an ultimatum to break their alleged conspiracy of silence or face dishonorable discharges, the president ordered the dismissal of all 167 black enlisted men and noncommissioned officers in the three companies of the Twenty-fifth Infantry. This executive action and Republican Senator Joseph Foraker's stubborn defense of the soldiers sparked a national debate, in which both Charles Culberson and John Garner played active roles. For a change, Joseph Bailey abstained from theatrical posturing on the floor of the Senate and contented himself with following Culberson's lead.

After Joseph Foraker introduced a resolution questioning the legality of the blanket discharge of the black soldiers and calling for a Senate investigation, Culberson offered a substitute, which endorsed the president's action. The Texas senator also delivered a major speech, in which he outlined the precedents for the dismissal. He devoted the bulk of his presentation, however, to defending the integrity of the people of Brownsville, who "are practically charged with rioting among themselves," and to demonstrating the guilt of the black infantrymen.[11] He not only cited the eye-witness accounts that the citizens' committee had compiled but also entered into the *Congressional Record* secret grand jury affidavits. Although Texas law forbade the release of grand jury testimony, James Wells had secured and mailed the transcripts to Culberson. Wells was aware that the senator intended to use the material in a public attack against Foraker's claims that the blacks were innocent.

Culberson's substitute met defeat, but the Republican leadership of the Senate pressured Foraker into accepting a compromise resolution that proposed an investigation of the Brownsville affray without challenging the "legality and justice" of the presidential initiative.[12] After conducting hearings over a period of several months and reviewing the evidence that other investigators had gathered, the Senate Committee on Military Affairs, on which Foraker served, submitted three reports. The majority report argued that the black troopers had committed the outrage, even though the individual culprits still eluded detection, and that President Roosevelt was justified in dismissing all the soldiers. The dissenters on the committee split. Two senators concluded that none of the inquiries had established the soldiers' guilt in a strict legal sense, while Foraker and another committeeman asserted that army ballistic tests had confirmed the men's innocence. Senator Foraker also introduced a bill that authorized the reinstatement of any discharged trooper who simply swore that he had not participated in the raid. After another Republican compromise in January 1909, the Senate passed a bill empowering the secretary of war to appoint a court of military inquiry to review the individual cases of the cashiered soldiers. The two Texas senators opposed both Foraker's original proposal for rehabilitating the infantrymen and the creation of this new investigative body. In his only remarks from the floor of the Senate on the Brownsville controversy, Joseph Bailey lambasted the GOP politicians for competing with one another to win the loyalty of the black electorate of the North.

The House of Representatives did not debate the question of the Brownsville raid until February 1909, when the bill to establish the court of military inquiry reached the floor. As early as December 1906, however, John Garner had taken legislative action. During the first session of Congress following the terrorist attack, Garner submitted a measure to repeal the legal authorization for the maintenance of the black regiments in the U.S. Army. He also proposed financial relief from the federal government for all Brownsville citizens who had suffered either physical injury or property damage as a result of the raid. Both bills died in committee, but the Uvalde representative reintroduced the ban against black enlistments in the military in 1907, 1910, and 1911. During the House debate of 1909, Garner's eagerness to use the issue of the Brownsville uprising to promote racist policies again surfaced, as he delivered a general condemnation of northern Republican interference in the racial caste system of the South and declared that "there is no power on earth that will make the African the equal of the white man."[13]

In assessing the Brownsville raid itself, Garner concluded that "there is not an innocent man in the battalion, for the reason that he either pulled the trigger or had knowledge of it, or had knowledge of facts that would aid the Government in ascertaining who was innocent or who was guilty."[14] Even the *Brownsville Herald* had conceded that some of the soldiers were innocent victims who had neither participated in the attack nor conspired to conceal the identities of the marauders. Most Southern Democrats joined Garner in voting against the revised legislation to establish a new board of review, but the proposal passed by a comfortable margin. This final congressional gesture had little practical effect, however. Despite the dearth of evidence against individual soldiers, the court of military inquiry exonerated only 14 of the 167 discharged infantrymen. Throughout the investigation of this case, the U.S. government denied the soldiers a fundamental guarantee of American law—the presumption of innocence until guilt has been proven. By any reasonable standard of justice, all the black soldiers were innocent.

For the citizens of Brownsville, the most disturbing long-term consequence of the raid was the closing of Fort Brown in September 1906. Almost a year earlier, the U.S. Army had made plans to abandon the post as part of a general program to concentrate at San Antonio the forces responsible for the defense of the South Texas border, but political pressure from Garner and others delayed the move. As local antagonism toward the military flared in the aftermath of the shooting spree, War Department officials perceived an opportunity to implement their scheme, despite charges that the Roosevelt administration was punishing the civilian population for protesting the outrage that they had suffered at the hands of the black soldiers. Troops returned to Brownsville in 1911 when President William Howard Taft ordered the mobilization of twenty thousand men in response to the escalating fighting in the Mexican Revolution. The army did not reactivate Fort Brown as a permanent base of operations until 1914, however.

Not even the Brownsville raid and its political repercussions could divert James Wells' attention from the problem of federal patronage. As the congressional debate over the terrorist attack continued through the final year of Roosevelt's presidency and the opening months of Taft's term, Wells participated in three major patronage disputes. The South Texas politico engineered the removal of Customs Collector John W. Vann and tried to block the confirmation of his successor, Rentfro B. Creager. Wells also opposed the appointment of Robert B. Rentfro, Jr., as the Brownsville postmaster. All three men posed serious threats to the democratic machines of the Lower Rio Grande Valley. Collector Vann was pressing for the prosecution of Starr County boss Manuel Guerra and his cohorts for the murder of customs agent Gregorio Duffy, while Creager and Rentfro had helped to arrange the conversion of the Red Club of Cameron County into the Independent party, which unified the Republican and dissident Democratic opposition to the Wells organization. In the fight to defeat the nominations of Creager and Rentfro, Wells relied on the congressional lobbying of John Garner. The campaign against Vann involved the fabrication of charges of misconduct and the possible corruption of a Treasury Department investigator.

When John Vann received his appointment to replace C. H. Maris as the Brownsville customs collector in 1906, James Wells applauded the move. After holding the position of Kerr County sheriff for ten years, Vann served under U.S. Marshal William Hanson, one of the few federal officeholders who maintained friendly relations with Wells. The Rio Grande chieftain believed that Vann would abstain from the political campaigning that had preoccupied his predecessors. The promise of an amicable relationship came to an abrupt end with the violent Starr County campaign of 1906, however. Vann allowed the customs officials at Rio Grande City to participate in the Republican drive to oust the Guerra machine from power. The contest led to the murder of Judge Stanley Welch, an armed confrontation on election day, a gun battle between GOP partisans and a force of Texas Rangers, and the killing of Gregorio Duffy in January 1907. Rather than retreating in the face of this mounting violence, the new customs collector took the offensive. Not only did he press for the federal investigation of Duffy's slaying, which eventually resulted in the indictments against Manuel and Deodoro Guerra and the Morales brothers for conspiring to commit murder, but he also charged that local Democrats were framing Alberto Cabrera, the accused murderer of Judge Welch. During the trial of Juan Morales at Laredo, the former sheriff provided armed protection for the prosecutors and witnesses. Vann and several of his agents attended the Cabrera trial as well, and when a fight threatened to break out between the chief prosecutor and the leading Republican spokesman of Starr County, Ed C. Lasater, the customs officials drew their pistols in the courtroom. The collector may have lacked Maris' skill as a political organizer, but Vann's willingness to resort to force and his unceasing agitation for legal retribution against the Guerras made him just as frightening to Wells.

With the legal battles stemming from the murders of Welch and Duffy still in progress, an anonymous "ex-customs officer" leveled charges of misconduct against John W. Vann in April 1908. After investigating the Brownsville customs house, special treasury agent W. S. Larner submitted a report that was highly critical of Vann and his employees. According to Larner, the financial records of the customs district were in disarray, and most of the officers neglected their duties. Instead of patrolling the Rio Grande and maintaining inspection posts at the main border crossing, they devoted all their time to politicking. The officials received their appointments as a result of their political connections, and they kicked back assessments from their salaries to pay for poll taxes for Hispanic voters. The most damaging part of the report concerned Vann's personal character and behavior:

> When the Collector was in Brownsville, his time was spent in the barrooms of that place, and he had little or no standing among the leading businessmen, or the reputable citizens of the community. He consorted with Mexican half-breeds and avowed bad men and gun-wielders. Numerous instances were

cited in which the Collector, who always went armed with a
Colt 45 in his hip pocket, had been engaged in brawls in saloons, and in one instance had called out all his armed Inspectors to protect himself against one of the municipal police
from whom he was attempting to rescue a bartender who had
been arrested by the policeman. On another occasion, he had
attempted to ride a horse into one of the saloons in broad
daylight, while under the influence of liquor.[15]

On the basis of this evaluation of the Brownsville customs operation, the secretary of the treasury removed John Vann from office in
June 1908, but the controversy continued. Vann denied the accusations, and Assistant U.S. Attorney Noah Allen argued that the local
bosses had conspired to discredit the collector because of his commitment to bring the murderers of Gregorio Duffy to justice. Allen
concluded that special agent Larner had been "unconsciously led
into a well laid scheme and . . . basely deceived by some traitors in
the camp and unscrupulous henchmen of the political czar of this
valley."[16] In response to these protests, two other Treasury Department representatives conducted another investigation, and their reports raised serious doubts about the credibility of Larner's findings.
R. W. Dowe, the collector at Eagle Pass who had refused to make any
contributions to the Scott campaign in 1902, completely exonerated
Vann. While praising the "good character" of the Brownsville collector, Dowe launched an attack against James Wells, whom he characterized as "dishonest and unscrupulous."[17] The investigator was
convinced that Wells was responsible for the slandering of Vann.
The fact that the most incriminating testimony in the Larner report
had come from A. Y. Baker reinforced this belief. A former Texas
Ranger and customs inspector, Baker was indebted to Wells for defending him against murder charges in 1903. Five years later, the two
men resumed their cooperation when Baker reversed his testimony
in the Duffy murder case to the advantage of the defendants. For this
service, Baker received the post of Hidalgo County treasurer. Because of the distortions in the original treasury report and because of
Larner's heavy reliance on dubious informants, such as Baker, Dowe
questioned not only Larner's judgment but also his honesty and
loyalties.

In a more balanced analysis of the Brownsville customs house,
agent Joseph D. Nevius cleared Vann of the charges of associating
with disreputable characters, brawling, excessive drinking, provoking fights with the police, and trying to ride his horse into a saloon.
A number of businessmen, bankers, and lawyers confirmed Vann's

standing as a respected citizen in the community. The involvement of the collector and his employees in local politics was undeniable, however. The customs force formed the organizational base of the opposition to the Democratic machines of the Valley, and Vann served as a party leader. Although only two officers claimed that they had paid compulsory assessments in order to retain their jobs, the rest of the force conceded that they had made political contributions on a voluntary basis. Tax records also revealed that customs officials had paid the poll taxes of Hispanic voters. In Vann's defense, Nevius pointed out that this kind of political activity conformed to a long-standing pattern among federal officeholders in South Texas and that the campaigning had not interfered with the performance of the customs employees' official duties. The number of seizures of smuggled goods compared favorably to the records of other customs districts along the Mexican border. Still, some administrative confusion and financial irregularities did exist.

After reviewing the Nevius report, President Roosevelt concluded that Vann was a "poor administrator" but "a mighty good citizen from the standpoint of the needs of the particular community where he dwelt." Rather than reinstating him as a customs collector, the president suggested that Vann should serve as a special agent for the Justice Department. His immediate assignment would be to assist with the prosecution of "that outfit of assassins down there who killed Duffy."[18] Thus, the removal of Vann from the collectorship represented only a token victory for Wells. In his new position, the former sheriff resumed his investigation of the Guerras and again shielded government witnesses from the harassment of Texas Rangers, local law officers, and other Democratic henchmen.

Even before this appointment, John Vann assumed a new political role as well. At the Republican congressional convention of 1908, he secured the district chairmanship and took charge of Dr. T. W. Moore's campaign against John Garner. Moore was a physician from Guadalupe County who had run against Garner two years earlier and had collected 36 percent of the vote. With the Republican state organization willing to invest most of its resources in the coming campaign, Moore appeared to be a more serious challenger in 1908. An apprehensive Garner appealed to the state Democratic executive committee for outside assistance and even consented to participate in two debates with Moore. In addition, the formation of the Independent party in Cameron County and Vann's decision to concentrate on the Lower Rio Grande Valley sparked vigorous campaigning on the part of James Wells.

Despite an upsurge of Republican strength in South Texas, John

Garner won reelection by a comfortable margin, and the Wells machine retained its control over Cameron County politics. Whatever sense of relief Wells and Garner derived from their victories was short-lived. In December 1908, Theodore Roosevelt placed the two politicians on the defensive again with the appointments of Rentfro B. Creager to the Brownsville collectorship and Robert B. Rentfro, Jr., to the office of postmaster. Earlier in the year, the president had nominated Rentfro, but Garner had managed to stall the confirmation proceedings until the close of the congressional session. Both men were anathema to James Wells. Rentfro was the son and namesake of Wells' old rival, who had run against William Crain for Congress in 1884 and had later headed the GOP forces along the Rio Grande. The younger Rentfro had served as a customs inspector for seven years and had participated in the founding of the Independent party. Wells' main concern, however, was the appointment of Rentfro B. Creager, the nephew of Robert B. Rentfro, Sr. Only thirty-two years of age, Creager was already a veteran of local Republican politics and one of the leaders of the new Independent party. Combining politics and the practice of law, he defended Alberto Cabrera against the charge of murdering Judge Welch, and he assisted in the extradition of Gabriel Morales from Mexico. Creager also held two federal jobs, U.S. commissioner and deputy clerk for the U.S. District Court for the Southern District of Texas. With the influx of unaffiliated voters into the Valley, James Wells was determined to block the appointment of a new collector whose political talents matched those of C. H. Maris.

The man responsible for the selection of Creager and Rentfro was the Republican state chairman, Cecil Lyon. Despite Lyon's failure to salvage the Scott congressional campaign of 1902 and despite the dramatic decline in the statewide Republican vote after 1900, Roosevelt continued to rely on the North Texan as his chief operative in the state. Roosevelt's confidence in Lyon rested on a close personal friendship and on Lyon's unfailing loyalty. Besides, the president was only marginally interested in the popular vote of Texas since the state invariably went Democratic. Instead, he depended on Lyon to deliver the Texas delegations at the national Republican conventions. In return for this support, Roosevelt authorized Lyon to act as his political "referee," who recommended federal appointees for Texas and settled all factional disputes over patronage. With this power, Lyon was able to establish his dominance over the state party by 1904 and to fashion a lily-white machine, which drew support from his hand-picked officeholders.

Cecil Lyon's interest in South Texas politics had not waned

since the Republican debacle in the Garner-Scott contest. Despite Garner's sweeps of the 1904 and 1906 elections, the presence of 160 federal officeholders along the border convinced Lyon that the fifteenth congressional district offered the best opportunity for a GOP breakthrough in the solidly Democratic state. During the 1908 campaign, the *San Antonio Daily Express* reported that Lyon intended to commit "the most powerful Republican guns available" to the candidacy of Dr. T. W. Moore.[19] Yet James Wells still posed a formidable obstacle to Republican success. After Lyon proposed Rentfro's initial nomination in February 1908, Garner warned his Brownsville ally that "there is no question but that [Lyon] is determined to do everything he can to destroy your influence along the Rio Grande."[20]

As John Garner lobbied against the appointments of Rentfro and Creager, he recognized the futility of trying to persuade Roosevelt to reject Lyon's recommendations, but he hoped to block the Senate confirmations until William Howard Taft assumed the presidency in March 1909. Although Lyon had compaigned vigorously for Taft, the Uvalde congressman anticipated that the president-elect might abandon the "referee system" and Lyon's control over Texas patronage: "It is an open secret that Mr. Taft does not fancy the one man power in the Southern states, and will do his utmost to select the best men for each place, regardless of politics; in this way try to build up his administration in the eyes of the best people of the South."[21] For almost three months, Garner waged a relentless fight to hold up Senate consideration of the appointments. He initially enjoyed the support of Senators Culberson and Bailey, both of whom occupied strategic positions in the confirmation process. Culberson served on the Post Office Committee, while Bailey held a slot on the Finance Committee, which oversaw the operation of the customs service. Garner also made direct appeals for postponements to the chairman of the Senate subcommittee that reviewed postal appointments for Texas. The representative's dilatory tactics succeeded during the closing session of the sixtieth Congress but only at the expense of his credibility among his colleagues. Garner conceded to Wells that "my requests in the future would not have the weight I would like for them to have" since the Uvalde congressman was unable to support his calls for delays with the presentation of specific charges against Rentfro and Creager.[22] When President Taft upset Garner's calculations and submitted the nominations of the two Brownsville Republicans, even Joseph Bailey refused to join the opposition. By the end of 1909, both men had received Senate confirmation.

For Garner, the appointments of Rentfro and Creager represented only a modest setback. As a result of his growing influence in Washington and his success at securing pork-barrel projects for South Texas, his congressional seat was safe. When Noah Allen, the dogged prosecutor in the Duffy murder case, challenged Garner in 1910, the Uvalde politico triumphed with 70 percent of the vote. Wells, on the other hand, faced grave political problems in the years ahead. The new customs collector, Rentfro B. Creager, took charge of the Independent party and engineered two consecutive victories in the Brownsville city elections. In 1910, the insurgents captured a majority of the seats on the Cameron County commissioners' court, while losing the countywide races. Two years later, only artful legal maneuvering to keep the names of the Independent candidates off the ballots for the general election prevented another strong Independent showing. Although Wells remained the dominant figure in Cameron County politics through the second decade of the twentieth century, these local attacks undermined his standing as the Democratic leader for all South Texas. Ironically, demographic changes, which Wells and his associates shaped through their promotion of railroad construction and irrigation, created the political opening for Creager and his Independent party.

As Wells' power declined, the relationship between the veteran Democratic organizer and his congressman underwent a subtle change. As late as the patronage battles of 1908 and 1909, Garner assumed an almost submissive posture toward Wells. Facing defeat in his campaign against the Creager and Rentfro appointments, he appealed to Wells to recognize the weakness of his lobbying position and to excuse his impending failure. The prospect of disappointing his mentor in an important political fight still made Garner uneasy. In years that followed, the South Texas representative continued to cooperate with Wells, but the deferential tone of Garner's correspondence disappeared. On occasions, he even questioned Wells' political judgment. The services that Garner later performed for Wells appeared as favors for a reliable ally, whose past support was much appreciated, but not as tribute to an all-powerful boss, whose present backing was indispensable.

8. Political Upheaval in South Texas

SINCE THE ARRIVAL of the first Spanish settlers in the Lower Rio Grande Valley in the late eighteenth century, the basic character of the land had remained unchanged. Despite the prevalence of dry grasslands and chaparral, which could sustain only cattle and sheep ranching, the potential for large-scale agricultural development was present. The region offered both rich soil and year-round growing seasons with its semitropical climate. Experimental projects in the 1870s and the 1890s had demonstrated the feasibility of irrigation to offset the limited rainfall. The missing ingredient in the economic equation was an efficient transportation system to deliver farm produce to the urban markets. Before 1900, the Valley lacked both a deep-water port and a railway link with the rest of the country.

The completion of the St. Louis, Brownsville, and Mexico Railway line from Corpus Christi to Brownsville in 1904 sparked an economic revolution. Almost immediately, development companies purchased ranchland, subdividing it into ten-to-forty-acre tracts, installing irrigation pumps along the Rio Grande, and digging drainage canals for the new farmsites. The price of land reached such extravagant heights that the ranchers of the Valley could not resist the temptation to sell substantial shares of their holdings. At the start of the boom, developers paid $5 to $50 per acre for unimproved pasturage, which had been worth $2 an acre only a few years earlier. By 1912, the price of irrigated farmland ran as high as $300 per acre.

The soaring land prices did not deter the influx of settlers. The developers hired Chicago- and Kansas City-based advertising agencies to mount massive promotional campaigns. These firms bought full-page ads in newspapers across the country, distributed thousands of leaflets, dispatched armies of traveling recruiters, and organized chartered railroad excursions to the Valley. Taking advantage of discounted fares as low as $25 for a round trip between Chicago and Brownsville, thousands of prospective buyers from the Midwest and other sections of the country toured the border region, where local promoters bombarded them with hard-sell promises. According to these pitchmen, any farmer could expect to earn annual profits of $300 to $500 on each acre of land.

Eight years after the construction of the St. Louis, Brownsville, and Mexico Railway, fifty pumps were drawing water from the Rio Grande to irrigate almost 60,000 acres of land. By 1921, the figure would reach 204,000 acres. Cotton and truck farming, and later fruit production, forced the rapid retreat of ranching from the river front to the country beyond the reach of the irrigation ditches. In 1913, the Valley farmers exported over four thousand carloads of vegetables. Despite these impressive statistics, serious economic problems accompanied the agricultural boom. Many of the new land purchasers lacked farming experience. Deceptive salesmen had convinced a wide variety of businessmen, professionals, craftsmen, and well-to-do industrial workers that all they had to do to succeed as farmers was "to sit quietly down, watch the crops grow, and collect their money."[1] During their apprenticeships, these novices committed grievous errors that eliminated any chance of their making quick profits. Even competent farmers suffered from the chaotic marketing conditions. Destructive competition prevailed over all proposals to establish cooperatives to influence prices through the regulation of the supply of vegetables and cotton available for sale. At the peaks of the harvests, railroad depots overflowed with produce, and serious shortages of freight cars developed. In the absence of local packing plants, the farmers did not even have access to standardized containers for shipping and marketing their vegetables. Nor were the forces of nature as benign as the promoters had claimed. Periodic frosts and floods ravaged much of the Valley farmland.

As large numbers of farmers fell victim to these misfortunes, the whole financial underpinning of the agricultural boom threatened to collapse. Most of the land transactions were based on credit. The developers borrowed money to purchase the ranchland and to construct irrigation facilities, and the new settlers made down payments covering only a fifth to a third of the prices of their tracts. The reliance on advertising agencies aggravated the problem of mounting indebtedness, since they charged fees that ranged from $65 to $100 for each acre sold. The farmers, the developers, and the note-holders all acted on the optimistic assumption that sizable profits from the sale of vegetables and cotton would supply the cash necessary to make the system work. With this money, the farmers could complete the purchase of their properties and pay for the use of the irrigation water, while the developers could in turn satisfy their creditors. When the anticipated profits failed to materialize, the settlers fell behind in their payments, and the land companies skidded toward bankruptcy. In fact, only one major private irrigation project escaped eventual receivership. During the second decade of the twentieth century, many farmers took advantage of new legislation to organize public irrigation districts and to float bond issues to buy out the private companies and their creditors.

Despite these financial difficulties, the farming population of the Lower Rio Grande Valley grew. In addition, over a dozen towns took root along the St. Louis, Brownsville, and Mexico Railway and its branch line through Hidalgo County. The same developers who furnished the irrigated farmlands also designated the sites for the new communities and sold town lots. Between 1900 and 1910, the population of Cameron and Hidalgo counties soared from 22,900 to 41,900, a gain of 83 percent. By 1920, the population of the two counties approached 75,000, even with the loss of territory through the creation of Brooks, Willacy, and Kenedy counties. Continuing immigration from Mexico accounted for much of the increase, as impoverished laborers sought employment opportunities in the expanding Valley economy. After 1911, the ravages of revolution and civil war in Mexico provided additional incentive for the flight across the border. Although this influx enabled the Hispanic population to retain its solid majorities in Hidalgo and Cameron counties, the Anglo citizenry reached sizable proportions for the first time. The new settlers had the potential to tip the political balance in closely fought contests, and most of these farmers and businessmen displayed little tolerance of the manipulation of the Hispanic vote by the competing political organizations of South Texas.

Prejudices against Mexican Americans often accompanied this opposition to election abuses. Many of the Anglo settlers of the nineteenth century had adapted to the Hispanic culture that they encountered along the Rio Grande by socializing and intermarrying with the leading Hispanic families, assuming paternalistic responsibilities in their relations with the common laborers, learning Spanish, and joining the Catholic church. The newcomers who poured into the Valley after 1904 displayed no inclination to make a similar adjustment. The pervasive illiteracy and the inability of many Hispanics to understand English appalled the Anglos, who refused to learn Spanish. Class consciousness heightened their feelings of superiority. Most of the settlers were well-to-do businessmen, farmers, and professionals, and they attributed the widespread poverty of the region to a lack of industriousness and ambition on the part of the Hispanic laborers. While Anglos were willing to take advantage of the low wage level for agricultural workers, they usually refused to provide any kind of paternalistic assistance. Economic and educational differences alone did not account for the hostility of the Americans, however. Convinced of the superiority of their own values and life-style, many even declined to associate with the affluent Hispanic ranchers, farmers, and businessmen. Racially segregated schools and residential patterns emerged in the new Anglo-dominated towns of the Valley. For Mexican Americans, the price of acceptance by the newcomers was the abandonment of their culture and way of life.

Not even the growth of the Hispanic population in the Lower Rio Grande Valley assured the continued dominance of the Democratic party. Few of the recent immigrants found employment with the established ranchers, who delivered blocs of voters for the Wells machine. Instead, the bulk of the newcomers worked for the small farmers and the land developers. The political affiliations of these employers varied, and the farmers showed little inclination to manage the voting of their workers. Besides, the short-term nature of the seasonal work on the farms and the attitudes of the Anglos precluded the development of strong personal ties between the employers and the laborers. While most of the migrants from south of the Rio Grande simply abstained from any kind of political participation, a large body of free-lance voters emerged. These Hispanics cast their ballots for whichever side paid their poll taxes and offered additional inducements. The Democratic party still controlled hundreds of Hispanic voters, but the electoral clout of this bloc diminished in the face of the demographic changes that overtook the Valley after 1904.

The political repercussions of agricultural development did not deter James Wells and his allies from participating in the frenzied business activity that sustained the economic boom. The prospect of collecting huge profits overrode any reservations that they might have had about the changing character of South Texas society. Besides serving as the general counsel for the St. Louis, Brownsville, and Mexico Railway and promoting the establishment of public utilities for Brownsville, Wells plunged into land speculation. Between 1900 and 1918, the Rio Grande boss bought and sold over 150,000 acres. Rather than organizing irrigation projects, he simply sold unimproved grazing land to developers. Wells also provided legal services for three major irrigation companies, and invested in the Chapin Townsite Company, which owned the site for the new county seat of Hidalgo County.

Despite the steady escalation of land prices for more than a decade after the chartering of the St. Louis, Brownsville, and Mexico Railway, James Wells' financial ventures ended in failure. Like other Valley entrepreneurs, he operated on credit and never overcame the burden of mounting indebtedness. As the result of campaign expenses, forfeited loans to business and political associates, and his reckless indulgence in land speculation during the 1880s and 1890s, Wells owed more than $80,000 to a single finance company even before the start of the era of rapid economic growth. The returns from his initial land transactions after 1900 enabled Wells to reduce this debt, but he continued to borrow from other sources to finance new deals. To meet his obligations to his creditors, he constantly had to sell recently purchased land at marked-up prices. When the outbreak of Mexican border raids in 1915 and 1916 temporarily stymied the demand for Valley land, Wells' delicate balancing act collapsed. Unable to pay either his property taxes or the interest on his debts, he had to sell over 90,000 acres at a loss. Even with this massive liquidation, the debt remained, and the veteran politician struggled for the remainder of his life to avoid bankruptcy.

John Closner, the political boss of Hidalgo County, played an even more conspicuous role than Wells in promoting the economic transformation of the Lower Rio Grande Valley. For almost thirty years, Closner shaped the political and economic destiny of his county. A native of Wisconsin, he arrived in the Valley in 1883 after losing his job on a railroad construction project in Mexico. Almost penniless, he secured employment as a stagecoach driver and then accepted an appointment to serve as the deputy sheriff of Hidalgo County, where lawlessness and political turbulence prevailed. Disgruntled with the endless feuding among the local Democratic leaders that occasionally degenerated into armed confrontations, James Wells supported Closner's election as sheriff in 1890 and his subsequent establishment of a machine that brought relative stability to Hidalgo County politics. Closner also attempted to eradicate the rampant cattle rustling that plagued his constituents. This law-and-order campaign provoked the only serious opposition that the sheriff faced until the organization of the Good Government League in 1914. According to Closner, two rival Democrats, who associated with the criminal gangs of the county, plotted his assassination twice during the 1890s. When the murder attempts failed, these men persuaded the governor to order a Ranger investigation of Closner's mistreatment of prisoners. Although he avoided indictment and suspension from office, the Hidalgo boss confided to Wells that "I went a little too far to make the suspects confess."[2]

While consolidating his political power and building a reputation as a hardline enforcer of the law, John Closner also devoted his attention to amassing a personal fortune, and, in the process, he laid the foundation for the economic development of Hidalgo County. During the 1890s, Closner bought over 45,000 acres of pastureland at prices as low as 25¢ an acre. Dissatisfied with the money-making potential of ranching, he converted 200 acres into a farmsite and installed the first modern irrigation system in Hidalgo County. He experimented with the production of cotton, sugar cane, alfalfa, and a variety of vegetables. His farming operation gradually expanded until he was cultivating 500 acres of alfalfa and 400 acres of sugar cane. In addition to pioneering the use of irrigation along the Rio Grande, Closner also promoted railroad construction. When the ranchers of his county failed to comply with an agreement to donate 20,000 acres of right-of-way land to the St. Louis, Brownsville, and Mexico Railway, Closner and two other landowners personally guaranteed the fulfillment of the bonus accord and salvaged the plan to build an extension line through Hidalgo County.

Once the land boom erupted, John Closner collaborated with James Wells in selling large tracts of unimproved ranchland to the irrigation companies, but Closner's main interest was the organization of his own development project. In 1906, the Hidalgo sheriff and a county commissioner named William F. Sprague planned the construction of an eight-mile railroad line from the Hidalgo branch of the St. Louis, Brownsville, and Mexico Railway to a location near Sprague's 300,000 acre ranch. They formed a partnership with another landowner, D. B. Chapin, to organize the 1,400-acre townsite of Chapin, which would serve as the northern terminus of the new line. Closner and Sprague's scheme also involved the purchase of 50,000 acres surrounding Chapin, the conversion of that land into farmsites, and the establishment of an irrigation system. In addition, the two entrepreneurs launched a drive to secure land bonuses and right-of-way privileges for the extension of their railroad from Chapin to Falfurrias. An existing railroad connected Falfurrias and San Antonio. The ultimate goal of the South Texas promoters was the creation of a thriving town and farming community with rail ties to both Brownsville and San Antonio.

After more than a year of preparation, the grandiose project languished in a state of limbo. The construction of the irrigation system had not begun; the negotiations for the railroad concessions had stalled; and Chapin remained a barren pasture. In an effort to revive their business venture, John Closner, William Sprague, and D. B. Chapin resorted to a political power play. They circulated a petition calling for a special election to authorize the shift of the county seat from the town of Hidalgo along the Rio Grande to Chapin. This transfer would ensure the settlement of their townsite and attract financial support for their railroad and irrigation schemes. With both William Sprague and W. B. Chapin serving on the county commissioners' court, the board approved the election request.

John Closner and his colleagues were able to present legitimate reasons for the relocation of the seat of government. Lacking rail service and located at the southern edge of a county that was the size of Rhode Island, the town of Hidalgo was not readily accessible to a large segment of the population. Moreover, floodwater from the Rio Grande periodically swept through the town and threatened to destroy the courthouse with all its public records. Although few citizens objected to the removal of the county government from Hidalgo, the designation of an alternative site aroused controversy. In defense of Chapin, the Democratic politicos argued that a major railroad line linking Brownsville and San Antonio would eventually pass through the town. They also donated free of charge four blocks of land for the use of the county government and promised to arrange the construction of modern utilities. These projections and pledges failed to impress the spokesmen for Mercedes, Donna, and the other recently created towns of Hidalgo County. While these communities were growing and prospering, the town of Chapin did not even exist. By the date of the election, October 10, 1908, a single building stood on the townsite.

Despite widespread opposition to the proposed establishment of the county seat at Chapin, the Closner machine carried the election handily, 422 to 90. Most of the dissenters had not lived in Hidalgo County long enough to fulfill the residency requirements for voting. When the opponents of the transfer announced their intention to seek an injunction, the sheriff and his allies decided to take quick action. As soon as the commissioners' court certified the referendum results on the Monday morning following the Saturday election, the Democratic leaders ordered the loading of all the county records onto a dozen mule-drawn wagons. By midnight, the procession reached Chapin. Although county officials had to conduct their business in tents until the completion of a temporary courthouse a month later, they had succeeded in confronting their critics with a fait accompli and stymieing any effective legal action. On December 12, 1908, the Democratic ring arranged the passage of a bond issue to finance the construction of a $75,000 courthouse. Only 165 voters participated in the election.

Not even the relocation of the county seat produced the business bonanza that Closner and his partners had anticipated. In 1909, the town of Chapin secured its link with the St. Louis, Brownsville, and Mexico Railway, but the plan to extend the line to Falfurrias collapsed. In addition, law suits and shortages of capital delayed the completion of the irrigation project. By 1911, when the name of the town was changed from Chapin to Edinburg, its population stood at only 400. After 1915, with the irrigation system finally in operation, the community experienced rapid growth. By that time, however, Closner's development companies had accumulated too many debts to avoid bankruptcy. A county audit later indicated that the Hidalgo boss embezzled over $100,000 from the public treasury as his business losses mounted. With this revelation, the transformation of Closner's public image was complete. Having won acclaim as a staunch upholder of law and order and as a visionary pioneer who introduced irrigation to Hidalgo County, he now appeared as a wheeler dealer, who indulged in reckless financial manipulation, used political influence for private gain, and even resorted to theft.

The contribution of the Democratic leaders to the economic development of the Valley went beyond their participation in ambitious but ill-fated business ventures. James Wells and his cohorts also campaigned for state legislation to combat the serious legal problems that interfered with irrigation along the Rio Grande. As competition for the water of the Rio Grande developed, the Valley Democrats promoted a compromise definition of water rights that would satisfy the interests of both the riparian titleholders, who owned land within the boundaries of the large Spanish land grants that once fronted the river, and the nonriparian owners, whose properties were located north of the river grants. The result of these efforts was the Burges-Glasscock Water Rights Act of 1913. While confirming the superiority of riparian claims, the law ended the legal monopolies of riparian owners over the use of water in streams. Irrigators servicing nonriparian lands could appropriate water when the available supply exceeded the needs of the riparian users. The law also established an order of priority for the rights of competing nonriparian owners on a first-come, first-served basis. Unfortunately, later legislation and court decisions upset this equitable arrangement and revived the uncertainty over water rights.

The financial instability of the irrigation companies aroused additional agitation for legislative redress. As an increasing number of development corporations succumbed to bankruptcy, the truck and cotton farmers of the Valley turned to the establishment of public irrigation districts as their only recourse for ensuring continued irrigation service. Even before the start of large-scale irrigation along the Rio Grande, the Texas Legislature made the creation of drainage districts feasible with the passage of a constitutional amendment that relaxed the limitations on public debt. Without the power to float large bond issues, these public enterprises could not have mustered the capital necessary to purchase the existing facilities of the private firms, to expand the systems, to make improvements, or to start new projects. In April 1905, just four months after the ratification of the amendment, the legislature enacted a comprehensive set of regulations for the organization and operation of public irrigation districts. By a two-thirds vote, the property-owning taxpayers of any locality could create a district with the power to levy taxes, to issue bonds, to penalize violators of district regulations, and to exercise the right of eminent domain.

Although the Valley Democrats made no significant contributions to the formulation and passage of the initial district law, Wells and his associates subsequently emerged as vigorous campaigners for improvements in the legislation. Legal problems plagued the implementation of the act because the lawmakers had copied it verbatim from a California statute without making any allowances for discrepancies between the constitutional limitations of Texas and California. While occupying the chairmanship of the House committee on irrigation, two South Texas legislators oversaw the passage of complete revisions of the district legislation in 1913 and 1917. James Wells supported these moves, but he made his main contribution to the promotion of irrigation districts with the drafting of the 1917 state constitutional amendment that provided the districts with unlimited bonding capacity. Even the relaxed restrictions of the 1904 amendment had hindered the operation of these public corporations in the Valley. Wells also spearheaded the successful drive to win public ratification.

The benefits of the drainage districts for Wells' constituents were undeniable. In fact, by 1920 only four private irrigation companies still operated in Cameron and Hidalgo counties. In the face of mounting financial crises, the districts not only guaranteed the continuation of irrigation service for the farmers but also provided compensation for the debt-ridden promoters. Because the private development corporations were more interested in selling land than in operating efficient irrigation systems, the quality of service generally improved after the shifts from private to public enterprise. At the same time, however, the drainage districts were vulnerable to manipulation by corrupt politicians. Although no evidence of scandal marred the management of the Cameron County districts during the Progressive Era, the Closner machine of Hidalgo County siphoned away tens of thousands of dollars from irrigation district funds, which had been deposited in the county treasury.

In promoting the economic development of the Lower Rio Grande Valley, James Wells and his Democratic allies helped to lay the groundwork for the social and demographic changes that would reshape the political balance of power in the region. With the influx of Anglo settlers and the continuing immigration from Mexico, the opposition to the Wells machine revived after 1906. The first indication of a changing political climate was the organization and the limited success of the Independent party of Cameron County. A few years later, the Good Government League emerged as the first serious challenger to the Hidalgo County ring since John Closner had consolidated his power in the 1890s.

The initial opening for the Valley insurgents came in 1908 when factional feuding erupted inside the Cameron County Democratic organization for the first time since Emilio Forto's defection in 1900. Intense competition for the offices of sheriff, tax assessor, district clerk, and county attorney strained the cohesiveness of the party to the breaking point. Because of James Wells' involvement in a series of trials at Corpus Christi, most of the responsibility for maintaining unity fell on the shoulders of José Canales and James A. Browne. Canales had won Wells' confidence during his four years of service in the state legislature, while Browne had played a central role in party affairs for over thirty years. The two politicos labored diligently to arrange a compromise ticket, but their peace-keeping maneuvers met with only partial success. Although they were able to persuade some candidates to withdraw and others to accept alternative positions, the compromise slate, which Wells endorsed, still faced opposition in the primaries, and the defeated dissidents showed little inclination to return to the party fold.

The Republican chieftains were determined to exploit the rebelliousness within the Democratic party and to test the political disposition of the changing Valley electorate. After the nominees of the GOP convention agreed to withdraw from their races in favor of a "nonpartisan" ticket, Rentfro B. Creager, Emilio Forto, Assistant U.S. Attorney Noah Allen, and Ex-Customs Collector John Vann established the Independent party of Cameron County. Although all the leading organizers came from the Republican party, three of the ten candidates for county offices had competed earlier for the Democratic nominations. The strength of the Independent movement was concentrated in Brownsville. Most of its officers, candidates, and public speakers were Brownsville professionals and businessmen. A few sympathetic ranchers and developers from outside the county seat also played a key role in this opening assault against Democratic supremacy by delivering blocs of Hispanic voters. The racial composition of the new organization resembled that of the Wells machine. Anglos filled most of the leadership positions, but the bulk of the rank-and-file membership consisted of Mexican Americans, and four of the local candidates were Mexican Americans.

Despite this preponderance of Hispanics among the party faithful, the insurgent spokesmen fashioned their campaign rhetoric to appeal to the Anglo settlers from the Midwest and other parts of the United States. The platform of the Independent party condemned the Democratic regime for indulging in "machine methods, bossism, corruption, and graft" and promised instead "honest, efficient, economic, and wise business methods . . . in the administration of local matters."[3] This initial bid for Anglo support, however, had little impact on the outcome of the election.

For the 1908 contest, the county commissioners' court organized voting precincts for three of the new Anglo communities, San Benito, Harlingen, and Raymondville. The election officials at Raymondville failed to report the vote count, but the returns from the other two towns offered a rough measure of the newcomers' response to the campaign. The Independents carried Harlingen by a wide margin but lost San Benito. The combined vote of both precincts provided the challengers with a net advantage of only fifty-four votes. Before the election, both parties conceded that the insurgent movement held a slight edge in Raymondville. The most striking feature of these returns was the low level of voter participation. The citizens of Harlingen and San Benito cast fewer than 200 ballots, and Mexican Americans accounted for a share of that vote. While many newcomers had not lived in Cameron County long enough to meet the residency requirements, others undoubtedly declined to vote because of skepticism over the claims of the Independent party. Although these farmers were disturbed about political practices along the border, especially the manipulation of the Hispanic vote, they questioned whether the insurgent movement offered a viable alternative. Aside from campaign rhetoric, the strategies of the two contending parties were indistinguishable. Both sides paid the poll taxes of their Hispanic followers and supervised their voting. While the Democrats exploited the resources of the county administration and the Brownsville city government to advance their cause, the Independents relied upon the electioneering of the customs house personnel.

Despite the failure of the insurgents to mobilize a sizable Anglo turnout on their behalf, the election was still close. Throughout the campaign, shortages of funds and the defections of some disgruntled Democrats hampered the operation of the Wells machine. The Brownsville boss made repeated appeals to the state Democratic executive committee for financial support. He also called on John Garner and other popular political figures to make appearances in the Lower Rio Grande Valley. The Democratic party managed to carry all the countywide races but by margins of only 150 to 250 ballots. At the precinct level, the Independents claimed three victories, including a seat on the county commissioners' court. Even in defeat, the Independent movement emerged as a formidable challenger with the potential to broaden its base of support.

Although many Anglo voters rejected the campaign pitch of the Independents, the narrowness of the election confirmed the political importance of the growing Anglo population. In the future, neither party could afford to rely solely on the delivery of blocs of Hispanic voters since a unified Anglo vote could tip the balance of power. The Independent oratory of 1908, with its call for efficient, businesslike government, would set the pattern for both insurgent and Democratic rhetoric in upcoming contests. The party in power would also have to devote more attention to improving public services. These adjustments, however, did not alter the basic pattern of South Texas politics. While competing for the favor of the Anglo farmers and businessmen, the Independents and the Democrats could not ignore the Hispanic majority or the expectations of the party workers who organized that vote. The traditional tactics that offended the newcomers were still more critical to election success than the attraction of Anglo support. Despite the danger of an Anglo backlash, the two parties continued to appoint political cronies to public office, to require campaign contributions from government employees, to finance poll tax payments, to corral and bribe Hispanic voters, and occasionally to resort to election fraud and displays of armed force.

After receiving his appointment as the Brownsville customs collector, Rentfro B. Creager consolidated his control over the Independent party. Under his skillful direction, the insurgents scored a breakthrough in the Brownsville city election of 1910. The Independent party's bloc of controlled voters increased as a result of the customs officers' campaign to recruit supporters from the swelling population of Hispanic laborers who had recently crossed the border. The Independents also capitalized on growing discontent in the Brownsville business community. Although the Wells-controlled city administration had overseen the establishment of a water works, an electric power plant, and a telephone system, many businessmen complained about the repeated delays in the implementation of the program. Mayoral nominee Benjamin Kowalski and the other Independent candidates responded to these protests by emphasizing the need for immediate improvements in city services. Their platform called for the paving of streets, the construction of a network of sidewalks, the expansion and more efficient operation of the water and light utilities, the establishment of a streetcar system, a more liberal policy of granting franchises, and "the fair and equal readjustment of property valuations for taxation" to finance the improvements.[4] To counter this appeal, the incumbent Democratic mayor, Dr. Frederick Combe, expressed his support for a similar set of policies, but the ploy failed to prevent business defections to the insurgent cause.

Drawing on both business and Hispanic support, the Independent party swept the election. The only Democratic survivor was James A. Browne, who won the post of alderman for the fourth ward. In the general election of 1908, most of the insurgent nominees had trailed in the Brownsville returns by approximately 50 votes. With an increase of 38 percent in the voter turnout, the Independent contestants in the citywide races now won by margins ranging from 124 to 297 votes. This election marked the first local defeat for the Wells machine since its inception in the mid-1880s.

As the general election of 1910 approached, the Independent party appeared to be capable of winning control of the county government and breaking the power of the Democratic ring. The victory in the municipal election had strengthened the insurgent movement by more than doubling the number of patronage jobs at its disposal. Independent loyalists who received city employment were obligated to make campaign contributions and to join with customs officers in corralling Hispanic votes. Mayor Kowalski even converted the Brownsville police into a partisan force to counter any strong-arm tactics on the part of the opposition or, if necessary, to apply its own brand of coercion. The mayor also manipulated short-term job offerings to bolster the standing of his party. A few weeks before the November election, the city administration hired over one hundred laborers to work on street improvements. For the first time, the patronage resources of the challengers were nearly equal to those of the Democratic incumbents in county government.

As a proven winner, the Independent party enjoyed another advantage over past opposition movements. The new party was more attractive to Democrats who were dissatisfied with their opportunities for advancement within the Wells machine. After Creager established his dominance over the Cameron County insurgency,

Emilio Forto and his followers returned to the Democratic party, but two new recruits for the Independent camp more than compensated for this loss. In exchange for nominations to the two most powerful county offices, José Canales and an influential irrigation promoter named Lon C. Hill joined the Independent party in the summer of 1910. After loyally representing Wells' interests in the state legislature for two terms, Canales had embraced the cause of prohibition and voted for the submission of a constitutional amendment in 1909. The Brownsville boss was unwilling to support Canales for reelection to the legislature but offered him instead the post of superintendent of county schools. When Creager promised to arrange his nomination for county judge, Canales switched parties.

A graduate of the University of Texas law school, Lon Hill moved to Cameron County in 1901 and played a major role in the economic boom that followed. He campaigned for railroad construction, engaged in land speculation, organized his own irrigation company, and established two townsites. One of the towns was Harlingen, which would emerge as a leading commercial center of the Valley after 1920. With his base of operations at Harlingen, Hill aspired for political prominence but received no recognition from Wells, except for an appointment as a delegate to the state Democratic convention in 1908. When Creager invited Hill to run as the Independent candidate for sheriff in 1910, the ambitious developer demanded the nomination for county judge. Although he soon relented and accepted Creager's offer, Hill's defiant gesture antagonized many of his new political associates. During the ensuing campaign, Hill acted as the hatchet man for the Independent party. His scathing personal attacks against James Wells, whom he characterized as an "absolute dictator," injected extra venom into an already bitter political struggle.[5]

In the campaign for the November election of 1910, the spokesmen for the Independent party again posed as reformers, but they went beyond their general indictment of the Democratic incumbents for practicing machine politics and leveled a series of specific charges. For decades the local ring had filled teaching positions in the county schools with political hacks who were incompetent, sometimes even illiterate. As a result of this practice, "95 percent"[6] of the Mexican American population of the county could not speak or understand the English language. According to the Independent critics, the management of the county road system was also unsatisfactory. The Democratic administration had failed to build enough new roads for a rapidly expanding population, and existing roads were in disrepair. Favoritism and discrimination marred the assessment of county taxes. José Canales cited the example of a development corporation that had rendered the value of its property for tax purposes at $50 per acre, while it was selling lots for $150 per acre. When the board of equalization raised the tax valuation of the land by almost $100,000, James Wells intervened to persuade the board members to limit the increase to a token amount. Similarly, the district court officials failed to apply an evenhanded standard of justice. Lon Hill complained that a gang of cattle thieves, whom he had apprehended in the act of branding his cattle, never came to trial. In another case, Hill had requested District Attorney John Kleiber to arrange the arrest of a notorious rustler, whose term in the state prison was about to expire. Although several indictments were still pending against the man, Kleiber refused to take any action. When Hill asked for an explanation, a court officer informed him that "Jim Wells doesn't want the man brought back here."[7]

The most serious charges confronting the Democratic machine dealt with criminal abuses in the handling of county finances. The Independent campaigners cited the apparent theft of $38,000 from revenues that had been collected during the 1880s and 1890s to pay for the construction of the county courthouse and jail. They also reviewed the outcomes of several civil suits that Rentfro B. Creager had instituted in 1901 to force the collection of delinquent taxes totaling almost $30,000. Although some of the defendants had conceded in sworn testimony that they owed back taxes, they subsequently presented receipts for the payment of taxes, and the cases collapsed. Creager contended that county officials had colluded with these men in committing tax evasion, but the Democratic-controlled grand jury refused to investigate the matter.

The Democratic politicians, recognizing the importance of the Anglo vote, maneuvered to counter the impact of these Independent accusations. While conceding that some irregularities had occurred in the past, they argued that the recent county administrations had compiled an admirable record of public service. The superintendent of public schools pointed out that all the teachers presently employed in the county system held certificates that confirmed their professional qualifications. In defense of his road program, the county judge asserted that "the county now has several hundred miles of first-class roads," and he identified fourteen new roads that the county had built since 1907.[8]

Democratic spokesmen reserved their strongest praise for the management of county finances. In the view of Francis W. Seabury, even the Cameron County officials of the prerailroad era, who had come under attack for alleged corruption, deserved credit for waging a Herculean battle to maintain the solvency of the local government. The *Brownsville Daily Herald* offered the following summary of Seabury's argument:

> All these counties [along the Rio Grande] had . . . in years past labored, and some of them still labor, under a terrible handicap. With a large territory to police and many miles of roads to build, a population mainly Mexican and wretchedly poor as poverty goes these days, and small taxable values, they have had to shoulder not only their own burdens, but to stand as a bulwark for the whole state against the inroads of criminals and infectious diseases from Mexico. Small wonder that, with a tax rate limited by law, they were for years behind in their payments, and that their credit and their warrants were depreciated. . . .
>
> But Cameron County, thanks to all honest and economical government, had practically overcome these handicaps before the railroad reached here. [9]

According to an editorial in the *Herald*, the performance of the present incumbents was just as impressive since the county finances were "in perfect condition, with its warrants at par, its bonded debt small and being paid as it falls due."[10]

The Democrats failed to answer all the charges against them, including the possible theft of revenue for the courthouse bond issue, but they argued that the accusations were out of date. "Such charges as have been brought for the purpose of besmirching the Democratic cause related to acts alleged to have been committed twenty years or more ago," said the *Brownsville Daily Herald*, "some involving the names of men long since dead and which, even if they were proven to be true, could have no bearing whatever upon present conditions or the pending election."[11] The Democratic platform appeared to confirm this break with the past. The party asserted its commitment to "efficient and progressive government" and promised to build more schools and roads and to promote new irrigation districts "without raising the taxes or assessments and without burdening the people with unnecessary bond issues."[12]

Despite all this rhetoric about a new beginning for the Democratic party, one man stood as an undeniable link to the past—James B. Wells. Any successful rehabilitation of the party's image depended on a strong defense of the Rio Grande chieftain. His apologists described Wells as an unselfish politician who had used his influence to support causes that he believed in and to advance the careers of other men. According to the *Corpus Christi Caller,* Wells "seldom . . . asked a favor in return from any of the beneficiaries of his generosities."[13] In contrast, critics like José Canales, who had profited from the Democratic leader's past support, were portrayed as nothing more than political opportunists and ingrates. The party spokesmen coupled these character sketches with emphatic denials that Wells had ever committed any unlawful acts or improprieties.

Not only did the Democrats survive the Independent assault, but they also managed to take the offensive against their rivals in the competition for Anglo votes. Wells and his associates argued that the main "menace to free institutions and good government" came not from Democratic boss rule but instead from the monopolization of power by the Independent party that already controlled the customs house and the Brownsville city government. Such a "political oligarchy" would inevitably result in "graft, corruption, and oppression." As evidence that the Independent party posed a threat, the Democratic campaigners cited the policies of the city government of Brownsville. According to these partisan critics, the Kowalski administration had doubled the tax burden on the citizens without providing the improved public services that the Independents had promised during the municipal campaign. "In a riot of extravagance," the city officials had used the increased revenue to finance patronage jobs for their political supporters.[14] The mayor and the city council had even tried to arrange secret pay raises for themselves, but the exposure of the scheme by the *Brownsville Daily Herald* had forced them to abandon the "salary grab."[15] The Democrats also charged that Mayor Kowalski had abused his emergency powers by hiring at least eleven special policemen. Denying the existence of any real emergency, the Democrats claimed that the Independent party intended to use these policemen to intimidate voters.

In certain respects, the Democratic criticisms of Mayor Kowalski and his colleagues were unfair and hypocritical. Charges that the new city administration had failed to fulfill its campaign pledges were premature, since the Independents had held power for only a few months by the time of the fall contest. In addition, the Wells machine had set the precedents for manipulating public employment and the police department for political purposes. As part of his defense, Kowalski pointed out that only "a few years" ago "the citizens of Brownsville, in order to cast a vote, were compelled to pass between double files of City Policemen and Deputy Sheriffs armed with Winchester rifles or shot guns and pistols besides." In contrast to these blatant efforts to coerce voters, the mayor argued that he had ordered the enlargement of the police force to cope with the legitimate problem of "the increased number of minor disturbances of the peace and disorders incident to the nearness of an election."[16] Nevertheless, this exchange of charges and countercharges tarnished the reformist image of the Independent party.

In response to appeals from representatives of both parties, the state adjutant general and a force of twelve Texas Rangers traveled to Brownsville to observe the voting and to ensure the maintenance of order. With the approval of the adjutant general, the Democrats and Independents organized their Hispanic supporters into separate lines and allowed them to cast their ballots on an alternating basis. In the face of a record voter turnout, the Democrats swept the countywide contests by margins ranging from 130 to 217 votes, while the Independents gained control of the commissioners' court and elected several constables and justices of the peace. The Wells machine was able to weather the Independent onslaught by retaining the support of a majority of the Hispanic electorate and splitting the Anglo vote. In the three precincts where the Anglo settlers formed solid majorities, the Independents claimed only 53 percent of the vote. Two of the communities, San Benito and Raymondville, even favored the Democratic ticket. The voter turnout for Harlingen and San Benito was 2.5 times greater than the level of participation in 1908. The Democrats also derived satisfaction from the fact that eight of their fourteen local candidates carried Brownsville by a handful of votes.

Despite the Democratic victory, the campaign proved to be a physical ordeal for James Wells. Already suffering from overwork because of his multiplying legal and business commitments, the sixty-year-old politico stepped down from the chairmanship of the fifteenth congressional district, but he continued to manage the Democratic forces at the local level. During a visit to Corpus Christi in late October, he became ill and remained bedridden for several days. Against the advice of his physicians, he returned to Brownsville to resume his campaign activities, and the effect on his fragile health was devastating. In the aftermath of the election, Francis Seabury reported that "Mr. Wells is completely down and under advice of doctors has gone away to San Antonio, where he will remain for some weeks, possibly months, to build up his shattered health."[17]

Although the Democrats had won all the countywide races and had claimed a respectable share of the Anglo vote, they had not completely broken the momentum of the Independent party. In fact, the insurgents stood at the height of their power. Not only did the new party control federal patronage and the Brownsville city government, but it also participated in the administration of county affairs with its three-to-two majority on the commissioners' court. Before challenging the Independent movement in another election, the Democratic organizers wanted to undercut the strength of their rivals. To avoid a premature confrontation, the Wells machine agreed to a compromise ticket for the city alderman election of 1911, even though the arrangement left the Independents in control of the municipal government. At the same time, however, James Wells, who had recovered from his physical breakdown, directed an attack against Rentfro B. Creager, the Brownsville customs collector and the leader of the Independent party.

In March 1911, Lawrence H. Bates, a former Brownsville city marshal and a close associate of James Wells, leveled a series of formal charges against Rentfro B. Creager and demanded a Treasury Department investigation. Besides citing the obvious fact that Creager used the customs service to advance the cause of the Independent party, Bates accused the collector of allowing his employees to neglect their official duties, encouraging these men to intimidate voters, offering appointments to unqualified persons to win their political support, defending his henchmen against criminal charges in the local courts, and arousing so much "bitter feeling" in the fall campaign "that it was necessary for the Adjutant General of the State and three companies of State Rangers to be present to preserve order."[18] Bates also pointed out that four customs inspectors had run for public offices in Cameron and Starr counties. Creager acknowledged the candidacies of his subordinates but denied all the other charges. He claimed that his relation with the Independent party was "a strictly personal one" and that "the Customs force . . . has had absolutely nothing to do with politics."[19] According to the Brownsville collector, any politicking on the part of his employees was voluntary and unrelated to their jobs in the service.

Facing pressure from Senator Bailey and Congressman Garner, the Treasury Department dispatched special agent W. M. Rice to investigate the case. Although he had previously expressed sharp criticism of Creager's management of the Brownsville customs house, Rice presented a balanced report. The agent conceded that Creager headed the Independent party of Cameron County and that his officers participated in local politics. He discovered that customs employees had paid the poll taxes for over five hundred Mexican American voters. He also questioned the qualifications of some of the collector's appointees, especially a Mexican American inspector who could barely speak English. Nevertheless, Rice concluded that "all of the ordinary and routine customs work was duly performed, [and] furthermore, it appears that the kind and character of the political activity in which the customs employees indulged might have been carried on without the neglect of their duties." In addition, the investigator vouched for Creager's good character and the generally "clean" record of the Independent party.[20] The customs collector had not condoned the intimidation of voters, and he had not indulged in any inflamatory rhetoric that threatened to provoke violence or disorder. Nor did Creager devote his law practice to the protection of criminal associates. In fact, Rice characterized Creager as one of the most respected lawyers in South Texas.

Despite these words of praise for the collector, agent Rice emphasized the need to reform the political conduct of the Brownsville customs force. On the basis of Rice's evaluation, the Treasury Department instructed Creager to "refrain from undue political activity" and to enforce civil service regulations for all his employees, even those not occupying classified positions.[21] The Brownsville collector responded to the new guidelines by prohibiting his subordinates from paying the poll taxes for other citizens, delivering speeches, running as candidates for elective office, and serving as officers in party organizations. These adjustments, however, did not stifle the political activism of the Brownsville customs house. Creager continued to direct the campaigns of the Independent party and to rely on his officers for support. The men still paid assessments, supervised Hispanic voting, and attended insurgent rallies. When the local Democrats filed additional charges at the start of the 1912 municipal campaign, the secretary of the treasury ordered another investigation, but the department failed to take any punitive action against Creager.

Although the Democrats failed to neutralize the political power of the customs house, the Independent party still faced serious problems in its fight to retain control of the Brownsville city government in 1912. During the fall campaign of 1910, the Wells machine had focused its attack on the Kowalski administration. The charges of excessive taxation, attempted "salary grabs," patronage abuses, misuse of the police force, and unfulfilled campaign promises had had a telling effect on the Anglo voters, and the Democrats had claimed a slight edge in the Brownsville vote. During the remainder of their term, Mayor Kowalski and his colleagues compiled an impressive record: the enlargement and overhaul of the municipal water and light systems, the completion of a sewage plant, the construction of a new city hall and public market, the establishment of a streetcar system, the paving of twenty-five blocks of streets, the laying of fifteen miles of concrete sidewalks, the installation of a drainage pipeline for overflow water, and the purchase of new equipment for the fire department. Nevertheless, the Independent strategists were convinced that Benjamin Kowalski was still an unpopular figure and that his renomination would guarantee the defeat of the party ticket. In addition, personal animosity had developed between the mayor and some of Creager's close associates. Lacking a base of support inside the Independent organization, Benjamin Kowalski signaled his formal break with the party when he signed a petition condemning the interference of Creager and other federal officials in local politics.

In place of Benjamin Kowalski, the Independent party nominated A. B. Cole, the U.S. commissioner for Brownsville. The incumbent mayor, however, decided to run as an unaffiliated candidate. The Independents were now in the awkward position of claiming credit for the accomplishments of the Kowalski administration while campaigning against his bid for reelection. Adding to their discomfort, the mayor charged that he was the victim of boss manipulation. With the self-proclaimed reformers feuding among themselves, James Wells perceived an opportunity to secure a larger share of the Anglo vote. The Democrats raised the same issues that had attracted Anglo support two years earlier. The party platform called for reduced taxation, economy in government, improved public services, and the "reformation of police methods."[22] By 1912, this recitation of reform promises had become a standard feature of Democratic campaigning, but Wells' choice for mayor was still unexpected. Rather than turning to a reliable hack, such as former mayor Frederick Combe, the Cameron County boss arranged the nomination of Louis Cobolini, a relative newcomer to Brownsville and the widely respected owner of a commercial fishing fleet.

Although Cobolini had supported the local Democratic party in each election since his arrival in 1907 and had run as one of the compromise candidates for the board of aldermen in 1911, his ties with the Wells machine were limited. Indeed, his past political record reflected a strong dedication to political and social reform. Born in Trieste in 1845, Louis Cobolini had fought under Giuseppe Garibaldi for Italian unification. After immigrating to the United States and settling in Galveston, he championed the cause of labor unionism and worked for the election of James Hogg to the governorship. Cobolini also promoted the construction of harbor and channel improvements along the Texas coast. As the secretary for the Brownsville Chamber of Commerce and a member of the Brownsville Waterways Association, he lobbied for federal financing for a proposed deep-water port at Brazos de Santiago.

Despite his popularity in the business community, the selection of Louis Cobolini to head the Democratic ticket upset some of Wells' associates. Even Wells' oldest surviving son, Joseph K. Wells, who had begun to play an active role in local politics, expressed reservations. After trying to persuade the mayoral challenger to endorse a protest against the political agitation of federal officeholders, Joseph K. Wells offered the following appraisal of Cogolini's response and his potential as a candidate:

> I wanted to have Cobolini sign the wire but did not know whether he would or not, so I asked, feeling my way, if he did not think the federal officials were politically active. He answered yes. I asked him further if he did not think it should be stopped, and he replied, "Well, they ain't done nothing yet." I responded that they had had meetings, selected candidates, and were busily working right now. He could not deny it . . . but looked away, shifted off, and mumbled something about waiting a few days and "see what we are going to do." I'll tell you right now, Papa, he won't do.[23]

The Democratic standard-bearer refused to wage a hard-hitting campaign against his rivals. Cobolini denied that the Independent city officials had engaged in any graft and credited each of his fellow aldermen with "doing his best." According to a press report, he even assured one gathering of Democratic partisans that "by a change [in government], they would not lose any of the good that the present administration had achieved." His main complaint was the absence of "new ideas" and efficient business methods in the management of city affairs.[24] This low-keyed approach failed to produce a Democratic victory. With the city election machinery under the control of the Independent party, A. B. Cole defeated Louis Cobolini by four votes. Competing without any organized support, Benjamin Kowalski collected only 59 of the 1,400 votes cast. While the Democrats broke even in the four aldermen contests, the Independent party won all but one of the citywide races.

The struggle for control of city government did not end with the counting of the ballots. The Democrats accused the victors of committing election fraud and filed five legal suits to challenge the outcome of the contest. Once again the two parties had agreed to organize their Hispanic supporters into separate lines and to permit them to vote in pairs, consisting of one Democrat and one Independent, but the defeated candidates argued that the Independent election officials manipulated this process to the advantage of their party. In the fourth ward, where the Democrats had mobilized overwhelming majorities in recent elections, the presiding officer halted the voting whenever a representative of the Independent party challenged the qualifications of a Democratic voter. Although several hundred citizens were waiting outside the polling station, only seventeen had voted by noon. The state adjutant general took charge of the election in the fourth ward during the afternoon to expedite the voting, but scores of patient Democrats still failed to gain admittance before the polls closed. In other wards, armed policemen occasionally halted the proceedings to give the Independent organizers an opportunity to replenish their depleted lines so that their voters could keep pace with the Democrats. A court ruling shortly before the election had required the listing of the unaffiliated candidates and the nominees of the Independent party in the same "independent column" of the ballot because of the failure of the Independent nominating convention to meet all the requirements of the Terrell Election law. Nevertheless, when illiterate Hispanic voters indicated a preference for the "independent" candidates, the election officials usually failed to inquire whether they meant the unaffiliated candidates or the choices of the Independent party. The officers simply marked the ballots of these voters for A. B. Cole and the rest of the Independent ticket. Other voters scratched out only the Democratic column on the ballot, and the election supervisors counted their votes for both the unaffiliated and the Independent party candidates. The Democrats also charged their rivals with failing to provide enough voting booths, voting Mexican aliens, and intimidating voters despite the presence of the Texas Rangers.

The trial for these suits, which did not begin until late November, revealed transgressions on the part of the Democrats as well as the Independents. Wells' henchmen had used delaying tactics of their own in the Independent strongholds, and many of the Blue partisans were unqualified to vote. In fact, a court-supervised recount of the legal votes widened A. B. Cole's margin of victory. Nevertheless, the fraudulent character of the Independent management of the election was undeniable. In reviewing the case, District Judge W. B. Hopkins condemned not only the unilateral abuses on the part of the Independent officials but also the agreement between the two parties to form separate lines for their Mexican American followers. Such an arrangement undermined the whole concept of a secret ballot. Although the judge declared the election "illegal and void," A. B. Cole remained in office for a full term because of the length of the appeals process.[25] By the time the Texas Supreme Court finally upheld Hopkins' ruling in November 1914, another city election had taken place, and Cole's successor had assumed office.

The ethical standards of the Independent movement were no lower than those of the Democrats, but the reformist image of the

new party lay in shambles. This resort to election fraud reinforced
the worst suspicions of the Anglo newcomers. The overriding concern of the Independent and Democratic leaders alike was the acquisition of political power, and both sides were willing to stoop to
any tactic in their pursuit of that goal. During the interim between
the city election and the November trial, another feature of South
Texas politics, even more appalling than the corruption of elections,
resurfaced and provided further proof that a moral vacuum existed.
The bitter rivalries among the Democrats, the Independents, and
even the unaffiliated campaigners produced a revival of political
violence.

On April 12, 1912, only ten days after the election, a gunfight
erupted in a Brownsville saloon. Three municipal policemen shot
and seriously wounded Andres Uresti, who had campaigned as an
unaffiliated candidate for city marshal. When city marshal Joseph
Crixell of the Independent party appeared at the county jail to interview the victim of the shooting, the Democratic deputy sheriffs arrested Crixell and held him incommunicado for a whole day, despite
protests from city officials. After Crixell's release on bond, the grand
jury indicted the city marshal and five of his officers for conspiring
to commit murder. Another outburst of gunplay four months later
prevented the marshal's case from ever coming to trial. After com-
pleting his nightly patrol of the streets of Brownsville on August 9,
1912, Joseph Crixell dismounted his horse in front of his brother's
saloon. Deputy Sheriff Paul McAllister was seated just outside the
door. As Crixell approached, neither man exchanged a word. Then,
without warning, McAllister drew his pistol and shot the city marshal six times. Crixell died ten minutes later with his gun still in his
holster. To forestall any possibility of mob action, the Texas Rangers
transferred the murderer to the county jail at Corpus Christi early
the next morning.

This pattern of political violence reached a climax on the night
of November 10, 1912, when three Rangers, a deputy sheriff, and Andres Uresti arrested a former city policeman named Ignacio Trevino.
Trevino was under indictment for the shooting of Uresti, but he had
fled across the border in April after raping a fourteen-year-old girl.
He was also charged with the recent murder of one of Lon Hill's employees. After receiving a report that Trevino had returned to his
house in Brownsville, Uresti and the four law enforcement officers
overpowered the fugitive without firing a shot. As they were escort-
ing the gunman to jail in a buckboard, the men encountered three
Brownsville policemen. Shooting broke out, and one ranger and one
policeman were wounded. After the city patrolmen fled, the Rangers

completed the delivery of their prisoner and then returned with reinforcements to investigate the incident. They arrested the wounded
Brownsville policeman at his home only a short distance from the
scene of the gunfight. In the meantime, a doctor had examined the
patrolman and had dressed a minor wound in his arm. A subsequent
examination by the same pyhsician at the county jail, however, revealed a serious bullet wound through the chest. Before his death
four days later, the city policeman charged that either a Ranger or a
deputy sheriff or Uresti had shot him in the back while he was under
arrest. The grand jury investigated the whole affair but failed to hand
down any indictments.

The election scandals of 1912 and the outright warfare between
opposing law enforcement agencies produced cries of protest from
the Brownsville business community. Business leaders were not only
concerned about their own personal safety and the security of their
families but also fearful that the specter of rampant lawlessness
would discourage prospective settlers from moving to Brownsville
and the surrounding region. To remedy this crisis, they demanded
the insulation of city government from the bitter partisan strife that
plagued the county. The Independent party responded to this agitation by calling for the formation of a compromise ticket for the 1914
municipal election and proposing the establishment of commission
government for Brownsville. The Democrats had agreed to a joint
slate for the board of aldermen election of 1913, but Wells was preparing to wage another full-scale political battle in 1914.

The fortunes of the discredited Independent party revived when
a leading Democratic organizer and his brother agreed to join the bipartisan ticket. James A. Browne and Augustus A. Browne were the
sons of one of the co-founders of the Blue Club, James G. Browne.
James A. Browne was also the son-in-law of the original Cameron
County boss, Stephen Powers. For over thirty years, James A. Browne
had stood as a loyal ally to James B. Wells. After the defection of
Emilio Forto in 1900, Browne emerged as the second most powerful
politician in the Democratic machine. From 1884 through 1896, he
had held the office of county tax collector, and presently he represented his party on the Independent-dominated city council. A. A.
Browne's political background was more ambiguous. Under both
Democratic and Republican collectors from 1889 to 1910, he had
served as the chief clerk and a deputy collector for the Brownsville
customs force. Three years after his resignation from the service, he
won election to the Brownsville board of aldermen as one of the
Democratic choices on a compromise ticket. Business success as
well as politics and public service accounted for the influence and

the stature of the Browne brothers. James A. Browne was a rancher, bank president, and director of two local companies, while A. A. Browne managed his father's $2 million estate and operated a brick factory. By the terms of the pact with the Independent leaders, James A. Browne ran for reelection to the board of aldermen as a compromise candidate, and his brother accepted the mayoral nomination.

The endorsement of commission government was also an important feature of the Independent strategy. All the bipartisan candidates agreed to promote the formulation of a new city charter and to relinquish their offices in the event the citizens of Brownsville later voted for the establishment of the new form of government. Introduced at Galveston, Texas, in the aftermath of the devastating hurricane of 1900, the city commission soon became a symbol of progressive reform at the local level. This scheme was designed to incorporate efficient, business techniques into municipal administration, to centralize authority, and to eliminate partisan competition. Under the existing system of government at Brownsville, the voters elected a mayor, eight aldermen, who joined with the mayor to form a legislative body, and six administrative officers. The Galveston plan reduced the slate of elected officers to five commissioners, who assumed both legislative and executive responsibilities. Most commission charters required nonpartisan elections to minimize the influence of political machines and to encourage unaffiliated businessmen and professionals, with proven managerial skills, to run for the commission seats. Despite current dissatisfaction with the heavy-handed tactics of the two Cameron County political organizations, the leading business figures of Brownsville had always exerted considerable influence over the operation of city government. The real change for Brownsville would not be in the caliber of men exercising power but in the composition of the electorate. The elimination of competition between the Democratic and Independent parties would remove the mass of the Mexican American citizens from city politics. Without the party organizers to pay their poll taxes and to supervise their voting, the illiterate Hispanic laborers would not participate in municipal elections.

The willingness of the Independent party to sacrifice the controlled Hispanic vote in city elections reflected both the intensity of the businessmen's reaction against partisan excesses and the desperation of the insurgent movement. Only a commitment to reform the rules of political competition could revive Anglo confidence in the progressive claims of the Independent party. For the county elections, the Independents would continue to rely on the support of blocs of Hispanic votes. During the hard-fought municipal campaign of 1912, the Democrats had made a token endorsement of commission government in their bid for Anglo support. Yet now, with the emergence of charter reform as the central issue, the Wells machine refused to reaffirm its support for the proposal.

When A. A. Browne and James A. Browne consented to campaign as compromise candidates, they acted without consulting James B. Wells. The Cameron County boss denounced the bipartisan slate as a front for the Independent party and threatened to field a separate Democratic ticket. The solid opposition of the business community to the renewal of bitter partisan conflict forced Wells to retreat, however. Although the Blue Club did select a set of candidates, the mayoral and aldermen nominations duplicated the choices of the Browne-Independent coalition. Even the Democratic opposition to the six other compromise candidates represented little more than a token gesture of defiance. The Wells machine made only a half-hearted effort to mobilize its bloc of Hispanic supporters, and the compromise nominees won the contested races by margins of two to one. Independent control over the city government became complete later in the year when the Browne brothers formally severed their ties with the local Democratic organization, and James A. Browne assumed the chairmanship of the Independent party.

As mayor, A. A. Browne fulfilled his promise to arrange the restructuring of city government. At a special election in the fall of 1914, the voters of Brownsville selected a slate of Independent candidates to form a charter committee. Although they retained the label of "commission" government for their proposal, the drafting committee actually opted for the city-manager plan. By the terms of the scheme, the electorate would choose five unsalaried commissioners, who in turn would appoint a professional manager to take charge of the city departments. From their own ranks, the commissioners would name a mayor, whose only additional responsibility would be to preside over commission meetings. While the elected officials would perform the legislative function of passing ordinances, all executive authority would rest with the city manager. Like the commission form of government, this plan was designed to provide business-style efficiency, but it imposed an even greater degree of centralization. The charter also called for nonpartisan elections and scheduled the contests for the Decembers of the odd-numbered years between the general elections.

At the dawn of a new era in city politics, the Anglo and educated Hispanic citizens of Brownsville ratified the charter by a majority of ten to one and elected five commissioners. In the absence of any organized Hispanic voting, the turnout for the December 1915 election was only 256 voters, less than one-fifth the level of participation in the volatile municipal contests of 1910 and 1912. All the candidates ran unopposed, and three of the men, including A. A. Browne and R. B. Rentfro, Jr., were prominent figures in the Independent movement. Even after the demise of the Independent organization, veterans of the insurgency continued to dominate the Brownsville city government. A. A. Browne retained the post of mayor until 1919, and his successor, A. B. Cole, served for ten years. R. B. Rentfro, Jr., followed Cole and held the office from 1929 through 1939.

Despite their success in city politics, the Independents still failed to win control of the county government. The 1912 general election ended in disaster for the insurgent cause. The Democratic charges of election fraud in the earlier municipal contest and the criminal indictments against six Brownsville policemen for conspiracy to commit murder had crippled the Independent party even before the start of the full campaign, but the fatal blows came from unfavorable rulings in two other legal cases. One suit concerned the appointment of election officials and the designation of election precincts by the Cameron County commissioners' court, and the other involved irregularities in the conduct of the Independent primary conventions.

After gaining a three-to-two majority on the commissioners' court in the 1910 election, the Independents were determined to use the power of that governing body to advance their political cause. In February 1912, the Independent commissioners appointed election judges, whom the Democrats characterized as "notoriously and openly avowed partisans."[26] Six months later, the three-member majority renewed its offensive by gerrymandering the boundaries of the commissioner, justice of the peace, and election precincts, increasing the number of election precincts from fourteen to twenty-one, and naming additional election officers. Following the resignation of one of the Independent commissioners, the balance of power on the court shifted, and the Democrats proceeded to reverse the earlier Independent actions. With one member abstaining, the court voted two to one to reestablish the old election precincts and to select new election judges. The Independent candidates for local office were able to secure a temporary injunction against the delivery of election supplies to the county precincts until District Judge W. B. Hopkins could arrange a hearing to consider the legality of the Democratic countermoves. Just five days before the general election, Hopkins ruled that the commissioners' court had acted lawfully, and he withdrew the injunction. Now Democratic rather than Independent partisans would oversee the voting and the counting of the ballots.

During the same court term, the Democrats pressed for the removal of the names of the Independent candidates from the official ballot because the insurgent party had failed to conduct its precinct and county conventions on the legally designated dates. The insurgent lawyers argued that the Independent chairman, C. H. More, had made an honest mistake and had not acted with fraudulent intent. According to the election law, errors in the scheduling of a primary did not invalidate an election that was conducted with fairness and honesty. The attorneys also contended that the Democrats were not even eligible to bring suit since they had suffered no legal injury as a result of More's action. Finally, the defense pointed out that the plaintiffs had failed to meet the deadline for contesting the legality of a primary convention. Despite the persuasiveness of these arguments, Judge Hopkins ruled in favor of the Democrats. The nearness of the election precluded any possible redress from court appeals. With the elimination of the names of the Independent nominees from the ballot, the insurgent campaign collapsed, and the Wells machine swept the election virtually by default.

The Independent party survived the humiliation of the 1912 general election and even received a boost with the election of Woodrow Wilson to the presidency. In response to the agitation of Wilson activists at both the local and state levels, the new administration appointed an anti-Wells Democrat to the collectorship in 1913. The recruitment of the Browne brothers one year later appeared to signal a full recovery for the beleaguered insurgency. Nevertheless, the basic contradiction in the behavior of the party persisted and undermined its chances for success. While appealing for Anglo support with promises of reform, the Independent movement continued to engage in the manipulation of the Hispanic vote and other practices that alienated the Anglo constituents. The Cameron County Democrats projected a similar dual image after they adjusted to the Independent threat by espousing their own brand of progressive rhetoric, but the problem was never as critical for the dominant party. Since the Wells machine still controlled a majority of the Hispanic electorate, its objective in wooing the Anglo voters was limited. The Democratic organization simply needed to blur the distinctions between the two parties and claim a respectable minority of the newcomers' votes. The Independents, on the other hand, faced certain defeat unless they could rally the support of the whole Anglo community. Not even the Independent promotion of nonpartisan, city-manager government for Brownsville satisfied the Anglo skeptics countywide.

The massive influx of Anglo settlers also sparked the rise of an insurgency in Hidalgo County. In contrast to the Independent party, the Good Government League of Hidalgo County consisted almost exclusively of Anglo farmers, businessmen, and professionals. Although the Democratic machine had aroused the resentment of the newcomers as early as 1908 when John Closner arranged the transfer of the county seat to Chapin, a reform party did not emerge until 1914. The reason for the racial homogeneity of the movement and the delay in its formation was the absence of any established base of opposition to the Closner ring. There was no viable Republican organization or dissident Democratic faction, controlling a large bloc of voters, with whom the new residents could align. Not even the customs force posed a threat to the Democratic regime. While over twenty customs agents were available for campaign duty in Cameron County, only four men held customs posts in Hidalgo, and their political influence was minimal. Before the introduction of large-scale irrigation, Mexican Americans formed over 90 percent of the population. Most of the men worked as laborers on the large ranches and cast their votes in accordance with the political dictates of their employers. Closner maintained the nearly unanimous allegiance of both Anglo and Hispanic stockmen by holding down property taxes, waging a vigorous campaign against cattle rustling, and promoting the economic changes that caused land values to skyrocket. In addition, the ranchers viewed Closner's one-man domination of local government as an attractive alternative to the violent partisan strife that plagued the county throughout the 1880s. During the first decade of the twentieth century, James Wells in Cameron County and the Guerras in Starr County faced serious challenges, but Closner's local tickets usually ran unopposed, and the Democratic nominees for district and state offices claimed over 90 percent of the Hidalgo County vote in all but one election. Despite their suspicions of pervasive corruption in county government, the politically inexperienced newcomers hesitated to challenge such a formidable organization.

Because of their lack of influence over the Hispanic electorate of Hidalgo County, the insurgents were more consistant than their Cameron County counterparts in advocating the purification of local politics, but they were also woefully short of votes. Even as late as 1914, only seven hundred Anglo farmers had paid their poll taxes, while the Democratic machine was capable of mobilizing over twelve hundred Hispanic followers. The exclusion of Mexican Americans from the reform movement also resulted in political attacks with strong racial overtones. The critics of the Closner regime frequently combined their charges of corruption and misconduct with condemnations of the influence of Hispanic officials over county government, even though Mexican Americans occupied only one-fourth of the elective posts and only two countywide offices. This strident rhetoric reflected the prejudices that many of the newcomers held toward the Hispanic majority and fueled racial tensions that would reach the boiling point in 1915 when Mexican bandit raids along the Rio Grande resumed.

Despite their lack of voting strength, the disgruntled farmers and businessmen of Hidalgo County attempted to launch a political offensive in 1914 when dissension developed within the Closner camp. After County Judge James Edwards appealed for Anglo support by promising to combat graft and to provide "an honest and economical administration of Hidalgo County affairs," John Closner and his associates dropped Edwards from the party ticket. The Anglo settlers responded to this purge by rallying behind Edwards' candidacy and organizing the Good Government League. The incumbent county judge, however, proved to be an unreliable ally. His correspondence with James Wells revealed the double-dealings of a consummate opportunist. Edwards alternately threatened to lead a reformist crusade and appealed to Wells to use his influence to arrange a reconciliation with Closner. Asserting that the Anglos regarded him as their "Moses," he outlined a program of driving the Hispanic officials from power, eliminating the "professional, non-tax-paying, and alien voter," and exposing the "rottenness" in county government. He contended that local officers had stolen thousands of dollars from the public treasury over the last ten years. Undeterred by the contradictions in his claims, Edwards also posed as Closner's loyal friend, who had lost the boss' support only because of the lies of "character assassins" like former County Judge D. B. Chapin. The erratic Edwards argued that he had discouraged the formation of an opposition party and that he was trying to shield the "courthouse gang" from legal prosecution.[27] In his most cynical move, he offered to sell his business holdings, withdraw from the race, and leave the county for $15,000. The only consistent theme running through his letters was his contempt for Hispanic officeholders.

James Edwards' failure to make a definite commitment to run as the reform candidate for county judge undermined the campaign of the Good Government League. After organizing a series of rallies, the league withdrew its ticket for the July primaries and later failed to fulfill its promise to field a slate of candidates for the fall contest. Despite the humiliating collapse of its initial bid for power, the Good Government League emerged as a potent force in Hidalgo County politics. Over the next four years, the reform movement instituted a series of legal suits to force the disclosure of the financial operations of the county government. Ironically, one of the first victims of the investigation was former County Judge James Edwards. In 1915, the auditor for the league uncovered evidence that Edwards had misappropriated $20,000 from the sale of drainage district bonds. The even more sensational revelations about the misconduct of John Closner surfaced in 1918 and brought his political career to an end, although the machine that he had fashioned would survive for another twelve years.

The Anglo farmers and businessmen who settled in the Lower Rio Grande Valley after the introduction of large-scale irrigation perceived a strange and forbidding social scene. The composition of the population and the pervasiveness of the Hispanic culture disturbed these newcomers, and the ruthless tactics of the competing political parties heightened their uneasiness. By the middle of 1915, this distress over social and political conditions gave way to sheer horror. The dramatic escalation of the Mexican border raids, which claimed over thirty Anglo lives and converted the region into a combat zone, brought the migration into the Valley to a halt and even forced thousands of families to abandon their farms and businesses. This crisis, however, only temporarily disrupted the development of Cameron and Hidalgo counties. Toward the end of the decade, massive settlement resumed. With the return of boom conditions, the campaigns against boss rule took on new force. The bandit pillaging and the Anglo resort to vigilante retaliation had intensified racial animosities, and the Anglo settlers were more determined than ever to overturn the domination of political organizations that relied on the manipulation of the Hispanic vote. Despite their skills as partisan operators, James Wells and John Closner could not escape the political consequences of the demographic revolution that they had helped to promote.

    After 1910, another political boss, Archer Parr of Duval County, also faced a serious insurgent challenge. Unlike Wells and Closner, Parr was not fighting a rearguard action to prolong the life of a faltering political organization. He was laying the foundation for a machine that would dominate the political, social, and economic affairs of his county until 1975.

9. Archie Parr and Duval County

AS JAMES WELLS STRUGGLED to maintain his control over Cameron County politics at the end of the first decade of the twentieth century, the most enduring of all the South Texas machines took shape in Duval County. Located north of Starr County and west of Nueces County, the region remained undeveloped and sparsely populated until the 1870s as the result of recurrent Indian raids. Although the Texas Legislature authorized the creation of Duval County in 1858, the local residents failed to organize a county government for another eighteen years. With the stationing of U.S. troops at San Diego, which became the county seat in 1876, and with the extension of a railroad from Corpus Christi to San Diego in 1879, American- and European-born stock raisers invaded the county to take advantage of the rich grasslands. By the early 1880s, Duval County had emerged as one of the leading sheep-producing areas of the state. The sheep boom collapsed in the mid-1880s because of falling wool prices and an epidemic that ravaged the flocks, but not even this setback stymied the growth of the county. Cattlemen replaced the sheepherders, and commerce prospered with the completion of the railroad line to Laredo. The discovery of oil at the Piedras Pintas field in 1903 offered the promise of further development, but large-scale production did not begin until the 1920s.

Between 1870 and 1900, the population of Duval County rose from 1,083 to 8,483. Although the Anglo-Americans and Europeans established their economic dominance with the acquisition of vast stretches of land, possibly as many as three hundred Hispanic families retained their ranches and farms. In addition, the Mexican Americans, most of whom worked as laborers on the ranches and in the few towns of the county, still formed over 90 percent of the population by 1900. During the nineteenth century, the only concentration of non-Hispanics existed at San Diego, where Anglos and migrants from Britain, Ireland, France, Spain, and Germany operated most of the local businesses. Even with an influx of Anglo farmers into the western section of the county after 1900, the overwhelming Hispanic majority remained intact.

Conforming to the pervasive South Texas pattern, Duval ranchers and businessmen managed the voting of their Hispanic laborers. Nevertheless, instability characterized the politics of the county from the mid-1880s through the first few years of the new century. Political power brokers regularly switched party affiliations, and a sizable body of Hispanic stockmen, farmers, and artisans remained independent of employer control. Personal loyalties and even bribery might still determine how they cast their ballots, but they did not necessarily vote consistently for the same party. Racial antagonism also complicated local politics. Unlike their counterparts closer to the Rio Grande, many of the American and European settlers in Duval County shunned the Hispanic culture and refused to assume paternalistic responsibilities for their workers. The lynchings of those charged with rustling and Hispanic resentment over the loss of land heightened tensions. Missing an opportunity to alleviate Hispanic disgruntlement, the Anglo politicians, who dominated both the Democratic and Republican organizations, allotted the Mexican Americans only token representation in county government. Before 1898, Hispanics occupied only three county wide offices: assessor of taxes for four terms, inspector of hides for two terms, and county judge for one term. Only once, in 1892, did they hold more than one seat on the five-man commissioners' court. In 1888, a veteran politician reported "how intensely bitter the feeling has been against the Gringo's."[1] This kind of ill will had no serious political consequences in the nineteenth century, but it laid the foundation for future political alignments.

For almost a quarter of a century, James O. Luby was the most influential figure in Duval County politics. An immigrant from England, who had served in the Confederate Army, Luby settled in Duval County after the Civil War and worked as a rancher, a lawyer, and a postmaster. Running as a Democrat, he became the first Duval County judge in 1876. When President Chester Alan Arthur appointed him collector of customs at Brownsville in 1884, Luby scrapped his ties with the Democratic party and took charge of R. B. Rentfro's congressional campaign. The collector's efforts to revitalize the GOP in South Texas through the distribution of federal patronage came to an abrupt end with the election of Grover Cleveland to the presidency, but Luby's political career revived when he returned to Duval County in 1885.

The fact that the Duval Democrats had swept every election except one since the organization of the county did not deter James O. Luby from pursuing his political ambitions. At the county convention of 1886, he engineered a split in the Democratic party. The bolters nominated Luby as their candidate for county judge, and he won the election with the support of both Republicans and maverick Democrats. Although he held the judgeship for only one term, his makeshift coalition transformed the once anemic GOP of Duval County. For the next eighteen years, the Republican party, or La Bota, fought the Democratic organization, or El Guarache, to a draw. The Duval Republicans not only captured a respectable share of the local offices but also carried the county for their congressional candidates in every election from 1892 through 1904.

Conflicting personal ambitions, and little else, accounted for the political battles in Duval County. Both sides favored low taxation and the promotion of schemes like railroad construction that would stimulate development. Nor did racial and class differences separate the two parties. Although the business community of San Diego provided solid backing for the GOP, the Republicans and Democrats alike drew their leadership from the successful Anglo-American and European ranchers, merchants, and professional men. By the turn of the century, both parties had made concessions to the well-to-do Hispanic families, who claimed three or more major county offices in each election from 1900 through 1906. Only with the emergence of Archer Parr as the Democratic boss of Duval County after 1907 did the character of the partisan strife change. Democratic dominance replaced the long-standing stalemate, and conflicts over race and government policies came to the forefront.

Archer (Archie) Parr was born on December 25, 1860, on Matagorda Island along the Texas Gulf coast. Because of the death of his father shortly after his birth, Archie Parr had to drop out of school and become a wage earner when he was only eleven years old to help support his mother and sister. He worked as a ranch hand for the Coleman-Fulton Pasture Company in San Patricio County and drove cattle along the Chisum Trail to Kansas. By the time he arrived in Duval County in 1882, he had seven years of experience as a cowboy. After a brief stint as foreman of a Duval ranch, Parr purchased his own tract of land and settled in Benavides. In 1891, he married Elizabeth Allen, and they eventually had six children, including George, the heir to the political empire that Archie Parr would forge after 1900.

Despite his generally even temperament and friendly manner, occasional outbursts of rage and arrogance became a Parr trademark. These displays of temper startled friends and enemies alike and revealed the intensity of a man who resorted to any means to gain and hold political power. The types of abuses that Archie Parr engaged in were no different from the practices of the other South Texas power brokers, but the Duval Democrat exhibited no sense of restraint, whether he was rigging an election, gerrymandering a new county, or stealing money from the county treasury. During the second decade of the twentieth century, progressives across the state came to regard Parr as the symbol of the worst qualities in Texas politics: corruption, violence, and intransigent opposition to reform.

Archie Parr's notorious political career had its beginning in Benavides. Located fifteen miles southwest of San Diego along the railroad connecting Corpus Christi and Laredo, the town emerged as the second-leading trading center for the ranchers and farmers of the county. Unlike San Diego, its population consisted almost entirely of Mexican Americans. Parr adapted to this Hispanic community by learning the Spanish language and acting as the *patrón* who looked after the special needs of his workers. When the former cowboy decided to enter politics, the local constituency rallied to his cause. For the Hispanic electorate, Parr was an ideal spokesman. As an Anglo, he won immediate acceptance from the Democratic chieftains and faced little resistance as he broadened his influence within the county organization. Yet, in contrast to most other Anglo politicians, he professed concern for the welfare of the Hispanic laborers and small-time farmers and stockmen. Parr offered more than coercion as an incentive for supporting his campaigns. In 1898 and 1900, he won election to the county commissioners' court, and he retained Benavides as his power base after he stepped down from the court in 1903. Parr's opportunity to take charge of the politics of the whole county came in 1907 with the assassination of the acknowledged leader of the Duval County Democratic party, John Cleary.

A land speculator, rancher, and oil promoter, John Cleary had served as the county tax assessor since 1900. Under his direction, the Democrats opened their party machinery to fuller Hispanic participation and welcomed Hispanic candidates for public office. This concerted appeal for Hispanic support paid off in 1906 with a sweep of the general election. El Guarache claimed every countywide office and all four commissioner seats and even prevailed in the congressional race for the first time since 1894. Charging that the Democrats had violated the new Terrell Election Law, embittered Republicans filed a legal suit to contest the elections of Cleary and three other officials, but to no avail.

On December 20, 1907, only a few days after the district court upheld the Democratic victories, a gunman shotgunned John Cleary in a San Diego restaurant. The local lawmen failed to take any action for over an hour because of their participation in a fiesta, and the assassin easily escaped. The officers claimed that fireworks and the noise of the celebrants had drowned out the sound of the shot and the commotion that followed the murder. After their arrival in San Diego the next morning, Rangers J. D. Dunaway and Sam McKenzie took charge of the investigation, and, in early April, they arrested three suspects: T. J. Lawson, a merchant; his son Jeff; and Candelario Saenz, a former deputy sheriff whom the Rangers accused of firing the fatal shot. The alleged involvement of the Lawsons in a conspiracy to murder Cleary did not resolve the question of whether or not the crime stemmed from the political strife that plagued the county. Although the Lawson family was affiliated with the Republican party, T. J. Lawson had also become embroiled in a dispute with Cleary over control of the Piedras Pintas oil field. Thus, even if the Lawsons were guilty, the motive for the killing remained clouded. In addition, the evidence against T. J. and Jeff Lawson was circumstantial, and the grand jury dismissed the charges against the two men and indicted only Candelario Saenz. Before Saenz' case could come to trial, two witnesses died of natural causes, and the last defendant went free. Ironically, four years later, a group of political insurgents killed Saenz in a gunfight while he was serving as a deputy constable for the regular Democratic organization.

Despite their subsequent release, the arrest of the Lawsons provided the Democrats with an opportunity to accuse the local Republicans of complicity in Cleary's murder. The GOP spokesmen responded by charging Rangers Dunaway and McKenzie with harassment and "the scandalous abuse and excess of authority."[2] The two sides sent competing petitions and letters to the governor and the adjutant general. While one set of correspondence praised the Rangers and called for the stationing of a Ranger force at San Diego, the other demanded an investigation of the lawmen's conduct. The Republicans even recruited the Democratic lieutenant governor of the state, A. B. Davidson, who was personal friend of T. J. Lawson, to press for the firing of Dunaway and McKenzie. As the controversy escalated, the Rangers revealed their suspicions about Republican responsibility for the killing. In a letter to Adjutant General J. O. Newton, Captain Tom Ross, the commander of the Ranger company for southeast Texas, argued that six of the local Ranger critics were "morally guilty of the John D. Cleary murder" and that most of the others were "relatives or sympathizers with the guilty parties."[3] When the adjutant general conducted his own investigation of the Rangers' actions, the Duval County Republicans retreated and ac cused Dunaway and McKenzie of nothing more serious than "toying" with their pistols as they questioned citizens.[4] Although the two officers remained in the service, Newton ordered Captain Ross to remove them from the Cleary case. No further arrests followed despite the investigators' belief that a conspiracy lay behind the murder.

Irrespective of who engineered the assassination of John Cleary, one man benefited more than anyone else—Archie Parr. After the elimination of Cleary, Parr took command of the Democratic machinery and established himself as the boss of Duval County. The key to his success was the Hispanic vote, which he controlled through a combination of paternalism, corruption, and coercion. In 1908, the Benavides rancher reclaimed his seat on the commissioners' court and arranged the conversion of the county treasury into a political slush fund. The county government provided short-term work for unemployed laborers on road and bridge projects, and the road supervisors deducted poll tax payments from the wages. Parr and his associates also financed poll taxes with their own money. To provide additional assistance for his constituents, the Duval politician resorted to a simple expedient. In violation of the state law, he issued orders to the county treasurer to make payments to individuals without specifying any services that the recipients had performed for the county. These informal welfare functions enabled Parr to broaden the base of Hispanic support beyond the blocs of voters that allied ranchers delivered and to reduce the Republican opposition to a permanent minority, despite its own controlled vote. The new political order even survived the defection of several influential Democrats, who objected to Parr's embrace of the Hispanic population and his indulgence in wholesale graft.

Not satisfied with increasing the Democratic vote, Archie Parr also maneuvered to limit the participation of his rivals and their followers in the political process. The tax collector sometimes refused to accept poll tax payments from Republican and Democratic spokesmen who agitated against the Parr machine. To prevent pockets of opposition at the precinct level from influencing the selection of Democratic party officials, the Duval County boss simply eliminated the precinct conventions and appointed his own men to serve as precinct chairmen and as members of the county executive committee. The stationing of armed guards at the polling places to intimidate citizens, the distribution of marked ballots to illiterate voters, and the occasional tampering with the returns completed the corruption of the election process.

Despite the thoroughness of his tactics, Archie Parr still faced challenges to his authority. In 1912, a rebellion developed within the Democratic organization. The county Democratic chairman, C. M. Robinson, tried to wrest control of the party machinery from Parr, and the ensuing struggle provoked a gunfight, led to a credentials contest at the state convention, and ended with the legal intervention of the district judge to restore the legitimacy of Parr's power. After winning the party chairmanship in 1910 as Parr's choice, Robinson recognized that the boss' illegal methods were a source of vulnerability as well as strength. When the former county chairman and the party secretary confirmed that no precinct chairmen had been elected in 1910, Robinson wrote the Texas attorney general to find out what course of action could be taken to correct the irregularity. On the adivce of the attorney general, the county chairman appointed his own precinct chairmen, who also formed the county executive committee for the Democratic party, and he scheduled precinct conventions in preparation for the county convention that would send delegates to the first state convention of 1912. Parr, in the meantime, picked his own county executive committee. To justify this move, he made the false claim that these men had won election as precinct chairmen two years earlier. When Robinson refused to join the Parr committee, the group chose Parr's brother-in-law, O. G. Allen, to serve as county chairman. The two Democratic factions organized separate conventions and selected competing delegations to attend the state convention that would name delegates to the national convention.

Less than two weeks before the delegations departed for the state convention at Houston, violence again erupted on the Duval political scene. Archie Parr had arranged an election for May 18, 1912, to authorize the incorporation of San Diego. The independent Democrats and the Republicans opposed the move because they realized that Parr would use the proposed city government as another source of revenue and patronage. Despite the concentration of Anglo-American and European-born citizens at San Diego, the Democratic boss' bloc of Hispanic voters could probably carry the city elections. On the morning of the referendum, C. M. Robinson, his brother, and two political cronies encountered three Hispanic county officials, including Candelario Saenz. C. M. Robinson and Deputy Sheriff Antonio Anguiano exchanged angry words, shooting followed, and all three Hispanics were killed. Before the bloodshed could spread, the sheriff of the newly created county of Jim Wells intervened, arrested three of the Anglos for murder, and transferred them to Corpus

Christi, where they went free on bond. The sheriff did not take C. M. Robinson into custody because he had not been armed during the fight.

The Parr camp claimed that the insurgents had provoked the gunplay in an effort to discourage the Hispanic voters from going to the polls. If this was the aim of Robinson and his allies, the ploy was successful. Only two hundred people participated in the election, and the incorporation proposal failed by a two-to-one margin. The Robinson supporters, on the other hand, argued that the three Hispanic officials had tried to murder their leader, and that his companions had acted in self-defense. In reality, however, neither side appeared to be prepared for the gunfight. After all, Robinson was unarmed when the shooting broke out, and Archie Parr was so shaken by the news of the bloodbath that he escorted his family to the safety of Corpus Christi before returning to counsel his Hispanic supporters to abstain from further violence. After several postponements and a change of venue to Richmond, Texas, the three Anglo gunmen came to trial in April 1914, and all won acquittals. The killings intensified the racial tensions within the county and solidified Parr's position as the spokesman for the Hispanic population. Although Hispanics and Anglos participated in both parties, the politicians and the public alike came to perceive the Democrats as the representatives of the Hispanic majority and the Republicans as the representatives of the Anglo-American and European minority.

In the aftermath of the gunfight, the contest at the state convention was almost anticlimactic, but the maverick Democrats won an important victory. After the state executive committee, on which Archie Parr served, recommended the seating of the Parr delegation, C. M. Robinson appealed to the credentials committee of the convention. With the reform-minded supporters of Woodrow Wilson in command, the committee and later the convention as a whole voted to recognize the insurgent representatives. Although both the Parr and Robinson factions supported Governor Judson Harmon of Ohio for president, the Texas Wilsonites regarded the Duval County machine as the antithesis of the progressive movement. In their view, Parr and the other South Texas bosses were arch corruptionists who pandered to an alien constituency at the expense of decent American citizens.

To counter this blow to the legitimacy of his political organization, Archie Parr turned to an ally outside Duval County, District Judge W. B. Hopkins of Corpus Christi. In response to a suit by O. G. Allen and the other members of the Parr executive committee, the judge issued an injunction on June 17, 1912, prohibiting C. M. Robinson from serving as the county chairman. When Robinson filed an application for a hearing to consider rescinding the injunction, Hopkins scheduled the proceedings for late October. This delay assured Parr's control of the July primaries and the selection of new party officials for the next two years.

With the restoration of Parr's full authority over the Democratic machinery in June, the insurgents' only recourse was to organize an independent slate for the general election, but the Duval county judge refused to include the names of the Robinson candidates on the official ballot. In their place, Parr arranged for the listing of a bogus opposition ticket that consisted of his own men. In the November election, the regular Parr ticket crushed his "independent" candidates as well as the Republicans. Despite the rigged character of the contest, a complication did arise. The election officials at Benavides became confused and reversed the totals for Parr and the Republican nominee for the county commissioners' court. When the officers failed to correct the mistake that threatened Parr's reelection, the Duval County boss altered the figures on the official tally sheet. This act technically qualified as election fraud and provided the grounds for a later state indictment against Parr.

After the collapse of the Robinson rebellion of 1912, Archie Parr's control over the Democratic party of Duval County became absolute. For the remainder of the decade, no county or party official dared to challenge his power. Even the Republicans and the independent Democrats outside the regular party organization abstained from running opposition tickets in the local races. This disappearance of election politicking, however, did not signal the total submission of Parr's opponents. Instead, the partisan struggle continued on two other fronts: the Texas Legislature and the courts. In these arenas, two issues dominated the public debate: the creation of new counties, both to provide refuge from Parr's domination and to extend his authority, and charges of corruption against Parr and other Duval County officials. As the legal and legislative battles raged, Ed C. Lasater emerged as Parr's leading antagonist. Since Lasater's ranching and farming empire extended into Duval County, his scheme to organize his own county aroused opposition from Archie Parr as well as the Guerra family of Starr County. Once Lasater secured the separation of his land from Starr County, he funneled his resources into the campaign for honest government in Duval County. Although the wealthy rancher scored several legal and legislative victories, Parr's grip on local politics remained as firm as ever.

Ed C. Lasater first proposed the establishment of Falfurrias

County, which would claim territory from Starr, Duval, Hidalgo, and Nueces counties, in 1907 after his failure to overturn the Guerra machine in the violent Starr County campaign of 1906. In defense of his proposal, Lasater emphasized the remoteness of Falfurrias from the county seat of Starr County and the desire of the Anglo residents for relief from boss domination. Although Lasater posed a real threat to the political order of Starr County and a potential one for Duval County, the regular Democrats of the two counties resisted his plan to organize a separate county. Both the prospect of an independent power base for the Republican party in South Texas and the loss of tax revenue from the farming and stock raising enterprises that Lasater promoted alarmed these politicians. As long as Archie Parr and the Guerra family remained united in their opposition, the proposal had little chance of passage in the Texas Legislature.

In 1911, however, Manuel Guerra withdrew his opposition to the scheme in order to prevent the formation of a coalition between Lasater's independent movement and a dissident wing of the Starr County Democratic party. Although the latest version of the Falfurrias County bill claimed land from only Hidalgo and Starr counties, not Duval County, Archie Parr was still dissatisfied because of the prospect of a Republican bastion next to his county. Yet, left alone to carry on the fight, Parr recognized the weakness of his position and offered Lasater a compromise. If the Falfurrias rancher would agree to limit his political activities to the new county, Parr would support the measure. Lasater rejected the proposition, but the bill passed anyway. Without the cooperation of James Wells and other Rio Grande power brokers, the Duval boss could not dictate legislative action on regional matters. Only one South Texas legislator opposed the measure, and his proposal to reshape the county to guarantee a Democratic majority failed. As a tribute to Representative J. A. Brooks, who had lobbied for the legislation for five years, his colleagues in the House renamed the county Brooks County. The same legislature also sanctioned the conversion of the western part of Nueces County into Jim Wells County and the conversion of the northern half of Cameron County into Willacy County.

The creation of Brooks County had a mixed effect on Parr's political fortunes. The ease with which the bill passed through the legislature not only revealed the limits of Parr's influence but also demonstrated how he could enlarge his power base. He perceived an opportunity to double the patronage at his disposal and to secure additional revenue by dividing Duval County. The new county would occupy the southern half of Duval County, and Parr's home town of Benavides would serve as its seat of government. In January 1913,

Representative Pat Dunn of Corpus Christi introduced the bill calling for the creation of Ross County, but the measure died when the House Committee on Counties submitted an unfavorable report. At the legislative hearing, a group of irate taxpayers exposed the proposal as a power grab on the part of the local machine. Undeterred, the Duval County chieftain persuaded Governor Oscar Colquitt, whom Parr had vigorously supported in two elections, to submit the question of creating new counties to the first special session of the thirty-third legislature. This action caught Lasater and his allies unprepared, and before they could resume their lobbying offensive, the bill swept through both houses in just one week. As the result of a House amendment, this new county also received the name of its sponsor, Pat Dunn.

During the earlier regular session of 1913, Ed C. Lasater suffered another setback. A wealthy rancher named W. W. Jones, who owned much of the land in the western half of Brooks County, lobbied for the separation of his domain from the Lasater-controlled county. Ironically, Jones' power play benefited from the protests of a group of Brooks County residents, who charged that Lasater dominated the politics of his county through the management of the Mexican American vote. According to these dissidents, the Falfurrias promoter had purchased hundreds of poll taxes for his Hispanic constituents. Both Parr and Lasater proved to be adept at adopting each other's tactics, but Lasater's experiment in boss rule resulted in the division of his county. In a heated debate in the House, the proponents of the bill to create Jim Hogg County used virtually the same arguments that the Lasater forces had advanced two years before in their advocacy of Brooks County. One representative, who recognized the cynical calculations that underlay this rhetoric, objected to the association of "the grand name of Jim Hogg" with any of the South Texas fiefdoms and suggested "Huerta or Díaz" as alternatives.[5] The rest of the legislators were unmoved, and the bill passed both houses with its name intact.

The struggle over the creation of new counties did not end with the 1913 legislative sessions. Archie Parr's lack of political restraint provided Lasater and his allies with a legal opening to challenge the organization of Dunn County. The Dunn County law empowered the Duval County commissioners' court to divide the new county into election and administrative precincts, to designate polling places, and to schedule an election for the purpose of choosing county officers and determining the location of the county seat. Parr took advantage of this authority to gerrymander the precinct boundaries shamelessly. While one county commissioner's precinct contained 550 qualified voters, the other three precincts combined contained only 140 voters, one as few as 20 voters. With a total electorate of 690 voters, a minority of 73 voters could elect three of the four county court commissioners. To ensure the selection of Benavides as the county seat in its competition with Realitos, the headquarters for Lasater's ranching interests in Dunn County, the Duval commissioners deprived Realitos of a voting box. The residents of Realitos would have to travel fifteen miles to Benavides to cast their ballots. The citizens of the town of Concepcion suffered an even worse fate. A precinct boundary split the community, forcing part of the population to travel twenty miles to Benavides and the rest to travel ten miles to the village of Mazatlan. Both Concepcion and Realitos had had voting boxes for more than thirty years.

In the face of this blatant abuse of power, several of Lasater's associates applied for an injunction to block the Dunn County election set for December 23, 1913. They argued that the action of the Duval commissioners' court "is violative and subversive to the principle of local self-government and deprives the great body of the citizens . . . of equal representation."[6] After Parr appealed to James Wells to use his influence with Hopkins, the district judge refused to grant the injunction and to declare the orders of the Duval officials null and void. The Fourth Court of Civil Appeals at San Antonio, however, reversed this ruling and instituted the injunction against the December election. While abstaining from dictating policy to the county commissioners, the appellate court suggested that these officers provide separate precincts for each of the three largest towns of Dunn County. Archie Parr and his colleagues simply disregarded the admonition of the court and devised an alternative gerrymandering scheme, by which 125 voters would choose two of the Dunn County commissioners, while over 500 citizens would elect the other two. In an exact repetition of the original litigation, Hopkins rejected the application for an injunction against a second election scheduled for January 15, 1914, and the Court of Appeals overturned his decision.

In the end, the broad questions of citizens' rights and equal representation did not determine the fate of Dunn County. Instead, the insurgents discovered that the legislation establishing Dunn County violated an obscure provision of the Texas Constitution, which required a minimum distance of twelve miles between the boundary of a new county and the county seat of the original county. The north line of Dunn County came within 11½ miles of San Diego, the Duval county seat. Not even Judge Hopkins could ignore this simple fact, and he declared the creation of the new county unconstitutional. Archie Parr refused to allow the issue to die, however. After his election to the state Senate in 1914, he promoted another division of Duval County. Although the bill passed the Senate with only one dissenting vote, Parr provoked strong opposition in the House when he boasted to the Committee on Counties that he was the boss of Duval County and that he intended "to stay boss."[7] He also admitted that he possessed over five hundred poll tax receipts. His only defense for his actions was to accuse Lasater and other rivals of resorting to the same tactics. As a result of Parr's arrogant performance, the House members killed the measure. Still seeking some breakthrough in his legislative confrontation with local Republicans and dissident Democrats, Archie Parr formulated a bill that would allow him to transfer the Duval county seat to Benavides, but the proposal failed in the House. The same fate befell still another county bill at the special session of the legislature in May of 1915.

The Lasater forces were not willing to allow Parr to monopolize the legislative initiatives on the question of reorganizing Duval County. Five hundred taxpayers petitioned the legislature at its regular session in 1915 to dissolve their county and to attach the territory to Live Oak County. Representative Frank Burmeister introduced the bill and persuaded the House Committee on Counties to submit a favorable report, even over the protests of the representative from Live Oak County, who argued that his county did "not want to wash Duval County's dirty linen."[8] No further action ensued. This charade of moves and countermoves reached its comic limit when Parr proposed the dissolution of Burmeister's home county of McMullen and its incorporation into Duval County. To the relief of the rest of the legislature, the question of eliminating or splitting Duval County did not resurface after 1915.

As Archie Parr fought to expand his power through the creation of a new county, he faced a series of legal suits that threatened to destroy his authority inside Duval County. The purpose of this legal offensive was to expose the corruption that pervaded the administration of the county government and to force the removal of county officials. The opening blows of the campaign came during the same week that Judge Hopkins nullified the establishment of Dunn County. On January 14, 1914, a group of dissident ranchers and businessmen, including Ed C. Lasater and James O. Luby, presented to the district court petitions that charged Duval officers with the misappropriation of public funds and called for a thorough audit of county finances. Although state law required annual audits of county governments, eleven years had passed since the last examination of the Duval County books. Many of the wealthiest ranchers in the county vowed to pay no more taxes until the completion of a financial review, and Lasater raised a fund of $3,000 to pay for the services of a professional accountant.

In the face of the mounting barrage of legal suits, Judge W. B. Hopkins abandoned his defense of Archie Parr. At his urging, the Duval County grand jury authorized the judge to select a committee of three citizens to audit the county financial records. After only one day of investigation, the group admitted its inability to fulfill the mandate and recommended the hiring of an expert. Hopkins forwarded the proposal to the Duval county commissioners' court, which complied by employing Thomas B. Dunn, the brother of Parr's legislative ally Pat Dunn. In late January 1914, Lasater's accountant, George Kidd of Houston, began an independent survey of the county books. On the basis of Kidd's preliminary findings, forty property owners applied for an injunction to block the collection of a special tax to finance the courthouse and jail fund. While authorizing only minor repair work on both buildings over the past five years, the county officials had collected $35,000 in taxes for the special fund. In violation of the state law, they had transferred all of this money to the general revenue fund and other accounts, in order to circumvent the constitutional limitations on county taxing power. Judge Hopkins issued the injunction and refused to dissolve it when the Duval County officials filed a counter suit.

In an effort to prevent further revelations of public misconduct, the Duval commissioners refused to allow Kidd to continue his survey of the county records. The resultant litigation, however, brought to light a broad range of financial irregularities. In early June, Lasater and his associates applied for a writ of mandamus to restore the accountant's access to the Duval County books. After four days of hearings, Hopkins again sided with the plaintiffs and issued an injunction against any interference with the citizen-sponsored audit. In explaining his ruling, the judge cited fourteen types of illegal activities that George Kidd had already uncovered. These abuses included the removal of account books, the failure to keep other financial records up to date, the merger of several specialized funds into one account at the county depository, the mismanagement of school funds, the improper withdrawals of thousands of dollars from the depository by Parr and the other commissioners, improper borrowing from local banks to finance county operations, and the failure to account for the disappearance of an $8,000 surplus from the county treasury.

Hopkins' order upholding the citizens' right to conduct a private audit did not force the surrender of Archie Parr and his colleagues but only encouraged them to resort to more unorthodox tactics of circumvention. When the insurgents brought suit in July 1914, to force the removal of six Duval County officers, including Parr, the defendants resigned and appointed trusted friends to serve as their successors. The district clerk for the county even refused to file the ouster petition with the court on the grounds that he had just resigned. Before the ends of their terms, several of the replacements resigned and allowed the original officials to reclaim their posts. Apparently, someone in the Parr organization even acted to eliminate the threat of Kidd's financial investigation. The Houston accountant could not resume his audit until the legal appeals had run their course. With the case still pending before the Court of Civil Appeals, a fire destroyed the Duval County courthouse during the early-morning hours of August 11, 1914. Despite assurances from the county judge that all the public records were safe in a fire-proof vault, Kidd later discovered that much of the material that he had intended to review had been lost in the fire. Parr and the other officeholders remained vulnerable to legal attacks, but the Lasater camp suffered a serious setback just as they appeared to be on the verge of exposing the full story of Duval County corruption.

In the midst of the escalating legal battles of 1914, Archie Parr launched his campaign for the state Senate. When the veteran senator for South Texas, John Willacy, decided to run for the governorship rather than to seek reelection, Parr informed James Wells that Lasater, Customs Collector Frank Rabb of Brownsville, and a clique of Nueces County Democrats had united behind the candidacy of Nueces County Judge Walter Timon. According to Parr, their aim was to destroy Wells' region-wide political influence, even though Timon had cooperated with the Cameron County boss in the past. As the most effective defense against this challenge, Parr advocated his own candidacy for the Senate seat. However seriously Parr took the threat to Wells, the Benavides politico was certainly more concerned with his own self-interest. Parr would gain significant political advantages from membership in the Texas Senate. As a matter of senatorial courtesy, the upper chamber would automatically pass his proposals on local questions. Similarly, he could effectively counter Lasater's lobbying for bills designed to undercut the Duval County machine. With the apparent weakening of Wells' position in his home county, Parr might even emerge as the leading spokesman for conservative Democracy in South Texas.

By the time Parr announced his candidacy in early April, Walter

Timon had decided not to run for the Senate. The Duval County chieftain still faced tough competition from Walter Perkins, the Jim Wells county judge. Although Perkins carried the majority of the counties in the district, Parr won the Democratic nomination by almost 1,500 votes. James Wells' backing provided Parr with his margin of victory. Despite his problems with the Independent party of Cameron County, Wells continued to dominate the Democratic primaries. He and his allies in Hidalgo and Starr counties rolled up a combined majority of over 2,100 votes for Parr. After this strong showing, Archie Parr ran unopposed in the general election.

Neither Parr's election to the state Senate nor the destruction of the county records deterred Ed Lasater and the other dissidents from continuing their attack against the Duval machine. Judge W. B. Hopkins revived the anti-Parr campaign in December 1914 when he named insurgents to serve as the jury commissioners, that is, the officers who prepared the list of prospective grand jurors for the county. The Parr forces had blocked criminal prosecutions against public officials for years through the manipulation of the local grand juries. When the sheriff learned that the jury commissioners had chosen mainly fellow insurgents as their candidates for grand jury duty, he refused to summon the prospective jurors for the opening of the district court session and organized a group of reliable alternates. The Lasater sympathizers appeared anyway and secured most of the seats on the grand jury. By the end of January, the independent-minded jurors returned twenty-six indictments against ten Duval officers, including the county judge, the treasurer, and the clerk. Over the strenuous objections of District Attorney John Kleiber, they even indicted Archie Parr. Because of the loss of so much evidence in the courthouse fire, the indictments scarcely reflected the full scope of wrongdoing on the part of the local officeholders. In fact, most of the charges against Parr appeared contrived. In three separate indictments, the grand jury accused him of extorting a grand total of $39 from the county. The minutes of the county commissioners' court indicated that Parr had unlawfully received his daily stipend of $3 for several days when the court did not meet. Other evidence revealed, however, that the county clerk had erred in compiling the official records. He frequently combined the minutes of more than one daily session in a single entry. In all likelihood, Parr had attended the meetings for which he received pay. The remaining allegation against the Duval boss stemmed from his alteration of the election returns in his 1912 race for county commissioner. Parr had clearly violated the law, but his offense was minor. He had simply corrected a mistake in the vote tabulation. The charges against the other officials ranged from election fraud to embezzlement.

Hopkins agreed to the postponement of the trials for several months, but this modest concession failed to placate Parr, who was incensed over the judge's role in the selection of the Duval County grand jury. As the legislature considered a bill to create a new judicial district for the Trans-Nueces, Parr decided to arrange the selection of a new judge for Duval County. Because of the growing backlog of untried cases, the lawyers of the region were campaigning for the division of the existing district. Pat Dunn's original bill proposed the separation of the courts at Corpus Christi and Brownsville, which had the busiest schedules. Judge Hopkins would continue to preside over legal proceedings for Nueces, Duval, Brooks, Jim Wells, and Jim Hogg counties, while Governor James Ferguson had tentatively agreed to appoint the incumbent district attorney, John Kleiber, to serve as the judge for Cameron, Willacy, Kleberg, Hidalgo, and Starr counties. After Dunn's measure passed the House, Parr surprised both his constituents and his colleagues in the legislature by submitting a complete revision of the bill, which would separate Duval County from Hopkins' jurisdiction and leave Nueces and Cameron counties in the same district. The Benavides politician hoped to persuade the governor to award the new judgeship to an ally, who would be more dependable than W. B. Hopkins in controlling the Duval County litigation. In order to salvage the legislation, Dunn accepted Parr's changes, and the revised version passed both houses.

Archie Parr failed to dictate the selection of either the judge or the district attorney for the new judicial district, but he still achieved his goal of legal protection. The choice of Volney M. Taylor for judge was acceptable to the Duval boss from the outset. Although District Attorney J. E. Leslie received his appointment over Parr's opposition, Leslie never posed any serious threat to Parr. At the start of the December court term for Duval County, the new district attorney conferred with Lasater's staff of lawyers about the indictments against Parr and the local officeholders. This cooperation came to an end when the prosecutor decided to request the dismissal of the extortion charges against the state senator. In Leslie's view, "the county clerk couldn't merely write a man into the penitentiary."[9] The district attorney was still willing to prosecute Parr for election fraud, the county judge for embezzlement, the treasurer for making improper payments, and several lesser officials on related charges, but he objected to the proposal of Lasater's lawyers for a change of venue to San Antonio or Amarillo. When Leslie and the attorneys failed to agree on a site for the trials, the judge chose Hidalgo County, where John Closner's political domination and Wells' influence undermined the prospects for convictions.

The insurgent cause suffered another blow when the district attorney accused the members of the grand jury of leaking information to and receiving instructions from Lasater's attorneys. At the prosecutor's request, Judge Taylor reprimanded the jurors and even threatened to put them in jail. Lack of respect for proper legal procedure was not limited to the Lasater camp, however. On December 9, 1915, Archie Parr and the Duval County sheriff stormed into the grand jury room and removed some financial records that the jurors and George Kidd were examining. Parr also berated the jury members for persecuting him. When the jury foreman reported the blatant violation of the law, Judge Taylor cited the Benavides politico and his accomplice for contempt of court, but the punishment was mild—a $100 fine and an hour in jail.

The prosecution of the Duval County officials reached an anticlimactic conclusion in Hidalgo County. By the opening of the court session, the insurgents had lost all hope for success. The combination of Leslie's lack of enthusiasm for the proceedings, the tradition of legal corruption in the Valley, and the weakness of several of the cases assured acquittals for Parr and his associates. Neither the Lasater lawyers nor the prosecution witnesses, except for George Kidd, even bothered to attend the scheduled trial. Leslie failed to issue subpoenas for the missing witnesses, and the judge dismissed all the charges.

Long before the resolution of the state cases against the Duval politicos, Ed C. Lasater pressed for federal action as well. On June 5, 1915, the federal grand jury at Corpus Christi indicted forty-two Nueces County Democrats, including District Judge W. B. Hopkins, for conspiring to corrupt the 1914 election. Perceiving an alternative to the delay-plagued state prosecution of Archie Parr, Lasater traveled to Washington and arranged a conference with Woodrow Wilson's attorney general, Thomas Watt Gregory of Texas. In response to Lasater's personal appeal and the detailed analysis of Duval County corruption that his chief lawyer submitted, the Justice Department called on U.S. Attorney John E. Green, Jr., to investigate the conduct of the 1912 general election in the South Texas county. The instructions to Green, however, warned him to avoid involvement in "matters purely local" and to seek indictments only if the misdeeds affected the outcomes of federal races.[10]

In September 1915, while U.S. Attorney Green was participating in the Corpus Christi trial of the Nueces County officials, a special agent for the Justice Department oversaw an eleven-day grand jury investigation of Duval County election abuses in 1912. The inquiry confirmed most of Lasater's charges: Archie Parr had posted armed guards at the polls, had paid for five hundred poll taxes, and had tampered with some of the election returns. Although the federal grand jury was willing to vote for indictments, Green opposed the prosecution of Parr because his actions had had almost no effect on the election of any federal officeholder. The acquittal of all but five of the Nueces County defendants also may have influenced the U.S. attorney's decision. When the grand jury failed to release a report or return any indictments by the end of its term, one of Lasater's attorneys, Chester Terrell, made an impassioned appeal to Thomas Gregory to review the case: "The white men of [this] section have spent three times more in two years to secure decent government and fair elections than the Federal Government has spent in the Nueces County prosecutions, where practically the only thing proven was the purchase of a few poll taxes and the buying of a few votes. There is as much difference between the corruption in Nueces County and Duval County as there is between petty theft and grand larceny."[11] At a Washington conference with Green and a Lasater representative, Gregory approved the U.S. attorney's stand. Two weeks later the deadline under the statute of limitations for prosecuting 1912 election cases passed.

In October 1915, with the prospects for federal prosecution fading and with the state indictments still pending, the anti-Parr forces launched another legal offensive. Six businessmen and ranchers filed suit to force the removal of most of the Duval County officers, including Archie Parr's son Givens, who had recently received an appointment to serve as county judge. From December 28, 1915, through January 8, 1916, Judge Volney Taylor conducted hearings to determine whether he should temporarily suspend Givens Parr and the four county commissioners until the final disposition of their cases at some later trial. The plaintiffs charged that the members of the commissioners' court had "been guilty of official misconduct in the administration of their offices, gross ignorance of their official duties, and gross carelessness in the discharge of their duties."[12] This broad indictment stemmed from thirty-seven specific allegations, which included the following: failing to audit all the county finances, ignoring proper procedures for dispersing county funds, refusing to sue county officials who owed money to the county treasury, violating antinepotism laws, paying officers extra fees for performing their official duties, creating new government jobs without legal authorization, approving insufficient bonds for local offi-

cials, designating a notoriously insolvent bank as the county depository, failing to collect all the interest due on the deposit of county
funds, mismanaging local construction projects, and paying Archie
Parr and other officeholders fees for serving as road supervisors, even
though Texas law forbade the appointment of state and local officials to these positions.

At the conclusion of the hearings, Judge Taylor ordered the temporary removal of the four county commissioners, but he allowed
Givens Parr to retain his county judgeship. Although Taylor selected
the four replacements for the ousted defendants, his actions had little effect on the conduct of public affairs in Duval County. None of
the appointees were participants in the insurgent movement, and
they all proved to be quite willing to preserve the status quo. In addition, the suit calling for the permanent removal of Duval officeholders never came to trial, and no other county officials suffered
even temporary suspensions.

Not only did Archie Parr and his henchmen survive the state indictments, the federal investigation, and the continuing barrage of
civil suits, but they also showed no inclination to reform their management of county government. Even as a deterrent against future
abuses, Lasater's legal campaign was a failure. In fact, the scope of
the financial wheeling and dealing broadened during this period of
frenzied legal activity. The two main sources of fiscal extravagance
and possible corruption were the construction of a new county courthouse and the road improvements program.

After the insurgents secured an injunction against a bond issue
of $100,000 to pay for the proposed courthouse, the county commis-
sioners contracted one of James Wells' longtime business associates,
L. G. Hamilton, to erect the building for $67,500. To finance the
venture, the Duval officials issued warrants, which were subject to
fewer state regulations than bonds. Although Judge Taylor imposed
a temporary injunction on the transaction in September 1915, he denied an application for a permanent injunction four months later
and allowed the construction to proceed. By the time the work was
complete, the commissioners owed Hamilton over $70,000. They
also concluded agreements with other businessmen to provide light-
ing, plumbing, sidewalks, fences, landscaping, and furnishings.
These costs totaled over $50,000. Alarmed at the level of spending
for the courthouse, Lasater and his associates hired independent
contractors to estimate the real value of the construction and related
activities. Allowing a 10 percent margin of profit for all the participants in the project, these analysts calculated that the builders and
the furniture suppliers had overcharged the county approximately

$40,000. Hamilton alone had received $25,000 in excess of the value of his work. The Lasater partisans never uncovered any evidence of kickbacks, but the pattern of awarding contracts to businessmen with close ties to the Democratic leadership of South Texas and allowing excessive profits aroused their suspicions.

A similar record of financial abuse marred the road improvement program for Duval County. In September 1915, the commissioners' court agreed to pay Marshall White $60,000 in county warrants for the construction and repair of a number of roads and bridges. When the dissident taxpayers filed suit to enjoin the contract, the Duval officials proposed an out-of-court settlement, which the plaintiffs accepted. In accordance with the understanding, the commissioners negotiated a supplemental contract with White that imposed a spending limit of $25,000. In addition, they appointed the taxpayers' own consulting engineer, Fred M. Percival, to supervise the project. This cooperation between the Lasater and Parr camps was short-lived, however. The county officers disregarded Percival's estimate that the proposed work was worth only $18,000 and instead paid White $25,000. Two subsequent contracts with White raised his earnings to $65,000, that is, $5,000 above the terms of the original contract. Despite the increase in spending, White failed to provide all the improvements that the contracts specified. These violations of the out-of-court settlement provoked another law suit, but the courts upheld the legality of the Duval County transactions. Still not satisfied with the size of the investment in road construction, the Parr machine secured the voters' approval of a bond issue worth $100,000 in July 1916. With James Wells acting as his agent, L. G. Hamilton purchased all the securities.

Additional bond issues for schools and other purposes increased the county indebtedness for 1915 and 1916 to $315,000. When Archie Parr introduced legislation to expand the authority of the Duval county commissioners and to convert them from part-time to full-time officials, the insurgent taxpayers delivered the following protest: "If [the commissioners] can run the county $315,000.00 in debt in about a year's time and devote only a part of their time to the county, we submit to the Legislature if they devote all their time to the affairs of Duval it will be cheaper to give them all the land than to try to pay the taxes."[13] The House rejected Parr's proposal, but the gesture hardly provided the Lasater forces with any relief from the financial chicanery of the local Democratic machine.

By 1917, the Republicans and the maverick Democrats recognized the futility of trying to break Parr's control over Duval County. Only one legal case, Lasater's suit to block the road improvement program, lingered in the court system. Archie Parr still faced another formidable challenge before the end of the decade, but it came at the district, not the local, level. In 1918, Governor William Hobby and the Texas Rangers joined forces with the self-styled reformers of the Trans-Nueces in an effort to defeat the Benavides politician in his reelection bid to the state Senate. Within Duval County, though, Parr's authority now went uncontested.

As newcomers revitalized the opposition to boss rule in Cameron and Hidalgo counties, Archie Parr remained secure in an unchanging social and political environment. After 1910, the population of Duval County leveled off, and by 1920 many of the demoralized Anglos, who had participated in the insurgent movement, had sold their land and left the county. Not even the oil boom and the spurt in population growth during the 1920s altered the basic composition of the population. It remained overwhelmingly Mexican American and loyal to Parr. The Duval chieftain had laid the foundation for a political dynasty that would survive until 1975.

Despite Parr's indulgence in wholesale corruption and the appeals of his critics for honest government, Duval County politics did not offer a clear-cut choice between villainy and virtue. While Archie Parr and his associates claimed the lion's share of the graft for their own personal benefit, they also used some of the proceeds to provide paternalistic services for their impoverished Hispanic constituents. In time of need, a faithful supporter could depend on the Duval boss for a modest handout from the county treasury. In addition, road building and other construction projects furnished short-term work for unemployed and underpaid laborers. The economy-minded opponents to the Democratic machine had no intention of creating an alternative to this informal welfare system. Their overriding concern was holding down taxes, not meeting the needs of the mass of the population. Nor was Parr the originator or monopolizer of unethical political conduct in the county. Long before his rise to power, both parties had manipulated the Hispanic vote. Parr's leading antagonist, Ed C. Lasater, tried to pay for hundreds of poll taxes for Duval County voters, usually without success, and he practiced his own brand of boss politics in Brooks County.

Yet even in this amoral political setting, Archie Parr's ruthlessness was exceptional. While his fellow politicians were guilty of their share of abuses, Parr carried corruption to extreme levels. He was willing to resort to almost any tactic to achieve his aims. At election time, he not only paid poll taxes and corralled voters to maximize his political support but also prevented the opposition from voting. Solid majorities failed to satisfy the Duval chieftain. Often he strived for unanimity in the vote count. Parr's techniques for siphoning money from the county treasury were just as thorough as his election practices. Earning thousands of dollars from the profits of inflated construction contracts did not prevent him from unlawfully claiming $150 for serving as a road supervisor. He overlooked no opportunities for enrichment, no matter how petty. When the Lasater-sponsored audit threatened to expose this thievery, the boss' henchmen simply destroyed the county records. Although Parr probably never ordered the murder of a political rival, he regularly used the threat of violence to intimidate voters. The bloodshed that claimed the lives of several political dissenters after Archie Parr's death had its roots in the attitudes and the actions of the man who consolidated Democratic dominance. He set the precedents for disregarding the law and relying on armed force.

For all of South Texas, the second decade of the twentieth century was a time of political unrest. In addition to Lasater's legal offensive against Parr and the influx of new settlers into the Valley, three other factors contributed to the turmoil: the patronage policies of the administration of Woodrow Wilson; the revival of border raids and military activity along the Rio Grande; and the statewide political battles over prohibition, women's suffrage, and James Ferguson. Under these stresses, the Wells machine of Cameron County finally collapsed.

10. The Wilson Administration and Federal Patronage

DURING THE ADMINISTRATION of Woodrow Wilson, the fortunes of the Wells machine were closely tied to the policies of the federal government. James Wells' opposition to Wilson's candidacy in 1912 produced more patronage woes for the aging boss and provided his local rivals with another opportunity to take the offensive. At the same time, the eruption of the Mexican Revolution and the revival of lawlessness along the border necessitated the intervention of federal troops to maintain order and to ensure the security of the Valley against the threat of a foreign invasion.

In 1912, Theodore Roosevelt accepted the nomination of the newly formed Progressive party and completed the destruction of Republican unity. This split in the GOP provided the Democrats with their first opportunity to reclaim control of the national government since the depression of the 1890s. Woodrow Wilson, the reform governor of New Jersey, Champ Clark, now Speaker of the House, Congressman Oscar Underwood, and Governor Judson Harmon of Ohio all competed for the Democratic nomination. Although the Democratic party could not escape the progressive-conservative tensions that plagued American politics, the ideological differences among the party's presidential aspirants were not sharply defined. Despite his impressive record of political and economic innovations during just one term as the New Jersey chief executive, Wilson was a recent and still somewhat cautious convert to progressivism. Conservative values also shaped the outlooks of Clark and Underwood, but, like Wilson, they were willing to accept moderate reforms. Only Judson Harmon, the least promising of the Democratic candidates, stood out as an uncompromising Bourbon.

In the competition for control of the Texas delegation to the national Democratic convention, Woodrow Wilson gained the upper hand. Texas progressives overlooked his ambivalence on the issue of prohibition and rallied behind his candidacy. Despite their recent setbacks with the election of Oscar Colquitt to the governorship in 1910 and with the defeat of statewide prohibition in a special 1911 election, these reformers remained a potent force in Texas politics. The Wilson presidential drive also received support from such pragmatic conservatives as Colonel Edward M. House and Congressman Albert Burleson, who were trying to recapture their lost political influence. After the reelection of Governor S. W. T. Lanham in 1904, Colonel House had retired from his leadership position in the state Democratic party. Now he harbored ambitions of serving as a confidant to a Democratic president in the same way that he had previously advised Texas governors. Although ill health prevented House from playing a central role in the state campaign for Wilson's nomination, a close personal relationship developed between the New Jersey governor and the former Texas "king-maker."

Under the leadership of Dallas progressive Thomas Love, the Wilson supporters fashioned an efficient organization that overwhelmed the opposition. Woodrow Wilson's conservative detractors failed to unite behind an alternative candidate, and only the Harmon backers attempted to wage a statewide campaign. Not even the strident attacks of Joseph Weldon Bailey, who had already announced his intention to retire from the Senate at the end of his present term, could reverse the Wilson tide. The coalition of progressives and House allies swept the precinct, county, and district conventions to secure a solid majority at the state convention.

Despite their statewide success, the Wilson forces met defeat in South Texas. Congressman John Nance Garner favored Champ Clark for the Democratic nomination, but the Uvalde politico abstained from active campaigning. The staunchest opposition to the Wilson effort came from James B. Wells, who promoted the candidacy of Judson Harmon. Wells took charge of the anti-Wilson movement in both Cameron County and the whole fifteenth congressional district. At the local level, the Rio Grande chieftain resorted to the crudest form of political manipulation. His henchman harassed Wilson organizers, and he even refused to inform the chairman of the Woodrow Wilson Club of the time and the site of the county convention. In the words of one embattled progressive spokesman, ". . . you would have thought we were a band of Highway men supporting an outlaw. [Wells] set his hounds on us and dogged us from start to finish."[1] Each of the Valley counties endorsed Harmon as its first choice for the presidential nomination, and the district convention chose a delegation of Wells loyalists to attend the state gathering. The district conferees also called upon the Texas convention to select Wells and Garner to represent the fifteenth congressional district at the national democratic convention.

The Wilsonites of South Texas turned to Frank Rabb, a wealthy Cameron County rancher and irrigation promoter, to lead the fight against the Wells machine. Once an ally and personal friend of the Democratic chieftain, Rabb became increasingly critical of Wells' political conduct and joined the insurgency. In cooperation with the Democratic members of the Independent party, Rabb established the Wilson Club of Brownsville and financed its operation. Later he attended a state organizational conference for the Wilson movement and secured the position of co-chairman for the fifteenth congressional district. His losses to Wells at the local and district levels did not deter Rabb from renewing the political battle at the state Democratic convention in Houston. Although Wells chaired the caucus of anti-Wilson delegates, his influence over the convention as a whole was minimal. The Texas progressives were determined to exploit their majority to the fullest. They rejected the recommendations of the anti-Wilson district conventions in the selection of delegates to the national convention and assigned all the posts to ardent backers of the New Jersey governor. The Wilsonites named Frank Rabb to serve as an alternate. The subsequent absence of the regular delegate enabled Rabb to participate with the Texas contingent at Baltimore.

Incensed over his defeat in Houston, James Wells tried to persuade other conservative Texas Democrats, who opposed Woodrow Wilson's quest for the presidential nomination, to level a formal challenge before the national convention. Wells argued that the state convention had exceeded its authority when it overturned the national delegate choices of several district conventions. He charged that this action was "utterly destructive of local self-government."[2] The Cameron County boss failed to muster enough support to continue this line of attack, but his last-ditch resistance to the Wilson campaign did produce political repercussions. Wells' maneuvering deepened the animosity of leading Texas Wilsonites, who would exercise influence over the patronage policies of the future Democratic administration.

Although Woodrow Wilson campaigned vigorously across the country, his presidential drive faltered outside Texas. By the opening of the national convention, Champ Clark had collected almost twice as many delegates as his New Jersey rival. Despite the heavy odds against their candidate, the Texas delegation held firm and contributed to his successful comeback. Congressman Burleson served as one of the two official floor leaders for the Wilson camp, while Thomas Love and Thomas Watt Gregory, another House associate, arranged an alliance with the Pennsylvania delegates to lobby for the defection of Clark and Underwood backers and to promote the Wilson cause generally. On the tenth ballot, Clark claimed over half the votes, but he never succeeded in gaining the necessary two-thirds majority. As the Speaker's offensive stalled on the following ballots, his support began to erode. By the forty-third ballot, Wilson controlled a majority of the delegates, and three ballots later he won the nomination. For their steadfast loyalty to the Democratic standard-bearer, the Texas delegation earned the title "The Immortal Forty."

After Woodrow Wilson's victory at the tumultuous Democratic national convention, the Texas campaign for his election in November proved to be anticlimactic. The New Jersey progressive carried the solidly Democratic state by a four-to-one majority. Even Democratic leaders who had opposed his bid for the nomination organized a fund-raising drive for the national ticket. When Governor Oscar Colquitt informed Wells that a contribution might enable him to exert "some influence with the national administration," the Brownsville politician donated $200 and promised to secure another $800 from his friends.[3] Nationwide, Wilson won the election with 43 percent of the vote, as Roosevelt and the Republican nominee, William Howard Taft, split the long-standing GOP majority. In the aftermath of the fall campaign, Wells professed his delight and announced to the press that "I will never get tired of crowing over [the Democratic triumph]."[4] The boss' belated conversion failed to impress local Wilsonites, who recalled that Wells had earlier ridiculed their candidate as a "boob" and "a school marm."[5]

In organizing his new administration, Woodrow Wilson continued to rely on the services of Texas Democrats. Despite Colonel Edward House's low profile during the campaign, Wilson had come to value his political judgment. After the election, House emerged as the president-elect's closest adviser. The colonel already had a long record of service as a political counselor, but his relationship with Wilson was quite different from his earlier associations with Governors Culberson, Sayers, and Lanham. House made the adjustment from manipulating weak public figures to subtly influencing a strong-willed president, who combined practical political skills, a commitment to moderate domestic reform, and visions of transforming the whole system of international relations. Not only did House adapt his pattern of political behavior to new circumstances, but he also discarded past allegiances with Texas Democrats who had not supported Wilson's candidacy for the Democratic nomination. He never exerted the slightest influence to assist James Wells during the prolonged battles over South Texas patronage. For a man playing the role of the president's alter ego, Wells' problems with federal appointees along the Rio Grande appeared remote and petty.

To the disgruntlement of the progressive Wilsonites, the Texans who claimed the choicest assignments in the Democratic administration were all associates of Colonel House. Most notably, Woodrow Wilson named Albert Burleson to serve as the postmaster general and Thomas Watt Gregory to serve as a special counsel in the Justice Department. One year later the president promoted Gregory to attorney general. The highest office that a Texas progressive without House connections secured at the start of Wilson's term was commissioner of Indian affairs. Having failed to capture what they considered a fair share of the high-level appointments, Texas Wilson men outside the House circle were determined to influence the distribution of postmasterships, collectorships, and other federal jobs in their home state.

As the postmaster general, with 56,000 positions at his disposal, Albert Burleson played a key role in shaping the patronage policies of the administration, but he showed little inclination to protect the interests of James B. Wells and the other South Texas bosses. Although Burleson and Wells shared many of the same conservative views, especially opposition to prohibition, they had not been close since 1908 when Burleson had publicly condemned Senator Bailey's conduct in the Waters-Pierce affair. The apparent decline of Wells' political power, his conspicuous role as the spokesman for the anti-Wilson delegates at the state convention, and the statewide agitation of progressives over the patronage controversies of South Texas reinforced the postmaster general's indifference toward his former ally. Moreover, Wells had committed an indiscretion that Burleson considered inexcusable. The Cameron County boss not only had opposed Wilson in the fight for the presidential nomination but also had made insulting remarks about the Democratic candidate.

With the organization of the new administration, James Wells faced a disturbing paradox. Although two of his past allies in Texas politics now occupied positions of enormous influence, Wells could not rely on either of them to back his choices for the Rio Grande collectorship and the other federal offices in South Texas. After battling Republican appointees through three consecutive GOP administrations, the Brownsville politico had hoped that the Democratic victory in the national election of 1912 would enable him to take charge of federal patronage and to eliminate the organizational base of his local opposition. As progressives across the state prepared to campaign for the patronage claims of South Texas insurgents, control over the federal spoils appeared as elusive as ever to Wells. For support, he turned to Senator Charles Culberson and Congressman John Nance Garner.

Senator Culberson had endorsed Woodrow Wilson for the presidency as early as October 1911 and had reaffirmed his support the following spring to counteract Bailey's attacks. At the national Democratic convention, he had rejected a proposal from Tammany Hall Democrats to stand as a compromise candidate as Champ Clark's drive collapsed. Because of his contributions to the Wilson campaign and his position as the chairman of the Senate Judiciary Committee, which shaped antitrust legislation, the senior Texas senator commanded the respect of the Democratic administration. In addition, his loyalty to James Wells remained intact. Nevertheless, Culberson's value to Wells during the opening round of patronage battles was minimal. In the spring of 1913, Culberson contracted Bright's disease, a kidney ailment, and withdrew to Connecticut for months of rest and seclusion. Although he eventually resumed his Senate duties, recurrent health problems brought on by years of excessive drinking undercut his effectiveness.

Culberson's incapacity forced James Wells to rely almost entirely on John Garner. At the outset of the Democratic presidency, the congressman's relations with the White House were strained. He had supported Champ Clark for the presidential nomination, and most of the Wilsonite progressives who represented Texas at the Baltimore convention regarded Garner as a reactionary. In 1913, Garner claimed a seat on the all important Ways and Means Committee, which managed tax and tariff legislation for the House. In addition, the Democratic members of this committee made all the other committee appointments for their party colleagues. Although Garner used his growing influence to support the major features of Wilson's New Freedom program, he still experienced patronage problems during Wilson's first term. When Garner proposed the appointment of a resident of his congressional district to a government commission in January 1917, he complained to the president's secretary that "not a single political crumb has fallen my way in the past four years."[6] Garner exaggerated his mistreatment at the hands of the administration, since he had sponsored most of the postal appointees in his district. Nevertheless, he suffered a number of setbacks, and one of his most conspicuous defeats affected the power of James B. Wells. In 1913, the office of customs collector for South Texas again went to one of Wells' rivals.

The customs service remained the most coveted federal patronage prize along the Rio Grande. Shortly before leaving office, President William Taft signed an executive order that provided for the reorganization of customs districts across the country. The decree placed the Corpus Christi, Brownsville, and Laredo customs houses in a single district, with its headquarters at Laredo. Brownsville and Corpus Christi retained their status as ports of entry, and the local staffs suffered only modest cutbacks. Any prospect that the transfer of the collector's office to Laredo would reduce the level of political activity among customs employees in Cameron County disappeared when Frank Rabb emerged as the leading candidate to manage the new district. Rabb's application for the Laredo collectorship provoked a complicated patronage struggle that lasted for more than four years and involved some of the most powerful figures in Texas politics and in the Wilson administration.

Progressive Democrats throughout the state campaigned for the appointment of Frank Rabb as the Laredo collector. The Treasury Department received almost eighty letters and petitions favoring Rabb's application, including endorsements from thirty-seven of the forty Texas delegates to the national Democratic convention. The roster of supporters boasted such prominent progressive names as Thomas Love and Thomas Campbell. In the view of many original Wilson men outside the House clique, this patronage fight represented one of the few remaining opportunities for the new administration to demonstrate its commitment to promoting reformist activism in the state. Their correspondence mixed praise of Rabb's integrity, competence, and allegiance to progressive Democracy with condemnation of his rivals as reactionaries and bosses. Even one of Colonel House's protégés, Thomas Watt Gregory, portrayed the contest as a reformist-conservative confrontation of statewide significance:

> The old Bourbon element of South Texas and in the entire state is making a desperate effort to defeat Rabb's appointment; it is impossible for them to say anything against his character, ability as a businessman, and general fitness for the place, and the fight is a purely political one and has behind it the very men over whose prostrate bodies we had to walk in order to reach Baltimore.
>
> In case he is not appointed to this place, it will be a severe blow to practically all the Wilson people of Texas and will be regarded throughout the state as a serious blow to progressive ideas and a triumph of reactionaries.[7]

The sharpest criticism of James Wells came from local insurgents. The chairman of the Cameron County Wilson Club offered the following assessment of Wells' political conduct: "What I want to say is that we have a Jim Smith [the leading Democratic boss of New Jersey] in South West Texas, whose nefarious schemes Jim Smith would blush with shame to undertake. His name is James B. Wells, an affable, pleasant gentleman who is my personal friend, but a political highwayman, whose slogan is, 'How many votes do you want?' meaning, 'I have thousands of Mexican votes at my command,' and he has, and many of them live in Mexico, but at his command."[8] Another South Texas Wilsonite was even more scathing in his denunciations. He characterized the Democratic ring as a "criminal element" that indulged in "murder and assassination . . . as a past-time."[9]

The anti-Rabb petitioners identified the applicant as a member of the "Republican Customs House–Independent Machine," but the administration regarded most of these critics with suspicion because of their failure to participate in the Wilson movement prior to the Baltimore convention.[10] An exception to this pattern was Harbert Davenport, the chairman of the pro-Wilson convention in Chambers County who subsequently moved to Brownsville and joined Wells' law firm. The young attorney provided a detailed account of the Independent party's resort to election fraud in the 1912 Brownsville election, their misuse of the city police force, and their effort to gerrymander the election precincts of Cameron County. Without directly implicating Rabb, another Brownsville Wilsonite accused the leaders of the local insurgency of plotting to lynch the deputy sheriff who had killed City Marshal Joseph Crixell. At the state level, Governor Oscar Colquitt protested Rabb's candidacy. The governor complained about the political activism of Republican federal officials along the border and argued that the maintenance of "law and order" depended on the appointment of men who were willing to cooperate with the state authorities.[11] Because of Rabb's "bitter opposition" to the governor's bid for reelection in 1912, Colquitt concluded that the independent Democrat was "an enemy of my administration" and unfit to hold the post of collector.[12]

Within the Wilson administration, the two most influential Texans, Colonel House and Albert Burleson, avoided any firm commitments. Both the opponents and the supporters of Rabb's candidacy claimed the ambivalent postmaster general as an ally. House rejected Rabb's request for an endorsement, but he suggested the possibility of "indirect services" on behalf of the Valley rancher.[13] Not even a direct appeal from Frank Andrews, once House's closest confidant on Texas political affairs, could induce the colonel to represent the interests of James B. Wells. Andrews argued that Wells' claims deserved serious consideration because of his record of "long and faithful service": "Considering yours [House's] and Culberson's relations to Jim Wells, I should regret beyond measure to see a man appointed whom he regards as a personal enemy. Jim talked to me with tears in his eyes about this last Sunday. Said he . . . would be overjoyed at the appointment of any decent man and urged me to appeal to you in his behalf."[14] Like House and Burleson, Secretary of the Treasury William McAdoo, the man directly responsible for making a recommendation to President Wilson, appeared uncommitted during the opening stage of the patronage fight.

Although no staunch opposition to Rabb's appointment developed inside the administration, only one high-ranking adviser, Secretary of State William Jennings Bryan, openly campaigned for the Brownsville insurgent. Personal friendship accounted for Bryan's endorsement. In 1909, the Nebraska Democrat purchased some land in Hidalgo County, and during his occasional trips to the Valley he stayed as a guest at Rabb's ranch. Additional support in Washington came from Texas Senator Morris Sheppard. After serving in the U.S. House of Representatives for ten years, the still-youthful advocate of prohibition and progressive reform had run for the Senate seat of the retiring Joseph Weldon Bailey in 1912. Despite his impressive victory in the preferential primary, Sheppard carried only a small percentage of the vote in the Lower Rio Grande Valley, and he attributed this regional setback to Wells' manipulation of the Mexican American electorate. Branding the Democratic bosses of South Texas as reactionaries who practiced "political slavery," Sheppard emerged as Rabb's most vigorous booster.[15]

John Garner acted as the Washington-based manager of the anti-Rabb campaign. He channeled protests to the administration, solicited support from various senators and congressmen, and regularly conferred with Treasury Secretary McAdoo. This conscientious lobbying, however, could not overcome all the obstacles that Garner faced. Besides the mobilization of Texas progressives in support of Frank Rabb, the Uvalde congressman had to contend with Wells' initial selection of alternative candidates for the collectorship. Incredibly, the Cameron County boss proposed his son Joseph and Archie Parr. Parr's reputation as a corrupt boss had reached statewide proportions in May 1912 when the Wilson forces expelled his Duval County delegation from the Houston convention. Only at the insistence of Garner and Frank Andrews did James Wells agree to promote Roger Byrne, a respected legislator from Central Texas and an original backer of Woodrow Wilson.

The success of this scheme to block Rabb's appointment and to install Byrne as a substitute depended on the intervention of Senator Charles Culberson. Garner explained to Wells that "without [Culberson's] support, I am helpless, because Secretary McAdoo would give little consideration to the endorsement of anyone not having the favorable consideration of one of the Senators."[16] Thus, Culberson's incapacitation with Bright's disease delivered a devastating blow to Garner and Wells' plans. The senator's secretary, C. W. Jurney, informed the Wilson administration of Culberson's dissatisfaction with Rabb and his inclination to support an alternative candidate. Neither Burleson nor McAdoo was willing to allow Jurney to endorse Byrne on the senator's behalf, but the Treasury Secretary agreed to delay any action on the matter until the expiration of the present Laredo collector's term in March 1914. Jurney anticipated the recovery of Culberson well before that time. A deepening crisis in relations between Mexico and the United States upset the timetable for settling the collectorship dispute, however.

In 1911, Francisco Madero, a Mexican revolutionary committed to the establishment of constitutional government in his country, toppled the thirty-year-old dictatorship of Porfirio Díaz. By the time Woodrow Wilson came into office, General Victoriano Huerta had staged a coup d'etat and arranged the murder of Madero. As a second revolutionary movement under Venustiano Carranza spread through most of northern Mexico, Wilson simultaneously offered to mediate the conflict and applied pressure to force Huerta from power. The American president's interference in Mexican politics succeeded only in offending the nationalistic sensibilities of both the Huerta regime and Carranza's Constitutionalist forces. In the midst of mounting tension between the two countries, Wilson decided to impose an arms embargo. To ensure the effective enforcement on this ban against the shipment of munitions into Mexico, the president and his advisers wanted to staff the customs houses along the Mexican border with officials completely loyal to the administration.

The Wells camp tried to take advantage of Wilson's concern over the turmoil in Mexico by challenging Frank Rabb's fitness to uphold American neutrality and to administer the customs laws impartially. In three separate petitions, sixty local officials of Cameron, Hidalgo, and Starr counties accused the independent Democrat of "active partisanship and constant association with the agents, officers, and soldiers of the Carranza army immediately preceding and following the battle of Matamoros."[17] Wells' law partner, Harbert Davenport, repeated the charge in more lurid terms: "Later the Rebels captured Matamoros, and the self-respecting Americans of Brownsville were treated with the amazing spectacle of Frank Rabb and others of his associates among the Independent leaders fawning upon and making great ado over the officers of the Mexican army at a time when the blood of young boys, guilty of no other offense than of having differed in their political convictions from the capturers of the city and of having defended their home against the invading army, dyed the walls of the Market Place, where they had been stood against the wall [and] shot."[18] In response to these attacks, Frank Rabb asserted that "the only interest that I have taken in Mexican matters is that which our Government stands for today."[19]

In selecting a new collector, the Wilson administration placed a premium on Frank Rabb's record of support for the president and discounted the charges of his meddling in Mexican affairs. On August 27, 1913, Woodrow Wilson announced the establishment of the arms embargo in an address to Congress, and the next day he sent to the Senate his nomination of Frank Rabb for the Laredo collectorship. Postmaster General Burleson informed the press that the emergency conditions along the border necessitated the immediate appointment of customs officials who completely supported the president's policies toward Mexico. The sudden reversal of Treasury Secretary McAdoo's prior agreement to postpone the selection of a collector until Charles Culberson's recovery prompted the senator's secretary, C. W. Jurney, to take counteraction. The aide persuaded several influential senators to arrange a delay of the confirmation proceedings for a few days to allow Culberson an opportunity to submit his recommendations on the matter. After the senator's wife informed Jurney that Culberson preferred not to obstruct the nomination at this stage, the Senate quickly approved Rabb's appointment.

The appointment of Frank Rabb as the collector for the Laredo district did not resolve the patronage battle. For the first three years of Rabb's four-year-term, Wells and Garner waged an unrelenting campaign to discredit the independent Democrat in the eyes of his Washington superiors and to limit his effectiveness as a local political organizer. Even after Rabb's influence over South Texas politics had crumbled, his two adversaries continued to scheme to arrange his replacement with someone sympathetic to their interests. Only when a more formidable rival to Wells made a bid for the collectorship in 1916, did the Democratic power broker express a willingness to allow Rabb to complete his term.

In January 1914, Wells wrote to Garner that the new collector "is very evidently working in Cameron, Hidalgo, and Starr Counties and . . . doing everything he can in the way of Customs changes and appointments, and promised increased force,—to rally every vote possible against you."[20] Another informant credited Rabb with control over the Democratic machinery of Zapata County, which borders Starr County on the west. Despite these pessimistic reports, Garner concluded by early February that his candidacy was "in good shape."[21] His own canvass of the entire district had revealed no widespread insurgency.

This renewed confidence in his prospects for reelection did not deter the Uvalde representative from pressing the attack against Rabb. When Senator Culberson's secretary Jurney first informed Woodrow Wilson of Rabb's plan to unseat Garner, the president acknowledged a feeling of friendship for the congressman and disavowed any support for such a scheme. Although Rabb denied the charges of partisan activity, Garner persuaded the president to order an investigation in June 1914. According to McAdoo, the inquiry exonerated Rabb of all practices beyond "the perfectly proper exercise of his rights as an American citizen."[22]

Although Frank Rabb posed no serious threat to John Garner's bid for reelection, the collector contributed to the revival of the insurgent movement in Cameron County. The general election campaign of 1912 had ended in disaster for the Independent party when a Democratic law suit had forced the removal of the names of the Independent candidates from the official ballot. Nevertheless, the Wells machine remained vulnerable to attack. In fact, the combination of Wells' failure to control the distribution of federal patronage along the border and the success of the Independent-backed compromise slate in the Brownsville municipal election of 1914 convinced many Republicans and maverick Democrats that the era of local boss domination was coming to a close. Brownsville Mayor Augustus A. Browne even decided to challenge Wells in the 1914 primary for the chairmanship of the Cameron County Democratic party, which the Rio Grande chieftain had held for thirty years. Five candidates entered the race for sheriff, and most of the Democratic incumbents faced primary opponents. The Browne faction changed its tactics, however, when James Wells refused to allow his Democratic rivals to influence the selection of the election judges for the July primary. Fearing election fraud, A. A. Browne, his brother James, and four other candidates withdrew from the Democratic contest and formally joined the Independent party. The dissident

Democrats quickly consolidated their control over the opposition organization, as James Browne claimed the chairmanship of the Independent party and A. A. Browne became the party nominee for county judge. Frank Rabb supported this political merger and used his influence to arrange the nomination of his brother-in-law, Fred Stark, as the Independent candidate for sheriff.

With the defection of the Browne wing of the Democratic party and with the customs service again in the hands of his opponents, James Wells realized that he faced a desperate fight to maintain his control over the county government. To broaden the appeal of the regular Democratic ticket among Anglo voters, Wells withdrew his support of the incumbent sheriff, C. T. Ryan, who had failed to curb the high incidence of crime in the rural areas of the county. Although the large-scale border raids would not begin until mid-1915, individual bandits, deserters, and half-starved refugees from war-torn northern Mexico were already stealing from the Anglo farmers near the border. In place of Ryan, the Cameron County boss picked W. T. Vann as his candidate. The former sheriff of Leon County, Vann had only recently moved to Brownsville to assume the post of deputy U.S. marshal. After the newcomer won the Democratic nomination, Sheriff Ryan resigned, and the county commissioners' court selected Vann to fill the office for the remainder of the current term.

During the fall campaign, the Independents again accused their Democratic opponents of corruption and submission to the dictates of one man—James B. Wells. The insurgents also criticized W. T. Vann for failing to reorganize the sheriff's department during his brief term of duty. To the dismay of the Independent politicians, Vann, who had held elective office for eighteen years in Leon County, proved to be an effective campaigner. In response to the charge that the number of deputy sheriffs exceeded the legal limit, he argued that a genuine emergency existed because of "the unprecedented amount of stealing and crime," and that the state criminal code "gives me the power and makes it my duty in emergencies to call to my assistance every citizen of the county, if necessary, to enforce the laws." Not satisfied with simply defending his own record, Vann took the offensive against his Independent critics. He reviewed the acts of fraud in the 1912 Brownsville city election and labeled R. B. Creager as the "boss" of the insurgent movement. The sheriff reserved his sharpest attacks for his opponent Fred Stark, however. As a customs inspector, according to Vann, Stark had failed to intercept the "hundreds of thousands of arms" that Independent party members had shipped into Mexico, but he was quite adept at apprehending "some poor humble Mexican" who was smuggling "two bits' worth of mescal across the river."[23]

Despite Vann's impressive performance as the spokesman for the Democratic ticket, James Wells still lacked complete confidence that his organization would carry the election. As an added precaution, he schemed to prevent representatives of the Independent party from serving as election supervisors. On Wells' instructions, County Judge H. L. Yates actually went into hiding so that Chairman James Browne could not submit the list of Independent election officials for the judge's approval. After searching for Yates in vain for ten days and failing to persuade the county commissioners to act in his absence, Browne and the Independent candidates filed suit in Judge W. B. Hopkins' district court to force the appointment of the Independent election supervisors. The county officers argued that the Independents had no right to choose election supervisors since their party had not formally existed at the time of the appointment of election officials in February. The attorneys for the plaintiffs pointed out, however, that the Terrell Election Law allowed a political party to apply for such representation at the polls as late as five days before the election. Yates' evasiveness shortly before that deadline indicated that the Democrats recognized the legitimacy of the Independent claims, but Judge Hopkins ruled against the Independent party. As a token gesture, County Judge Yates then agreed to allow members of the opposition party to serve as election officials in less than half the precincts. With the election machinery under the control of the Wells ring, the Democratic ticket swept the countywide contests by majorities ranging from 895 to 1,056 votes. Vann defeated Stark 1,811 to 812.

In the wake of the Independent defeat, James Wells dismissed Frank Rabb as a "figurehead without any influence whatever . . . who could not hurt us."[24] The Cameron County boss might have been premature in making this judgment, but the collector's political standing in Washington and the Lower Rio Grande Valley deteriorated steadily after the 1914 election. The two main problems that plagued Rabb were the exposure of his involvement in the national politics of Mexico and Garner's persistent lobbying to force the removal of the independent Democrat.

Although Frank Rabb's appointees in the customs service actively participated in the Cameron County contests of 1914, the Laredo collector missed much of the fall campaign because of two extended trips into Mexico. In early August and again in October, the Treasury Department granted Rabb thirty-day leaves of absence, but his superiors did not realize that he had traveled south of the border until they received a telegram from Mexico City in November requesting an extension of his second leave. When the department rejected his appeal, two of Rabb's companions sent messages claiming that the collector was sick and could not travel. In direct violation of instructions to resume his official duties as customs collector immediately, Rabb remained in Mexico City until the second week in December. Already dismayed over this act of defiance, officials in the Wilson administration experienced an even greater shock ten days after Rabb's belated return to his post at Laredo. On December 23, 1914, the *New York World* reported that the Rio Grande customs chief had been lobbying to advance General Lucio Blanco's presidential ambitions and to secure valuable economic concessions for a syndicate of wealthy Texans. General Blanco had captured Matamoros for the Constitutionalist movement in April 1913, but since the fall of the Huerta regime in July 1914, his loyalties had vacillated between support for Venustiano Carranza and support for the Constitutionalist leader's most powerful rival, Francisco (Pancho) Villa. The newspaper exposé also identified Congressman Garner, Senator Sheppard, and Secretary of State Bryan as Rabb's confederates.

The claim of cooperation between Rabb and Garner was obviously false, and President Wilson's private secretary, Joseph Tumulty, tried to discredit the whole story by citing the congressman's repeated protests against Rabb's political activities in the border counties. Sheppard, Bryan, and Garner all professed complete ignorance of the alleged scheme to influence Mexican politics and to arrange economic concessions, but Rabb's response was ambiguous. While denying any connection with a Texas syndicate, the collector admitted that he had campaigned for General Blanco.

Rabb's association with Lucio Blanco and other Mexican generals eventually destroyed the last vestiges of his influence in South Texas politics. After the outbreak of bandit raids from Mexico in mid-1915, the Anglo residents of the Valley became convinced that the Carranza government was encouraging the plundering and the killings. Those Anglos who had previously endorsed the Constitutionalist cause became the targets of scorn and suspicion. No one had been more conspicuous in his advocacy of the revolutionary upheavals in Mexico than Frank Rabb.

Rabb's foray into Mexican politics had a more immediate impact on his relations with the Wilson administration. The article in the *New York World* provoked a second Treasury Department investigation into the conduct of the Laredo collector. In contrast to the earlier evaluation, the report of January 1915 was highly critical of Rabb, both for his misuse of customs personnel in local campaigning and for his entanglement in Mexican affairs. Although the South Texas district employed more mounted customs inspectors for every hundred miles of border than any other district on the Mexican frontier, Rabb had repeatedly sought authorizations to hire additional riders. The supervising investigator for the department contended that these requests stemmed from the practice of using mounted inspectors "to influence the vote of the Mexican portion of the border population."[25] Political calculations also determined the pattern of promotions, transfers, and firings among customs personnel. On the subject of Rabb's trip to Mexico, the report cited his failure to explain his absences from his post, his failure to comply with orders to return to the United States immediately, and the complaints of a State Department representative in Mexico City that the collector was interfering with the diplomatic activities of the United States government.

As the charges against Rabb from official and unofficial sources mounted, John Garner stayed on the offensive. Prior to the publication of the *New York World* story, the Uvalde representative introduced a congressional resolution calling for the disclosure of all the Treasury Department documents on the Laredo collector. In January 1915, Garner reached an understanding with Wilson's secretary, Tumulty. In return for Garner's pledge to drop the resolution, Tumulty agreed to arrange for the president to review the collectorship case personally. Moreover, Garner persuaded Senator Culberson to endorse Joseph Wells for the position in the event of a vacancy.

Despite Garner's pressure and Rabb's growing notoriety, the insurgent Democrat survived the crises of late 1914 and early 1915. Within the Wilson cabinet, William Jennings Bryan and Thomas Watt Gregory, who was now the attorney general, still supported Rabb. Although the assistant secretary of the Treasury in charge of the customs service advocated Rabb's dismissal, McAdoo declined to take any action. When Garner advised Wells to confer with Burleson during the postmaster general's trip to Austin at the end of 1914, the South Texas boss discounted any possibility of his influencing Burleson on the collectorship question. Never an enthusiastic booster of Frank Rabb, the postmaster general was simply unwilling to press for the collector's removal. Wilson's most influential adviser, Colonel Edward House, remained aloof from the whole controversy.

Although the *New York World* exposé had embarrassed Morris Sheppard with its charge that he had sponsored Rabb's activities in Mexico, the junior senator from Texas still stood as Rabb's strongest supporter. For Sheppard the issue remained the same as it had been in 1913. When Treasury Secretary McAdoo asked Sheppard to review the case against the Laredo collector, the senator claimed that Rabb was the victim of conservative, anti-Wilson intrigues. Perhaps Sheppard's attitude was the key to understanding the reluctance of McAdoo and Burleson to disturb Rabb's tenure. Throughout 1914, Governor Oscar Colquitt had attacked the Wilson administration for allegedly tolerating Mexican atrocities against U.S. citizens along the border and for failing to order an invasion of Mexico. To preserve a solid base of support in Texas for the president's policies, Wilson had to have the cooperation of the progressive Democratic movement, which still regarded Rabb's appointment as one of its few rewards for rallying behind the Wilson banner in 1912.

With his failure to dislodge Frank Rabb during the early months of 1915, John Garner turned to low-keyed tactics. The veteran congressman limited his campaign to soliciting protests from Texas allies and to encouraging the agitation of the assistant secretary of the Treasury, who favored Rabb's removal. This lull in the customs dispute lasted until mid-1916 when one of Wells' closest associates broke with the boss and launched his own drive for the collectorship.

Lawrence Bates had served James Wells as a loyal ally since 1899 when the Uvalde native resigned from the Texas Rangers to assume the position of Brownsville city marshal. The next year Wells used his influence with his brother-in-law, District Attorney John Kleiber, to clear Bates of a murder charge. The close association between the Cameron County boss and the former Ranger continued even after Bates received an appointment as a special agent for the Treasury Department in 1905. Although his official assignment was to investigate smuggling operations, he devoted much of his attention to collecting evidence of political misconduct against the Republican customs collectors at Brownsville. In 1910, Bates resigned from the federal service to assist Wells, who was on the verge of a physical breakdown, in the management of the fall campaign against the Independents. After unsuccessful bids in 1912 to reclaim the post of city marshal and to secure an appointment as a U.S. marshal, Wells' versatile lieutenant staged a comeback by winning a seat in the Texas House of Representatives in 1914. Once in Austin, Bates began to display uncharacteristic independence. He joined Governor James Ferguson's staff and subsequently announced his intention to run for the office of Cameron County sheriff against the Wells-backed incumbent, W. T. Vann. Fearing a direct challenge to his own authority from this formidable political operator, Wells proposed a quid pro quo deal. In return for Bates' promise to withdraw from the sheriff's race, Wells arranged his selection as a delegate to the national Democratic convention. The accommodation soon collapsed, however, when Bates resumed his drive for sheriff and revealed his ambition to replace Frank Rabb as the customs collector for the Laredo district.

Although Wells was confident that Sheriff Vann could defeat Bates in the Democratic primary of 1916, the aging boss viewed his former ally as a serious competitor for the collectorship. In correspondence with Representative Garner, Wells expressed the fear that Governor Ferguson had accompanied Bates to Washington to arrange his appointment to the Laredo post. For Wells, the prospect of Bates' succeeding Rabb was appalling. In place of a pathetic figure, who "does not really control a dozen votes in this entire Congressional District," the Rio Grande chieftain would have to contend with a politician who had demonstrated his organizational abilities through sixteen years of faithful service for the Democratic machine. Bates' ties with Governor Ferguson would enable him to exert influence over the distribution of state patronage as well. Moreover, the new challenger enjoyed the support of a few key Democrats on the local scene, including County Judge H. L. Yates. In an emotional appeal to Garner, Wells asserted that "if an *Enemy Must* hold the position of Collector of Customs . . . , Rabb is a thousand times in preference to any other such,—and especially Bates."[26]

John Garner's response was strangely ambiguous. On the one hand, he reassured Wells that Ferguson had not accompanied Bates to Washington, and he questioned how much influence the demagogic governor exercised over the Wilson administration. At the same time, however, Garner took Bates' threat seriously enough to suggest a second effort at reconciliation. During a conference with the former city marshal at the national convention, the Uvalde congressman called on Bates to set aside his ambitions for the offices of sheriff and collector and urged him to run for reelection to the Texas House, where he could defend Garner's interests in the legislative fight over congressional redistricting. In striking contrast to Wells' bitter condemnations of Bates' character and conduct, Garner formed a favorable opinion of the man. The South Texas representative informed Wells that Bates "expressed no feeling against you whatever —simply said that your age and health did not permit you to look after the political situation as you once did." Garner added, "I sincerely hope it can be arranged so there will be no division in your forces."[27] Rather than acting as a Wells partisan, Garner appeared to be gravitating toward the role of mediator. Perhaps the veteran congressman had developed his own doubts about Wells' continuing effectiveness as a political leader and was reluctant to antagonize any politician who might displace Wells as the Democratic boss of Cameron County. Any inclination to compromise his ties with Wells vanished, however, when Sheriff Vann overwhelmed Bates in the Democratic primary. After that defeat, Lawrence Bates never reemerged as a major force in Valley politics.

Although Frank Rabb had survived Garner's attacks from 1913 through 1915 and Bates' challenge in 1916, the collector's prospects for reappointment at the end of his term in October 1917 were nil. Even after the subsidence of the uproar over Rabb's meddling in the Mexican Revolution, high-ranking officials in the Treasury Department continued to express dissatisfaction with his performance as a customs collector. In his final report on the operation of the Laredo district, the chief of the Division of Customs stated that "Rabb lives in Brownsville, is very seldom in his office [at Laredo], and pays little attention to the customs business."[28] The supervisor also noted that the expenses of the South Texas district actually exceeded the revenue from the collection of duties by $20,000 in 1916.

Another barrier to Rabb's reappointment was the special relationship that developed between John Garner and the Wilson administration after American entry into World War I in April 1917. Claude Kitchin of North Carolina, who held the positions of Democratic majority leader in the House and chairman of the Ways and Means Committee, voted against the declaration of war against Germany and showed little inclination to lead the fight for the passage of the revenue bills needed to finance the war effort. To offset Kitchin's break with the administration, the president recruited Garner to serve as his spokesman on the Ways and Means Committee. The Texas representative not only lobbied for Wilson's tax and bond proposals before the committee and the whole House, but he also contributed to the formulation of those policies through regular consultation with the president and his leading advisers.

John Garner's role as a congressional confidant to the president naturally strengthened his bargaining position on patronage matters. Both Burleson and McAdoo refused to support Frank Rabb's application for reappointment, and the Treasury secretary asked Garner to suggest a suitable replacement. For a time, even Attorney General Gregory appeared receptive to Garner's influence. When the South Texas congressman tried to arrange the appointment of Joseph K. Wells to serve as a lawyer in the Judge Advocate's Department of the Army, Thomas Gregory withdrew the name of his candidate as a gesture of appreciation for Garner's legislative services. Gregory's gratitude had its limits, however. He subsequently wrote a series of letters to promote support for Rabb, but to no avail. The only influential endorsement from outside the administration came from Senator Morris Sheppard, who restated his familiar portrayal of Rabb as a courageous supporter of Woodrow Wilson in 1913. In the face of Frank Rabb's embarrassing performance over the past four years, the other spokesmen for progressive Democracy in Texas apparently regarded their debt to the Valley insurgent as paid in full.

By mid-August, Garner expressed confidence that "the Collector will not be reappointed, and that . . . the Secretary [of the Treasury] will take the man that I recommend."[29] However, neither the congressman nor James Wells was taking any chances. Garner had already advised his ally to choose "a high class, efficient businessman" as his candidate and to arrange a letter-writing campaign on the part of "bankers and leading commercial men in our section of the state."[30] Throughout the collectorship struggle, Wells had regarded his son Joseph as the ideal choice, but after his failure to secure an appointment in the Judge Advocate's Department, Joseph Wells had joined the regular army and was now serving in France. Further complications arose when the Wilson administration ordered another reorganization of the customs districts of Texas just a month before the end of Rabb's term. The plan called for the merger of the Eagle Pass and Laredo districts and the establishment of the district headquarters at San Antonio. After learning of this move, John Garner suggested the candidacy of Thomas Coleman, a wealthy rancher who lived in San Antonio. James Wells replied that the customs appointments under Coleman "would be the same, as if I were the Collector, and making them myself."[31] Although Senator Sheppard abandoned Rabb and endorsed an original Wilson man who had served as Senator Culberson's campaign manager in 1916, Garner persuaded Culberson, McAdoo, and President Wilson to accept his choice. On September 20, 1917, the president appointed Thomas Coleman to the collectorship for the new San Antonio district.

Ironically, the effect of Coleman's appointment on South Texas politics was minimal. Rabb's disrepute and ineptitude had already neutralized the political influence of the customs force along the border. In addition, the new collector refused to bow to Wells' dictates on the selection of customs personnel for the Brownsville office. When the friend of a discharged inspector appealed for assistance from Wells in 1919, the frustrated boss admitted that Coleman "has not appointed anyone of the several persons that I have warmly recommended,—for what reasons I do not know."[32] The prolonged patronage dispute, which was supposed to represent a struggle between the forces of reform and reaction and to determine the future course of Valley politics, ended with a whimper. In fact, as the Rabb controversy dragged on, far more consequential events overtook the Lower Rio Grande Valley—events that disrupted the economic boom, caused dramatic shifts in population, deepened the involvement of the federal government in local affairs, and simultaneously destroyed the Independent party and speeded the demise of the Wells machine. These cataclysmic developments were the revival of Mexican border raids on a massive scale and the murderous vigilante response of the Anglo residents of the region.

11. Tension along the Border, 1911–1918

THE MEXICAN REVOLUTION produced a new era of lawlessness along the border that was reminiscent of the days of Juan Cortina. Because of repeated war scares, Mexican raids, and American counterattacks, the delicate racial accommodation in the Lower Rio Grande Valley, which James Wells and his allies had labored to maintain for thirty years, eventually collapsed. The political repercussions for both the Democratic machine and the Independent party of Cameron County were staggering.

From the time of the fall of the Díaz regime in 1911, the farmers and ranchers of South Texas reported a steady increase in the theft of livestock and equipment. In the words of one Anglo farmer, "everything that [was] not tied down and watched with a shotgun" soon disappeared.[1] The Anglo residents blamed the refugees from the war-torn country to the south and local Hispanics for the stealing, but racial antagonism intensified only gradually. Four years passed before organized bands of Mexican marauders launched a campaign of terrorist attacks in the Lower Rio Grande Valley and provoked a backlash of lynchings and summary executions. When President Taft mobilized a force of thirty thousand troops to patrol the boundary with Mexico in 1911, South Texans appeared to be more concerned over the threatened reassignment of black soldiers to their region than over the prospect of raids from Mexico. After only five months, Taft withdrew the army and left the border virtually unprotected. Widespread agitation for the reintroduction of federal troops along the Rio Grande did not develop until General Victoriano Huerta ordered the arrest and murder of President Francisco Madero in 1913. The subsequent outbreak of fighting between the armies of Huerta, on the one hand, and those of Venustiano Carranza, Pancho Villa, and Emiliano Zapata, on the other, generated fears that the violence of the Mexican Revolution might engulf the whole border region, the U.S. side as well as the Mexican.

Developments in Matamoros in February 1913 alarmed Cameron County officials. When the military revolt against Madero erupted in Mexico City, the commander of the Matamoros garrison declared his allegiance to the deposed dictator Díaz, who had fled the country two years earlier. Within a week, the officer ran out of money to pay for the maintenance of his force and appealed to the residents of the Mexican city for a loan. When the local merchants and businessmen failed to donate enough funds, the commander threatened to withdraw his troops and to leave the town at the mercy of looters and bandits. Rumors circulated that the Mexican military also intended to imprison American citizens living in Matamoros, who refused to comply with these demands for money. After conferring with the U.S. consul in Matamoros, Cameron County Sheriff C. T. Ryan and County Judge E. H. Goodrich called on Governor Colquitt to dispatch the Texas National Guard to prevent any outburst of lawlessness from spilling across the border. A local captain in the state militia even wanted to use the troops to rescue endangered American citizens in Matamoros. While refusing to sanction armed intervention in Mexico, Colquitt did send five troops of cavalry to Brownsville. In a display of jingoistic bravado, he also authorized the local officials to "notify the Mexican commander at Matamoros . . . that if he harms a single Texan, his life will be demanded as a forfeit."[2]

The Mexican garrison at Matamoros, which quickly adandoned Díaz in favor of the new Huerta regime, remained in the city and maintained order. Although Colquitt claimed credit for the peaceful resolution of the crisis, some Americans along the border charged that the governor and the Cameron County officials had overreacted. The U.S. consul at Matamoros denied that he had made an appeal for protection and accused Ryan and Goodrich of exaggerating the seriousness of the situation. Dissent also came from some South Texas businessmen who feared that the news of military deployments to Brownsville would discourage land purchases and undercut the economic boom that the Valley had been experiencing since 1905. While conceding the need for stationing troops in the Valley, the Brownsville Chamber of Commerce cautioned that "our business interests demand conservative action and reason in any display of protection."[3]

The most important consequence of the moves of Governor Colquitt and the Cameron County officials was the return of the United States Army to the Lower Rio Grande Valley. After the murder of Madero, President Taft ordered the organization of a force of ten thousand troops at Galveston, but the War Department initially refused to send any soldiers to Brownsville. When false reports reached Washington that Colquitt planned to allow the state militia to cross the border, the Taft administration instructed the commander at Fort Sam Houston in San Antonio to dispatch a single troop of cavalry to the border town. Although no trouble developed, the army decided to retain a small force in the Lower Rio Grande Valley as part of a general plan to commit seven regiments to the protection of the whole boundary from the Gulf of Mexico to the Pacific coast. The presence of federal troops at least temporarily reduced the anxieties of Valley residents. Even in the face of a Carrancista offensive against Matamoros in June 1913, the population on the U.S. side of the border did not panic. In fact, just a few days before the battle in which the Constitutionalists gained control of Matamoros, over two hundred American sightseers, many of them prospective land buyers, visited the threatened city.

This period of relative calm was short-lived. Once the Constitutionalist forces consolidated their power along the border, South Texans became uneasy over the proximity of large concentrations of Mexican soldiers. In a letter to the secretary of war of the new Wilson administration, Congressman Garner denounced the failure of the army to assign more troops to the border as "criminal negligence." The representative pointed out that there were almost twelve thousand Mexican soldiers within "easy striking distance" of Laredo and another eight thousand near Brownsville.[4] He warned that reinforcements from San Antonio could not reach the border fast enough to prevent the sacking of these towns in the event of Mexican attacks. Although President Wilson denied the existence of any immediate danger, he agreed to enlarge the border patrols, mainly for the purpose of allaying the fears of the residents of the region.

The deployment of a limited number of additional troops failed to satisfy the farmers and ranchers of South Texas, and they turned to Governor Oscar Colquitt as their spokesman. When the *New York Sun* solicited the views of several governors on the issue of relations with Mexico in November 1913, Colquitt's response created a sensation. In contrast to Wilson's application of diplomatic pressure against the Huerta regime, the Texas chief executive called for armed intervention to restore order in the strife-torn nation. Tension between the governor and the Wilson administration mounted three months later when a group of Mexican soldiers kidnapped and murdered a Webb County rancher named Clemente Vergara, who was trying to recover some stolen cattle. Colquitt requested permission for the Texas Rangers to cross the Rio Grande to rescue the rancher, but Secretary of State Bryan rejected the proposal. After the return of Vergara's body to the American side of the border, ambiguous reports suggested that the Rangers had staged a raid into Mexico to recover the corpse. Although Colquitt denied that the Rangers had entered Mexico, he subsequently threatened to provoke another international incident by offering a $1,000 reward for the apprehension of the Mexican soldiers who had killed Vergara.

Ironically, when President Wilson engaged in his own brand of limited military intervention, panic overtook the residents of South Texas. To avenge the inadvertent and temporary arrest of several U.S. sailors at the Mexican port of Tampico and to block the shipment of German arms to Huerta's troops, Woodrow Wilson ordered the American seizure of the port city of Vera Cruz. From the outset of the crisis, pleas for military protection flooded the office of Governor Colquitt and the San Antonio headquarters of General Tasker Bliss, the commander of the Southern Department of the U.S. Army who supervised military operations along the entire border with Mexico. A letter from Hidalgo County Judge James Edwards, who was preparing to lead an insurgent revolt against the Closner machine, reflected the anxieties and prejudices of the recently settled Anglo farmers of the Valley: "A band of mounted men could easily swoop down upon any one of the numerous and populous but unprotected towns of the county, and with torch and flame, wipe it out of existence in a night, killing and massacring men, women, and children while they slept. There is no need to tell you what the Mexican race is. Indian warfare, divested of a few horrors, is the kind the Mexican wages."[5] Other residents expressed their fear of uprisings on the part of their Mexican American neighbors or the mass of refugees who had flooded the region. Local politicians even overcame their factional differences and made joint appeals for more troops. The military command at Fort Sam Houston also perceived a serious threat. The day before the attack against Vera Cruz, General Bliss proposed the American occupation of all the major Mexican border towns in the event Huerta's and Carranza's forces united to resist U.S. intervention. In Bliss' view, "if [these] Mexican towns are allowed to be occupied by unfriendly troops, all women and children and other noncombatants must be ordered to leave the American [border] towns as their only safety."[6]

Despite General Bliss' concern for the safety of the border towns, the War Department decided to send only two additional troops of cavalry to Brownsville. This reluctance to take strong action offered Governor Colquitt another opportunity to upstage the U.S. Army. With only three hundred soldiers present to patrol the whole Valley, the Texas governor ordered the movement of over one thousand state militiamen to Brownsville and then arranged the re-assignment of half of these troops to seven other Valley towns. As soon as the Texas guardsmen started for the border, Secretary of War Lindley Garrison abandoned his previous claim that no reinforce-ments were available and proposed the replacement of the state troops with a comparable number of regular army personnel. The first contingent of federal troops did not reach Brownsville until ten days after the arrival of the militia, and the guardsmen continued to patrol the other towns of Cameron and Hidalgo counties for another week. In the eyes of his South Texas constituents, Colquitt not only forced the hand of the federal government but also provided the first line of defense at the height of the crisis with Mexico. In the long run, however, the security of the Lower Rio Grande Valley depended on the presence of the U.S. Army. For the remainder of the era of armed conflict in Mexico, the Wilson administration maintained a sizable force along the border. The troop strength in the Valley never dropped below one thousand men and increased spectacularly from mid-1915 through 1916. The Texas militia did not return until July 1916 when President Wilson mobilized the national guard through-out the country and placed the state troops under the direct control of the regular army.

Despite Huerta's resignation from the Mexican presidency in July 1914 and the withdrawal of U.S. troops from Vera Cruz four months later, tension along the border rose dramatically in 1915. The collapse of the Huerta military dictatorship simply led to a split between Venustiano Carranza and Pancho Villa, and large-scale fighting resumed throughout the country. The Villista forces gained control of all northern Mexico except for a few scattered enclaves along the border, including the region around Matamoros. As a Vi-llista army of 4,000 soldiers prepared to launch an assault against Matamoros in March 1915, reports that both sides intended to use heavy artillery frightened the citizens of Brownsville. Although two miles separated Brownsville and Matamoros, the American town lay within range of any misdirected shells. To discourage reckless ac-tions on the part of either Mexican army, Secretary of War Garrison ordered the dispatch of 450 men and twelve field guns to Browns-ville. The press reported that the opposing Mexican factions were "doing much to avert any movement that might result in danger to the citizens on the American side of the Rio Grande."[7] Because of these precautions, the feared catastrophe did not take place. In the climactic battle for Matamoros, which followed a three-week siege, the outnumbered Carrancista defenders relied exclusively on rifle and machine gun fire as they turned back the Villista attack. Villa's partisans fired only twenty-five artillery shells, all of which landed on Mexican territory. Following the failure of their assault, the Villista troops withdrew from the border region.

Although the Carrancista victory at Matamoros placed this faction in complete control of the Mexican side of the Lower Rio Grande Valley, peace and order did not return to the region. Instead, the long-standing fears of the Americans were finally realized. A wave of lawlessness and violence swept across the border and left social and economic turmoil in its wake. From July through October 1915, bands of Mexican marauders staged approximately thirty raids into U.S. territory. Appeals for military protection came from communities as far north as Kingsville, one hundred miles from the border, but the depredations were concentrated in Cameron and Hidalgo counties. The bandits operated in groups ranging in size from ten to one hundred men, and they attacked farms, ranches, irrigation stations, trains, military units, and even small towns. They killed over thirty American civilians and soldiers and wounded approximately the same number. Despite this fairly modest level of casualties, the raiders' reputation for hating Anglos and murdering defenseless victims without provocation horrified ranchers and farmers, who had already endured four years of widespread stealing and recurrent panics over developments in Mexico. Thousands of residents abandoned their homes and property in outlying areas. They moved into the more secure towns or left the Valley altogether. Land sales collapsed, and the economic boom of the region came to an abrupt halt.

The causes of the raids were complex. Many of the participants were simply outlaws, deserters, and impoverished refugees from the Mexican Revolution, whose sole aim was to steal from the affluent Anglo settlers of the Valley. Evidence also indicated that the Carrancista commander at Matamoros, General Emiliano Nafarrate, tolerated and possibly even sanctioned some of the raids. Until Nafarrate's removal in October 1915, the Mexican army made no effort to suppress the marauders, who used the Mexican side of the border as a sanctuary. Two of the most notorious bandit leaders openly recruited followers in Mexico, and at least one pro-Carranza newspaper published appeals for Mexican citizens to join the raiders. A few of the brigands even wore the uniforms of the Carrancista army and carried official military passes.

At the time of the escalating lawlessness along the border, Venustiano Carranza was seeking American recognition as the legitimate ruler of Mexico, but his repeated refusals to submit to Woodrow Wilson's guidance had alienated the U.S. president. After the outbreak of civil war between the Carranza forces and those of Pancho Villa, U.S. policy shifted from a brief, initial embrace of Villa's cause to a course of strict noncommitment. In his drive to establish diplomatic relations with the United States, Carranza took advantage of the border raids by claiming that his military commanders could not cooperate with the U.S. authorities as long as his regime went unrecognized. When the Wilson administration finally extended de facto recognition in October 1915, the Mexican army immediately cracked down on the bandit activity.

Conditions on the American side of the Rio Grande also contributed to the bandit upheaval of 1915 since Hispanic residents of Texas as well as Mexican nationals participated in the raids. In fact, the two leading organizers of the raiding parties were well-to-do Mexican Americans: Luís de la Rosa, a Brownsville grocer, and Aniceto Pizaña, the owner of a small ranch in Cameron County. After 1905, the level of racial antagonism in the Trans-Nueces rose sharply with the influx of settlers from other parts of Texas and the United States. Many of the newcomers displayed open contempt for all Hispanics, regardless of their class standing, and imposed blatant forms of discrimination in the new towns and farming communities of the Valley. The Anglo farmers not only disavowed any paternalistic responsibilities for their workers but often engaged in merciless exploitation. Wage rates were low, and Mexican American laborers complained that their employers still shortchanged them. The arrival of thousands of migrants from Mexico and the exposure of local Hispanics to the egalitarian rhetoric of the Mexican Revolution, which called for an end to the feudalistic exploitation of the *peones* of that country, also had an unsettling effect on race relations in South Texas. Nevertheless, only a small minority of the Mexican American population joined or actively supported the marauders, and some of the collaborators acted only out of fear of bandit retaliation. Unfortunately, panic-stricken Anglos lashed out against innocent as well as guilty Hispanics. As hundreds of Mexican Americans fell victim to Anglo vigilante action, race hatred along the Rio Grande soared, and the base of support for the raids grew.

The first warning of impending border trouble came in February 1915 when Sheriff Deodoro Guerra of Starr County arrested a Mexican national named Basilio Ramos, who had once worked as a beer distributor in San Diego, Texas, and who had more recently served time in a Mexican jail. Ramos had in his possession documents that revealed a farfetched irredentist scheme called the Plan of San Diego. Anti-American zealots at San Diego had fashioned the plan and later circulated it among Huerta sympathizers in a Mexican prison. The program called for a general uprising of the Hispanic population of five southwestern states, including Texas, the eventual reunification of this territory with Mexico, and the conquest of six additional states, which would serve as a buffer zone between Mexico and imperialistic United States. The Mexican revolutionaries intended to solicit the support of blacks and Apache Indians and to kill all Anglo males over the age of sixteen. The whole scenario was so preposterous that neither the authorities nor the South Texas populace took the conspiracy seriously at first. In early August, however, one month after the start of frequent, large-scale raids, a cavalry patrol captured documents that indicated that at least some of the marauders were committed to the implementation of the Plan of San Diego. Later de la Rosa and Pizaña made a public announcement of their aim to liberate Texas and the other border states. Although the objectives of the plan still appeared ludicrous, the new revelations fueled the mounting hysteria of the Valley residents.

For the first month of the escalating bandit activity, General Frederick Funston, who commanded the Southern Department from his headquarters at Fort Sam Houston in San Antonio, declined to send massive reinforcements to the Lower Rio Grande Valley. Several factors accounted for his restraint. In March 1915, James Ferguson had replaced Oscar Colquitt as the governor of Texas, and the new chief executive showed no inclination to resort to Colquitt's tactic of deploying the state militia to prod the U.S. Army into action. The fact that none of Funston's troops came under fire or suffered any casualties in July also caused the general to down play the seriousness of conditions in the Valley. Another reason for his refusal to take strong action was his belief that the local politicians were responsible for the turmoil in the border counties:

> From the best information obtainable, the situation in Cameron, Hidalgo, and Starr Counties, Texas, appears to be due to a political feud with headquarters in Brownsville, both parties having organized bands of more or less lawless men to intimidate the other by means of robbery and murderous attacks on ranches belonging to the other.
>
> The activities of these bands of cut-throats have now gotten beyond the control of leaders, and bands have inaugurated a campaign of vengeance against enemies who have incurred their enmity.[8]

When federal officials leaked the report to the newspapers, James Wells, Chairman C. H. More of the Independent party, and fifty other Cameron County politicians wired an indignant protest to the Washington offices of the Associated Press: "We represent all shades of political belief and all local political factions, and we absolutely know that the statements made are untrue. All factions are cooperating as American citizens to restore order and obtain adequate protection for our families and property."[9]

Although the political parties of the Valley had long records of fostering violence, no evidence emerged to substantiate Funston's sensational claims. As the politicians' rebuttal to the charges indicated, the mounting crisis along the border was generating an uncharacteristic willingness on their part to form a united front. Furthermore, Funston drastically revised his views on the origins and the potential dangers of the raids in response to a startling chain of events during the second week in August. The first skirmish between U.S. Army troops and bandits did not take place until August 2, but the increasingly brazen marauders launched three more attacks against military patrols from August 8 through August 10. During the last of these clashes, the soldiers seized the documents that revealed the link between the raids and the Plan of San Diego. Two days later a seventy-five–year–old Hispanic employee of the King Ranch testified that a party of fifty armed men had forced him to participate in a raid. According to the informant, half of the group consisted of Mexican soldiers who professed their allegiance to Carranza. Their ultimate objective was to restore lost territory to Mexico. Funston also received reports indicating that more than a thousand Hispanics were pledged to fight for the Plan of San Diego. In the face of these disclosures, Governor Ferguson, Congressman Garner, and local officials stepped up their agitation for greater military protection.

All these developments forced the commander of the Southern Department to discard his earlier contention that the bandits were agents of the competing political parties of the Lower Rio Grande Valley. On August 13, Funston informed the secretary of war that "it is now established beyond doubt that [a] considerable portion of [the] band of outlaws came from Mexico and were officers and soldiers of Carranza's forces, doubtless acting without the authority of their chiefs."[10] The next day, the general even implicated the Mexican military chief at Matamoros and predicted that Nafarrate might respond to any military clash along the border with an attack against Brownsville. Overcome with this new sense of urgency, Funston secured authorization from the War Department to assign over a thousand additional soldiers to the Brownsville region. By the end of October, the troop commitment for the Lower Rio Grande Valley reached five thousand men.

With the rapid buildup of military strength in the Valley in mid-August, the raids subsided but then resumed in full force a few weeks later. Feeling as insecure as ever, the citizens of South Texas and their political leaders continued to campaign for more state and federal protection. These efforts came to a head in late October when Brownsville Mayor A. A. Browne organized a conference of representatives from every town in Cameron and Hidalgo counties, plus spokesmen from Brooks, Willacy, and Kleberg counties. Over two hundred people attended the meeting, and the delegates voted to create a committee to meet with state and national officials for the purpose of explaining the seriousness of the threat along the Rio Grande. The spirit of bipartisan cooperation still prevailed, since the committee included such diverse political figures as Ed C. Lasater, Rentfro B. Creager, and James B. Wells. In their meetings with Governor Ferguson and General Funston, the South Texas representatives called for increased diplomatic pressure on the Carranza government to police the border, the pursuit of bandits into Mexico, the establishment of martial law in the border counties, and the offering of liberal rewards for the apprehension of the bandit leaders. Although officials in the Wilson administration promised to give the suggestions serious consideration, the political offensive had little impact on federal policy. Even before the Brownsville convention, the president had recognized the Carranza regime as the de facto government of Mexico and had renewed his appeals for cooperation in fighting the bandit menace. Until the intentions of Carranza and his commanders along the border became clear, the U.S. government was unwilling to implement more extreme measures.

In their appeals for assistance, the Valley spokesmen invariably portrayed the Anglo citizenry as the target of Mexican aggression. Their accounts focused on the threats of raids and invasions from Mexico and uprisings by their Mexican American neighbors. Although these fears were genuine, the Anglos' actual suffering and hardships paled beside the horrors that they inflicted upon the Hispanic population. In their hysteria over the bandit attacks, the Anglo residents turned to vigilante action, and a bloodbath that claimed from two hundred to three hundred Hispanic lives ensued.

Some of the Anglo responses to the border crises were legitimate acts of self-defense. Alarmed citizens patrolled the streets of the Valley towns at night, organized caravans of automobiles to scout the countryside, formed posses to assist local law enforcement officers, and provided federal troops with automobile transportation. Regrettably, the campaign to curb bandit depredations went beyond these legal measures. Anglo gangs burned houses, forced Hispanic families to flee their farms and ranches, and confiscated their weapons, but widespread lynchings overshadowed all of these practices. Vigilante committees compiled "black lists" of suspected raiders or collaborators and marked them for death.[11] According to a correspondent for the *St. Louis Post-Dispatch*, "when a certain man . . . is captured or killed in . . . a raid, his brothers, half-brothers, and brothers-in-law are assumed to be guilty and are immediately killed or arrested."[12] Not even the arrest of suspects assured their protection from vigilante retribution. At San Benito alone, mobs dragged at least fifteen prisoners from the jail and shot or hanged them. By the middle of September, the *San Antonio Daily Express* reported that "the finding of dead bodies of Mexicans . . . has reached the point where it creates little or no interest."[13]

Much of the blame for the proliferation of these crimes rested with the lawmen of South Texas. Not only did they fail to conduct serious investigations of the killings of Hispanic suspects, but some of the officials even participated in the lynchings and summary executions. When the officers returned from their manhunts bearing bullet-riddled corpses, they usually contended that the victims had been killed while resisting arrest. These claims were difficult to disprove, since probably few real bandits were willing to surrender peacefully. Some posses, however, made no pretense of acting in self-defense and hanged their prisoners. Sheriff W. T. Vann of Cameron County refused to condone or engage in wanton killings, but even Vann was slow to fire his San Benito deputies, who repeatedly refused to defend their prisoners against mob violence.

The most blatant abusers of police power were the Texas Rangers. The size of the Ranger force along the border increased from fifteen men at the time of the Tampico incident in 1914 to sixty men by the end of October 1915. Although the Anglo residents of the Valley appreciated the presence of the U.S. Army, many of them believed that the Rangers were more effective than the military in pursuing Mexican raiders. In contrast to the cavalry, the state lawmen knew the country well, traveled fast, and were adept at taking the bandits by surprise. The ruthlessness of the Rangers also appealed to their admirers. The *Corpus Christi Caller and Daily Herald* offered the following account of Ranger tactics: "All armed Mexicans that are slow to explain their identity and purpose are in immediate danger throughout the disturbed region, and if any one makes a threatening move, his life is forfeited. Officially the number of Mexicans killed [since a raid against a branch of the King Ranch at Las Norrias in Cameron County on August 8] is between fifteen and twenty, but it is known that many more have been shot to death while resisting arrest."[14] One well-informed Brownsville citizen reported that the Rangers "began a systematic manhunt and killed, according to a verified list, 102 Mexicans" in the aftermath of the Las Norrias raid.[15]

Sheriff Vann's testimony before a legislative committee in 1919 confirmed that the Rangers were capable of committing cold-blooded murder. The Cameron County sheriff related an incident that occurred in October 1915, following a bandit attack against a train, in which the engineer, a soldier, and a civilian passenger were killed:

> The morning we came out there and arrested those four men, [Ranger] Captain Ransom had them and walked over to me and says, I am going out to kill these fellows, are you going with me. I says no. . . . He says, if you haven't got guts enough to do it, I will go myself. I says, that takes a whole lot of guts, four fellows with their hands tied behind them, it takes a whole lot of guts to do that, and I went up the road four or five miles. . . . When I went back, Ransom had killed his men, and I told my deputy, you take these men [whom Vann had arrested in the meantime] and put them in the car and carry them to town. . . . Ransom says he is going to kill them too. I says, no, they are my two, he hasn't enough Rangers to kill my two . . . , and we . . . put them in jail, and they were proved to be innocent.[16]

Although the *Corpus Christi Caller* reported at the time of these killings that the Rangers and the civilian posses had "executed" at least ten Hispanics, the state government failed to investigate the matter or to take any punitive action.[17] In fact, in his biennial review for 1915 and 1916, the adjutant general asserted that "the work of the Ranger force from the inception of the border troubles . . . was of the highest order and worthy of the best traditions of the Ranger force."[18]

The chief effects of this reign of terror against the Hispanic population were twofold: the flight of thousands of Hispanics from their homes and the fueling of racial enmity on both sides of the border. Many of the Mexican Americans from outlying areas sought refuge in the towns of the Valley, while others fled into Mexico. The Anglos who had refused to panic and abandon their farms and ranches now faced severe labor shortages. The problem became so acute that the mayors of six Valley towns passed a resolution to reassure Hispanic workers that they were secure as long as they did not give "aid and sympathy to the invaders."[19] A San Benito developer even tried to promote "better feelings" between the races by urging local Hispanics to surrender their weapons.[20] These appeals failed to stem the tide of fleeing Mexican Americans, who understood all too well how safe they would be if they gave up their guns and relied on the goodwill of local lawmen for protection.

The abuses of vigilante groups and law enforcement officers not only spawned racial hatred among the persecuted Hispanic residents of South Texas but also incited the Mexicans south of the border. José Canales pointed out that "every relative" of the Hispanics whom the Rangers had killed "would go to Mexico with his tale of woe." Their stories aroused support for the bandits and contempt for the Anglos "to the extent that practically the whole Mexican border on the other side was at war with us."[21] Rentfro B. Creager speculated that the intensity of anti-American sentiment among the general Hispanic populace influenced General Nafarrate's decision to support the bandit activity. As American charges of his complicity in the raids mounted, the Matamoros commander launched a public attack against the Rangers for brutalizing Hispanics living in South Texas and for firing shots across the border. Belatedly, even the Wilson administration acknowledged that the mistreatment of Hispanics in the Valley was contributing to the tension between the United States and Mexico. On October 31, Secretary of State Robert Lansing appealed to Governor Ferguson to use his influence with state and county officials "to allay race prejudices and restrain indiscreet conduct."[22] The secretary argued that an improvement in race relations in South Texas would bolster his efforts to persuade the Carranza government to take action against the bandit gangs.

James Wells and his allies failed to take a strong stand against the anti-Hispanic violence that swept through the Lower Rio Grande Valley. Only the independent-minded José Canales called on Governor Ferguson to halt the abuses of the Texas Rangers. All the other appeals from county officials and leading Democrats dealt solely with the threat of the Mexican bandits. Although Sheriff Vann condemned the Rangers for murdering their prisoners, he did not attempt to arrest any of the state policemen, and he failed to apprehend any of the local participants in vigilante terrorism. Hidalgo County Sheriff A. Y. Baker, who had replaced John Closner in 1914 when the aging boss decided to run for county treasurer, was a former Ranger and cooperated closely with the state force. Even after a political split developed between Wells and the Rangers in 1918, the Cameron County chieftain had nothing but praise for the Ranger performance during the bandit upheaval of 1915. Before a legislative committee in 1919, Wells testified that "two or three companies of Rangers did more good than all those federal troops."[23] When a state senator inquired about the killings of "innocent men," the veteran Democrat offered the following reply: "There is no doubt about that. I know a number. I want to add that there were a lot more that should have been killed."[24]

The callous response to the terrorist campaign against the Hispanic population stemmed in part from the Democratic politicians' own sense of insecurity. The racial conflicts of the post–Civil War era had left their mark on many of the old-timers and their families, who never overcame their fear of the volatility of the Hispanic masses. Over the years, strong support for the Rangers had accompanied the politicians' and ranchers' adaptations to the Mexican culture, their paternalistic care for Hispanic laborers, and their cooperation with well-to-do Hispanic landowners and businessmen. For Wells and his associates, this hard-line, often brutal police force had always represented the first line of defense in the event of a renewal of racial hostilities. James Wells' brother-in-law, District Attorney John Kleiber, expressed the ambivalence that many established residents felt toward their Mexican American neighbors. While defending "the ordinary Mexican" as a "law-respecting and law-fearing man" under normal circumstances, Kleiber conceded that these people could be aroused by outside agitators and their patriotic attachment to their homeland.[25]

Even the veteran Democrats who had complete faith in the loyalties of their longtime constituents looked upon the recent migrants from Mexico with suspicion. Thousands of these newcomers lived outside the supervision of either political party, and their sympathies remained a mystery. As the bandit activity intensified, the bosses and their lieutenants were in no position to discount reports that over a thousand Hispanics supported the Plan of San Diego and collaborated with the raiders. Facing a possible rebellion of this magnitude, the politicos were willing to tolerate ruthless countermeasures, even if such actions meant the sacrifice of some innocent Mexican Americans. While the Democratic organizers regretted the harassment or killing of any of their faithful supporters, they felt no sense of responsibility for the welfare of the recent arrivals from Mexico.

Economic considerations also may have shaped the attitudes of the Democratic leaders. Wells, Closner, and their colleagues had invested heavily in the economic development of the Valley, and they paid dearly when the outbreak of bandit raids caused the collapse of the local boom. Confronted with impatient creditors and mounting taxes on land that they could not sell, these political entrepreneurs were desperate for a quick end to the crisis. Again the resort to brute force appeared as a tempting solution to their problem.

The same concerns influenced many of the Independent politicians as well. In addition, the Independent party was far more dependent on the Anglo vote than the Democratic machine was, and the insurgents could hardly afford to offend their panic-stricken constituents with condemnations of the mistreatment of the Hispanic population. Not even past grievances over Ranger collaboration with the Wells faction prompted the Independents to attack the practices of the state police. In 1919, R. B. Creager charged that "90% of those [Hispanics] killed were as innocent as you or I of complicity in those bandit outrages," but at the time of the raids, he abstained from making any public criticisms of the Rangers, local lawmen, or vigilante groups.[26] Another Wells adversary, Lon Hill, was in the forefront of the agitation for a crackdown on Hispanic traitors. He served as a special Ranger and a vigilante organizer and later asserted that "every Mexican in the country was in sympathy" with the raiders.[27]

Contrary to the expectations of local politicos, neither the Ranger executions nor the vigilante hysteria that gripped the Anglo residents of the Valley brought the bandit raids to a close. Not even the presence of the U.S. Army was decisive. Instead the critical factor was the decision of the Carranza government to mount a military campaign against the marauders. With recognition from the United States imminent, Carranza removed Nafarrate as the commander at Matamoros in early October and appointed General Eugenio López. Although two spectacular raids occurred later that month, López began to cooperate with the U.S. forces that patrolled the border. Shortly after the extension of de facto recognition on October 19, the bandit activity ended, and peace returned to the border region for five months. The Mexican government even paid Pizaña and de la Rosa $50,000 to stop organizing raids and awarded the latter a commission in the regular army. In November, Venustiano Carranza visited Matamoros and conferred with Governor Ferguson and General Funston. The Mexican president pledged his full support of American efforts to combat lawlessness along the Rio Grande. He subsequently assigned General Alfredo Ricaut, an outspoken proponent of improved relations with the United States, to take charge of the garrison at Matamoros. Under Ricaut's direction, the Mexican troops thwarted several attempts to launch raids into U.S. territory.

The revival of tension between the United States and Mexico in

1916 resulted from the outrages of Pancho Villa, whose beaten armies had retreated to his native state of Chihuahua, south of New Mexico and West Texas. When the Wilson administration recognized the Carranza regime as the de facto government of Mexico, Villa felt betrayed and decided to take his revenge against U.S. citizens in northern Mexico and along the border. He also hoped to provoke an armed conflict with the United States that might rejuvenate his declining military and political fortunes. In January 1916, his partisans shot sixteen American passengers on a train traveling through Chihuahua, and two months later he staged a murderous attack against Columbus, New Mexico. The raiders burned the town and killed nineteen Americans. In the face of a national outcry, President Wilson ordered the formation of an army to capture or destroy Villa's force in Mexico. General Funston assembled the "Punitive Expedition" of five thousand soldiers and, on instructions from the War Department, he placed General John Pershing in command. As the elusive Villa drew Pershing's troops hundreds of miles deep into Mexican territory, Carranza adamantly demanded an immediate withdrawal.

From the outset of Pershing's campaign in Mexico, military strategists expressed concern over the security of Brownsville and the other border towns. To bolster the defense of Brownsville, General Funston dispatched a battery of artillery and urged Sheriff Vann to organize a "home guard" of local citizens. Although no major raids occurred in the Lower Rio Grande Valley until June, tension remained high. General Ricaut at Matamoros still professed his commitment to maintaining order along the border, but his troops became unruly. On one occasion, Mexican soldiers threw four "reputable" San Benito citizens into jail, where the guards robbed them and threatened them with death. After releasing the Americans, the soldiers fired shots at them. At a later date, a group of U.S. soldiers on leave were victims of the same kind of abuse. In early May, part of the Matamoros garrison rebelled and looted several stores before Ricaut could reassert his control.

Developments outside the Valley appeared even more ominous to the local residents. After a Mexican raid against two isolated towns in West Texas, Glen Springs and Boquillas, a small force of U.S. soldiers pursued the bandits into Mexico and remained there for almost two weeks. In response to this incident, President Wilson placed the national guards of Texas, Arizona, and New Mexico in the federal service and assigned 4,500 militiamen to patrol duty along the border. On the Mexican side of the confrontation, Carranza ordered Ricaut and the commander at Nuevo Laredo to attack any U.S. troops that entered their military districts. In addition, negotiations between the Mexican war minister and representatives of the U.S. Army at Ciudad Juárez, Mexico, broke down when Carranza refused to accept a tentative agreement calling for a gradual American withdrawal. The Mexican president objected to the conferees' failure to specify a definite date for the complete evacuation of Pershing's army. In a later note to the U.S. State Department, Carranza denounced American intervention as an act of aggression against his nation and argued that only an immediate withdrawal could dispel the suspicion that the United States was trying to provoke a war.

Just one day after the collapse of the Ciudad Juárez conference, the capture of two Villista officers at Kingsville revived fears of a general Hispanic uprising throughout South Texas. The federal agents who made the arrests charged that the suspects had been recruiting Mexican Americans to sabotage railroad lines and to plant bombs in San Antonio, Kingsville, Mission, and Brownsville. Local officers at Kingsville subsequently arrested thirty alleged conspirators, and the Texas Rangers intervened with their own special brand of justice. During a transfer of prisoners from Kingsville to Brownsville, the Rangers killed the two ringleaders as they "tried to escape."[28]

In June, the center of action in the unfolding drama of American-Mexican relations returned to the Lower Rio Grande Valley. Luís de la Rosa reappeared on the Mexican side of the border as a bandit organizer. Although General Ricaut arranged the arrest of de la Rosa and several of his followers in Monterrey on June 11, most of his gang escaped capture and launched a new campaign of raids into South Texas. On June 15, a band of sixty Mexican marauders attacked an American military patrol in Webb County and killed four soldiers. The next day a detachment of soldiers fired on another group of raiders a few miles from San Benito. Ricaut announced that his troops would "shoot the first American soldier crossing the Rio Grande," but this warning failed to deter the new commander for the Brownsville district, General James Parker.[29] He ordered a force of four hundred cavalrymen to follow the second band of raiders into Mexico. During the expedition, which lasted only one day, the U.S. troops fought a minor skirmish with a few bandits and avoided any encounters with Ricaut's forces. When Parker received a pledge from the Mexican general to apprehend the raiders, the U.S. commander instructed his troops to withdraw. Following Parker's provocative action, serious bandit activity in the Valley again ceased. The subsequent introduction of thousands of national guardsmen into the Brownsville military district, which extended from the Gulf Coast into Zapata County, ensured the preservation of order along the southeastern end of the border for the remainder of 1916. Not even the return of General Nafarrate to take charge of the Matamoros garrison led to any new disturbances.

Although the June crisis came to a quick end at the local level, the brief revival of Mexican raids and Parker's intervention had serious consequences for the general course of Mexican-American relations. The incident coincided with an exchange of threatening notes between General Pershing and the Carrancista military commander for Chihuahua and served as one of the catalysts that "set war machinery in motion on both sides."[30] On June 18, President Wilson mobilized all the national guard units in the country for service along the border. The order affected over 125,000 men. During this same period, Secretary of State Lansing sent a scathing diplomatic message to the Mexican government. He condemned the regime for its failure to prevent raids against American territory and warned that any Carrancista attacks against Pershing's forces or any other U.S. troops would "lead to the gravest consequences."[31]

The momentum toward war reached its climax on June 21, when a reconnaissance party from Pershing's army attacked a force of 250 Mexicans at the town of Carrizal in northern Chihuahua. The Mexican soldiers held their ground, killed twelve Americans, and captured twenty-three others. Only Carranza's prompt release of the prisoners in response to an American ultimatum prevented President Wilson from delivering a war message to Congress. Since the United States already faced the threat of war with Germany over the issues of submarine warfare and American economic support for the Allied cause in World War I, Wilson could not afford to ignore Carranza's conciliatory gesture. Both leaders then made impassioned pleas for peace and, within a few weeks, arranged for the establishment of a joint commission to study the differences between the two countries and to make recommendations for a settlement. The commission met from September 1916 into January 1917, and, all the while, Pershing's expedition remained in Mexico.

Although the immediate threat of war passed during the first week of July 1916, the U.S. military remained in the state of readiness for large-scale action. As a result of the calling out of the whole national guard, 150,000 soldiers were patrolling the border by mid-July. The arrival of a division of New York guardsmen in late June raised the troop level in the Lower Rio Grande Valley to almost 30,000 men. Despite this spectacular increase in military strength and the cessation of the bandit raids, Valley spokesmen still expressed dissatisfaction over border security. Now the issue was the distribution of the new forces. A protest from James Wells and a Brownsville banker to Garner revealed the intensity of the competition among the Valley towns for troop deployments. The two men complained that "only one regiment of . . . troops has been sent to Brownsville" while "many thousands of them have been . . . located at McAllen, Mission, and other unimportant points." In Wells' view, Brownsville was "the only really important point upon the Rio Grande border this side of El Paso" and "decidedly the best point at which to concentrate a large number of troops."[32] Garner, Charles Culberson, and Morris Sheppard all lobbied on Wells' behalf, and General Funston promised to send additional forces to the Brownsville area. At the request of General Parker, the Democratic chieftain and one of his clients even allowed several militia units to establish a base on 265 acres of their land "free of any charge."[33]

Economic concerns as well as competing security claims underlay Wells' appeal. With the economy of the region still depressed from the effect of the bandit raids of 1915, the businessmen of the different Valley towns were desperate for the trade of the incoming guardsmen. Not only did the soldiers, who eventually totalled forty thousand, make individual purchases, but the army quartermasters ordered some of the supplies for their military units from local merchants. The army also deposited substantial sums of money in local banks. The two Brownsville banks received $50,000 each. The long-range consequence of this infusion of soldiers was almost as dramatic as its immediate impact. As José Canales later pointed out, the exposure of thousands of militiamen from all parts of the country to the Lower Rio Grande Valley "constituted the greatest free advertizement that this area has ever got."[34] When the land boom resumed after World War I, former guardsmen and their friends participated in the new wave of settlement.

Although the peace commission failed to formulate a settlement that Carranza would accept, the Wilson administration ordered Pershing to begin withdrawing his troops in January 1917, and the evacuation was complete by February 5. Pancho Villa remained at large, but Carrancista forces had crushed his army in early January. In addition, Carranza had arranged the popular election of a constitutional convention to lay the foundation for the establishment of a democratic government. After Carranza's election to the presidency on March 11, the United States extended de jure recognition to the new government. Even before the withdrawal of American troops began, tension along the U.S.-Mexican boundary had diminished so dramatically that the War Department had started releasing some of the national guard units from active duty. On February 18,

1917, Wilson demobilized the fifty thousand guardsmen still remaining on the border and left the boundary defense in the hands of fifty thousand regular troops.

As the size of the border patrol shrank, General James Parker expressed doubts about the capacity of his troops to protect the Lower Rio Grande Valley from future attacks. In early February, he informed James Wells that only four regiments of soldiers would remain in his district after the departure of the guard, and warned that, "if raids come, this is not enough."[35] Despite the present calm along the Rio Grande, Parker's apprehension was not unreasonable. Subsequent events demonstrated that the establishment of constitutional rule in Mexico did not mean the restoration of order throughout the country. Turmoil soon returned to the northern states of Chihuahua and Tamaulipas, which borders the Lower Rio Grande Valley. In the spring of 1917, a volatile gubernatorial campaign in Tamaulipas degenerated into an armed confrontation between the competing factions and eventually led to a rebellion against the national government. In Chihuahua, Pancho Villa staged a modest comeback. Even more disturbing to American observers than these domestic upheavals were the efforts of Germany to promote open conflict between the United States and Mexico, as the U.S. gravitated toward intervention in World War I on the Allied side.

Six weeks before the U.S. declaration of war against Germany, British intelligence agents intercepted a startling message from the German foreign minister, Arthur Zimmerman, to his ambassador in Mexico. Zimmerman called on the Mexican government to form an alliance with Germany and possibly Japan and to participate in a joint war effort against the United States. As a reward for fighting this country, the minister promised Mexico the return of her "lost" territory in Texas, New Mexico, and Arizona. The publication of the Zimmerman telegram created a public uproar and reinforced the willingness of most Americans to enter the war against Germany. For South Texans, the scheme revived memories of the Plan of San Diego and heightened their anxieties over the reduction of U.S. military strength along the border.

Although Carranza rejected Zimmerman's proposition, the Mexican president's sympathies lay with the German cause. German agents and propagandists had operated along the U.S.-Mexican border since the start of World War I, and Carranza allowed the practice to continue after the United States entered the conflict in April 1917. Still, both the United States and Mexico carefully avoided any overt actions that might provoke a military confrontation. The Wilson administration continued to assert the right of the U.S. Army to pursue bandits across the border, but the War Department imposed severe restrictions on how far into Mexico the military units could travel and how long they could stay.

Neither Carranza's hostility toward the United States nor the paramilitary struggle in Tamaulipas produced a resurgence of unrestrained violence in the Lower Rio Grande Valley. The only panic came in March 1918 when the new commander of the Brownsville district informed a citizens' meeting that General Nafarrate intended to proclaim himself the provisional governor of Tamaulipas and to launch an attack against Brownsville. The assault never materialized, and Nafarrate was killed a month later in Tampico. Cattle rustling and other forms of theft remained serious problems for the settlers, and a few minor skirmishes between soldiers and Mexican bandits disturbed the peace along the border. Yet no large-scale raids occurred in Cameron and Hidalgo counties. In fact, German spies replaced Mexican desperadoes as the main concern of the Texas Rangers. Although some of their suspects may have been legitimate German agents, the Rangers arrested or harassed anyone with a German name or a German accent.

Valley residents continued to agonize over the security of the border during World War I, but their most pressing problem was a severe labor shortage. Fear of military conscription and rumors of an impending conflict between the United States and Mexico sparked another massive exodus of Hispanic workers from South Texas to their native land. Local spokesmen charged that the dissemination of German propaganda incited the panic, but the Hispanic population hardly needed encouragement from outside agitators to flee from the draft of a country in which they had been the victims of discrimination, labor exploitation, police abuses, and vigilante violence. The loss of workers became so serious that Governor Ferguson appealed to President Wilson to deliver "a proclamation at once exempting all Mexicans from registration and selection during the year 1917."[36] Although Wilson rejected the proposal, he pledged that his administration would do its "best through other means to reassure the laborers of South Texas and remove wrong impressions from their minds."[37] The migration continued, however, and the labor scarcity persisted throughout the war.

Despite the dislocations that the war produced, James Wells and his Valley allies supported American involvement in the European conflict. With two sons serving in France, the sixty-seven–year–old boss refused to tolerate expressions of dissent about the war effort. When he heard an army officer "very strongly espousing the cause of Germany," he lost his temper and told the man to "change his opinion, or his uniform."[38] In the same spirit, Sheriff Jacobo Guerra urged his constituents in Starr County to "refrain from public discussion of questions involved in the present crisis," and he warned them that "any act, however slight, tending to give aid and comfort to the enemy is treason."[39] The South Texas legislators voted for the state Loyalty Act of 1918, which was designed to curb criticism of the national government and its war policies. Representative José Canales, who reclaimed his house seat in 1916 with Wells' backing, appeared before a legislative committee to endorse a proposed ban against the teaching of German in the public schools. In addition, Governor Ferguson appointed James Wells and three other residents of the Trans-Nueces to serve on the State Council of Defense, which encouraged the citizens of Texas to participate fully in the wartime mobilization and informed the federal authorities of the defense needs of the state.

Only on the issue of Hispanic draft evasion did the South Texas Democrats show any tolerance. While blaming German propagandists for the failure of thousands of Hispanics to register or to report for duty, Wells and his associates bore little ill will toward the draft dodgers and their families. In fact, James Wells had opposed the passage of the Selective Service Act at the outset of the war. He subsequently represented applicants for deferments and lobbied for the reduction of the draft quota for Cameron County. The most serious infractions of the selective service law occurred in Starr County. Sheriff Jacobo Guerra tempered his stern warning against giving "aid and comfort to the enemy" with an assurance that "no foreigners of whatever nationality should have any fear of being forced into the military service."[40] At the second draft call in September 1917, only four of the twenty-eight draftees from Starr County complied with the summons. In late 1918, a federal grand jury indicted G. A. Guerra, who had just won election to replace his uncle as sheriff, for filing a false affidavit to escape the draft.

Almost five years of border disturbances and wartime dislocations took their toll on the politics of South Texas. The immediate effect of these upheavals was to eliminate the Independent party of Cameron County and to provide the Wells machine with some temporary relief, but, in the long run, the Democratic organization suffered as well. In 1916, several factors discouraged the Independents from fielding a county ticket. After the flight of thousands of Anglos and Hispanics in 1915 as a result of the raids and the vigilante retaliation, the population of Cameron County remained in a state of disarray. Collector Frank Rabb's ineptitude as a political operator further undercut the Independents' prospects of mobilizing a sizable

Hispanic vote. The insurgents could no longer rely on the customs force as their organizational base. In addition, their most effective political strategist, Rentfro B. Creager, was running for the gubernatorial nomination of the anemic state Republican party, and he had little time to devote to the preparation of a local campaign. Overshadowing all these considerations was the psychological impact of the racial violence of recent years. So much bitterness and distrust now separated the Anglo and Hispanic communities that it was impossible for the Independent party to revive its past strategy of appealing for the support of the bulk of the new Anglo settlers while corralling Hispanic voters. The Independent party never mounted another campaign. Future challenges to Wells' domination of county affairs depended on exclusive Anglo support and took place in the Democratic primaries.

With the demise of the Independent party in 1916, James Wells faced only one immediate threat—the political maneuvering of Lawrence Bates. While lobbying for an appointment to serve as the Laredo customs collector, Wells' former ally launched a campaign against Sheriff W. T. Vann in the Democratic primary. Bates tried to outflank the Democratic machine by appealing for the support of Hispanic voters and capitalizing on their resentment over the recent mistreatment that they had received from lawmen and vigilante groups. The combination of Wells' continued control over a sizable bloc of Hispanic voters and the Anglo backlash against Bates' strategy produced a landslide victory for Vann. During the heated contest, Wells warned that Bates' tactics might provoke a "race war," and the Cameron County boss called on "every intelligent, sane, and right-hearted person, Mexican or American, [to] do everything to prevent such a suicidal movement."[41] Bates' campaign may have been as dangerous as Wells charged, but the Democratic chieftain's belated appeal for racial peace could not conceal his own responsibility for the racial hatred that had overtaken the Valley. During the bloodbath of 1915, he had failed to use his influence to defend the Hispanic population against lynchings, summary executions, and other horrors.

Unprecedented competition erupted in the Democratic primaries of 1918. In the past, Wells' control over the party machinery had usually deterred his rivals from challenging his slate of candidates in the primary conventions or elections. After the collapse of the Independent party, however, insurgents from the Anglo-dominated communities of San Benito and Harlingen showed no inclination to develop a new party organization and launched individual campaigns in the Democratic primaries. As a result, six Wells-backed incumbents now faced opposition in their bids for nomination. In addition, the 1912 Democratic candidate for mayor of Brownsville, Louis Cobolini, ran against Wells for the chairmanship of the Cameron County Democratic party. The recent enactment of women's suffrage for the primaries and two other election reforms, which were designed to limit Hispanic voting, added another element of uncertainty to the local contests. Lacking effective countywide organizations, the local challengers failed to forge a united front of Anglo support, but they still managed to give the Wells machine a scare. Although Wells and Sheriff Vann won handily, three regular Democratic candidates, including the county judge, barely escaped defeat.

The outcome of one of the district races was particularly disturbing to James Wells because it involved the apparent defeat of one of his closest allies and revealed the potential strength of a united Anglo vote. In an effort to offset charges that he was an uncompromising reactionary and to retain some influence over state patronage, Wells supported the campaign of the popular reform governor of Texas, William Hobby, who had come to power in 1917 when the state legislature impeached James Ferguson. The identification of the regular Democratic organization with Hobby undoubtedly helped to split the Anglo vote. In the contest for the state senate seat, however, a clear choice existed between a Hobby-backed candidate, D. W. Glasscock, and a Ferguson supporter, Archie Parr. The widely publicized charges of pervasive corruption in Duval County also hurt Parr's cause. Despite Wells' mobilization of his Hispanic voters for Parr, the state senator lost Cameron County by almost five hundred votes. This result indicated that the repeated displacements of population since 1915 and the partial enforcement of the new election laws had left the Anglo voters with a numerical edge. Wells' and Parr's subsequent resort to election fraud to salvage the senator's renomination proved to be a fatal mistake for the Cameron County boss. First Parr in the general election of 1918 and then Wells in the primary of 1920 became targets of reformist campaigns that cast them as the architects of Hispanic domination and boss rule. Archie Parr survived the assault, but James Wells did not.

In Hidalgo County, the Democratic machine still controlled a large enough bloc of Hispanic voters to discourage the Anglo population from mounting a local campaign. In February 1918, an audit of the county finances indicated that Treasurer John Closner had misappropriated over $150,000 from the county, several drainage districts, and the school district. Although this revelation forced Closner to resign, his political allies retained firm control over local politics. The legal challenge came to an end one month later when the district judge dismissed an ouster suit against the other members of the Hidalgo County government. The only political change to result from this confrontation was the emergence of Sheriff A. Y. Baker as the new boss of the Democratic organization. This former Ranger and customs agent, who had closely cooperated with James Wells ever since his arrival in South Texas around the turn of the century, kept the Anglo settlers at bay for another twelve years through a combination of voter manipulation, election fraud, and large-scale graft.

The years of the Wilson presidency were disastrous for James Wells. Both the patronage policies of the Democratic administration and the continuing tension along the border sapped his political strength. By the end of the decade, he was no longer able to cope with the political effects of the changing composition of the Valley population and the hardening of racial hatred. During this same period, Wells and his South Texas allies suffered a number of setbacks in state politics as well. After the impeachment of James Ferguson in 1917, Wells' influence over state government disappeared. Ferguson's successor, William Hobby, not only revived the reformist spirit in the Texas Legislature but also ordered the intervention of the Rangers to combat election abuses in the Trans-Nueces. The result of all these developments was the eventual downfall of the Wells machine.

12. State Politics: The Closing Battles

THE CENTRAL ISSUES of Texas politics during the second decade of the twentieth century were prohibition, woman suffrage, and James Ferguson's performance as a candidate and as governor. James Wells persisted in his uncompromising opposition to election and liquor reforms, but he was ambivalent toward the conservative chief executive, who shared Wells' views on these questions. After opposing Ferguson's initial bid for election in 1914, Wells reached an accommodation with the flamboyant politico. When Ferguson fell from power in 1917, the Rio Grande boss abruptly abandoned his cause and embraced his progressive successor, William Hobby. Despite these opportunistic shifts, Wells failed to maintain his influence over state political affairs. Archie Parr, on the other hand, remained loyal to Ferguson, and Parr's stubborn defense of the impeached governor provoked the climactic political confrontation of the Progressive Era in South Texas.

After sweeping a special set of elimination primaries and conventions, a Houston lawyer named Thomas Ball claimed the united support of the prohibitionist forces in the state and emerged as the favorite to win the Democratic gubernatorial nomination in 1914. His only serious rival was a previously obscure opponent of prohibition, James Ferguson. Despite the poverty of his youth, Ferguson had amassed a personal fortune through marriage, shrewd real estate dealings, and, eventually, the opening of his own bank in Temple, Texas. He had actively participated in local and state politics from 1908 on, but he did not seek election to public office until his entry into the 1914 gubernatorial race. While asserting his intention to veto any liquor legislation that reached the governor's desk, Ferguson focused his attention on another issue—farm tenancy. Between 1880 and 1910, the percentage of tenants among the farmers of the state rose from 37 percent to 52 percent, as a result of the agricultural depression of the 1890s, the continuation of an oppressive farm credit system, and the rising cost of land. Most of these farm laborers faced grinding poverty and perpetual indebtedness, and they had little hope for a better life for their children. With his promise to push for the enactment of a legal maximum on land rent payments, the Temple banker won a strong following among the rural voters of Central and North Texas. To reinforce his appeal, he played the part of "Farmer Jim," who spoke the language of his semiliterate constituents and articulated their aspirations, fears, and biases.

Ferguson's candidacy split the ranks of the conservative Democratic spokesmen of Texas. His opposition to prohibition, his pledge to conduct a businesslike administration, and the failure of his wet rivals to arouse much popular support induced many conservatives to join the Ferguson campaign. Other Old Guard Democrats, such as Joseph Bailey, regarded the candidate as a radical demagogue and reluctantly endorsed his dry opponent, Thomas Ball. One of the most scathing denunciations of Ferguson came from James B. Wells: ". . . the election of Ferguson as Governor will be a statewide public calamity with his wild socialistic views as embodied in his Land Tenancy Plank of his platform, which will necessarily unsettle, and practically take the ownership of land and all other property . . . from the owners,—and in addition, I assure you as my friend there is no comparison between Ball and Ferguson,—and every motive of patriotism and love of our state, and its future welfare, and the Democratic party prompts us to decisively defeat Ferguson."[1] Ball's past support of Bailey, his opposition to the passage of a national constitutional amendment on prohibition, and his long service as a corporation lawyer provided additional incentives for conservatives to reject Ferguson. These same features of Ball's record, however, undercut his support within the progressive-prohibitionist wing of the Democratic party.

During the early stages of the primary contest, Thomas Ball appeared to be unbeatable in the Lower Rio Grande Valley. The candidate enjoyed the support of not only James Wells and his allies but also independent Democrats like Frank Rabb and José Canales. In April, Wells informed the Democratic front-runner that "I have everything in Cameron, Hidalgo, Starr, Willacy, San Patricio, Jim Wells, Kleberg, and Jim Hogg going splendidly, and also everything looking good in Nueces County."[2] The Ball campaign suffered an almost complete collapse in South Texas three months later, however, when the moderate prohibitionist called for legislation to remove illiterate Hispanics from the election process. According to the *San Antonio Daily Express*, Ball "uttered the prophecy that liquor and

Mexicans will go from Texas politics simultaneously and rest together forever in death."³ Through mid-July, Wells tried to reassure
his allies along the border that Ball was still the preferable candidate,
but Ball partisans persisted in their attacks against the Hispanic
vote. By election day, July 25, 1914, Wells himself had abandoned the
campaign.

Thomas Ball's setbacks were not limited to South Texas. His
opposition to nationwide prohibition and Joseph Bailey's endorsement of his candidacy antagonized progressive voters. In addition,
the Ferguson camp launched a series of vicious personal attacks,
which cast Ball as an adulterer, an alcoholic, and a hypocritical
member of a private club that served liquor and allowed gambling.
The Temple politico also exploited the widespread resentment of
"political preachers," who were actively campaigning for both Ball
and a prohibition proposal on the primary ballot. Not even the belated endorsements of Woodrow Wilson, William Jennings Bryan,
and Albert Burleson could salvage Ball's faltering drive for the governorship. In fact, the combination of Governor Colquitt's praise for
Ferguson and the intervention of the Wilson administration contributed to the demise of the Ball campaign in the Valley. The Anglo settlers along the border credited Colquitt with ensuring their safety
during the Vera Cruz crisis, and many were reluctant to vote for a
candidate whose victory might be interpreted as an endorsement of
the cautious military policies of the national government.

James Ferguson swept the state with a record total of 237,000
votes to 191,000 votes for Ball. The withdrawal of the Democratic
machines from the Ball camp and the weakening of his base of Anglo
support produced a Ferguson landslide in the Lower Rio Grande Valley. "Farmer Jim" carried Cameron, Hidalgo, and Starr counties by a
majority of almost 1,500 votes. The statewide defeat of submission
by a margin of 22,000 votes added to the frustration of the prohibitionist leaders, who had anticipated a major breakthrough for their
cause in the 1914 primary.

The absence of sharp ideological differences on most issues, Ferguson's patronage policies, and his agitation for the deployment of
more federal troops along the border paved the way for a reconciliation between the governor and the South Texas Democratic leaders
following the political infighting of 1914. Despite Wells' earlier hysterical claims that Ferguson's tenancy proposal posed a threat to
property rights, State Senator Archie Parr and the representative for
Starr, Hidalgo, and Brooks counties voted with the legislative majority to impose a maximum land rent of one-third of the value of the
grain and one-fourth of the value of the cotton that a tenant farmer

raised. Wells' handpicked representative for Cameron and Willacy counties, Lawrence Bates, was absent during the roll call votes on the bill. The practical effect of the law was minimal, and the Texas Supreme Court overturned it in 1921. The legislators from the Trans-Nueces also displayed flexibility on the other modest reforms that the chief executive favored. Bills establishing compulsory school attendance, allowing local school districts to supply free textbooks, providing one million dollars for the improvement of rural schools, requiring the licensing of employment agencies, and regulating mines all passed with only one dissenting vote from the South Texas legislative delegation.

On the overriding questions of prohibition and election reform, Governor Ferguson and the Wells-Parr faction stood united. Ferguson's pledge to veto any liquor legislation stymied the narrow dry majorities in both houses. They had no hope of mustering the two-thirds majorities needed to override the governor's veto or to circumvent it with the passage of a constitutional amendment. Facing this obstacle, the progressive-prohibitionist coalition decided to concentrate on the enactment of new election laws, but this effort failed as well. Convinced that middle-class women would form a solid front for prohibition and other reforms if they had the right to vote, dry activists introduced a constitutional amendment to establish woman suffrage. They also tried to break the power of the conservative bosses by pressing for legislation to curtail assistance to illiterate voters at the polls. Both of these measures lost in the House of Representatives.

As the president of the Texas branch of the National Association Opposed to Woman Suffrage, James Wells' wife, Pauline, directed the lobbying campaign against the voting rights proposal. In an address before a special night session of the legislature, she argued that the establishment of women's suffrage would lead to the destruction of the family, black rule in the South, socialism, and anarchy. According to Mrs. Wells, most women lacked the experience and the temperament to make responsible political decisions. Besides, the move to enlarge the franchise represented an insult not only to the men of the state but also to the mothers, who had reared and shaped the values of the male voters. Although a majority of the House members supported the resolution for woman suffrage, they fell short of the necessary two-thirds majority. The two Valley representatives divided on the issue.

Political favors, as well as general agreement on state policies, strengthened the accommodation between James Ferguson and the South Texas bosses. In making patronage appointments for the Valley counties, Ferguson relied on the recommendations of James Wells. The governor even selected a Wells confidant, Representative Lawrence Bates, to serve on his personal staff. Only later, after Bates broke with Wells, did this appointment generate tension. When Archie Parr arranged the formation of a new judicial district for Duval and several other Trans-Nueces counties, Ferguson appointed a judge and a district attorney who helped the Duval chieftain escape conviction for election fraud and extortion. The Temple politico also won the gratitude of the Rio Grande Democrats with his response to the border crises of 1915 and 1916. Ferguson refused to follow the Colquitt strategy of prodding the federal government into action with the mobilization of the Texas National Guard, but his alternative approach of coupling strong support of Wilson's Mexican policies with insistent appeals for additional troops proved to be equally effective. Ferguson could claim at least partial credit for the spectacular military buildup in the Valley after the start of the large-scale Mexican raids. In addition, the governor ordered a dramatic enlargement of the Texas Rangers and assigned virtually the whole force to the border region.

Despite Wells' suspicion that Ferguson was encouraging Bates' local insurgency in 1916, the Cameron County boss and Archie Parr supported the governor's campaign for reelection and played active roles in the Ferguson-Bailey coalition that dominated the two state Democratic conventions that year. At the May gathering in San Antonio, the conservative and progressive forces battled over the selection of delegates to the national Democratic convention, the election of a new national committeeman for the state, and the formulation of the party platform. The two sides were evenly matched, but the Old Guard gained the upper hand when it won the allegiance of the temporary chairman, W. C. Wear, and recruited another dry moderate, William Poindexter, to run for national committeeman against the dedicated reformer Thomas Love. Wear filled the platform committee with antiprohibitionists and named Wells to serve as chairman of the panel. Wells in turn allowed Bailey and Ferguson to write the party document. The product of their collaboration was a general endorsement of the Wilson administration and strong statements of opposition to national amendments on prohibition and woman suffrage. Because of the appeal of Bailey's states rights rhetoric to some of the dry delegates, the platform passed by a comfortable margin. The conservatives also claimed a majority of the delegates to the national convention, and Wells arranged the selection of Bates in return for the legislator's promise not to challenge Wells' candidate for Cameron County sheriff in the July primary. In the climactic contest for national committeeman, Poindexter won by a disputed vote of 400 to 396 over Love.

After its defeat at the May convention, the progressive wing of the Democratic party failed to muster a serious challenge to conservative supremacy for the remainder of the primary season. Although a narrow majority of the electorate voted for submission in the July primary, Ferguson's partisans controlled the August state convention and excluded from the platform any reference to a state constitutional amendment on prohibition. Wells' main concern during the summer campaigning was neither the liquor referendum nor Ferguson's renomination, which was never in doubt, but instead Charles Culberson's fight to retain his seat in the United States Senate.

Wracked by the effects of alcoholism and various physical disorders, Culberson had made only rare appearances in the Senate since mid-1915, and he was unable to participate in his own campaign for renomination. The senator's obvious vulnerability attracted a bevy of competitors. The front-runner among the challengers was Oscar Colquitt, who continued his attack against President Wilson's Mexican policy and emphasized his opposition to national prohibition. In an appeal for German American support, he also called for an end to the escalating arms trade between the United States and the Allied nations in World War I. Although Archie Parr threw his support behind Colquitt, James Wells remained loyal to his long-time ally in Congress. The Cameron County boss joined with other conservative leaders across the state and a few Wilson sympathizers to manage Culberson's campaign while the incapacitated senator stayed in Washington.

Despite Colquitt's popularity among the Anglo voters along the border, Wells succeeded in delivering solid majorities for Culberson in Cameron, Hidalgo, and Starr counties. The flight of thousands of settlers as a result of the Mexican border raids of 1915 and the continuation of chaotic conditions throughout the Valley drained Colquitt's base of support and precluded any effective political organization on his behalf. Late returns from South Texas contributed to Culberson's come-from-behind victory over the leading prohibitionist candidate and enabled the incumbent to claim a place in the run-off election against Oscar Colquitt, who led the field with 33 percent of the vote. Duval County stood out as one of the few Colquitt strongholds in the Trans-Nueces. The former governor carried Archie Parr's fiefdom by a vote of 802 to 1 for Culberson. None of the other candidates received even a single vote.

A broad-based coalition emerged to promote Charles Culberson's candidacy in the senatorial runoff. Colquitt's denunciation of proposals for nationwide prohibition and his call for a repudiation of the Wilson administration drove progressives and dry activists into the Culberson camp. Although President Wilson declined to make a public endorsement, Postmaster General Burleson and Attorney General Gregory provided behind-the-scenes support for the ailing senator. Governor Ferguson also boarded the Culberson bandwagon. In a preview of the nativistic demagoguery that would flourish after U.S. intervention in World War I, the senator's surrogate campaigners cast the election as a choice between a loyal and influential friend of the president and a sympathizer with Imperial Germany. The combination of these patriotic appeals and cooperation between leading conservative and progressive Democrats lifted Culberson to a landslide victory. Again benefiting from a light voter turnout, the incumbent carried the Lower Rio Grande Valley by the impressive margin of 1,340 to 161. Of the twelve counties forming the southeastern tip of Texas, only Duval and Jim Wells counties favored Colquitt.

Although the Republican party posed no serious threat in the general election, the race for governor generated local interest along the border because Rentfro B. Creager had received the GOP nomination. The South Texas Republican endorsed woman suffrage, straddled the issue of prohibition, accused Governor Ferguson of misusing public funds, and condemned President Wilson's policies toward Mexico. These vigorous attacks against the Democratic party had almost no effect on the Texas electorate, however. James Ferguson swept the election by a margin of six to one. Although Creager carried only one South Texas county, Zapata, his showing in Cameron County was at least respectable. He lost the county by less than one hundred votes, while the rest of the GOP state candidates trailed by almost one thousand votes.

Another notable feature of the 1916 election was the return of José Canales to the Texas House as the representative for Cameron, Willacy, and Kleberg counties. After serving as a faithful Wells partisan in the legislature from 1905 through 1908, Canales broke with the Valley boss in 1909 over the issue of prohibition and campaigned as the Independent candidate for county judge in 1910. Two years later, he returned to the Democratic fold and won election as the school superintendent of Cameron County. His moves to improve the quality of teaching, to expand the facilities of the rural schools, and to curtail the use of Spanish in the classroom bolstered Wells' efforts to attract Anglo voters to the Democratic party. During the border raids of 1915 and 1916, Canales organized a company of Hispanic scouts to collect intelligence for the U.S. Army. At the same time, he stood out as the only prominent local Democrat who called for an end to Ranger and vigilante brutalities against the Hispanic population. In 1916, Wells again backed Canales in his bid for the legislature, but the Cameron County chieftain was never able to control Canales' voting. For the next four years, the Mexican American politician followed a wildly contradictory course. While defending the rights of his Hispanic constituents against the abuses of the Rangers, he appealed for Anglo support by embracing such reformist causes as prohibition, women's suffrage, and even restrictions on Hispanic voting. His most dramatic maneuver came in 1919 when he demanded a legislative investigation of the Texas Rangers and the reorganization of the force. This initiative placed Canales at the center of a desperate struggle between the Wells-Parr faction and a coalition consisting of local insurgents, the Rangers, and the governor of Texas.

At the conclusion of the election campaign of 1916, James Wells' position in Texas politics appeared secure. To be sure, he exercised much less influence than he had during the reign of Colonel Edward House, but he remained one of the leading spokesmen for South Texas conservatism. He had reached an accommodation with the dominant political figure in the state, James Ferguson, and he had retained his ties with Joseph Bailey, who had staged a modest comeback in 1916. In addition, Wells' old friend Charles Culberson had won reelection to the U.S. Senate. Although the progressive-prohibitionist forces maintained their majorities in the Texas Legislature, Ferguson's veto power still held the reformers at bay on the vital questions of liquor and election legislation. Lawrence Bates' rebellion in 1916 and the election of the independent-minded José Canales to the House that same year signaled the end of Wells' control over the Valley legislative delegation, but Archie Parr remained an influential and loyal ally in the state Senate. The disagreement between Wells and Parr over the Colquitt-Culberson Senate race did not affect their cooperation on other political matters.

The appearance of conservative domination was deceptive, however. Despite the recent gains of the Old Guard, Wells and his associates were more vulnerable than they ever imagined. Texas politics stood on the brink of an upheaval that would drive James Ferguson from office and unleash a new wave of reform. The progressive resurgence at the state level would also spark an insurgent campaign to block Archie Parr's reelection to the state Senate and contribute to the eventual collapse of the Wells machine in Cameron County. The event that triggered this chain reaction of conservative reversals was Ferguson's attack against the University of Texas.

Despite his commitment to the improvement of rural education in the state, Governor Ferguson displayed outright hostility toward the University of Texas. In Ferguson's view, the faculty and administrators were elitist snobs, who looked down upon less educated common people, engaged in questionable financial practices, and plotted against his state administration. He also calculated that an attack against the arrogance and extravagance of the university community would enhance his popularity and provide an effective issue for his planned campaign for the U.S. Senate in 1918. In response to Ferguson's interference in university affairs, a group of influential ex-students organized a lobby to defend their alma mater and to conduct an investigation of charges that Ferguson had misused public funds. Proponents of prohibition and woman suffrage joined the anti-Ferguson campaign. The confrontation intensified dramatically in early 1917, as the following developments unfolded in rapid succession: a House investigation of Ferguson's personal finances, the governor's removal of two members of the board of regents, Ferguson's veto of the university appropriation bill, the firing of several professors, the House Speaker's charge that the governor had offered him a $5,000 bribe, and grand jury indictments against Ferguson and his aids for the misappropriation of public funds and embezzlement.

After Governor Ferguson called a special session of the legislature for August 1917, the House of Representatives instituted impeachment proceedings. The governor's refusal to reveal the source of a $150,000 loan, which he had used to cover his indebtedness to his own bank in Temple, sealed his fate. On August 24, the House members approved twenty-one articles of impeachment. The charges included perjury, Ferguson's abuse of his authority over the University of Texas, his use of public revenue for his personal benefit, and the deposit of state funds in banks in which he held stock or to which he owed money. José Canales voted for the first nine impeachment articles and then left the House chamber. The other Valley representative voted against all twenty-one articles. The House member from Corpus Christi, who also represented Duval County and usually cooperated with Archie Parr, supported two of the charges. At the conclusion of a three-week trial, the Texas Senate upheld ten of the charges and voted not only to remove Ferguson from the governorship but also to bar him from holding any state office in the future. Parr was one of only four senators who opposed conviction on every count.

James Wells refused to participate in the impeachment controversy. When Ferguson's critics initially agitated for an investigation
of the governor's finances during the regular session of the legislature, Wells promised to support his cause, but by June 1917, he had
retreated from this position. Wells informed former Governor Joseph
Sayers that "as I am a friend of both Governor Ferguson and The
University of Texas, I will not take any active interest in the matter."[4] The Cameron County boss may have calculated that the revelations about Ferguson's misuse of public money and the backlash
against his attack on the university had already destroyed his effectiveness as a political leader, regardless of the outcome of the campaign to force him from office. Wells' support for the governor had
always rested on his respect for Ferguson's political power. The
South Texan's suspicions that Ferguson had backed Bates' drives for
sheriff and customs collector in 1916 precluded any deep-seated
commitment from Wells. The Rio Grande chieftain would defend
Bailey and Culberson however heavy the odds against them, but not
Ferguson. Besides, the prospect that Lieutenant Governor William
Hobby might replace Ferguson did not disturb Wells. The owner of a
Beaumont newspaper and son-in-law of a conservative Texas congressman, Hobby had relied on such Old Guard Democrats as Frank
Andrews to promote support for his initial campaign for lieutenant
governor in 1914. Just before the primary that year, Wells had described his politicking for Hobby as "a labor of love."[5] None of the
publisher's actions during his first three years of state service fore-
shadowed his subsequent conversion to progressivism.

Ferguson's fall from power was not the only problem that conservative Democrats faced in 1917. American entry into World War I
in April was just as destructive to their cause. In the midst of the
anti-German hysteria that swept the state and the nation, the identification of conservative wet politicians with the German American
families who controlled the brewery industry now appeared to be
disreputable, if not somehow treasonous, in the eyes of many voters.
Claims that the production of alcoholic beverages diverted vital
resources from wartime mobilization and demands that soldiers
be shielded from drinking and other vices also widened the appeal
of the prohibitionist movement. Even the Wilson administration,
which had previously resisted agitation for prohibition, now pressed
for the creation of dry zones around military bases. In December
1917, Congress passed a constitutional amendment calling for the
creation of national prohibition. Furthermore, the increasing reliance on women to fill civilian jobs strengthened the suffragists' arguments that women deserved the right to vote.

When William Hobby became governor in September 1917, he hoped to avoid taking an immediate stand on statewide prohibition and to attract support from both moderate wets and drys. However, mounting pressure from prohibitionists and Ferguson's plans to ignore the legislative disqualification and to run for governor in 1918 soon forced the new chief executive to choose sides. In February 1918, Hobby called a special session of the legislature and authorized the lawmakers to act on a wide range of reform measures. The progressive-prohibitionist majorities in both houses seized this opportunity, as they ratified the national prohibition amendment, banned prostitution and the sale of liquor near army bases, and imposed statewide prohibition by statute, rather than by constitutional amendment. Although José Canales favored all the antiliquor measures, he did make one concession to his wet constituency in the Lower Rio Grande Valley. During the debate over state prohibition, he argued that the legislation should remain in effect only until the end of the war, but the House rejected his proposal. In the Senate, Archie Parr voted against every restriction on the sale and manufacture of alcoholic beverages.

The conservative forces also suffered serious defeats on the question of election reform. Another vigorous lobbying effort by Pauline Wells failed to block the enactment of a bill providing women with the right to vote in the primaries and to participate in the party conventions. Even more ominous to the bosses of South Texas was the passage of two bills aimed at curbing the voting of their Hispanic constituents. One measure prohibited election judges from assisting voters in the preparation of their ballots, unless the voters were over sixty years old, suffered from physical disabilities, or had been citizens for at least twenty-one years. This last provision was designed to exempt illiterate native-born Anglos from the application of the law. The other threat to Hispanic political participation came from a bill that established U.S. citizenship as a prerequisite for voting in the primaries. The enforcement of this law would curtail the long-standing practice of recruiting Mexican nationals, arranging their applications for citizenship, and manipulating their voting. In the fight over election qualifications and procedures, Canales once again defied the conservative Democratic leaders of his section. Although he was absent during the roll call votes on the two bills that established literacy and citizenship as voter qualifications, he supported woman suffrage and served on the conference committee that formulated the final version of the voter assistance act. In addition, the maverick legislator even proposed an amendment to limit the extension of female suffrage to native-born women. The amendment failed. Not surprisingly, Archie Parr opposed all the election reforms that the legislature considered during its special session.

The prospect of a Ferguson comeback prompted yet another effort to alter the election laws of Texas. Although the legislature had disqualified James Ferguson from holding any state office, his supporters still controlled the state executive committee for the Democratic party, and they were willing to approve the inclusion of his name on the Democratic primary ballot. Fearing that a split in the progressive movement might allow the impeached chief executive to win the gubernatorial race with less than half the vote, Hobby partisans in the House introduced a bill to require majority nominations for all state and district officeholders. In the event that no contestant received a majority of the primary vote, the two leading contenders would face each other in a run-off. Until the enactment of this law, only the candidates for the U.S. Senate nomination had to compete in a run-off when no one claimed a majority in the primary. As an added precaution, progressives in the Senate offered amendments that authorized the Texas Supreme Court, rather than party officials, to pass final judgment on the eligibility of any disputed candidate. These provisions provoked an angry response from Archie Parr, who engaged in the following exchange with Senator O. S. Lattimore of Fort Worth:

> Parr: "You want to put these disqualification amendments in the bill because you are afraid of Ferguson running for governor."
> Lattimore: "Not at all. We provide that he and any other person can take the issue into the courts and let the courts pass on it."
> Parr: "Why aren't you willing to let the people say? You must be afraid."
> Lattimore: "Why do you object to putting this question in the hands of the court? Are you afraid of the courts?"
> Parr: "I don't know whether I am or not. I won't say [laughter]. But I do say you will not dare to have Ferguson go before the people for their decision, whether he was rightly impeached. There are some of you in the chamber who would have voted to impeach him no matter what the evidence was."
> Lattimore: "That is true, but there are Senators here who would have voted not to impeach him regardless of the evidence."[6]

Despite Parr's protests, the Senate adopted the disqualification amendments, but the conference committee later removed them. The final version of the bill passed both houses by overwhelming majorities.

William Hobby's promotion of the reform legislation of 1918 was not the only cause for concern among James Wells and his allies. Just as disturbing to these politicians was the governor's management of the Texas Rangers. For decades, the Rangers had provided the Democratic machines with armed support whenever partisan violence had erupted along the border. Wells had carefully cultivated this relationship by sponsoring applicants to the force, promoting legislation favorable to the Rangers, and providing free legal defenses for Rangers who faced criminal charges. Not even the Ranger atrocities against the Hispanic population in 1915 had weakened Wells' commitment to the state police. During the Hobby administration, however, the composition and the political posture of the law enforcement agency underwent a dramatic transformation. The governor and his adjutant general, James Harley, raised the number of regular Rangers from 73 to over 130 with the creation of six new companies and the enlargement of the existing six. The governor also discharged many of the veterans from the force. In addition, the new administration took advantage of two pieces of legislation to create the Loyalty Ranger Force. While Ferguson was still in office, the legislature authorized the recruitment of unpaid special Rangers to help meet emergencies that might arise following U.S. entry into World War I. The total number of regular Rangers and special Rangers could reach as high as 1,000 men. A year later during Hobby's called session, the legislators passed the Loyalty Act, which empowered state officials to arrest anyone who criticized U.S. war policies or engaged in other "disloyal" activities. At the suggestion of Ranger Captain William Hanson, Governor Hobby appointed three special Rangers in each county of the state to form an intelligence network. These Loyalty Rangers cooperated with federal and local authorities in the investigation of cases involving draft evasion, desertion, sabotage, spying, the dissemination of anti-American propaganda, and even cattle stealing.

The key man in the reorganization of the Texas Rangers was William Hanson, a former Republican U.S. marshal and assistant marshal for the Southern District of Texas. Hobby named Hanson to serve as both the inspector for the regular Rangers and the director of the Loyalty Ranger Force. In his role as inspector, Hanson reviewed the activities of the full-time Rangers, investigated charges against them, and made recommendations on the hiring and firing of these men. He also exercised considerable influence over the deployment of the Ranger companies. During his term of duty as a federal appointee from 1898 through 1906, Hanson had maintained friendly relations with James Wells despite their affiliations with different political parties. After Hanson had resigned from his federal post and had moved to Mexico to engage in cattle raising and oil speculation, he had even allowed the Starr County deputy sheriff, who had fled across the border to escape arrest for the killing of Customs Inspector Gregorio Duffy, to stay at his ranch. Hanson's past cooperation with Wells had no effect on his conduct as a Ranger captain, however. He purged the Ranger force of Ferguson sympathizers and arranged the appointment of men whose loyalties lay with William Hobby, not the bosses of South Texas. In addition, the ex-marshal converted the Loyalty Ranger Force into a campaign organization for the governor. During the gubernatorial race of 1918, Hanson sent a list of the special Rangers to Adjutant General Harley with the following recommendation:

> I will suggest that you at once furnish "Hobby Headquarters" with this copy . . . in order that they can take such steps as they see fit towards putting these people actively to work. I will further suggest that each one be given a bunch of Hobby literature for distribution and that a letter be addressed to each of them asking their opinion as to whether Governor Hobby will carry that county and further asking them for a full report of the county and their opinion as to how is the best way to carry it in case it is doubtful. . . . In case you find any of them that are not all right, kindly let me know.[7]

William Hanson also arranged for the regular Ranger captains along the border to report on political developments.

This overhaul of the Texas Rangers produced a sudden change in their political stance in the Lower Rio Grande Valley. Frank Rabb received one of the special Ranger commissions for Cameron County. In addition, Adjutant General Harley dispatched a newly created company under Captain Charles Stevens to police Hidalgo and Cameron counties. Just two months after the arrival of this unit, the manager of the King Ranch, Robert J. Kleberg, demanded the transfer of Stevens because of reports that the captain intended to run against Hidalgo Sheriff A. Y. Baker in the Democratic primary. Stevens denied the accusation and retained his post. A bitter conflict also developed between Stevens and Cameron County Sheriff W. T. Vann. Following the capture of several suspected rustlers, the Ranger captain asked Vann to refuse to release the men on bond, but Vann replied that he was under a legal obligation to accept the bail payments that the judge in the examining trial had set. Stevens accused Vann of dereliction of duty and began delivering all his prisoners to the military guardhouse or to the jail in Hidalgo County. Stevens' policy of indiscriminately searching the homes of Mexican American citizens, including a deputy sheriff, and confiscating their arms generated additional tension. This practice even angered James Wells, who had become more sensitive to the rights of his Hispanic constituents since the passing of the border raid crisis. On one occasion, Wells threatened to shoot Stevens "between the eyes" if the Ranger ever tried to break into his house.[8] The feud between Stevens and the Rio Grande Democrats intensified again in late May of 1918 when Vann ordered the arrest of three Rangers for the murder of a Hispanic prisoner. Two months earlier these Rangers had taken the man into custody, and no one saw him again until the discovery of a skeleton with traces of his clothing on it. Because of uncertainties over the identity of the remains, two grand juries refused to issue indictments.

Throughout his controversial term of service along the border, Captain Stevens claimed that he enjoyed the full support of the prosperous Anglo farmers of the Valley, who were dissatisfied with the performance of Sheriff Vann and his deputies. Despite his frequent public criticisms of the sheriff, Stevens refused to play an active part in the 1918 primary campaign in Cameron County, and Vann won renomination handily. In the aftermath of the primary, however, the presence of an antagonistic Ranger force became a real threat to the political power of James Wells and Archie Parr.

The gubernatorial race overshadowed all other contests in the Democratic primary. Governor Hobby's approval of all the major reforms of the special legislative session of 1918 assured him the full backing of the revived progressive wing of the Democratic party, but he still faced a serious challenge from James Ferguson. As expected, the state Democratic executive committee sanctioned Ferguson's candidacy for the governorship. The earlier dismissal of the criminal indictments against "Farmer Jim" now enabled him to argue persuasively that his impeachment had been nothing more than a political power play on the part of his enemies. Nevertheless, the ex-governor remained vulnerable on one important question. He still refused to reveal the names of his benefactors who had loaned him $150,000 to pay off his notes to the Temple State Bank. Relying on highly ambiguous testimony before a U.S. Senate committee, Hobby partisans asserted that Ferguson had received the money from an organization of German sympathizers called the German-American Alliance. With this charge, the loyalty issue came to the forefront of the campaign.

While cooperating closely to promote Parr's bid for reelection to the state Senate, the Duval County boss and James Wells divided over the Hobby-Ferguson race. Having vigorously defended Ferguson's right to participate in the primary, Parr now intended to deliver the Duval County vote to the former chief executive. Although Wells opposed the reforms of 1918 and resented his loss of control over the Rangers in the Valley, both expediency and a lingering personal affection for Hobby prompted him to embrace the recent convert to progressivism. The regular Democratic candidates for public office in Cameron County faced stiff opposition, and the Rio Grande chieftain calculated that their identification with the popular governor would attract Anglo support. In addition, Wells' support of Hobby might forestall any effort on the part of the Rangers to enforce the new restrictions on Hispanic voting. In his correspondence with the chairman of the Hobby campaign committee, Wells characterized himself as "a lifelong friend of Governor Hobby" and vowed that "my whole heart is with him." Despite their professions of commitment to progressive reform, the Hobby managers urged Wells to secure the support of the other bosses along the border and welcomed his promise to mobilize "a large majority of Mexican voters."[9]

The solidarity of the progressive movement, the women voters' overwhelming support for Hobby, and the charges of corruption and disloyalty produced a humiliating defeat for James Ferguson. William Hobby carried the primary by a margin of two to one. In Cameron County, where the corralled Hispanic vote and the Anglos formed a united front for the incumbent, the result was even more one-sided, 2,245 to 192. Wells also managed to persuade A. Y. Baker of Hidalgo County and the Guerra family of Starr County to abandon Ferguson in favor of Hobby. Except for Duval County, the governor swept the whole southeastern tip of the state.

Not only did Archie Parr's campaign for James Ferguson flounder outside Duval County, but his conspicuous identification with the disgraced ex-governor nearly cost him his seat in the Texas Senate. In one of the most bitterly fought races of the Progressive Era, Parr faced opposition from a broad-based regional insurgency, the governor, the managers of the state party organization, and the Texas Rangers. Only by resorting to election fraud, the manipulation of the

Senate district convention, and the recruitment of a friendly judge to overturn his apparent defeat in the Democratic primary did Parr survive this onslaught. His accomplice throughout the struggle was James B. Wells.

The 1918 senatorial contest began quietly enough. After some initial indecision over whether or not to seek reelection, strong statements of support from Wells and two of the leading ranchers of the district persuaded Parr to make the race. Just a few days before the filing deadline, a group of Valley insurgents recruited McAllen lawyer D. W. Glasscock to run against the senator. By 1918, Glasscock was a veteran participant in South Texas politics. He did not move to Hidalgo County until 1912, but during his first year along the border, he helped James Wells prepare a series of legal suits challenging the Independent victory in the Brownsville city election and ran for the Texas House with the backing of both Wells and Closner. Serving as the chairman of the House Committee on Irrigation, he co-authored the comprehensive water rights law of 1913. After just one term, Glasscock retired from the legislature, resumed his law practice in Hidalgo County, and assumed the post of receiver for the Mission Canal Company. Despite his past association with Wells and Closner, Glasscock presented himself as a reformer and an ardent supporter of Governor William Hobby in 1918.

For most of the primary campaign, D. W. Glasscock did little to advance his candidacy. In fact, shortly before the election, Assistant Adjutant General Walter Woodul offered to arrange Glasscock's withdrawal from the race if Parr would throw his support behind Governor Hobby, but the state senator refused. Despite the insurgent's inactivity, both Parr and Wells were concerned about the outcome of the primary because of the introduction of women's suffrage. On July 18, 1918, Wells informed Parr that "in Cameron County, . . . between 1000 and 1100 [women] have registered,—and no one on earth can either tell how they are going to vote, or control them,—but it is generally known that they will be largely for Glasscock."[10] After the Duval County boss received similar reports from other counties in the district, his exasperation surfaced in a letter to Wells: "The Lord only knows what these women are going to do. You ought to be able to vote all the Mexican women. Though I know they do not want to go to the polls."[11]

Two days before the election, D. W. Glasscock launched his only major assault of the campaign. In an address at Brownsville, the McAllen lawyer characterized James Ferguson as a disloyal citizen, who had cooperated with the German-American Alliance in exchange for bribes, and he denounced Archie Parr for his support of the impeached governor. He also recounted Parr's record of election abuses. The speech came to a hysterical climax as the candidate discussed Ferguson's refusal to disclose the source of the notorious $150,000 loan to cover his bank notes:

> Jim Ferguson says that his promise of silence is "written in blood," he has never said in whose blood the promise is written, his or our boys over there. In Texas right now there are only two kinds of people, there is not even a No Man's Land between them, there is no dividing fence or middle ground, they are either disloyal or loyal. I don't believe in interring spies and traitors and pampering them for the war, I believe in standing them up against a stone wall and shooting them. If you are an American, I'm for you. If you are a hyphenated American, I am against you.[12]

Besides the women's vote and his association with Ferguson, Archie Parr faced one other problem in the 1918 senatorial race—the intervention of the Texas Rangers. With the assistance of Glasscock partisans, Captain William Hanson and several of his men conducted a systematic campaign in Corpus Christi to discourage the Hispanic population from voting. The Rangers informed the Hispanic residents that they would go to prison if they were illiterate and still tried to vote. In addition, Hanson dispatched several officers to Duval County to observe the management of the primary election. In contrast to these activities, Ranger interference in the Valley primaries was limited. Acting on their own initiative, some of Captain Stevens' men arrested a Cameron County commissioner whom they suspected of planning to distribute liquor to the voters of his precinct. To prevent Wells from arranging the prisoner's release on bond, Stevens ordered his men not to inform the local authorities of the commissioner's arrest and to move him around the county until the election was over. The only other action on the part of the Valley Rangers was quite proper. Captain Stevens assigned officers to the polling station in Mercedes after he learned of an effort to block the voting of the members of the local Ladies Hobby Club. Wells' support of Hobby probably accounted for the generally low profile that the Rangers maintained along the border on election day.

Although Wells and his allies were able to mobilize the Mexican American electorate of the Lower Rio Grande Valley on Parr's behalf, D. W. Glasscock staged an apparent upset in the July 27 primary. After the tabulation of all the returns, except those from Duval County, Glasscock held a lead of 1,200 votes. His impressive showing resulted from the solidarity of the Anglo voters throughout the district and the increase in their number with the advent of woman suffrage. Parr's own record of corruption and the taint of disloyalty stemming from his support of James Ferguson had a galvanizing effect on these citizens. Glasscock swept the seven counties that had Anglo majorities, and he claimed most of the Anglo precincts in the border counties. The white backlash even produced a startling defeat for Parr in Cameron County, where he lost by a vote of 1,406 to 909. Women's suffrage and the repeated displacements of population since mid-1915 overturned the long-standing Hispanic majority among the voters of Wells' county. Despite Glasscock's formidable lead, the outcome of the election remained in doubt because Archie Parr refused to allow the release of the returns from his home county until the opening of the Senate district convention, almost a month after the election.

Uncertainty over the vote count in Duval County gave rise to maneuvering on the part of both Parr's supporters and opponents. Although Glasscock carried Cameron County, James Wells retained his position as the Democratic county chairman and still exercised considerable influence over the county convention. Since a large number of Glasscock's followers attended the local gathering, Wells could not simply pack the delegation to the Senate district convention at Corpus Christi with his cronies. Instead, the chairman allowed anyone who expressed a willingness to participate in the district convention, irrespective of factional affiliation, to serve as a delegate. The result of this ploy was the selection of an oversized delegation of eighty-two men and women, who would cast the county's five district votes. The county convention instructed the delegates to support the choice of D. W. Glasscock as the Democratic nominee. Whether this guideline obligated the delegates to favor Glasscock's interests in any dispute that might arise was unclear. Wells' associates formed a minority of the delegation, but the veteran organizer anticipated that only a fraction of those chosen would actually travel to Corpus Christi. In that event, the Wells contingent could control the Cameron County votes. These regular Democrats intended to side with Archie Parr on the critical question of whether or not to accept the Duval County results.

D. W. Glasscock and his lieutenants were afraid that Parr might try to steal the primary with inflated returns from his home county, and they persuaded the governor to order a Ranger investigation of election irregularities in Duval County, as well as the Hispanic precincts of Cameron and Hidalgo counties. The state police uncovered a pervasive pattern of election fraud. In violation of the 1918 voter assistance act, election officers had prepared the ballots for illiterate Hispanics. Wells' brother-in-law, District Attorney John Kleiber, who was not even an election official but instead a candidate for renomination, had marked ballots in one of the rural precincts of Cameron County. The participants in the primary included aliens, many of whom had not even filed for naturalization papers, and citizens who had failed to pay their poll taxes. The residents of Benavides, Parr's hometown, had cast 376 votes, but the Rangers estimated that no more than 76 of these men and women were qualified to vote. Later, the state comptroller reported that the number of votes from Duval County surpassed the number of poll tax payments and exemptions by 392.

The suspense over the Duval County returns ended on August 24, 1918, at the meeting of the Democratic executive committee that preceded the district convention. The fears of the Glasscock supporters were realized. A Duval County representative submitted an official vote count of 1,303 for Parr and 23 for Glasscock. These results gave the incumbent senator a majority of 118 for the entire district. All but two of the county chairmen, who comprised the executive committee, were Parr backers, and they voted to declare their candidate the nominee of the Democratic party. They also scheduled the convention for four o'clock in the afternoon and recommended the selection of James Wells as chairman of the proceedings. In order to overturn the committee's verdict on the primary election, the Glasscock delegates needed the support of the Cameron County conferees. The other counties that D. W. Glasscock had carried in the primary controlled only fourteen of the thirty-three convention votes. The five votes from Cameron County would determine the outcome of any floor challenge.

Shortly after the adjournment of the executive committee session, the managers of the Glasscock campaign received two pieces of information that prompted them to take drastic action. Although the committee had announced that the convention was to begin at four o'clock, one of the pro-Glasscock county chairmen had received a letter from the district chairman ten days earlier, which set the time at two o'clock. Since the Terrell Election Law required compliance with the dates and times in the official notices to the county chairmen, the insurgents suspected that the four o'clock announcement was a Parr trick to block their participation in the district convention. The Glasscock partisans also learned that eight of Wells' associates had just arrived by train from Brownsville. Because only a handful of the Glasscock delegates of Cameron County had decided to attend the convention, Wells now had an opportunity to deliver the votes of his county to the Parr camp. Fearful that they no longer enjoyed the support of the majority of the delegates and suspicious of the intentions of the Parr operators, Glasscock and his followers decided to organize their own convention.

Acting without the sanction of the district executive committee, delegates from eight counties, including Glasscock's supporters from Cameron County, assembled at two o'clock and declared the McAllen lawyer the Democratic nominee of the twenty-third Senate district. They also passed a resolution that nullified the returns from Duval County and cited the findings of the Ranger investigation of election abuses in that county. Two hours later, James Wells presided over the Parr convention, which confirmed the nomination of the Duval County boss. Rather than settling the race for the Texas Senate seat, the convention process had merely opened a new round of political infighting. In the competition that followed, serious handicaps plagued both sides. The legality of the Glasscock convention was questionable, while the evidence of widespread election fraud made a mockery of Parr's claims to a popular majority.

In their drive to establish the legitimacy of D. W. Glasscock's nomination, the insurgents of South Texas turned to the state party organization for support. At the state Democratic convention of 1918, which the Hobby forces controlled, Lon Hill and Glasscock's lawyer, Claude Pollard of Houston, persuaded the credentials committee to oust the delegation from Duval County. The convention as a whole upheld this decision and passed a resolution that condemned the "irregularities, fraud, and corruption" in the Duval County primary and called upon the Texas secretary of state to certify D. W. Glasscock as the regular nominee of the Democratic party.[13] Three weeks later, the secretary of state complied with this request.

To counter the intervention of the secretary of state, Archie Parr filed a law suit, in which he challenged the legality of the Glasscock district convention and requested an injunction to prevent the inclusion of Glasscock's name on the official ballots for the general election. The case came to trial in Hidalgo County before a district judge, whose own legal and political problems bore a striking resemblance to Parr's. Judge F. G. Chambliss normally presided over the judicial district to the north of the seventy-ninth district, in which Parr brought his suit. In Chambliss' 1918 bid for renomination, he met apparent defeat but afterward contested the outcome of the primary with the argument that the recently passed woman suffrage act was unconstitutional. Rather than formally disqualifying himself from trying his own case and allowing Governor Hobby to appoint a special judge, Chambliss made an arrangement with Judge Volney

Taylor of the seventy-ninth district to exchange benches for the duration of the primary suit. This transfer raised questions about the impartiality of the judges in both the Chambliss and the Parr cases. In the first instance, the plaintiff, Judge Chambliss, chose the person who would decide his case. On the second day of the hearing, Judge Taylor upheld his colleague's contention that the establishment of female suffrage for the primaries violated the Texas Constitution, and he threw out the women's votes. The subsequent recount gave the incumbent a nineteen-vote majority.

Two circumstances accounted for the pretrial suspicions of judicial prejudice in the Parr case: the similarity between Parr's and Chambliss' suits, and the fact that the same lawyer represented both Glasscock and Chambliss' primary opponent. Once the legal proceedings began, the judge's biases became all too apparent. Over the objections of Glasscock's lawyer, Chambliss postponed the trial so that it overlapped with the hearing of his own case in San Patricio County, almost 150 miles north of the Hidalgo county seat. As a result of this ruling, the chief counsel for the defense, Claude Pollard, was unable to attend the Parr trial. In addition, Chambliss limited the scope of the election case to consideration of the competing district conventions. He refused to admit any evidence concerning Parr's resort to election fraud and his delay in allowing the release of the Duval County returns. On the narrow grounds that the Glasscock convention failed to conform to the requirements of the Terrell Election Law, the judge certified Parr as the legal nominee of the Democratic party and issued an injunction that compelled the county officials to delete Glasscock's name from the ballots and insert Parr's.

Although this decision dealt a devastating blow to the Glasscock campaign, the candidate and his supporters refused to surrender. On October 20, 1918, Charles Flato of Kingsville, who had headed the Hobby organization for the twenty-third Senate district during the primaries, announced the formation of the Hobby-Glasscock Club. The aim of this group was to promote a write-in drive for the McAllen insurgent. Both the retention of the ban against woman suffrage in the general election and the complications of writing in a candidate's name made a sharp reduction in the Anglo vote inevitable. Thus, to have any chance of success, the Glasscock forces not only had to arouse the full support of the eligible Anglo voters but also had to deter the voting of the machine-controlled Hispanic blocs.

Glasscock's appeal to the Anglo citizenry of the district stressed his claim to be the genuine Democratic nominee and the need to overthrow boss domination. With a campaign fund of $4,600, the insurgents distributed thousands of circulars with instructions for recording Glasscock's name on the ballot, and they ran frequent newspaper advertisements. Their political broadsides reviewed the evidence of Parr's offenses in the primary, cited the actions of the state Democratic convention and the secretary of state on Glasscock's behalf, blasted Judge Chambliss' decision, and presented letters of endorsement from Governor Hobby, the chairman of the state executive committee, and even former chairman Frank Andrews, who had long supported Wells' political causes. Glasscock also returned to the themes of his brief primary campaign, as he linked Parr's brand of corruption to the menace of "Fergusonism" and raised the loyalty issue: "While the world is being made safe for democracy by the annihilation of the Hun 'over there,' the democratic party shall be made safe by the eradication of Kaiser bossism 'over here.'"[14]

To cope with the overriding problem of the Hispanic vote, the Glasscock camp pursued three lines of action. As part of their crusade against boss rule, the self-styled reformers appealed for racial solidarity among the Anglo citizens and agitated for the removal of the illiterate, illegal voters from the political process. In a display of blatant hypocrisy, the insurgents also made a limited effort to secure Hispanic support. The election officials in Webb and LaSalle counties, who favored Glasscock, systematically marked the ballots of illiterate Mexican Americans. Along with the Anglos, Hispanic voters throughout the district received sample ballots in the mail with Parr's name scratched out and Glasscock's written in. Parr's operatives reported instances in which Hispanics copied these marked ballots at the polls in violation of the law. The ultimate weapon of the Glasscock forces against the mobilization of the Hispanic electorate in support of Parr, however, was the intervention of the Texas Rangers.

Protests over Captain Stevens' denial of bond to the Cameron County commissioner, whom his men had arrested the day before the primary, resulted in the captain's transfer from the Valley in late August. Nevertheless, the Ranger involvement in regional politics escalated as the general election approached. In September, Governor Hobby ordered further investigations of the irregularities in the primaries of Starr and Hidalgo counties. Captain Hanson openly consulted with Glasscock's campaign managers at their headquarters in Kingsville. Under Hanson's general command, a large force of regular officers and special Rangers observed the conduct of the November elections in most of the Hispanic precincts of Duval, Nueces, Cameron, Hidalgo, and Starr counties. Although these state policemen took little direct action to prevent anyone from voting, the mere presence of armed Rangers at the polling stations had an intimidating effect on the Hispanic population, which had suffered so many abuses at the hands of these law enforcement officers. To Parr's chagrin, six Rangers showed up at the precinct station where he cast his ballot.

The impact of the Ranger intervention became clear when the ballots were counted. Parr's vote total in Starr County surpassed the primary figure by a few ballots, but his support declined sharply in the other counties in which the Rangers monitored the election: from 1,366 to 843 in Hidalgo County, from 865 to 499 in Nueces County, and from 909 to 401 in Cameron County. The most dramatic drop of all came in Duval County, as Parr's vote tumbled from 1,303 to 226. The senator's spokesmen charged that Ranger intimidation deterred at least 500 voters from exercising their rights. Yet Parr weathered the Glasscock assault. The elimination of the women's vote, which barely affected Parr's total, cut deeply into the challenger's returns, but the decisive factor was the control that Parr's allies exercised over the election machinery in several counties. They not only continued to allow ineligible Hispanics to vote but also threw out hundreds of Glasscock ballots because of the misspelling of his name, the use of incorrect initials, and minor errors in the write-in procedure. With both sides claiming victory, the returning officer for the twenty-third Senate district, who was a Parr loyalist, canvassed the ballots and declared the Duval County chieftain the winner by a margin of 624 votes. Glasscock subsequently decided to carry his fight to the Texas Senate, where he intended to contest the seating of Archie Parr.

During the 1919 regular session of the state legislature, Archie Parr and James Wells battled their district opponents and the Hobby administration on two fronts. As the Duval boss fought to retain his seat in the Senate, José Canales agitated for an end to Ranger lawlessness and a complete overhaul of the force. Although the maverick legislator had not been aligned with Parr in the 1918 senatorial contest, Canales' attack placed the governor and his adjutant general on the defensive, at least temporarily, and Wells and Parr supported the representative's efforts. Because of their preoccupation with these two confrontations, the South Texas conservatives failed to offer any resistance to Hobby's campaign to complete the reform program that he had launched a year earlier.

At a preliminary hearing before the Senate Committee on Elections and Privileges, D. W. Glasscock and his lawyers appealed for a full Senate review of Archie Parr's reelection. Relying on Ranger reports, they disclosed a pattern of corruption in the general election that matched the level of abuses in the primaries. In Cameron and Hidalgo counties alone, six hundred Mexican Americans voted without presenting their poll tax receipts, and at least one thousand illiterate voters received assistance from election officers. Many of the election judges in the Hispanic precincts across the district were illiterate and unqualified to vote. At one Valley polling station the presiding officer served liquor to the voters, and officers at two other precincts, where Glasscock received a majority of the votes, simply refused to report their returns. Officials discarded approximately four hundred Glasscock votes in Nueces, Cameron, and Hidalgo counties for minor errors. Another common practice was the illegal payment of poll taxes for Hispanic voters by county officeholders and candidates. Because of the pervasiveness of the irregularities and the impossibility of distinguishing the legal votes from the illegal ones, Glasscock's lawyers called for the nullification of all the returns from Cameron, Hidalgo, Willacy, Starr, and Duval counties. In their view, Glasscock had clearly received a majority of the legal votes. Archie Parr responded to these claims with an outburst that caught even his own attorneys by surprise. Shaking his finger at one of the opposing lawyers, he shouted that "every affidavit and deposition in your possession was secured by State Rangers at the points of revolvers."[15] This display of temper and the reasoned arguments of Parr's chief counsel, Marshall Hicks of San Antonio, who had distinguished himself as a vigorous supporter of Woodrow Wilson in 1912, left the committee unmoved. They voted to investigate every phase of the senatorial contest from the primary campaign through the general election and to expand the membership of their committee to include all the members of the Senate except Archie Parr.

For one month, the Senate devoted most of its afternoon sessions to holding hearings on the Parr-Glasscock case. The enlarged Committee on Elections and Privileges listened to 148 witnesses and reviewed piles of documentary material, including the reports of the Texas Rangers. Although the Glasscock legal team was able to substantiate most of its charges of election chicanery, three revelations undercut the challenger's cause. Marshall Hicks introduced evidence to show that some of the insurgent organizers had manipulated the Hispanic vote just as flagrantly as the Parr operators. Even more damaging to Glasscock's personal reputation was the disclosure that during his term in the Texas House he had voted against the Boehmer bill of 1913, which had been designed to eliminate assistance to illiterate voters. The McAllen lawyer offered the explanation that he had lived in the Valley for only a year at the time of the vote and that he had been unaware of the scope of election abuses along the border. This rationalization collapsed, however, when Hicks pointed out that prior to Glasscock's election to the legislature he had prepared a law suit that charged the Independent party with the illegal manipulation of Hispanic voters and other offenses in the 1912 Brownsville city election. The seemingly irrelevant accusation that Glasscock had cheated his irrigation customers in Mission, Texas, also tarnished his reformist image. Mission was the only Anglo precinct in the Valley that had voted overwhelmingly for Parr.

By the end of the hearings, Marshall Hicks had convinced many of the senators that D. W. Glasscock and his organizers were just as unethical as the Duval chieftain. Once the choice appeared to be only between varying degrees of corruption, rather than between corruption and reform, Archie Parr was able to take advantage of the political ties and friendships that he had formed in the legislature. A growing number of converts decided to allow their wayward colleague to retain his seat. During the floor debate over whether to affirm Parr's election or to require a new election, only one senator defended Parr's integrity, but several argued that Glasscock had not come "into this contest with clean hands."[16] The most sanctimonious expression of this willingness to accept Parr back into the fold came from Senator F. M. Gibson of Bonham: "The story of the accused woman brought before Christ is parallel to this one. I think this Senate should ask: Is the accuser without sin? The proper decision would be to say to Parr: 'Go Thou, and sin no more.'"[17] Parr's critics continued to argue that the Senate should take strong action to uphold the election laws of the state and to eliminate the corruption that pervaded South Texas politics, but all to no avail. After a preliminary committee vote that left the issue in doubt because of two absentees, the whole membership of the Senate voted sixteen to fourteen to seat Parr.

In a strictly legal sense, the verdict of the Senate was unjust. Although the Glasscock camp had abused the election process, their offenses were modest in comparison to the activities of Parr and his cronies, who had violated the election laws in every way imaginable. The Rangers had conducted their investigations in a partisan spirit, but the corruption that they had uncovered was undeniably real. Glasscock's lawyers were correct in their contention that their candidate had received a majority of the legal votes in both the primary and the general elections. At the very least, D. W. Glasscock deserved an opportunity to challenge Parr again in a new election.

Any endorsement of the Glasscock cause must be qualified, however, because of the racial implications of the insurgent uprising in South Texas. The election laws that Parr and Wells treated with such contempt were discriminatory against the poor, illiterate Hispanic masses, who still formed a majority of the population of the region. The Glasscock reformers shared and exploited the racist prejudices of their Anglo followers. For the Mexican Americans, a new Anglo order would mean labor exploitation, untempered by paternalistic concessions, and complete exclusion from the political process. Wells, Parr, and the other bosses had failed to satisfy the needs of their Hispanic constituents in important respects, but most Mexican Americans along the border still preferred the traditional combination of paternalism and manipulation to reform.

Just before the Senate Committee on Elections and Privileges voted to conduct an investigation of the Parr-Glasscock race, José Canales launched his attack against the Texas Rangers. Ever since the Ranger atrocities of 1915, he had regarded the force as "a shame and disgrace to my native state," but on two previous occasions state officials had convinced him that they would take corrective action.[18] When the United States entered World War I, Governor Ferguson appealed to the legislature to raise the limit on the number of regular and special Rangers to one thousand men. To prevent Canales from lobbying against the bill, the governor gave his personal assurance that he would fire anyone who abused the Mexican American citizens of South Texas. Captain William Hanson made a similar pledge for the Hobby administration in February 1918. The later removal of Captain Stevens from the Valley appeared to confirm Hanson's good faith, and Canales delivered a loyalty speech to his Hispanic constituents, in which he declared that the Rangers no longer posed a threat. The Brownsville representative even arranged the appointment of his brother, who lived in Jim Wells County, to serve as a special Ranger. This cooperation with the Rangers was short-lived, however.

Two incidents in October 1918 revived Canales' uneasiness over the conduct of the state police. While following the trail of some stolen cattle, one of Canales' relatives, Santavo Tijerino, encountered a posse of Rangers, who accused him of participating in a smuggling operation but never pressed formal charges. The lawmen cursed Tijerino repeatedly and made insulting remarks about his family. The relative believed that the Rangers were trying to provoke a fight so that they could shoot him for resisting arrest. Later that month, Captain Hanson showed Canales the written statement of a Ranger who had mistaken an innocent Hispanic resident of Starr County for a draft evader and had killed the man. When Canales concluded that the affidavit amounted to a confession of manslaughter and possibly even second-degree murder, Hanson became indignant and insisted that the Ranger was innocent of any wrongdoing. This exchange convinced the Mexican American legislator that the captain's main concern was to shield his men from prosecution rather than to curtail their abuses.

A frightening sequel to the Tijerino incident prompted José Canales to press for a legislative solution to the Ranger problem. In December, a Ranger named Frank Hamer met Canales on a street in Brownsville and berated him for complaining to Captain Hanson about the mistreatment that Tijerino had received. The officer then warned the legislator that he was "going to get hurt" if he did not stop criticizing the force.[19] After Hamer repeated the threat in front of a witness, Canales turned to Sheriff Vann for protection. According to Canales, Vann gave the following reply: "My advice to you is take a double-barreled shotgun and I will give you a man and go over there and kill that man. . . . No jury would ever convict you for that."[20] Canales declined to follow the sheriff's suggestion and, instead, wrote a letter of protest to Governor Hobby. In his complaint, the South Texan charged that "Hanson did nothing [about the Tijerino incident] but instead told these Rangers that I was making complaints against them and evidently . . . instructed them, as the best way to stop complaints, to threaten me."[21] Canales also informed Adjutant General James Harley that Hanson's investigation of the Ranger killing in Starr County had been a whitewash. When Hobby and his adjutant general failed to take any punitive action against Hamer or Hanson, Canales gave up all hope that the executive branch would reform the Rangers on its own initiative.

At the start of the regular session of the legislature in 1919, José Canales introduced a bill calling for the reorganization of the Texas Rangers and the imposition of tight controls on their operation. The measure would eliminate the Loyalty Ranger Force and limit the size of the regular force to twenty-four men "in time of peace" and eighty men during an emergency. Only U.S. citizens over twenty-five years of age and with two years of experience as peace officers could qualify to serve in the state police. An applicant would have to submit "evidence from the County Commissioners' Court of his county that he is and has been a peaceful and law-abiding citizen." The most controversial features of the Canales proposal concerned local controls and bonding requirements. A Ranger would have to deliver his prisoners without delay to the sheriff's department of the county in which he had made the arrests. Any complaint from the sheriff, county judge, and county commissioners that a Ranger had mistreated a prisoner would result in the dismissal of the officer from the force. These same local officials could petition the governor or the adjutant general to remove Texas Rangers from their county. If the state administration failed to comply with this request within ten days, the Rangers would "cease to be peace officers in said County."[22] Like sheriffs and their deputies, the state lawmen would also be subject to civil damages for any abuse of their power, and they would have to post bonds ranging from $15,000 for captains to $5,000 for privates.

During the opening round of the House debate over his bill, José Canales declared that "my life is threatened by a Ranger now in the service of the State of Texas because I have dared to insist on reform measures." The Brownsville representative also charged that "the Rangers of Texas have committed crimes equal to those of the Germans in Belgium . . . , by spilling the blood of innocent men who were accorded no right under the law while in their hands."[23] These remarks generated widespread newspaper coverage of his proposal and attracted the attention of his South Texas constituents, who divided over the issue of disciplining the Rangers. James Wells and Sheriff Vann both endorsed Canales' move. In fact, Vann had tried earlier to promote support within the Sheriffs' Association of Texas for the abolition of the state police. The Anglo farmers and most of the independent politicians, on the other hand, bitterly opposed the bill. They organized mass meetings in several Valley towns and flooded the House with protest messages. A shortage of state funds had already forced personnel cuts within the law enforcement agency, including the dissolution of one of the two Valley companies, and the protesters were afraid that the additional restrictions in Canales' legislation would lead to the complete withdrawal of the Rangers from the region. In their view, the presence of these officers was essential to the maintenance of order along the border. They also argued that the Rangers alone had demonstrated a commitment to enforce the election laws in the Trans-Nueces. Canales' critics, both in the Valley and in the legislature, suspected that he was serving as a front man for Archie Parr, whose defense in the Senate rested, at least in part, on the claim that the Rangers had deterred hundreds of legitimate voters from going to the polls. Although Parr and Canales now had a common interest in curbing the power of the Rangers, the representative's past record of political independence and his personal grievances against the state lawmen indicated that he was acting on his own initiative. At the same time, however, Canales welcomed the support of the South Texas bosses.

After the Hobby partisans in the House attached several crippling amendments to the Ranger bill, José Canales agreed to send his proposal back to the Committee on Military Affairs for further consideration. Despite this setback, the Brownsville politico was able to force a joint House-Senate investigation of the activities of the state police. Canales' attack against the agency had received so much publicity that now even the defenders of the Rangers were eager for an inquiry so that they would clear the name of the lawmen. During the first week of the hearings, Canales submitted nineteen charges against the Texas Rangers and the adjutant general. All of the accusations dealt with offenses that had occurred since the start of the Hobby administration, and the crimes ranged from drunk and disorderly conduct to the massacre of unarmed Mexican American villagers. The most despicable incident under review had taken place in the West Texas county of Presidio. A posse of Rangers had entered a small Hispanic community, dragged fifteen men from their homes, accused them of participating in a raid, and executed them on the spot. Six other charges involved the killing of suspects. Canales also attacked Adjutant General Harley and Captain William Hanson for their inadequate supervision of the state force. The representative again accused Hanson of covering up Ranger crimes, and he criticized the adjutant general for hiring disreputable gunmen, assigning the Rangers to protect the ranches of the "political pets of the administration," and generally failing to eliminate Ranger abuses.[24]

The hearings did not turn into a one-sided assault against the Texas Rangers. The joint committee refused to review the charges against the adjutant general and often appeared to be more interested in the motives of Canales and the other Ranger critics than in the misdeeds of the state officers. Canales failed to substantiate some of his charges, and his shameful manipulation of the evidence to discredit every action on the part of Captain Hanson and Adjutant General Harley further undercut his case. When Harley pointed out that he had fired all the men involved in the Presidio massacre and had forced the resignation of their commanding officer, Captain J. M. Fox, Canales cited Fox's selfserving letter of resignation as evidence that the captain had been removed for political reasons. The representative conveniently ignored the fact that Fox had based his charge of partisanship on the claim that his men were innocent of any wrongdoing. A parade of friendly witnesses, who applauded the Ranger campaign to combat banditry and theft along the border, also bolstered the cause of the state agency.

Despite the attitudes of the committeemen, the praise for the state police, and Canales' shortcomings as an unofficial prosecutor, the hearings did expose the full scope of Ranger lawlessness. A sordid tale of abuse of power, partisan favoritism, brutality, and unprovoked killings emerged. The formal charges dealt only with the recent offenses of the force, but Sheriff Vann, Rentfro B. Creager, and other witnesses discussed at length the Ranger outrages during the border raids of 1915. Even supporters of the agency, such as Lon Hill, hinted that the officers had gone far beyond the limits of legal action. No one disputed the claim that the state lawmen and the vigilante groups of the Valley had killed over two hundred Hispanics. The only point of contention was whether or not this wanton slaughter had been necessary to restore order.

James Wells was perhaps the most ambivalent witness to appear before the committee. While professing his continuing loyalty to the Rangers, he endorsed the main provisions of the Canales bill, especially the bonding proposal, which would afford citizens some protection against arbitrary arrests and police brutality. Wells' review of the record of the Rangers, however, did not reflect any consistent concern for the rights of citizens. The Rio Grande boss expressed indignation over Captain Stevens' confiscation of the arms of Hispanic residents in 1918 and his illegal detention of the Cameron County commissioner before the July primary, but he was willing to excuse the far more serious Ranger offenses of 1915 as necessary emergency actions.

The conclusions and recommendations of the joint committee represented an awkward attempt to arrange a political compromise. On the one hand, the legislators expressed their gratitude to José Canales for his "fair, prompt, and considerate" conduct during the hearings and defended his motives in leveling the charges against the Rangers. Only later did their real sentiments toward the Mexican American representative surface. The investigators also concluded that many of the accusations of unwarranted violence and disregard for the law "have been established by sufficient and competent evidence." Undaunted by the contradictions in their analysis, the committeemen turned around and applauded the "great service that has been rendered by many of the State Rangers."[25] The legislative probers claimed that the force had made an indispensable contribution to law enforcement along the border. They exonerated Adjutant General Harley and Captain Hanson of any wrongdoing and even commended Harley's efforts to raise the standards of competency and integrity within the agency. Along these same lines, the panel suggested that the best way to reform the Rangers was to grant more authority to the governor and the adjutant general to control the lawmen. The only proposal that the committeemen borrowed from the Canales bill was a call for a reduction in the size of the force, but they were willing to allow the governor to appoint as many officers as he deemed necessary in the event of an emergency.

All hope of a compromise settlement of the battle over Ranger reorganization disappeared when José Canales urged the House to reject the report that the joint committee had prepared. The Valley representative criticized the panel for endorsing Harley's performance as adjutant general after it had ruled out any investigation of the charges against him. Canales' condemnation of the inquiry provoked an angry rebuttal from the chairman of the committee, W. H. Bledsoe of Lubbock, who had previously maintained a public posture of neutrality in the Ranger controversy: "While the committee exonerated Representative Canales of any wrongful motive in bringing his charges, it is our belief that he has been misled in some ways and influenced unduly by a 'man higher up.' I may go further and say that in order to throw obstacles in the path of the men charged with the administration of the laws of this state a whole coterie of politicians along the border has been willing to sink the best interests of the state and the county in order to achieve personal ends."[26] In more explicit terms, another representative charged Canales with trying to destroy the Rangers in order to block the investigation of political corruption in South Texas and to protect his relative whom the lawmen suspected of "collusion with bandits on the other side of the border."[27] At the conclusion of these exchanges, the Brownsville legislator suffered an overwhelming defeat, as the House adopted the report by a vote of eighty-seven to ten.

With the backing of the adjutant general, Representative Bledsoe submitted a complete revision of Canales' Ranger reform plan. The Bledsoe substitute eliminated the bonding requirement and allowed the retention of the special Rangers. The chairman's only concession to the concept of local control was the stipulation that a state lawman had to deliver his prisoners promptly to the county jail. Although any charge of abuse of power could lead to a discharge hearing before a local magistrate, only the adjutant general had the power to institute such proceedings.

As the debate over the Canales bill and the Bledsoe substitute progressed, tension mounted. After Canales accused his adversary of misrepresenting the provisions of his original reform, the two men almost came to blows on the floor of the House. The *San Antonio Daily Express* offered the following account of the confrontation:

"Mr. Canales," threatened Representative Bledsoe, walking from the head of the table in the center aisle of the House of Representatives to the chair where the member from Cameron was seated, bending over and shaking his fist in Canales's face, "if you dare again to open your mouth to intimate that anything I may say is an untruth, I will slap you on the jaw if it costs me my seat in the House."

"Go ahead and slap it," Canales challenged; and the two for a minute looked unflinchingly in each others' eyes, while the Speaker rapped like a trip hammer with his gavel, and the sergeant at arms advanced down the aisle to interpose, and members stood and half rose from their seats the better to see what would happen. A full minute, it seemed, they confronted each other, then the Lubbock man straightened up and returned to his former station.

"I offer my apologies to the membership of this House," said Bledsoe, his voice trembling with emotion, "but when one has sat for weeks, day after day, listening to a man guilty of the things this man has done, seeing him using every method to accomplish personal ends instead of representing his people, as he has sworn to do, patience ceases to be a virtue."[28]

Racial animosity probably accounted for the intensity of the reaction against Canales' commitment to reform the Rangers. Many legislators shared the view of the Anglo settlers along the border that the Rangers stood as the first line of defense for white civilization against Mexican barbarism to the south. The representatives also appreciated the efforts of the state police to curb the manipulation of the Hispanic vote, which they regarded as the source of the political corruption that plagued South Texas. Although the joint investigating committee had condemned the worst excesses of the Rangers, its members subsequently led the fight to block the imposition of effective controls on the force. If these lawmakers prevailed, the Rangers would be free to combat any future border raids with whatever tactics they considered necessary. The fact that Canales was a Mexican American heightened the resentment of his legislative opponents. Despite his record of support for a wide range of reforms and his cooperation with the U.S. Army in suppressing the bandit trouble of 1915, Canales' critics publicly denounced him as an agent of corruptionists and criminals. Not even Archie Parr, whose reputation for political chicanery was unrivaled, ever provoked the kind of emotional, almost violent outburst that Canales faced.

After W. H. Bledsoe's bitter harangue and his threat to strike Canales, the House vote on the Ranger bill was anticlimactic. The legislators passed the Bledsoe substitute by a majority of ninety-five to five. The measure met only token opposition in the Senate, where Archie Parr was maintaining a low profile following the narrow de-

feat of Glasscock's challenge. The Duval boss did not even participate in the roll call votes on the bill. In the final balloting, only one
senator cast a dissenting vote. Despite the revelations of the Ranger
hearings, the victory for both the Hobby administration and the
state police was now complete. Bledsoe's revision of the Canales reform proposal left the governor and his adjutant general with a free
hand to run the Rangers as they saw fit, and the overwhelming majorities in both houses provided the lawmen with a strong vote of
confidence.

The emasculation of the Ranger reorganization bill was not the
only setback that James Wells and Archie Parr suffered during the
regular legislative session of 1919. The progressive forces of the
House and Senate staged a major breakthrough with the passage of
two long-sought constitutional amendments. One amendment provided for statewide prohibition to cover the interval before the
implementation of national prohibition, while the other extended
voting rights to women for the general elections as well as the primaries. The female suffrage resolution also contained a provision
that excluded aliens from the election process. Only persons who
had been born in this country or who had become naturalized citizens would be eligible to vote. Before either of these amendments
could go into effect, the measures had to receive the approval of the
voters of Texas in a special election scheduled for May 24, 1919. In
another move to tighten restrictions on Hispanic voting, the legislature enacted a statute that required election officials to use only English in assisting voters and permitted such aid only for people over
sixty years old and those who were physically disabled.

When each of these reforms came before the Senate for debate,
Parr's colleagues were still considering the Glasscock challenge to
his election, and the Duval boss made an effort to avoid offending
any of the members of the progressive majority. Parr voted for statewide prohibition and the woman suffrage resolution with its ban
against alien voting. Just before the balloting on the measure to restrict voter assistance, he left the Senate chamber. In conformity
with his past record, Canales supported prohibition and women's
voting rights, but he refused to commit himself on the third reform.
During the roll call votes on voter assistance, he simply answered,
"Present."

Wells, Parr, and other Old Guard Democrats had an opportunity
to recoup some of their recent legislative losses in the special election on May 24, which would determine the fate of the two constitutional amendments. The conservative leaders of the state decided to
concentrate their efforts on the defeat of the female suffrage pro-

posal, and Pauline Wells again headed the campaign of the Texas Association Opposed to Woman Suffrage. Her co-workers distributed over 100,000 circulars, which contained their familiar arguments that the extension of voting rights to women would lead to socialism, black rule in the South, and the destruction of the family. James Wells contributed to the drive by soliciting financial contributions and appealing to Joseph Bailey to deliver a series of speeches on the issue. Although the prohibition amendment carried the state by a comfortable margin, woman suffrage and the accompanying ban on alien voting met defeat by a vote of 166,893 to 141,773. The proponents of women's voting rights argued that a large turnout of alien voters was responsible for the outcome of the election, but the suffrage amendment prevailed in seven of the twelve counties forming the southeastern tip of Texas. Only in Duval and Starr counties did the antisuffrage forces claim one-sided majorities, and, even in those counties, the turnouts were light. Once again, Wells was unable to deliver his own county in an important political battle. The prohibition amendment fared as well as the voting rights measure in South Texas.

Following the defeat of women's suffrage at the polls, conservative spokesmen demanded the repeal of the statute providing female voting rights in the primaries. The reformers, on the other hand, called for the legislative ratification of the national constitutional amendment on women's suffrage, which Congress passed in early June. After Governor Hobby summoned a special session of the legislature, Wells, Parr, Ferguson, and over one hundred other conservative Democrats signed an appeal to the legislators to respect the verdict of the May election and to uphold the southern tradition of states rights, but the petition had little effect. The national amendment passed the House easily and survived a filibuster in the Senate. Parr voted with the opposition, while Canales supported the measure. This legislative action completed the route of the Democratic Old Guard at the end of the second decade of the twentieth century.

The resurgence of Texas progressivism after 1917 not only destroyed James Wells' influence over state government but also speeded the collapse of his power base in Cameron County. The establishment of woman suffrage and the partial enforcement of the restrictions on Hispanic voting contributed to the formation of the new Anglo majority within the local electorate. At the same time, Wells' active participation in the disputed senatorial contest of 1918, the attack against the Rangers, and the drive to defeat women's suffrage convinced his Anglo constituents that he was an unrepentant corruptionist and reactionary. Ever since the emergence of the Anglo population as a significant factor in Cameron County politics, Wells had maneuvered to capture a share of the newcomers' vote with the recruitment of new candidates and promises of improved public services from the county government. In 1918, he had defeated a strong challenge from an independent slate by embracing the candidacy of the popular progressive governor, but Wells' conspicuous opposition to reform causes since then eliminated any possibility of the successful repetition of this ploy in 1920. Shortly before the general election of 1918, the *Brownsville Daily Herald* reviewed Wells' role in the Parr-Glasscock race and issued a prophetic warning to the Democratic leader: "The *Herald* believes that Judge Wells has made a great big mistake—a mistake which will rise up and confront him in the future."[29]

Conclusion: The Last Hurrah for James Wells

JAMES WELLS' DOWNFALL came in 1920. For the past five years, his bloc of Hispanic followers had shrunk as a result of the massive exoduses of 1915 and 1917 and the campaign of the Texas Rangers to deter illegal voting in 1918. After the conclusion of World War I, Mexican workers again poured into the Valley, but most of them were newcomers who had no loyalty to the Wells machine. The Democratic organizers could no longer depend on employers to recruit new supporters since the Anglo farmers, who hired the migrants, opposed Wells' leadership and Hispanic participation in the election process. By 1920, the Anglo voters outnumbered the ring-controlled Hispanic voters by a majority of almost two to one. Facing the prospect of defeat and troubled by serious health problems, the seventy-year-old boss wanted to retire from the post of county Democratic chairman after thirty-six years of service. Nevertheless, he remained politically active through June because of his strong support of Joseph Bailey's bid for the governorship and his opposition to the man who had the best chance of succeeding him as county chairman, Francis W. Seabury.

During the 1890s and the first decade of the twentieth century, Seabury had cooperated with the Wells organization. As a Valley representative and as the Speaker of the Texas House, he had consistently opposed election reforms that threatened Wells' power. He had also managed the Democratic forces in the volatile Starr County contest of 1906, which had ended with the murder of Judge Stanley Welch and an armed confrontation on election day. After serving as the chairman of the Democratic campaign in the Brownsville city election of 1912, Seabury withdrew from politics for almost eight years and concentrated on his law practice. With most Cameron County voters only vaguely aware of his past association with Wells, the former Speaker decided to stage a political comeback in 1920. He formed an alliance with a clique of independent politicians from San Benito and emerged as the leading critic of the Democratic machine.

The first collision between James Wells and Francis Seabury occurred in the spring. Wells supported Joseph Bailey's campaign to mobilize a rebellion against the progressive Democratic leadership at the state and national levels. Bailey's immediate objective was to take charge of the state Democratic convention that would select delegates to the national convention. Despite Wells' forecast that he would carry Cameron County for the Bailey cause, Seabury and his associates controlled a majority of the precinct conventions. Conceding defeat, Wells allowed his rival to chair the county convention, which endorsed Woodrow Wilson's record as president. The Bailey initiative floundered throughout Texas. His partisans prevailed in only a few counties and formed a bloc of fewer than fifty votes at the state convention.

After the dismal showing of his forces in the opening round of the political competition of 1920, James Wells appealed to Seabury to rejoin the regular Democratic organization and to run for the county Democratic chairmanship in the July primaries as the boss' chosen successor. Seabury rejected the overture because he realized that the real power in local politics now lay outside the Wells machine. In addition, the insurgent was unwilling to support Wells' choice for governor, Joseph Bailey, whose uncompromising conservatism was unacceptable to the reform-minded Anglo voters of the Valley. Seabury favored the leading progressive aspirant, Pat Neff. In June, Seabury launched his independent campaign for the county chairmanship. At the same time, he expanded his law firm to include District Judge Volney Taylor as a partner, and he persuaded one of his junior colleagues to run for county attorney. The Rio Grande boss was afraid that Seabury was maneuvering not only to destroy the Democratic ring but also to replace Wells as the most influential lawyer in the Valley.

To counter Seabury's threat, James Wells once again resorted to a devious political strategy. He announced his candidacy for reelection to the Democratic chairmanship and recruited a San Benito politician named Samuel Spears to enter the race as a third competitor. Spears had supported progressive causes in the past, but he had fallen out with the San Benito independents who were backing Seabury. He was determined to prevent his former allies from establishing their dominance over county politics. Wells hoped that Spears would split the Anglo electorate and allow Wells to retain his post with a plurality of the vote. Even this ploy failed. In late June, Wells fell ill and sought medical treatment at a hospital in New Orleans. Although he was able to return to Brownsville two weeks later, his doctors ruled out any additional campaigning, and he withdrew from the race. In his last desperate effort to influence the outcome of the contest, he directed the party regulars to work for the election of Samuel Spears.

The final stage of the 1920 campaign produced a complete repudiation of Wells' political leadership. Francis Seabury called for an end to boss rule, denounced Spears as a Wells pawn, and warned the Anglo voters about the planned mobilization of the Hispanic electorate on his opponent's behalf: "Preparations were being made for a grand outpouring of the Mexican vote, illegal as well as legal, in favor of Judge Spears. To this end, the county officers are being assessed for funds; bailes are being planned, cows are being killed, the faithful are being called to the colors, and in the midst of it all, the Mexican voters, in those precincts, do not know that they are to be voting for Judge Spears, but still believe that Judge Wells is in the race."[1] Recognizing the liability of his identification with the Wells camp, Spears began to indulge in the same kind of rhetoric. Three days before the election, he condemned "the political dictatorship of Judge Wells" and accused Seabury of receiving his "political tutelage under Judge Wells."[2] The aging boss' continued willingness to deliver the Hispanic vote for Spears even in the face of this attack revealed the full measure of Wells' desperation and humiliation.

Spears was able to attract enough Anglo support for a respectable total, but he still lost to Seabury by a vote of 922 to 806. The election also produced a dramatic turnover within county government. Only four of the thirteen major officeholders retained their positions. Most of the incumbents were aware of the odds against them and simply refused to run for reelection. In the five races in which Wells' allies faced challengers, the insurgents won three county offices. Only Sheriff Vann, who had always been an effective campaigner, and the county commissioner from Brownsville survived independent opposition. The races for governor and district attorney provided the clearest tests of strength for Wells and his opponents. Although approximately 1,500 ballots were cast in each contest, Joseph Bailey and Wells' brother-in-law, John Kleiber, who had held the position of district attorney since 1892, received only 457 and 412 votes, respectively. Kleiber fared almost as poorly in the two other populous counties in the district and lost to a reformminded Brownsville lawyer. Because of the division of the progressive vote among three gubernatorial candidates, Joseph Bailey claimed a narrow statewide plurality, but his success was short-lived. The progressive wing of the Democratic party united behind Pat Neff in the run-off campaign, and the Waco prohibitionist overwhelmed Bailey with 60 percent of the vote. Neff carried Cameron County in both the initial primary and the run-off.

Although James Wells remained politically active after his fall from power, he entertained no illusions about his prospects for a comeback. He understood all too well the fundamental changes that had overtaken his county. Shortly before the 1922 Democratic primary, Wells described the new political order to Archie Parr: "Cameron County has ceased to be the 'Banner' Democratic stronghold, since it got into the hands of F. W. Seabury, as Chairman of the Executive Committee,—and it is now, 'Anybody's and Everybody's County,'—which is due, also, to the fact that the 'Snow-Diggers' are in the majority, and fast increasing."[3] With even more bitterness, Wells warned Joseph Bailey that "the Ku Klux Klan and the Bolsheviki are entirely in the saddle in this part of the state, and the Democrats, who think, and feel, as yourself and myself do, are entirely, and vastly, in the minority, and unheaded."[4]

Wells used the term "Bolsheviki" maliciously as a label for progressives and anyone else to the left of center on the political spectrum, but his reference to the Ku Klux Klan was quite literal. During the 1920s this organization emerged as a formidable force in Texas politics, and its anti-Catholic, nativistic bigotry appealed to the Mexican-hating Anglos along the border. When Charles Culberson made his bid for a fifth term to the U.S. Senate in 1922, he faced competition from five Democratic challengers, including Railroad Commissioner Earle Mayfield, who was openly sympathetic to the Klan. With the Anglo vote of Cameron County split among several candidates, Wells' campaigning enabled Culberson to edge out Mayfield by a vote of 641 to 616. Statewide, however, the recurrently ill incumbent finished third. In the run-off, Wells sided with former Governor James Ferguson, but the pro-Klan candidate rolled up a staggering majority of 1,436 to 694 in Cameron County and carried the state as well. Wells, who was a devout Catholic, hated the Ku Klux Klan so intensely that he abandoned his career-long adherence to party regularity in the general election and supported the independent candidacy of George Peddy. For once, Rentfro B. Creager and Wells stood on the same side in a political contest. As the state chairman of the Republican party, Creager persuaded the regular GOP nominee to withdraw and arranged for the state executive committee to endorse Peddy. Nonetheless, Mayfield swept the state and Cameron County.

James B. Wells' political career came to a close in 1922. That year he campaigned not only for Charles Culberson but also for John Garner, who faced a surprisingly strong challenge from a novice politician from the northwestern end of the district, and for Archie Parr, who barely survived a three-man race for the Democratic nomination for state senator. To prevent a recurrence of the Ranger interference of 1918, Parr threw his support behind Governor Neff's bid for reelection and was able to defeat his opponents with huge Duval County majorities in both the primary and the run-off. Ignoring Parr's reputation as an arch corruptionist and the lingering resentment over his theft of the 1918 election, Wells attributed the strong showings of the senator's challengers to "the vote of the Ku Klux Klan [and] the Bolsheviki."[5] As an expression of gratitude for two decades of loyalty, support, and guidance, Archie Parr arranged for the Duval County Democratic convention to select Wells as one of its delegates to the state convention. This gesture turned out to be the dethroned boss' last political honor. Throughout 1923, Wells' health deteriorated. By November, he was too weak to leave his house, and he died on December 21.

Although political machines continued to operate in South Texas after 1923, James Wells' death and the earlier collapse of his Cameron County organization marked the end of an era. For almost four decades, Wells was the dominant political figure in the border region. His machine served as a model for the Democratic rings that emerged in Duval, Starr, and Hidalgo Counties, and his support helped to launch the careers of Archie Parr, John Closner, A. Y. Baker, and Manuel Guerra. The Rio Grande chieftain also made an impact on state and national politics. After the restoration of conservative rule in Texas in the mid-1890s, Wells cooperated closely with the leading architects of the new political order, Colonel Edward M. House and Joseph Weldon Bailey, and served as the state Democratic chairman for four years. Despite his willingness to reach accommodations with the two progressive governors who revived the reform movement in the state, Wells remained a stubborn opponent of the foremost goal of Texas progressives—prohibition. The role of the one-sided South Texas votes in the recurrent defeats of antiliquor referendums accounted for the constant clamor in the state legislature for election reforms to eliminate the manipulation of the Hispanic electorate. Wells' one significant contribution to the shaping of national political history was his promotion of John Nance Garner's initial campaign for Congress in 1902 and his continued support for the representative over the next two decades. By the start of the Wilson administration, Garner had already established himself as one of the most influential Democrats in the House. He held a seat on the all important Ways and Means Committee and continued his service as majority whip. When Wells tried to persuade Garner to run for the Senate in 1922, the Uvalde representative revealed his ambition to become Speaker of the House —a goal that he would achieve in 1930, two years before his election to the vice-presidency.

The key to Wells' long-term success was his sensitivity to constituent needs. The Valley Democrat maintained the allegiance of the powerful ranchers by holding down property taxes, defending their land titles in the courts and the legislature, and lobbying for the stationing of Rangers and federal troops along the border. His promotion of railroad construction and irrigation development coincided with the interests of the ranchers and land speculators, who envisioned the subdivision of their vast holdings into small farmsteads, and the business community of Brownsville, which had suffered a prolonged depression since the completion of the railroad lines from San Antonio and Corpus Christi to Laredo in the early 1880s. Wells' allies also included the well-to-do Hispanic families, who had managed to retain their lands and businesses in the face of the Anglo economic onslaught after the Civil War. The boss provided legal services for the Mexican American gentry and allowed their representatives to hold important county offices. To mobilize the lower-class Hispanic laborers, who formed the overwhelming majority of the population, Wells enlisted the cooperation of their employers and established his own informal welfare system. The Rio Grande chieftain failed to arrange any general avenue of upward mobility or to facilitate the assimilation of the Hispanic masses into Anglo society, but his modest relief payments in times of special need and his respect for Mexican social customs earned him the loyalty of these impoverished constituents. For almost a decade, Wells even attracted some support from the new Anglo settlers with his pledges to improve the public services of the county government.

Paternalistic care for the Hispanic laborers and their families was the indispensable component in the operation of each of the Democratic machines, but Wells and his allies also relied on other, less benevolent, practices to bolster their causes. Corruption and violence pervaded the politics of South Texas. All the bosses systematically violated the election laws of the state by paying for the poll taxes of their Hispanic followers, recruiting ineligible aliens to vote, marking the ballots of illiterate voters, and tampering with the results when necessary. In Duval County, Archie Parr even refused to conduct precinct and county conventions and simply appointed his trusted henchmen to serve as party officials and delegates to district and state conventions. The regular Democrats, as well as the Republican and independent insurgents, hired gunmen to intimidate voters and the opposition, and a grim record of armed confrontations and political killings unfolded. In addition, the machine politicians embezzled funds from the county treasuries. Although the Cameron County Democrats exercised considerable restraint after the influx of Anglo farmers, their earlier escapades included the theft of $38,000 from revenue that they had collected to finance the construction of the courthouse and jail. The foremost practitioners of graft were Archie Parr, whose financial manipulations produced an awesome public debt of $315,000 for his underdeveloped county, and John Closner, who had to resign as Hidalgo County treasurer after the exposure of his misappropriation of $160,000. The bosses and their associates used the money both for their personal enrichment and for such political purposes as subsidizing poll taxes and supplying relief payments to their hard-pressed constituents. In contrast to Parr, Closner, and the Guerras, James Wells never faced formal criminal charges, but he set the precedents for manipulating the legal system to prevent the prosecution of loyal Democrats.

Despite the repeated campaigns on the part of progressive Democrats to strengthen the election laws of Texas, the state government did little to curb the election abuses and other forms of corruption along the border until William Hobby's intervention in 1918. The conservative, wet administrations appreciated the solid electoral support that the South Texas bosses furnished, while reform Governor Thomas Campbell preferred accommodation to confrontation with Wells and his allies. The special relationship between Wells and the Texas Rangers stood as another barrier to the investigation and eradication of political corruption. Hobby's reorganization of the Rangers and his drive to block Archie Parr's bid for reelection to the state Senate proved to be an aberration rather than a turning point in the policies of the state government. For the next three decades, state officials continued to tolerate the criminal activity of the Trans-Nueces bosses, who generally pursued an opportunistic strategy of supporting Democratic front-runners and incumbents in state races, regardless of their ideologies. Only at the federal level did the South Texans face the threat of prosecution.

The opponents of Democratic boss rule at the local level were hardly models of public virtue. The Valley Republicans and the Independent party of Cameron County manipulated the Hispanic vote in the same way that their Democratic counterparts did, but with much less success. After the Independents took charge of the

Brownsville municipal government in 1910, they exploited their control of the election machinery to rig the next contest, and they converted the city police into a partisan force that became involved in a series of gunfights with sheriff deputies and Texas Rangers. The suspects in the John Cleary and Judge Welch murder cases were all affiliated with local GOP organizations. The Good Government League of Hidalgo County and the independent Democrats of Cameron County, who challenged Wells' tickets in the 1918 and 1920 primaries, were determined to eliminate corruption and election abuses, but their solution was the disfranchisement of most of the Hispanic electorate. Racial prejudices as well as disgust with the political practices of the regular Democratic organizations underlay the reformist crusade that toppled Wells from power.

In two important respects, James B. Wells was the architect of his own destruction. He not only participated in the development schemes that attracted thousands of Anglo settlers to the Valley but also failed to come to the aid of his Hispanic constituents in their hour of greatest need. When the Texas Rangers, local lawmen, and vigilante groups terrorized the Mexican American residents of Cameron and Hidalgo counties in 1915, Wells refused to use his influence with the state government and local officials to curb the atrocities. Left defenseless, a large percentage of Wells' followers fled across the border. After the population displacements of 1915 and 1917, the Democratic organization never regained enough electoral strength to withstand the Anglo insurgency of 1920.

Hidalgo County underwent the same demographic changes that transformed Cameron County politics, but the Anglo population of this neighboring county still lacked the necessary political experience, leadership, and aggressiveness in 1920 to stage a similar coup. Boss rule persisted in Hidalgo County until the death of Sheriff A. Y. Baker in 1930. Despite the arrival of Anglo farmers with the belated introduction of irrigation in Starr County, the overwhelming Hispanic majority remained intact, and the Guerras continued to dominate the county until the post–World War II era when another Hispanic organization took charge. Although Archie Parr lost his seat in the Texas Senate in 1934 after the federal government filed a civil suit against him to recover thousands of dollars in unpaid taxes, the Parr family retained its control over Duval County until 1975. Not even the fall of the Parrs from power signaled the end of boss politics in South Texas. This remarkably resilient combination of paternalism, corruption, and tyranny has survived to the present day in Duval and Starr counties and in scattered communities throughout the Trans-Nueces.

Notes

Because of the need to reduce publishing costs, I have decided to eliminate all the notes except those for direct quotations, and to present a brief bibliographical essay. Anyone interested in studying the full documentation of my book can consult two sources: a footnoted copy of my manuscript at the Barker Texas History Center, University of Texas at Austin, or my dissertation, "Bosses under Siege: The Politics of South Texas during the Progressive Era" (Ph.D. dissertation, University of Texas at Austin, 1978), which is available through University Microfilms International. The dissertation contains 120 pages of single-spaced footnotes; the manuscript, 76 pages of double-spaced footnotes.

Introduction

1. Robert Merton, *Social Theory and Social Structure* (Glencoe, Ill.: Free Press, 1957), pp. 70–81; Joel Arthur Tarr, *A Study in Boss Politics: William Lorimer of Chicago* (Chicago: University of Illinois Press, 1971), pp. 11, 17–22, 35, 45–46, 66, 72–75; Zane Miller, *Boss Cox's Cincinnati: Urban Politics in the Progressive Era* (New York: Oxford University Press, 1968), pp. 57–73, 92–93, 97–110; and Seymour Mandelbaum, *Boss Tweed's New York* (New York: John Wiley and Sons, 1965), pp. 50–58, 67, 71–75.
2. Samuel P. Hays, "The Politics of Reform in Municipal Government in the Progressive Era," in *Twentieth-Century America: Recent Interpretations*, ed. Barton J. Bernstein and Allen J. Matusow (New York: Harcourt, Brace and World, 1969), pp. 34–57.

1. The Wells Machine

1. Florence Johnson Scott, *Historical Heritage of the Lower Rio Grande Valley* (San Antonio: Naylor Co., 1937), p. 156.
2. *Glasscock* vs. *Parr*, Texas Legislature, *Supplement to the Senate Journal*, 36th Legislature, Regular Session, p. 848.
3. Ibid., p. 862.

4. Harbert Davenport to Sam Rayburn, June 20, 1913, Frank Rabb Appointment File, Treasury Department, National Archives, RG56.
5. James Wells to E. K. Butler, July 10, 1901, James B. Wells Papers, University of Texas Archives.
6. Constitution of the State of Texas, 1875, p. 13.
7. James Wells to E. M. House, August 14, 1896, Edward M. House Papers, Yale University Library.
8. Ibid.
9. B. O. Hicks to James Wells, May 2, 1884, Wells Papers.
10. James Wells to William Hobby, July 30, 1918, Wells Papers.

2. The Customs House Gang

1. R. B. Rentfro to Thomas Ochiltree, [no date], 1884, Collector of Customs Applications, James O. Luby, Treasury Department, National Archives, RG56.
2. James Edwards to the president, June 28, 1897, Collector of Customs Applications, Texas, C. H. Maris, Treasury Department, National Archives, RG58.
3. J. C. Cummings to the secretary of the treasury, October 25, 1904, Maris File.
4. Affidavit by H. M. Field to James A. McEnery, November 22, 1901, Wells Papers.
5. J. C. Cummings to the secretary of the treasury, October 25, 1904, Maris File.
6. Stanley Welch and John Kleiber to Joseph Sayers, September 27, 1901, Wells Papers.
7. Affidavit by H. J. Wallace to James A. McEnery, November 22, 1901, Wells Papers.
8. Affidavit by C. H. Maris to James A. McEnery and Henry Terrell, [no date], 1901, Wells Papers.
9. George B. Cortelyou to L. J. Gage, January 27, 1902, Maris File.
10. James Wells to Thomas Scurry, April 26, 1902, Wells Papers.
11. J. C. Cummings to the secretary of the treasury, October 25, 1904, Maris File.

3. Assault against the Guerra Machine of Starr County

1. *Brownsville Daily Herald*, October 6, 1906.
2. F. W. Seabury to James Wells, October 6, 1906, Wells Papers.
3. J. C. Guerra to James Wells, July 8, 1906, Wells Papers.
4. *San Antonio Daily Express*, November 15, 1906.
5. James Wells to George West, November 7, 1906, Wells Papers.
6. *Brownsville Daily Herald*, November 8, 1906.
7. Noah Allen to Lock McDaniel, March 6, 1907, U.S., Department of Justice, *U.S.* vs. *Manuel Guerra et al.*, File 100579, National Archives, RG60.

8. Lock McDaniel to the U.S. attorney general, November 16, 1908, *U.S. vs. Manuel Guerra et al.*

9. Theodore Roosevelt to Cecil Lyon, December 1, 1908, Theodore Roosevelt Papers, Library of Congress.

10. Noah Allen to Lock McDaniel, January 31, 1908, *U.S.* vs. *Manuel Guerra et al.*

11. Lock McDaniel to the U.S. attorney general, February 4, 1908, *U.S.* vs. *Manuel Guerra et al.*

12. *The State of Texas, ex rel, W. E. Caldwell* vs. *Manuel Guerra*, May 3, 1909, Wells Papers.

13. Monta J. Moore to T. M. Campbell, May 9, 1909, Wells Papers.

14. J. R. Monroe to James Wells, April 5, 1910, Wells Papers.

15. T. B. Skidmore to James Wells, July 24, 1910, Wells Papers.

4. Wells and State Politics: The House Years

1. James Hogg to James Wells, June 9, 1900, James Stephen Hogg Papers, University of Texas Archives.

2. *Dallas Morning News*, January 19, 1901.

3. Albert Burleson to Edward House, July 17, 1900, House Papers.

4. Ibid.

5. Edward House to Frank Andrews, September 8, 1901, cited in James Tinsley, ed., "Letters from the Colonel: Edward M. House to Frank Andrews, 1899–1902," *Texas Gulf Coast Historical Association Publication* 4 (December 1960): 13.

6. Ibid., September 4, 1901, p. 12.

7. Ibid., September 8, 1901, pp. 13–14.

8. W. E. Moore to James Wells, May 20, 1901, Wells Papers.

9. Jeff McLemore to James Wells, July 2, 1901, Wells Papers.

10. Ibid.

11. Ibid.

12. James Wells to Edward House, July 10, 1901, Wells Papers.

13. Albert Burleson to Edward House, February 10, 1902, House Papers.

14. Ernest W. Winkler, ed., *Platforms of Political Parties in Texas*, University of Texas Bulletin, no. 53 (Austin, 1916), p. 431.

15. Albert Burleson to Edward House, January 22, 1902, House Papers.

16. *Dallas Morning News*, February 27, 1902.

17. Albert Burleson to Edward House, May 21, 1902, House Papers.

18. Joe Lee Jameson to James Wells, April 11, 1902, Wells Papers.

19. Albert Burleson to Edward House, February 10, 1902, House Papers.

20. *Dallas Morning News*, July 14, 1902.

21. Joe Lee Jameson to Edward House, July 21, 1902, House Papers.

22. Winkler, *Platforms of Political Parties in Texas*, p. 450.

5. Wells and State Politics: The Progressive Challenge

1. *Dallas Morning News*, February 5, 1905.
2. Ibid., January 22, 1905.
3. Ibid., January 11, 1905.
4. Ibid., January 12, 1905.
5. R. Baker to James Wells, June 12, 1901, Wells Papers.
6. *Dallas Morning News*, August 15, 1905.
7. Winkler, *Platforms of Political Parties in Texas*, pp. 493–496.
8. James Wells to Thomas Berry, October 31, 1906, Wells Papers.
9. *Dallas Morning News*, October 25, 1902.
10. *San Antonio Daily Express*, November 6, 1902.
11. *Dallas Morning News*, March 18, 1905.
12. Ibid., March 29, 1905.
13. James Wells to Joseph Bailey, October 6, 1906, Wells Papers.
14. J. T. Canales to James Wells, January 20, 1907, Wells Papers.
15. Texas Legislature, *House Journal*, 30th Legislature, Regular Session, pp. 1630–1631.
16. *Dallas Morning News*, March 1, 1907.
17. James Wells to J. T. Canales, April 27, 1908, Wells Papers.
18. George P. Huckaby, "Oscar Branch Colquitt: A Political Biography" (Ph.D. dissertation, University of Texas, 1946), p. 203.
19. *Dallas Morning News*, July 30, 1911.
20. Ibid., July 25, 1911.
21. Ibid., March 9, 1913.
22. Ibid.

6. The Election of John Nance Garner to Congress

1. *Corpus Christi Weekly Caller*, May 16, 1902.
2. John Garner to James Wells, February 12, 1902, Wells Papers.
3. Ibid., March 20, 1902.
4. The editorial was reprinted in the *Seguin Enterprise*, June 6, 1902.
5. *San Antonio Daily Express*, August 22, 1902.
6. Ibid., August 29, 1902.
7. Ibid., September 7, 1902.
8. Ibid., July 29, 1902.
9. *Corpus Christi Weekly Caller*, September 12, 1902.
10. *Houston Post*, October 28, 1902.
11. Ibid., October 21, 1902.
12. *San Antonio Daily Express*, November 6, 1902.

7. Trouble with Washington

1. *Dallas Morning News*, November 1, 1915.
2. U.S. Senate, *Senate Documents*, 60th Congress, First Session, "Brownsville Affray," vol. 20, p. 2530.

3. Ibid., p. 2382.
4. Ibid., vol. 23, p. 3274.
5. *Brownsville Daily Herald*, August 18, 1906.
6. John Bartlett, etc. to S. W. T. Lanham, August 18, 1906, Texas Adjutant General Correspondence, Texas State Archives.
7. "Brownsville Affray," vol. 23, p. 2397.
8. Albert B. Paine, *Captain Bill McDonald, Texas Ranger: A Story of Frontier Reform* (New York: J. J. Little and Ives Co., 1909), p. 349.
9. S. W. T. Lanham to William McDonald, August 24, 1906, Governor's Papers, S. W. T. Lanham, Texas State Archives.
10. "Brownsville Affray," vol. 23, pp. 3297–3298.
11. *Congressional Record*, 59th Congress, Second Session, vol. 41, part I, p. 613.
12. John D. Weaver, *The Brownsville Raid* (New York: W. W. Norton, 1970), p. 137.
13. *Congressional Record*, 60th Congress, Second Session, vol. 43, part IV, p. 3393.
14. Ibid.
15. W. S. Larner to the secretary of the treasury, April 18, 1908, John Vann Appointment File, Treasury Department, National Archives, RG56.
16. Noah Allen to Theodore Roosevelt, July 30, 1908, Vann File.
17. R. W. Dowe to the secretary of the treasury, August 19, 1908, Vann File.
18. Theodore Roosevelt to Cecil Lyon, December 1, 1908, Roosevelt Papers.
19. *San Antonio Daily Express*, October 3, 1908.
20. John Garner to James Wells, February 12, 1908, Wells Papers.
21. Ibid., December 19, 1908.
22. Ibid., January 4, 1909.

8. Political Upheaval in South Texas

1. Merle Elliot Tracy, "The Romance of the Lower Rio Grande Valley, Part III: What Is Being Reaped," *Texas Magazine* 8, no. 4 (August 1913): 372.
2. John Closner to James Wells, September 11, 1899, Wells Papers.
3. *Brownsville Daily Herald*, August 17, 1908.
4. Ibid., April 2, 1910.
5. Ibid., October 17, 1910.
6. Ibid., October 10, 1910.
7. Ibid., October 17, 1910.
8. Ibid., October 25, 1910.
9. Ibid., October 24, 1910.
10. Ibid., November 7, 1910.
11. Ibid.
12. Ibid., October 29, 1910.
13. The editorial was reprinted in the *Brownsville Daily Herald*, November 4, 1910.
14. Ibid., November 3, 1910.

15. Ibid., October 24, 1910.
16. Ibid., November 5, 1910.
17. F. W. Seabury to J. C. Guerra, November 11, 1910, Francis W. Seabury Papers, University of Texas Archives.
18. L. H. Bates to the secretary of the treasury, March 7, 1911, R. B. Creager Appointment File, Treasury Department, National Archives, RG56.
19. R. B. Creager to the secretary of the treasury, March 21, 1911, Creager File.
20. W. M. Rice to the supervising agent, May 27, 1911, Creager File.
21. Memorandum for the secretary, June 10, 1911, Creager File.
22. *Brownsville Daily Herald*, March 4, 1912.
23. Joseph K. Wells to James Wells, March 15, 1912, Wells Papers.
24. *Brownsville Daily Herald*, March 28, 1912.
25. Ibid., January 2, 1913.
26. Harbert Davenport to Sam Rayburn, June 20, 1913, Rabb File.
27. James H. Edwards to James Wells, January 27 (first, third, and fourth quotations), May 5 (sixth quotation), and June 23 (second and fifth quotations), 1914, Wells Papers.

9. Archie Parr and Duval County

1. James O. Luby to James Wells, October 24, 1888, Wells Papers.
2. Petition (C. F. Stillman, etc.) to Thomas Campbell, May 5, 1908, Texas Adjutant General Correspondence.
3. Tom Ross to J. O. Newton, May 26, 1908, Texas Adjutant General Correspondence.
4. Report by J. O. Newton, "Investigation of Conduct of Rangers J. D. Dunaway and Sam McKenzie, San Diego, Texas," May 30, 1908, Texas Adjutant General Correspondence.
5. *San Antonio Daily Express*, March 25, 1913.
6. Ibid., December 14, 1913.
7. *Corpus Christi Caller and Daily Herald*, February 3, 1915.
8. *Austin American*, March 6, 1915.
9. *Glasscock* vs. *Parr, Supplement to the Senate Journal*, 1919, p. 756.
10. William Wallace to John E. Green, Jr., August 4, 1915, U.S. Department of Justice, File 177325, National Archives, RG60.
11. Chester Terrell to T. W. Gregory, September 29, 1915, ibid.
12. *Corpus Christi Caller and Daily Herald*, January 9, 1916.
13. Petition to the 35th Legislature, 1917, "Has the Average Citizen of Duval County a White Man's Chance?" p. 25, Texas State Archives.

10. The Wilson Administration and Federal Patronage

1. D. P. Gay to Woodrow Wilson, December 21, 1912, Woodrow Wilson Papers, Library of Congress.
2. *San Antonio Daily Express*, June 9, 1912.

3. Oscar Colquitt to James Wells, September 25, 1912, Oscar Branch Colquitt Papers, University of Texas Archives.
4. *Houston Post*, December 20, 1912.
5. Martin Slattery to William McAdoo, June 2, 1913, Rabb File.
6. John Garner to Joseph Tumulty, January 16, 1917, Wilson Papers.
7. Thomas Gregory to William McAdoo, March 18, 1913, Rabb File.
8. D. P. Gay to Woodrow Wilson, December 21, 1912, Wilson Papers.
9. John Holbein to Woodrow Wilson, January 29, 1913, Rabb File.
10. Petition from the officials of Cameron County to William McAdoo, June 18, 1913, Rabb File.
11. Oscar Colquitt to Woodrow Wilson, January 7, 1913, Colquitt Papers.
12. Oscar Colquitt to William McAdoo, March 11, 1913, Colquitt Papers.
13. Frank Rabb to Edward House, December 15, 1912, House Papers.
14. Frank Andrews to Edward House, April 11, 1913, House Papers.
15. *Congressional Record*, 63rd Congress, 2nd Session, vol. 51, p. 4533.
16. John Garner to James Wells, June 4, 1913, Wells Papers.
17. Petition from the officials of Cameron County to William McAdoo, June 18, 1913, Rabb File.
18. Harbert Davenport to Sam Rayburn, June 20, 1913, Rabb File.
19. Frank Rabb to William McAdoo, August 21, 1913, Rabb File.
20. James Wells to John Garner, January 18, 1914, Wells Papers.
21. John Garner to James Wells, February 3, 1914, Wells Papers.
22. William McAdoo to Woodrow Wilson, July 23, 1914, Wilson Papers.
23. *Brownsville Daily Herald*, October 27, 1914.
24. James Wells to John Garner, December 27, 1914, Wells Papers.
25. "Memorandum for the Customs Division for Assistant Secretary Peters Relative to Matters Pertaining to the Customs District of Laredo, Texas, during the Period That Mr. Frank Rabb Has Been the Collector of Customs," January 30, 1915, William G. McAdoo Papers, Library of Congress.
26. James Wells to Mrs. John Garner, June 7, 1916, Wells Papers.
27. John Garner to James Wells, June 19, 1916, Wells Papers.
28. Memorandum from F. M. Halsten to Harper, August 16, 1917, Rabb File.
29. John Garner to Thomas Coleman, August 18, 1917, Wells Papers.
30. John Garner to James Wells, July 27, 1917, Wells Papers.
31. James Wells to John Garner, August 30, 1917, Wells Papers.
32. James Wells to O. E. Cannon, October 21, 1919, Wells Papers.

11. Tension along the Border, 1911–1918

1. *San Antonio Daily Express*, April 10, 1914.
2. Oscar Colquitt to Captain Head, February 24, 1913, Colquitt Papers.
3. *San Antonio Daily Express*, February 26, 1913.
4. Ibid., August 20, 1913.
5. James Edwards to Oscar Colquitt, April 21, 1914, Colquitt Papers.

6. Tasker H. Bliss to General Wotherspoon, April 23, 1914, Wilson Papers.
7. *Brownsville Daily Herald*, March 31, 1914.
8. Frederick Funston to L. M. Garrison, August 9, 1915, Wilson Papers.
9. *Corpus Christi Caller and Daily Herald*, August 12, 1915.
10. Frederick Funston to L. M. Garrison, August 13, 1915, Wilson Papers.
11. "Proceedings of the Joint Committee of the Senate and the House in the Investigation of the Texas State Ranger Force," 36th Legislature, Regular Session, p. 355, Legislative Papers, Texas State Archives.
12. The article was reprinted in the *Brownsville Daily Herald*, November 27, 1915.
13. *San Antonio Daily Express*, September 11, 1915.
14. *Corpus Christi Caller and Daily Herald*, August 14, 1915.
15. Frank C. Pierce, *A Brief History of the Lower Rio Grande Valley* (Menasha, Wis.: Collegiate Press, George Banta Publishing Co., 1917), p. 114.
16. "Proceedings . . . in the Investigation of the Texas State Ranger Force," pp. 575–576.
17. *Corpus Christi Caller and Daily Herald*, October 21, 1915.
18. *Biennial Report of the Adjutant General of Texas*, January 1, 1915–December 31, 1916, p. 11, Texas State Archives.
19. *San Antonio Daily Express*, September 9, 1915.
20. Ibid., September 8, 1915.
21. "Proceedings . . . in the Investigation of the Texas State Ranger Force," p. 865.
22. *San Antonio Daily Express*, November 1, 1915.
23. "Proceedings . . . in the Investigation of the Texas State Ranger Force," p. 691.
24. Ibid., p. 763.
25. U.S. Senate, *Investigation of Mexican Affairs, Senate Documents*, 66th Congress, 2nd Session, Document no. 285, p. 1278.
26. "Proceedings . . . in the Investigation of the Texas State Ranger Force," p. 355.
27. *Investigation of Mexican Affairs*, p. 1254.
28. *Corpus Christi Caller and Daily Herald*, May 24, 1916.
29. Ibid., June 17, 1916.
30. Arthur Link, *Wilson: Confusions and Crises* (Princeton: Princeton University Press, 1964), p. 300.
31. Ibid., p. 303.
32. James Wells and John Fernandez to John Garner, July 7, 1916, Wells Papers.
33. James Wells to C. G. Morton, April 27, 1917, Wells Papers.
34. "Personal Recollections of J. T. Canales," April 28, 1945, p. 20, Harbert Davenport Papers, Texas State Archives.
35. James Parker to James Wells, February 3, 1917, Wells Papers.
36. James Ferguson to Woodrow Wilson, May 29, 1917, Wilson Papers.
37. Woodrow Wilson to James Ferguson, May 31, 1917, Wilson Papers.
38. James Wells to J. H. Slocum, July 13, 1918, Wells Papers.
39. *Corpus Christi Caller and Daily Herald*, May 5, 1917.

40. Ibid.
41. James Wells to Mrs. John Garner, June 7, 1916, Wells Papers.

12. State Politics: The Closing Battles

1. James Wells to A. M. Bruni, July 15, 1914, Wells Papers.
2. James Wells to Thomas Ball, April 4, 1914, Wells Papers.
3. *San Antonio Daily Express*, July 12, 1914.
4. James Wells to Joseph Sayers, June 11, 1917, Wells Papers.
5. James Wells to William Hobby, July 24, 1914, Wells Papers.
6. *San Antonio Daily Express*, March 21, 1918.
7. William Hanson to James Harley, June 27, 1918, Texas Adjutant General Papers.
8. "Proceedings . . . in the Investigation of the Texas State Ranger Force," p. 686.
9. James Wells to O. S. Carlton, June 12, 1918, Wells Papers.
10. James Wells to Archie Parr, July 18, 1918, Wells Papers.
11. Archie Parr to James Wells, July 25, 1918, Wells Papers.
12. *Brownsville Daily Herald*, July 26, 1918.
13. *Glasscock* vs. *Parr, Supplement to the Senate Journal*, 1919, p. 839.
14. *Brownsville Daily Herald*, November 4, 1918.
15. *San Antonio Daily Express*, January 17, 1919.
16. Ibid., March 13, 1918.
17. Ibid.
18. "Proceedings . . . in the Investigation of the Texas State Ranger Force," p. 869.
19. Ibid., p. 886.
20. Ibid., p. 887.
21. Ibid., p. 888.
22. House Bill no. 5 by Canales," Wells Papers.
23. *San Antonio Daily Express*, January 24, 1919.
24. "Proceedings . . . in the Investigation of the Texas State Ranger Force," p. 126.
25. Texas Legislature, *House Journal*, 36th Legislature, Regular Session, pp. 535–539.
26. *San Antonio Daily Express*, March 2, 1919.
27. Ibid.
28. Ibid., March 8, 1919.
29. *Brownsville Daily Herald*, November 4, 1918.

Conclusion

1. *Brownsville Daily Herald*, July 21, 1920.
2. Ibid., July 22, 1920.
3. James Wells to Archie Parr, July 20, 1922, Wells Papers.
4. James Wells to Joseph Bailey, August 30, 1922, Wells papers.
5. James Wells to Archie Parr, August 30, 1922, Wells Papers.

References

Bibliographical Essay

In writing this book, I have relied mainly on primary sources: manuscript collections, government documents, and contemporary newspaper accounts. Probably the single most important source is the collection of the James B. Wells Papers in the University of Texas Archives in Austin. Wells was the central political figure in South Texas throughout the late nineteenth century and the Progressive Era, and he left a legacy of two hundred boxes of political, business, legal, and personal correspondence. Joe Robert Baulch thoroughly researched these papers in preparing his informative biographical dissertation on Wells, "James B. Wells: South Texas Economic and Political Leader" (Ph.D. dissertation, Texas Tech University, 1974), but his failure to study a wide variety of alternative sources with equal thoroughness resulted in a partisan account, which endorses Wells' position in almost every political controversy. The appointment files of the U.S. Treasury Department in the National Archives offer a valuable source of correspondence from the opponents of the Democratic machines for the whole period under review. The Republicans, Independents, and maverick Democrats regularly launched letter-writing campaigns to influence the selection of customs officials along the border, and their correspondence is filled with detailed criticisms of boss rule in South Texas. In addition, Treasury Department agents conducted numerous investigations of charges of corruption and partisanship on the part of the customs officials and collected testimony on general political conditions from representatives of all the political factions.

The brief introduction on the political, social, and economic background of the Trans-Nueces is based largely on secondary sources. The best general study of the region is LeRoy P. Graf, "The Economic History of the Lower Rio Grande Valley, 1820–1875" (Ph.D. dissertation, Harvard University, 1942). Other useful works include Jovita Gonzalez, "Social Life in Cameron, Starr, and Zapata Counties" (M.A. thesis, University of Texas, 1930); Florence Johnson Scott, *Historical Heritage of the Lower Rio Grande Valley* (San Antonio: Naylor Co., 1937); Tom Lea, *The King Ranch* (Boston: Little, Brown, and Co., 1957); and Ozzie Simmons, "Anglo Americans and Mexican Americans in South Texas: A Study in Dominant-Subordinant Group Relations" (Ph.D. dissertation, Harvard University, 1952).

O. Douglas Weeks provides an excellent brief introduction to the study of border politics with his article "The Texas-Mexican and the Politics of South Texas," *American Political Science Review* 34 (August 1930). In addition to Baulch's dissertation, two accounts by Harbert Davenport furnish valuable background information on Wells: "The Life of James B. Wells," University of Texas Archives and "Reminiscences of Judge James B. Wells," interviewed by William A. Owens, July 12, 1952, *Oral History: Pioneers in Texas Oil*, University of Texas Archives. Most of my information on the operation of the Wells machine in Chapter 1 comes from the Wells Papers. Other important primary sources include the Minutes of the Cameron County Commissioners' Court, vols. H and I, County Courthouse, Brownsville, Texas; *Glasscock* vs. *Parr*, Texas Legislature, *Supplement to the Senate Journal*, 36th Legislature, Regular Session; and the Frank Rabb Appointment File, Treasury Department, National Archives, RG56. For general economic conditions in Cameron County, W. H. Chatfield, *The Twin Cities of the Border and the Country of the Lower Rio Valley* (New Orleans, 1893), is a useful contemporary source. Weeks, Simmons, Arthur Rubel with his book *Across the Tracks: Mexican-Americans in a Texas City* (Austin: University of Texas Press, 1966), and Paul Taylor with his book, *An American-Mexican Frontier: Nueces County, Texas* (Chapel Hill: University of North Carolina Press, 1934) offer insights into ethnic relations in South Texas. Baulch provides detailed analysis of Wells' private business dealings.

The most valuable sources for the study of the political activities of the Republican customs officials from the 1880s through 1906 are the Treasury Department files on the following Brownsville customs collectors: James O. Luby, Robert B. Rentfro, and C. H. Maris. Although Rentfro B. Creager held the position of collector after the period covered in Chapter 2, his correspondence provides information on the general operation of the customs house.

The *Brownsville Daily Herald*, the *San Antonio Daily Express*, and the *Corpus Christi Caller* all provided full coverage of the turbulent events in Starr County that culminated in the murders of Judge Stanley Welch in 1906 and Gregorio Duffy in 1907. Conflicting points of view are available in the Wells Papers and the U.S. Justice Department file, *U.S.* vs. *Manuel Guerra et al.*, in the National Archives. The letters from the U.S. attorney for South Texas and his assistants not only describe all the legal actions taken against the suspected murderers of Duffy but also contain strong criticisms of Democratic rule along the border. The later split in the Guerra machine is covered in the Wells Papers.

The three best secondary accounts of Texas state politics during the Gilded Age and the Progressive Era are Alwyn Barr, *Reconstruction to Reform: Texas Politics, 1876–1906* (Austin: University of Texas Press, 1971), Lewis Gould, *Progressives and Prohibitionists: Texas Democrats in the Wilson Era* (Austin: University of Texas Press, 1973), and James Tinsley, "The Progressive Movement in Texas" (Ph.D. dissertation, University of Wisconsin, 1953). My general interpretation of progressive politics in Texas is based on the work of Lewis Gould. Both the *Dallas Morning News* and the *San Antonio Daily Express* offer detailed analysis of state politics. In addition to the Wells Papers, two other sources provide important information on Wells' abortive campaign for the governorship: Edward M. House Papers, Yale University Library, and James Tinsley, ed., "Letters from the Colonel: Edward M. House to Frank Andrews, 1899–1902," *Texas Gulf Coast Historical Association Publication* 4, no. 1 (December 1960). For the legislative battles over Joseph Weldon Bailey, prohibition, and election reform, both the newspapers and the House and Senate journals for the state legislature serve as valuable sources. Useful studies on some of the leading politicians of the era include Robert C. Cotner, *James Stephen Hogg: A Biography* (Austin: University of Texas Press, 1959); Rupert Richardson, *Colonel House: The Texas Years*, Hardin-Simmons University Publications in History (Abilene, Tex., 1964); Sam Hanna Acheson, *Joe Bailey: The Last Democrat* (New York: Macmillan Co., 1932); Charles K. Chamberlain, "Alexander Watkins Terrell, Citizen, Statesman," (Ph.D. dissertation, University of Texas, 1956); and George Huckaby, "Oscar Branch Colquitt: A Political Biography" (Ph.D. dissertation, University of Texas, 1946). The Colquitt Papers at the University of Texas Archives shed light on his gubernatorial campaigns, the continuing fight over prohibition, and patronage practices. Other letter collections include the James Stephen Hogg Papers at the University of Texas Archives and the Governors' Papers at the Texas State Archives.

All the biographies of John Nance Garner are inadequate, but the least objectionable of the group is Bascom Timmons, *Garner of Texas: A Personal History* (New York: Harper and Bros., 1948). Alwyn Barr has written an informative article, "John Nance Garner's First Campaign for Congress," *West Texas Historical Association Yearbook* 48 (1972). Valuable primary sources on the 1902 election include the *San Antonio Daily Express*, the *Corpus Christi Caller*, and the *Seguin Enterprise* from Joseph Dibrell's home county. The *Houston Post* covers the split among the state Republican leaders at the end of John Scott's campaign. The Wells Papers contain extensive correspondence with Garner and provide much information on both the congressman's campaigns and his services for the South Texas bosses. The *Congressional Record* and various *House Reports* and *House Documents* reveal the full dimensions of Garner's efforts to secure pork-barrel projects. The material on the Brownsville raid is voluminous. The Senate investigating committee compiled five volumes of testimony on the incident: U.S. Senate, *Senate Documents*, 60th Congress, First Session, "Brownsville Affray." Of several secondary accounts, John D. Weaver, *The Brownsville Raid* (New York: W. W. Norton, 1970), provides the most thorough and persuasive analysis.

A number of sources cover the economic development of the Lower Rio Grande Valley during the first two decades of the twentieth century: Merle Elliot Tracy's three-part article, "The Romance of the Lower Rio Grande Valley," appearing in the June, July, and August 1913 issues of *Texas Magazine* 8, nos. 2–4; Edwin J. Foscue, "Land Utilization in the Lower Rio Grande Valley," *Economic Geography* 8, no. 1 (January 1932); William Leshner, "In the Lower Rio Grande Valley," *Texas Magazine* 2, no. 6 (October 1910);

Samuel Evans, "Texas Agriculture, 1880–1930" (Ph.D. dissertation, University of Texas, 1960); William Kenneth Mathews, "A History of Irrigation in the Lower Rio Grande Valley" (M.A. thesis, University of Texas, 1938); J. L. Allhands, *Gringo Builders* (privately printed, 1931); and J. Lee and Lillian J. Stambaugh, *The Lower Rio Grande Valley of Texas* (San Antonio: Naylor Co., 1954). Most of the material in Chapter 8 on the insurgent challenges to Democratic boss rule in Brownsville and in Cameron and Hidalgo counties comes from the Wells Papers, the *Brownsville Daily Herald*, the Rentfro B. Creager Appointment File in the Treasury Department papers at the National Archives, and the Hidalgo County File at the Barker Texas History Center, University of Texas at Austin. The *Brownsville Daily Herald* provides thorough coverage of all the city and county election campaigns from 1908 through 1920, the outbreak of political violence in Brownsville after the 1912 election, and the establishment of commission government in 1915.

Dudley Lynch offers a brief but informative introduction to Duval County politics with his book *The Duke of Duval: The Life and Times of George B. Parr* (Waco: Texian Press, 1976), which contains background material on Archer Parr's earlier reign. In 1919, the Texas Senate conducted an exhaustive investigation into Archer Parr's resort to election fraud to win his senate seat the year before. The one thousand pages of testimony cover not only the campaign but also general political conditions in Duval County after 1900. The reports and letters of Texas Rangers in the Texas Adjutant General Correspondence at the Texas State Archives in Austin provide detailed information on the murder of John Cleary. Another valuable primary source is the U.S. Justice Department file at the National Archives on the federal investigation of the 1912 Duval County election. Both the *San Antonio Daily Express* and the *Corpus Christi Caller* offer thorough coverage of all the court proceedings dealing with Duval County corruption. These newspapers along with the *Dallas Morning News* and the Senate and House journals cover the legislative battles over the creation of new counties in the Trans-Nueces. The views of local insurgents appear in two pamphlets that were originally submitted to the Texas Legislature as petitions of grievance: "Remarkable Conditions in Duval County: Protest by Citizens against Proposed Division," Barker Texas History Center, and "Has the Average Citizen of Duval County a White Man's Chance?" Texas State Archives.

The main source of information on the controversy over the appointment of Frank Rabb to the South Texas collectorship is the Frank Rabb Appointment File in the Treasury Department records at the National Archives. Other useful letter collections include the Woodrow Wilson Papers at the Library of Congress, the William G. McAdoo Papers at the Library of Congress, the Edward M. House Papers at the Yale University Library, the Oscar Branch Colquitt Papers at the University of Texas Archives, and the Wells Papers. The *Brownsville Daily Herald* covers the county election of 1914. The best secondary account of the Wilson movement in Texas is Gould's *Progressives and Prohibitionists*.

Three articles provide excellent analyses of the Mexican border raids of

1915 and 1916: Charles Harris and Louis Saddler, "The Plan of San Diego and the Mexican–United States War Crisis of 1916: A Reexamination," *Hispanic American Historical Review* 58 (August 1978); Charles C. Cumberland, "Border Raids in the Lower Rio Grande Valley—1915," *Southwestern Historical Quarterly* 57 (January 1954); and James A. Sandos, "The Plan of San Diego: War and Diplomacy on the Texas Border," *Arizona and the West* 14 (Spring 1972). Other secondary accounts include Clarence Clendenen, *Blood on the Border: The United States Army and the Mexican Irregulars* (London: Macmillan Co., 1969); Arthur Link, *Wilson: The New Freedom* (Princeton: Princeton University Press, 1956), *Wilson: The Struggle for Neutrality* (1960), *Wilson: Confusions and Crises* (1964), and *Wilson: Campaigns for Progressivism and Peace* (1965); Walter Prescott Webb, *The Texas Rangers: A Century of Frontier Defense* (Austin: University of Texas Press, 1965); William Sterling, *Trails and Trials of a Texas Ranger* (Norman: University of Oklahoma Press, 1959); and Frank C. Pierce, *A Brief History of the Lower Rio Grande Valley* (Menacha, Wis.: Collegiate Press, George Banta Publishing Co., 1917). The primary sources on the border troubles during the Mexican Revolution are also extensive: *Investigation of Mexican Affairs*, Senate Documents, 66th Congress, Second Session, Document no. 285; the Woodrow Wilson Papers; the Oscar Branch Colquitt Papers; the Texas Adjutant General Correspondence; and "Proceedings of the Joint Committee of the Senate and the House in the Investigation of the Texas State Ranger Force," 36th Legislature, Regular Session, Legislative Papers, Texas State Archives. The most graphic descriptions of Ranger atrocities against the Hispanic population appear in the Texas legislative hearings. The *San Antonio Daily Express*, the *Corpus Christi Caller*, and the *Brownsville Daily Herald* provide full coverage of the military deployments and the violence along the border. Material on the political repercussions of the border turbulence is available in the Wells Papers and the newspapers.

Gould's *Progressives and Prohibitionists* is indispensable to understanding state politics during the administrations of James Ferguson and William Hobby. The Wells papers, the newspapers, and the House and Senate journals cover Wells' involvement in state politics from 1914 through 1919. The main sources of information on the reorganization of the Rangers under William Hobby and the legislative investigation of the Rangers are the Ranger correspondence in the Texas Adjutant General Correspondence and the "Proceedings of the Joint Committee of the Senate and the House in the Investigation of the Texas State Ranger Force," 36th Legislature, Regular Session. The legislative committee collected over sixteen hundred pages of testimony and evidence. Legislative hearings also provide the most complete account of Archer Parr's fraudulent reelection campaign of 1918: *Glasscock vs. Parr*, Texas Legislature, *Supplement to the Senate Journal*, 36th Legislature, Regular Session. Additional information on that campaign appears in the Wells Papers, the *San Antonio Daily Express*, the *Dallas Morning News*, the *Brownsville Daily Herald*, the *Corpus Christi Caller*, and the Texas Adjutant General Correspondence.

The Wells Papers, the Francis W. Seabury Papers at the University of

Texas Archives, and the *Brownsville Daily Herald* serve as the main sources of information on the collapse of the Wells machine in 1920 and the final years of Wells' life.

Primary Sources

MANUSCRIPTS

Burleson, Albert Sidney. Papers, University of Texas Archives, Austin.

Campbell, Thomas M. Papers, University of Texas Archives, Austin.

Closner, Jonn. Biographical file, Barker Texas History Center, University of Texas, Austin.

Colquitt, Oscar Branch. Papers, University of Texas Archives, Austin.

Conner, J. E. "A History of the Parr-Glasscock Election Contest of 1918–1919." University of Texas Archives, Austin.

Davenport, J. Harbert. "The Life of James B. Wells." University of Texas Archives, Austin.

———. Papers, Texas State Archives, Austin.

———. "Reminiscences of Judge James B. Wells." Interviewed by William A. Owens, *Oral History: Pioneers in Texas Oil*, University of Texas Archives, Austin.

Hidalgo County. County file, Barker Texas History Center, University of Texas, Austin.

Hogg, James Stephen. Papers, University of Texas Archives, Austin.

House, Edward M. Papers, Yale University Library, New Haven, Connecticut. Microfilm copies at the Barker Texas History Center, University of Texas, Austin.

Kleberg, Rudolph. Papers, University of Texas Archives, Austin.

Lanham, S. W. T. Governors' Papers, Texas State Archives, Austin.

Lasater, Edward C. Biographical file, Barker Texas History Center, University of Texas, Austin.

McAdoo, William G. Papers, Manuscripts Division, Library of Congress, Washington, D.C.

McLemore, Atkins Jefferson (Jeff). Papers, University of Texas Archives, Austin.

Parr, Archer (Archie). Biographical file, Barker Texas History Center, University of Texas, Austin.

Roosevelt, Theodore. Papers, Manuscripts Division, Library of Congress, Washington, D.C. Microfilm copies at the University of Texas Library, Austin.

Seabury, Francis W. Papers, University of Texas Archives, Austin.

Taft, William Howard. Papers, Manuscripts Division, Library of Congress, Washington, D.C. Microfilm copies at the University of Texas Library, Austin.

Wells, James B. Papers, University of Texas Archives, Austin.

Wilson, Woodrow. Papers, Manuscripts Division, Library of Congress, Washington, D.C. Microfilm copies at the University of Texas Library, Austin.

UNITED STATES GOVERNMENT DOCUMENTS
Bureau of the Census. *Ninth Census of the United States: 1870. The Statistics of the Population of the United States*, vol. I. Washington: Government Printing Office, 1872.

———. [Manuscript Census.] "Tenth Census of the United States: 1880. Brownsville, Cameron County, Texas; Duval County, Texas." Microfilm copies at the Barker Texas History Center, University of Texas, Austin.

———. *Tenth Census of the United States: 1880. Statistics of the Population of the United States*, vol. I. Washington: Government Printing Office, 1883.

———. *Eleventh Census of the United States: 1890. Report on Population of the United States*, vol. xi, part I. Washington: Government Printing Office, 1897.

———. *Twelfth Census of the United States: 1900. Population*, vol. I, part I. Washington: Government Printing Office, 1901.

———. *Twelfth Census of the United States: 1900. Agriculture*, vol. V, part I. Washington: Government Printing Office, 1902.

———. *Fourteenth Census of the United States: 1920. Population*, vol. III, Washington: Government Printing Office, 1922.

———. *Fifteenth Census of the United States: 1930. Population*, vol. III, part 2. Washington: Government Printing Office, 1932.

Congress. *Congressional Record*, 56th Congress–65th Congress, vols. 33–55. Washington: Government Printing Office, 1900–1917.

———. *House Journal*. 59th Congress, 2nd Session. Washington: Government Printing Office, 1907.

———. Senate. *Senate Documents. The Brownsville Affray.* S. Doc. no. 389, 5 vols., 60th Congress, 1st Session. Washington: Government Printing Office, 1908.

———. ———. *Senate Documents. Investigation of Mexican Affairs.* S. Doc. no. 285, 2 vols., 66th Congress, 2nd Session. Washington: Government Printing Office, 1920.

Department of Justice. Applications and Endorsements, 1901–1933, Texas, Southern District, Applicants for U.S. Marshal, Lawrence H. Bates. National Archives. Record Group 60.

———. Duval County Election Investigation, File 177325. National Archives. Record Group 60.

———. Nueces County Election Cases, File 176178. National Archives. Record Group 60.

———. Thomas Watt Gregory File, File 190470. National Archives. Record Group 60.

———. *U.S. vs. Manuel Guerra et al.*, File 100579. National Archives. Record Group 60.

Department of State. *Papers Relating to the Foreign Relations of the United States, 1913*. Washington: Government Printing Office, 1920.

Treasury Department. Collector of Customs Applications, Texas, J. J. Cocke. National Archives Record Group 56.

————. Collector of Customs Applications, Texas, James O. Luby. National Archives. Record Group 56.

————. Collector of Customs Applications, Texas, Charles H. Maris. National Archives. Record Group 56.

————. Collector of Customs Applications, Texas, R. B. Rentfro. National Archives. Record Group 56.

————. Presidential Appointments, 1833–1945, Thomas A. Coleman Appointment File. National Archives. Record Group 56.

————. Presidential Appointments, 1833–1945, Rentfro B. Creager Appointment File. National Archives. Record Group 56.

————. Presidential Appointments, 1833–1945, Frank Rabb Appointment File. National Archives. Record Group 56.

————. Presidential Appointments, 1833–1945, John W. Vann Appointment File. National Archives. Record Group 56.

————. "Register of Customs Officers in the District of Brazos de Santiago, Port of Brownsville, Texas." Customs Employees, Baltimore–New Orleans, 1864–1909, vol. 2, no. 11. National Archives. Record Group 56.

————. "Register of Customs Officers in the District of Brazos de Santiago, Port of Brownsville, Texas." Small Ports, Customs Officers, vol. 4, no. 92. National Archives. Record Group 56.

TEXAS GOVERNMENT DOCUMENTS

Adjutant General. *Biennial Report of the Adjutant General of Texas, January 1, 1915–December 31, 1916*. Austin: Von Boeckmann-Jones Co., Printers, 1917.

————. Correspondence. 1906–1909, 1912, 1915–1919. Texas State Archives, Austin.

Cameron County. Minutes of the Cameron County Commissioners' Court. Vols. H and I. August 1891–November 1905. Cameron County Courthouse, Brownsville.

————. Record of Election Returns for Cameron County. Book B. Cameron County Courthouse, Brownsville.

Constitution of the State of Texas, 1875. Galveston: *News* Steam Book and Job Establishment, 1875.

Constitution of the State of Texas. J. W. Moffet, annotator. Austin: Gammel's Book Store, 1922.

Legislature. *General Laws of the State of Texas*. 28th Legislature, Regular Session. Austin: Von Boeckmann-Jones Co., State Printers, 1903.

————. *General Laws of the State of Texas*. 29th Legislature, Regular Session and First Called Session. Austin: State Printing Co., 1905.

————. "Proceedings of the Joint Committee of the Senate and the House in the Investigation of the Texas State Rangers." 36th Legislature, Regular Session. Legislative Papers. Texas State Archives, Austin.

————. House of Representatives. *House Journals*. 26th Legislature–36th Legislature, 1899–1919.

————. ————. *House Journal. Proceedings of House Investigating Com-*

mittee. 32nd Legislature, First Called Session, vol. II. Austin: Austin Printing Co., 1911.

————. Senate. *Senate Journals*. 27th Legislature–36th Legislature, 1901– 1919.

————. ————. *Senate Journal. Proceedings and Findings of Senate Investigating Committee*. 32nd Legislature, Regular Session, vol. II. Austin: Austin Printing Co., 1911.

————. ————. *Supplement to the Senate Journal. D. W. Glasscock, Contestant* vs. *A. Parr, Contestee*. 36th Legislature, Regular Session. Austin: A. C. Baldwin and Sons, State Printers, 1919.

Secretary of State. *Biennial Reports*. 1872–1920.

PAMPHLETS

Citizens of Duval County. "Has the Average Citizen of Duval County a White Man's Chance?" Petition to the 35th Legislature, 1917. Available at the Texas State Archives, Austin.

————. "Remarkable Conditions in Duval County: Protest by Citizens against Proposed Division." Petition to the 34th Legislature, 1915. Available at the Barker Texas History Center, University of Texas, Austin.

Seabury, Francis W. "Legislative Reform" No publisher or place of publication cited; 1903. Available at the Barker Texas History Center, University of Texas, Austin.

Wells, Mrs. James B. "Why I Am Opposed to Woman Suffrage." Address before the State Senate, Austin, Texas, February 23, 1915. Available at the Barker Texas History Center, University of Texas, Austin.

NEWSPAPERS

Austin American, 1915, 1917.
Brownsville Daily Herald, 1890–1920.
Corpus Christi Caller, 1900–1918.
Dallas Morning News, 1901–1919.
Galveston Daily News, 1918.
Houston Post, 1902, 1909–1913, 1919.
San Antonio Daily Express, 1890–1924.
Seguin Enterprise, 1902.

Index

DATE DUE
